Merchants and Luxury Markets

The Marchands Merciers of Eighteenth-Century Paris

Victoria and Albert Museum Studies in the History of Art and Design

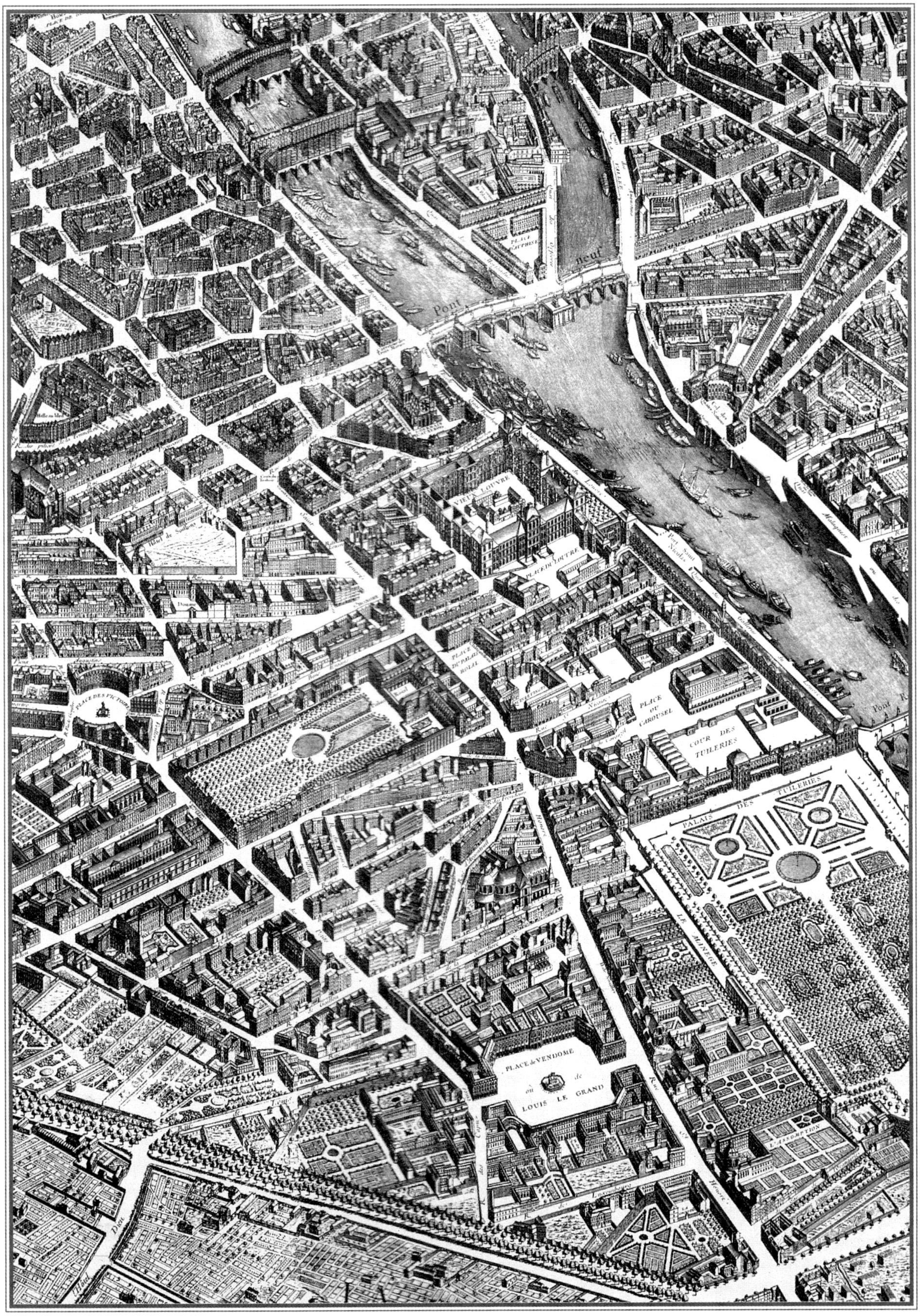

The rue St Honoré, detail from the Plan Turgot, Paris, 1739. Bibliothèque Nationale de France, Paris.

Merchants and Luxury Markets

The Marchands Merciers of Eighteenth-Century Paris

Carolyn Sargentson

Victoria and Albert Museum
in association with the J. Paul Getty Museum

First published by the Victoria and Albert Museum, London, 1996
in association with the J. Paul Getty Museum, Malibu, California

The Victoria and Albert Museum
London SW7 2RL

The J. Paul Getty Museum
17985 Pacific Coast Highway, Malibu, California 90265-5799

Carolyn Sargentson asserts her moral right to be identified as author of this book

Victoria and Albert Museum Edition ISBN: 1 85177 176 X
A catalogue record for this book is available from the British Library

J. Paul Getty Museum Edition ISBN: 0 89236 295 2

Produced by Alan Sutton Publishing Ltd, Stroud, Gloucestershire.
Printed in Great Britain by Butler and Tanner, Frome, Somerset.

On dit proverbialement, A petit Mercier, petit panier, pour dire, que les petits gens peuvent vivre de leur trafic en réglant leur dépense à leur gain. On dit aussi d'un homme fort emporté de colère, qu'il tueroit un Mercier pour un peigne. On dit aussi encore qu'au jour du Jugement chacun sera Mercier, qu'il portera son panier, pour dire, qu'il répondra de ses fautes.

(*Dictionnaire Trevoux*, Paris, 1752, 467)

Le Mercier, *French, late 17th/early 18th century, Jean-Baptiste Bonnart. Bibliothèque Nationale de France, Paris.*

CONTENTS

ACKNOWLEDGEMENTS

I would like to thank the British Institute in Paris and the University of Glasgow (David Carritt Scholarship) for substantial grants in support of research undertaken in the Paris archives between 1987 and 1990. The Owen Taylor Research Fund, the Pasold Research Fund, the Maison des Sciences de l'Homme Networks Scheme/ESRC and the Whistler Foundation also generously supported travel expenses and photocopying costs. The Victoria and Albert Museum and De Montfort University, Leicester jointly funded a post in the Research Department of the V&A to allow the much-needed time for the book to be written. I am grateful to my friends and colleagues in the Furniture and Woodwork Department at the V&A who gave me leave to spend time away from my usual duties in order to write this book.

Pierre Verlet's 1958 article on the *marchands merciers* was in many ways the starting point for the project, although the influence of several others directed me towards this area of research. Neil McGregor's inspired teaching at the University of Reading around 1980 first motivated me to think of working on French art and design. Much later, Michael Sonenscher suggested the subject of the *marchands merciers* whilst I was a student on the V&A/RCA MA Course in Design History, and he guided the research from its inception in 1987. His knowledge of the French archival system made this project possible and his published work on the eighteenth-century French trades has been a lesson in working with such source material. I am grateful to him and to Juliet Kinchin and Alan Tait at the University of Glasgow for their supervision of the Phd thesis which forms the basis of this work. I am indebted to Lesley Miller for sharing her research and thinking during 1994 and 1995, when we worked together on the commercial and design relationships between Paris and Lyon, the results of which form a substantial part of chapter 5. I would also like to thank Malcolm Baker for his sympathetic and immensely constructive readings of the text in more recent months, and Paul Greenhalgh, Mary Butler, and especially Fiona Elliott for their help in putting the book together.

The ideas expressed in this book owe much to the example and guidance of these individuals, and also to the teaching on the V&A/RCA MA in History of Design under the direction first of Charles Saumarez-Smith and later John Styles, both of whom offered thought-provoking material through the course, and much personal encouragement besides. The conferences in Paris and Oxford organized by the Achievement Project on the skilled workforce in early modern Europe were extremely useful in persuading me to write up various parts of the research and in providing a framework for thinking about the organization of the trades in relation to the products of the workshops. The conference on textiles organized jointly by the Institut d'Histoire Moderne Contemporaine in Paris and the University of Rouen was a fruitful and stimulating opportunity to work with French historians in this field. I thank Daniel Roche especially for his encouragement.

A project which began as an interrogation of the written evidence in the French archives has evolved and altered course through the experience of working with the collections and curators in many museums. I have learned a tremendous amount both from my colleagues at the V&A and from Gillian Wilson at the J. Paul Getty Museum, whose support of the project has been manifold. I hope that the result of this path through various institutions, academic disciplines and collections is a book which both establishes some new ways of looking at the eighteenth-century French luxury trades, and opens the subject of the *marchands merciers* for further research and debate. Any faults in the book are, needless to say, my own.

Many institutions have been generous with time, advice and information. I would like to thank in particular the staff and curators of the Archives Nationales in Paris, Archives de Paris and the Bibliothèque Nationale de France. I am also indebted to the following individuals who helped in many ways with advice and information: Daniel Alcouffe, Christian Baulez, Geoffrey de Bellaigue, Frank Berendt, Riccienda Binney, Françoise Bonnardel, Clare Browne, Judith Crouch, Theodore Dell, Richard Edgecumbe, Anita Ellis, Roland de l'Espée, Odile Falieu, Nadine Gasc, Robert Gibbs, Henry Hawley, Mark Haworth-Booth, Peter Hughes, Jolyon Hudson, Oliver Impey, Claude Jollin, Rose Kerr, Ulrich Leben, Patrick Leperlier, Claude Lévy, David Maskill, Sarah Medlam, Thomas Monck, Michael Moss, Tessa Murdoch, Angela O'Shea, James Parker, Alexandre Pradère, Tamara Préaud, Daniel Roche, Xavier Salmon, Adrian Sassoon, Rosalind Savill, Katie Scott, Barry Schifman, Michael Snodin, Don Spaeth, Paul Stirton, Kate Ware, John Whitehead, Christopher Wilk, Elaine Williamson, Ghislaine Wood, Lucy Wood and Hilary Young.

For help with photographs at the V&A, I would like to thank especially Jennifer Blain, and also the Photo Studio, Picture Library, the Furniture Conservation Department and colleagues in the National Art Library, and the Textiles and Dress, Metalwork, Ceramics, Prints, Drawings and Photographs and Furniture and Woodwork Departments. At the J. Paul Getty Museum I am indebted to the museum photographers, conservators, Charissa Bremer-David, Jeffrey Weaver and Gillian Wilson. For their efficient and generous help with other photographs my thanks are due to Christie's and Sotheby's, M. Baudry, Elizabeth Conran, Rosamund Griffin, Joanna Hashagen, Brigitte Lainé, Sylvie Rabusseau, Lydia Romain, Conrad Waldersee, Ulrich Leben, Elaine Sullivan and Jessica White.

A number of people gave special help which enabled me to continue with the research and writing and I would like to thank Clive Bates, Erica Knighton, Mrs Jean Lloyd, Kevin Rogers, Jude Ruff, and Elizabeth and Jeremy Young. Sarah Medlam's help, as always, exceeded the normal bounds of duty, and I also owe very many thanks to David Maskill for his constant support, and for his companionship and help in the archives. My parents offered unfailing encouragement of my research over the years, and it is to their memory that I dedicate this book.

List of Abbreviations

AN	Archives Nationales, Paris
AN MC	Archives Nationales, Minutier Central
AVP	Archives de Paris
BF	Bibliothèque Forney, Paris
BHVP	Bibliothèque Historique de la Ville de Paris
BM	British Museum, London
BML	Bibliothèque Municipale, Lyon
BMP	Bibliothèque Mazarine, Paris
BNF	Bibliothèque Nationale de France, Paris
BNF Est	Bibliothèque Nationale de France, Département des Estampes
BNF Mss	Bibliothèque Nationale de France, Département des Manuscrits

Units of Measurement

The *livre* was the French money of account and from 1726 6 *livres* equated to 1 silver *écu*, and 24 *livres* to 1 *louis d'or*. One *livre* comprised 20 *sous*, and each *sol* was worth 12 *deniers*.

The *livre* as a measure of weight was equivalent to 8 *onces*, or 489.5 grams.

The *aulne* (the rod held in the right hand of the *mercier* as illustrated on front of jacket) was the standard measure for fabrics, of 3 *pieds*, 7 *pouces*, 10½ *lignes*, or 1.188 metres.

Estimated Incomes in France 1726–1790

(After Sgard 1982)

Although the classification of work and professions, and the establishment of accurate wage bands in eighteenth-century France is problematic, the following figures provide some context for the sums of money discussed in this book, such as the capital funds of businesses, the price of property and offices and the profits of individual mercers.

Annual income (*livres*)	Work/standard of living
100–300	Labouring poor (eg. 200 days' work @ 10 *sous* a day).
300–1,000	Salaried manual work including skilled work (eg. gilder/cabinet-maker, *c*. 400–750 *livres*).
1,000–3,000	Professional worker/office holder (eg. tutors employed by the academies or by princely houses, 2–3,000 *livres*).
5,000–20,000	Salaried professionals and those with income from investments (eg. wealthy doctor, 8–10,000 *livres*).
40,000–100,000	Noble standard of living (eg. bishops, 40–100,000 *livres*).
over 100,000	Princely standard of living (eg. the income of the Duc de Villeroy, 377,175 *livres*).

INTRODUCTION

Dans la théorie, l'opinion commune est contraire au luxe, dans la pratique tout le monde s'y livre.[1]

The *commerce de luxe* in Paris has long been part of the city's economic, social and visual identity. By the early eighteenth century the city had a reputation not only for the scale of consumption of the king and aristocracy, but also for the luxury goods on sale in the Parisian shops and markets. The production and circulation of goods was dependant on a high degree of specialization in terms of retailing as well as manufacturing skills. This book is about a group of merchants, the *marchands merciers*, who played a pivotal role within the luxury market place, and who were largely responsible for the introduction into Paris of a range of new goods. Their merchandise was manufactured in Paris, the French provinces, Europe, the colonies and the Orient. Through their shops they supplied the court, residents of the city and tourists with objects of fine craftsmanship and fashionable design. Despite their involvement in almost all aspects of Parisian commercial life, the history of the mercers has remained largely obscure. This book is about their role in the importation, transformation, design and marketing of luxury goods, and thereby about some of the practical workings of the Parisian luxury economy.

The spheres of retailing and marketing – merchant activity as opposed to the organization of production – have been little treated by historians of the French economy, either at the level of the Parisian luxury trade corporations, or of the economic history of seventeenth- and eighteenth-century France. In the late seventeenth century, Jean-Baptiste Colbert set out to transform France into a great manufacturing and trading nation, a system which came to be called 'mercantilism'. Central to his policies was the luxury economy. His encouragement of this sector extended to manufacturing (the Manufactures Royales) and to the corporation of mercers, who were given rights to trade more freely than any other Parisian corporation. The mercers had traditionally played a strong role in the luxury economy since their incorporation in the twelfth century, trading especially in imported goods. From the seventeenth and eighteenth centuries they were also extremely active in the distribution of luxury goods made in Paris and other regions of France. As Sabel and Zeitlin have argued, fashion goods can be priced competitively at the beginning of the product cycle, when an extremely high premium can be charged for novelty and fashion, and at the end of the cycle when they can be sold cheaply either in centres of fashion or in more distant markets which are less sensitive to changes in fashion. Many goods combining valuable materials and high quality craftsmanship held their value for considerable periods of time within a second-hand economy for luxury goods, before they were sold at knock-down prices or broken down for their material content. Although they did not engage in manufacturing, the mercers' access to the best designers and manufacturers, to imported materials denied to other trades, and their rights to finish goods, enabled them to manipulate these fashion markets.

This study is based on the inventories of some forty families. Although the mercers lived and traded in their thousands across the city, the subject of this book is the mercers who had retailing premises in or around the rue Saint Honoré. This quarter, still known for the trade in haute couture, luxury accessories and antiques, emerged during the eighteenth century as the principal area for the retailing of silks, fine furnishings and fashionable dress.[2] In 1715, a visitor described its shops

> dont le luxe n'était dépassé que par le flux de paroles gracieuses et de civilités empressées qui s'y disputaient sa bourse.[3]

The inventories provide many details about the mercers, their stock, their families and their finances. The book is as much about the process of working with such documents as the information which they contain. Inevitably, the chapters leave out much detail about individual mercers, in particular the details of the objects described in their inventories, and biographical information. Whilst some of this wealth of detail is included here in footnotes, most of it will be published elsewhere in the form of articles.

The mercers' activities have a place within a number of historiographical traditions which have emerged from disparate institutions and academic disciplines. These include the histories of the Parisian trade corporations[4] and their members, the history of design and collecting, and debates about consumption and markets in early modern Europe.[5] Recent research in these areas has demonstrated the usefulness both of an extensive range of French archival sources, and of a number of lines of enquiry and interpretation which are drawn on here with the aim of looking at the mercers in the widest contexts.

The first chapter considers the mercers in terms of their collective institutional identity through the limited surviving documentation of their corporation.[6] Studies of the complexion of individual corporations have traditionally been restricted to artisanal rather than merchant groups.[7] Consequently, they have spoken little of the distinctions and relations between these and the merchant bodies. The issues of labour and skill have dominated these histories, resulting in a view of the trades which hardly takes into account the complex relations between merchants and artisans, and the significance of groups which specialized in marketing rather than making. The emphasis on the social and economic conditions of Parisian artisans has meant that the trading practices of the mercers have been little integrated into the view of the *ancien régime* Parisian economy. The corporation's statutes, however, reveal that the mercers were intended to act as retail outlets for many of the city's workshops, and in some cases even to supply them with raw materials and labour.

The history of the corporation was partly written in 1911 by Vidal and Duru, themselves members of the corporation, and in an unpublished thesis on the corporation from the twelfth to sixteenth centuries.[8] The former is limited to somewhat anecdotal detail, though Cleret's study gives a commentary on the rapid expansion of the corporation over a period of several centuries. First documented as a body in the twelfth century, the mercers were governed by statutes which prohibited them from manufacturing but allowed them wide trading rights until a restructuring of the Parisian corporations in 1776. The corporation made sizeable loans to the King in return for commercial privileges, and defended its rights to free trade against the other corporations. However, despite (or perhaps because) the total membership numbered over 2,000 mercers engaged in some twenty different branches of commerce, the corporation served less the personal interests of individual mercers or specialist groups, but rather its own programme. This extended to the commissioning in 1674 of a painting for the church of the *confrérie* which symbolized the mercers' relationship with the King and his minister, Colbert. Its wealth, trade and artistic patronage placed it, by the end of the seventeenth century, as a significant force within the merchant corporations of Paris, the Six Corps.

After dealing with the official face of the

corporate body, and the theoretical controls laid down in its statutes, chapter 2 turns to the circumstances of individual mercers. Using the collective evidence of a range of inventories, it considers the ways in which their businesses were financed and managed in practice. Like artisanal groups, the mercers operated within networks of small units of production, distinguished by corporate regulations and linked by the movement of goods, labour and credit. Unlike artisanal corporations, the mercers were allowed and indeed encouraged to trade widely, in many markets, in competition with local workshops which nevertheless depended upon them for custom. Their inventories provide detailed information on family relationships and business interests. To some degree, they make it possible to reconstruct the sources of family and investment capital, short-term income and credit, and raw materials, labour and finished goods. Each mercer was at the centre of a fragile web of suppliers and customers, held together by a series of credit arrangements across geographical boundaries and time. The inventories record the credit which allowed the mercers to establish far-reaching networks of supply and to lay out large sums for the acquisition of goods.

The inventories represent a 'snapshot' of a business at a point of change in the circumstances of a merchant or family, whether death, marriage, partnership or bankruptcy. The business at such a moment may not have been running typically: for example, a mercer at the end of his or her life may have been operating on a reduced scale. However, should the business have been handed over to a son or daughter, or sold as a going concern, the inventory drawn up for the purpose of recording the precise terms of the agreement may represent a reasonably unexceptional state of affairs. Although bankruptcy may seem an extraordinary episode in the life of a business, the balance of debt against assets was very often extremely fragile, and some of the most highly reputed mercers went bankrupt at some point in their careers. It was usual to continue to trade under the governorship of a syndicate of creditors until the balance of accounts could again be deemed healthy, a process which could take some years.

Daybooks offer useful but rare information about the workings of a business over time. The daybook of Lazare Duvaux, which spans a ten-year period from 1748 to his death and his wife's control of the business, records the sales of porcelain, furniture, clocks and snuff boxes to a prestigious clientele.[9] Since his inventory also survives, it is possible to get a sense of both the stock and the turnover, and more information about suppliers. His daybooks recording supplies of work and goods have not been found. The publication of the daybook has allowed many surviving objects to be linked with individual makers and clients, and has been confined largely to the discussion of prices within catalogue entries for porcelain.[10] The implications of this data for an understanding of the mercers' business cycles is considered in chapter 2, alongside evidence from other surviving daybooks.

Inventories of stock may each list several hundred objects. Only in a relatively small number of cases can surviving objects be linked to these descriptions, and although the outstanding debts are listed, the objects and services for which an individual client owed money at the time of the inventory are not detailed. Although the professions of the mercers' suppliers of labour, materials and finished goods are listed in the inventories, in only a few cases is it possible to assume that a specific individual made any single item in stock. It is also unwise to assume that the output of any of these individual suppliers was homogeneous enough to predict the way the objects might have looked. Given that a cabinet-maker may have supplied a number of private clients as well as a number of mercers during the course of his business, and that he may have sub-contracted work to a number of workshops, it is important to approach the manuscript descriptions with caution.[11] Certainly the mercers' inventories yield less precise information about individual objects than the royal household accounts or the sales registers from Sèvres. However, the fact that the complete stock is described and valued, including raw materials, damaged and old goods, partly finished and finished goods and work temporarily away from the shop premises gives a much fuller picture of the business than has previously been possible.

The inventories are particularly unhelpful on the subject of design. Designers are rarely listed as creditors to the mercers, and few designs can be linked with certainty to mercers or the objects which they sold. The evidence for attributing certain innovations and models to the mercers is summarized in chapter 3, which outlines the various ways in which they intervened within the design process.

The literature on the decorative arts has long acknowledged the mercers' importance as designers. In the late nineteenth century, Louis Courajod published Lazare Duvaux's daybook, with a companion volume on the eighteenth-century commerce in luxury goods.[12] More recently, Pierre Verlet drew attention to the significance of the mercer's activities for the study of decorative arts in a seminal article of 1958. He used in particular the registers of suppliers to Versailles and the royal residences.[13] Francis Watson followed suit in 1965[14] and since then several writers have taken up the subject of the mercers' influence on design and taste. Svend Eriksen again placed the mercers in a central role in early neoclassicism in France.[15] Geoffrey de Bellaigue included biographies of Daguerre, Duvaux, Granchez and Poirier in the catalogue of the collection at Waddesdon Manor, which includes a number of pieces which can be associated with individual mercers.[16] De Bellaigue went on to publish on the mercers' role in bringing French objects and taste to Britain, particularly through the mercer Daguerre.[17] The mercers feature in many other studies of individual objects, mercers or makers, and their names now appear regularly in the ever more detailed provenances recorded in auction house catalogues. The result of this interest and scholarship is the identification of a number of mercers through documents and marks on surviving objects, and a clear sense that the mercers were highly important in the history of design. However, the combined evidence of chapters 2 and 3 suggests that their control of the look, quality and value of the objects in their stock owed as much to their powerful position within trading networks as to their design ability or capacity to employ skilled designers.

Chapters 4 and 5 are each dedicated to a group of mercers trading in specialist markets. The lists of stock are used in some detail here to examine the retailing of imported and domestically produced goods (porcelain and lacquer from China and Japan, and patterned silks woven in Lyon). As specialists in these branches of commerce, the mercers developed a close understanding of the languages of connoisseurship and fashion which gave them significant power to create new fashions and control demand.

Chapter 4 looks at the ways in which the mercers acquired oriental imports in bulk, and sold them to clients who used them for furnishing or to embellish their collections. Here the consumption of large volumes of oriental porcelain in the eighteenth century needs to be seen in terms of a pattern of collecting and display established earlier, particularly at Versailles. By the early eighteenth century, the mercers were developing this market by altering lacquer and porcelain imports to produce new forms and decoration. By re-mounting oriental lacquer panels onto modern Parisian furniture and cutting down and setting porcelain vessels into elaborate gilt bronze mounts, the mercers created new types of goods and integrated oriental objects into the Parisian registers of fashion and taste. As European factories started to produce imitations of the oriental materials, the mercers entered agreements as exclusive or multiple outlets for these products. They also traded in antique porcelain and lacquer wares, which were highly valued on the newly-emerging antique market of the second half of the eighteenth century.

In chapter 5 the relationship of the mercers to the Lyonnais silk industry is considered in the light of various theories of consumption in the eighteenth century which have emerged from research on élite markets driven by fashion.[18] France has been held up as a paradigm of court culture, a society whose consumption is driven by the observance of the behaviour of the court and the emulation of it by city consumers.[19] In the case of the Lyonnais silk industry, the court clearly served as a means of authorizing new designs, and was exploited by the Lyonnais as such, though the intent of the Parisian populace to emulate, as opposed to imitate, the aristocracy is hard to prove.[20] The chapter uses the case study of the market for patterned silks, and argues that the concept of novelty was shaped within the Parisian market place, rather than in the centre of production in Lyon. Alongside the design and manufacture of brand new lines, minor design changes to existing patterns satisfied the demand from Paris for frequent change.

The final chapter, based largely on the inventories of a mercer named Granchez, looks at another aspect of the history of consumption – the design, environment and use of the shop.[21] The chapter charts the way in which he, like others, created a specific identity for a business (in this case an English-style shop) during the 1770s and 80s, a period of *anglomanie* in Paris. Through the design of the interior and exterior of the shop, the production of a shop sign, trade cards and regular advertisements, his stock of English-style wares was given a coherent identity and thus powerfully marketed. Granchez manipulated fashion and generated almost metaphorical allusions to his shop, Le Petit Dunkerque, amongst the social circles of the pre-revolutionary Parisian élite. Like his *confréres*, Granchez had an interest not only in controlling the way things looked, but also the context within which they were sold.

Granchez was not atypical, and his business was certainly comparable to those of the mercers trading at the top end of the market in the rue Saint-Honoré. Apart from their corporate rights and interests, the mercers had in common trading practices which were often high risk, and led them to tread a fine line between solvency and bankrupcy. Motivated by potential profits and dynastic advancement, many of them engaged in the speculation associated with long-distance commerce and the marketing of highly fashionable goods. Their relations with other corporations were complex. They were similar to artisanal enterprises in some ways, yet distinct in others, dependant on them for labour and goods but in competition with them for custom. Their success depended partly on the management of capital, goods and credit but also on marketing skills. These ranged from a connoisseurship which guaranteed the quality of stock and a close relationship with consumers, to the presentation of merchandise in a seductive environment.

Although most studies of consumption and commercial developments in early modern Europe have looked to Britain as a model of a 'consumer society', historians are beginning to look at consumer behaviour in Paris, particularly within the luxury market place.[22] Whether or not France witnessed a consumer revolution of its own is debateable, and is perhaps too large a question to be answered in this book. However, the activities of the mercers indicate that, during the eighteenth century, retailing skills and commercial innovations were integral to the practical organization of supply and the control and development of demand.

NOTES

1. *Théorie du luxe; ou traité dans lequel on entreprend d'établir que le luxe est un ressort non seulement utile mais même indispensable nécessaire à la prosperité des Etats*, 1771 (London, 1775), attributed to Dumont or Butel-Dumont, cited in Galliani 1989, 346. The books and pamphlets on the subject of luxury, such as that cited above, are too numerous to list here. The critical literature on the eighteenth-century luxury debate includes Gaffiot 1926, Galliani 1986 and 1989, Labriolle-Rutherford 1963, Morisette 1941, Neuman 1982, Ross 1975, Saisselin 1992, Sekora 1977, Sombert 1967.
2. For the geography of eighteenth-century Paris, particularly areas populated by the specialist trades, see Burstin 1977, Furet 1961, Garrioch 1986, Hilairet 1956, Monnier 1981, Roche 1981. For the history of the rue Saint Honoré, see Henard 1908–9 and de Segur 1897.
3. Liger *Le Voyageur fidèle* 1715, cited in Henard 1908–9, 377.
4. Although the Parisian counterpart to the guilds was a hierarchy of both *corporations* (of merchants) and *communautés* (of artisans), the term 'corporation' will be used in this book to describe both.
5. The literature is vast, but for a recent and comprehensive discussion of debates on consumption and commerce in Europe, particularly in Britain, see Brewer and Porter 1993, and also Braudel 1979, Campbell 1987, McKendrick, Brewer and Plumb 1982. The literature on European trade and commerce in the eighteenth century is also extensive, but is rarely directly relevant to the discussion of Parisian luxury markets. For texts with a more direct bearing on consumption and the trade in art and luxury goods, and in some cases biographies of individual merchants, see also Bailey 1984, Bonnaffé 1895, Casselle 1982, Chatelus 1973, Courajod 1873, Fairchilds 1993, Grivel 1986, Joullain 1786, Montias 1987, Pardhailé-Galabrun 1988, Parker 1979, Perrot 1981, Peyrot 1973, Pomian 1987, Reddy 1984, Reitlinger 1961–3, Roche 1987 and 1989, Schaeper 1983, Schoeser-Boyce 1981, Scott 1995, Sonenscher 1993, Wildenstein 1962, Verlet 1958, Watson 1965 [2].
6. The literature on the corporations includes Coornaert 1966, Franklin 1968, Gaston 1910, Lespinasse 1892, Olivier-Martin 1937 and Saint-Léon 1922. For more recent arguments about the the corporations in *ancien régime* France see Bossenga 1988, Kaplan and Koepp 1986, Kaplan 1986, Sewell 1981 and 1986, Sibalis 1988, Sonenscher 1983, 1986 and 1987 [1], Sonenscher and Garrich 1986, Vardi 1988. For debates more closely focused on the luxury economy see Kaplan 1981, Sturmer 1979 and Walton 1986 and 1989. See also Sonenscher 1989, 210–243, for a discussion of the economy of the bazaar (after Clifford Geertz).
7. For example see Baulez 1995 and Verlet 1987 on the bronze-workers, Alcouffe 1962 and Pradère 1989 on the cabinet-makers and Sonenscher 1987 [2] on the hatters.
8. Vidal and Duru 1911 and Cleret 1941.
9. Courajod 1874.
10. For example, see de Bellaigue 1974. Rosalind Savill has recently used the daybook in conjunction with the sales registers from the factory at Sèvres to demonstrate Duvaux' prominent role in retailing porcelain (Savill 1988).
11. For example, for a discussion of Giles Joubert as subcontractor, see Roberts 1972.
12. Courajod 1874.
13. The Journal du Garde Meuble de la Couronne. Verlet had by then started to publish his work on French Royal Furniture, which represented a major step forward in the identification of royal pieces through linking the numbers on the furniture with entries in the Journal du Garde Meuble (Verlet 1990–94).
14. Watson 1965 [2], and in French in 1967 [1].
15. Eriksen 1974.
16. De Bellaigue 1974, 858–863.
17. De Bellaigue 1968 and 1995. This subject has also been treated by Watson 1967 [1] and John 1995.
18. See Brewer and Porter 1993, especially the essay by Sissie Fairchilds 1993, Delpierre 1966, Jones 1973, Lemire 1991, Robinson 1963.
19. Particularly by Elias 1983 but earlier also by Sombert 1967 and Fairchilds 1993. Veblen's classic text on conspicuous consumption (1912) also has some bearing here.
20. See C. Campbell 'Understanding traditional and modern patterns of consumption in eighteenth-century England; a character-action approach' in Brewer and Porter 1993, 40–57, for a convincing argument that the consumption of goods which imitate more valuable objects consumed by a social élite is not necessarily driven by a desire to emulate the élite, and for a discussion on the character and motivation of consumers. He argues that such consumers may not be attempting to live an aristocratic lifestyle through this form of consumption, and points out that the demonstration of an individual's wealth and status is the result, rather than necessarily the motivation for their acquisition. Other forms of satisfaction may be gained from the consumption of clothing, furnishings and food and drink (Campbell uses the case of tea, coffee and chocolate).
21. The literature on the history of shops is limited, and largely centred on London: Adburgham 1981, Davis 1966, Mui 1987, Todd 1989, Walsh 1995. For shops in France in the eighteenth and nineteenth centuries see Franklin 1898, Hartmann 1909, Miller 1981, Word 1986.
22. Fairchild's essay on 'populuxe' goods in eighteenth-century Paris is particularly relevant here since she proposes that 'urban France did experience a consumer revolution in the eighteenth century' (Fairchilds 1993, 228).

1 The Corporation of Marchands Merciers

Le corps de la mercerie est celui qui, par l'étendue des objets qu'il embrasse, exige le plus intelligence et de connoissance . . . Il méritoit par cette raison d'être regardé comme le premier corps de Marchands.[1]

The aim of this chapter is to give a brief history of the corporation of mercers since it was first recorded in the twelfth century until the late eighteenth century, and to comment on some of the ways in which it presented itself and acted as a body. The history of the merchant corporations (distinct from the artisanal bodies) has been little documented. Their finances, function and meaning are not easily defined, due in part to the scarcity of evidence[2] but also because the significance of some of their language and activities seems, to modern eyes, elusive.[3] This is true also of the *confréries* associated with the corporations.[4] Though much of the internal workings and symbolism of the mercers' corporation may remain obscure, surviving papers of the merchant body document at least its official remit. Statutes defining trading rights indicate the mercers' expanding trade horizons, and the occasional re-organization within the corporation reveals something of the thinking behind the corporation's management of its members and interests.

The extent to which any of the Parisian corporations served the specific interests of their members is debatable. In the case of the mercers, the corporate body frequently lobbied for privilege and used litigation as a means of protecting its rights against commercial competition from other groups. Except at these points where corporate and individual concerns intersected, the corporation appears to have operated in other spheres independently of the disparate needs of its members. Given a membership in the eighteenth century estimated at between two and three thousand, the high degree of specialization practised within the group, and the variety in the scale of trading assets of its members, it is hardly surprising that it did not engage actively in the pursuit of individual causes.

The Six Corps of Merchants

A sphere of more or less independent activity was the Six Corps, the group of six merchant corporations of Paris. This body, described in 1724 by Sauval as 'une sorte d'aristocracie industrielle' was identifiable from 1431, and remained at the top of the hierarchy of the Parisian corporations from its inception to the Revolution.[5] It participated in a number of various ceremonial and symbolic events in the city of Paris, and the rank of its six members was expressed by the order in which they stood for official processions which accompanied French and foreign royalty into the city of Paris.[6] From 1531, the mercers took third place within the sequence of the Six Corps (fig. 1). In 1725, they represented over half of the total membership of the Six Corps (fig. 2). The mercers finally reached the top of the hierarchy in 1776, when they joined ranks with the drapers (fig. 3).

1.	*Drapiers*	merchant drapers
2.	*Epiciers*	spice merchants
3.	*Merciers*	mercers
4.	*Pelletiers*	furriers
5.	*Bonnetiers*	merchant hosiers
6.	*Orfèvres*	merchant goldsmiths

Fig 1. The Six Corps, 1531–1776.[7]

1.	*Drapiers*	190
2.	*Epiciers*	640
3.	*Merciers*	2,167
4.	*Pelletiers*	47
5.	*Bonnetiers*	540
6.	*Orfèvres*	500
	TOTAL	4,084

Fig 2. The membership of each of the Six Corps, 1725.[8]

1.	*Drapiers/merciers*	drapers/mercers
2.	*Epiciers*	spice merchants
3.	*Bonnetiers/pelletiers/ chapeliers*	hosiers/furriers/ hatters
4.	*Orfèvres/batteurs d'or/ tireurs d'or*	goldsmiths/and workers of gold
5.	*Fabricants d'étoffes/ tissutiers/rubanniers*	textile and ribbon manufacturers
6.	*Marchands de vin*	wine merchants

Fig 3. The Six Corps from 1776.[9]

Allusions to the nobility of the mercers both from inside the corporation and as part of a commentary on the trades and Parisian commerce were frequent. The corporate identity of the mercers rested partly on their status as merchants rather than manual workers, 'marchands de tout, faiseurs de rien'.[10] The mercers considered themselves unique as a corporation of individuals which did not work with their hands, and they employed this distinction to position themselves within the hierarchy of the Six Corps. Although the other five corporations within the Six Corps were all merchant bodies, many were engaged in manufacturing. The mercers were considered

> plus nobles que les autres corps qui sont mixtes, tenans un peu de l'Artisan.[11]

However, despite the mercers' insistence on their singular status within the Six Corps, the body represented itself as a closely-knit group with strong allegiance to a single identity. Its emblem was a seated figure of Hercules attempting, in vain, to break apart a tied bundle of six batons. Its motto was 'Vincat concordia fratrum'. The assemblies of the Corps were attended by the thirty-six guards of the six merchant corporations, and presided over by a representative of the top-ranking corps (the drapers).

A number of positions within the administration of the city of Paris were appointed from the Six Corps, including two of the four *échevins* (magistrates) and the judges and consuls of the Parliament. In addition, one representative from the Six Corps was appointed to the Conseil de Commerce of Paris (established in 1700) in order to

> veiller sous les ordres du Sr Lieutenant Général de Police, à tout ce qui peût intéresser le commerce de ce capitale, le rendre plus florissante et donner encore plus de perfection et d'activité à ses fabriques.[12]

The Six Corps was also a source of capital for the king. Contributions towards war expenditure by the Parisian corporations were not uncommon.[13] In 1567 the mercers offered armed men in support of Charles IX,[14] and in 1636 they gave the king 16,000 *livres*. In 1674 they made a gift of 50,000 *livres* towards Louis XIV's war expenses, at his request. In 1762, five years into the Seven Years War, the Six Corps contributed a total of 700,000 *livres* for the construction of a ship.[15]

In the early seventeenth century, each of the Six Corps was granted by royal act a new armorial, designed around the central motif of sailing ships, which had been used for centuries as the emblem of Paris. The designs were intended to represent the linked fortunes of the Six Corps and the city of Paris. Each of the Six Corps was allocated a new design using the number of ships which corresponded to their rank within the Six Corps. The mercers' armorial was given in 1629, and comprised three silver ships below a banner and gold sun, and surrounded by the blazons of the seven guards. It was to be used 'tant qu'aux ornements de leur chapelle quen toutes occasions quils en auront besoin'.[16] Many high-quality copies were printed in 1674 (plate 1). However, according to Sauval, the mercers chose to continue to use as their symbol the image of St Louis, their patron saint.[17] Both images were used on the medals of the corporation (plate 2).

Plate 2. Jetons *(medals or coins), 1704, struck for the mercers' corporation. Bibliothèque Nationale de France, Paris.*

European merchants were frequently depicted as itinerant pedlars, travelling between fairs and towns (plate 3). Early images of the mercer represented him, in the tradition of the *cris de Paris*, (plate 4) selling portable wares, dressed cheaply and without regard to fashion, and apparently far from prosperous. By the late seventeenth century, however, alternative images of Parisian merchants emerged. For example, the cover illustration presents the mercer as embodied by the merchandise and *attributs* of his trade. Other prints of this date depicted the mercers as fashionable shopkeepers, specializing in retailing and looking not unlike their customers (plates 5 and 6). The virtue of nobility and the aspiration to status, adopted by the corporation as a means of claiming their place in the hierarchy of the Parisian trades, were also powerful assets to an individual who depended on a public image of credit-worthiness and social superiority to develop his business relationships with suppliers and clients alike. When the mercer Sautreau was attacked as a result of a dispute with a merchant outside the corporation, he was subjected to a form of humiliation which could only damage his reputation. He was a guard of the corporation, and had presumably provoked his attacker Jannart's wrath when the guards of the mercers' corporation compounded goods from his shop. Two weeks later, on 2nd October, 1691, a bailiff accompanied by fifteen archers went to Sautreau's shop. He alleged

> Qu'ils lont scandaleusement enlevé de sa Boutique, et trainé par les rues à pied et sans chapeau, jusqu'au prisons de Fort-Leveque, ou

Plate 1. Armorial of the corporation of marchands merciers, *printed in 1674. Bibliothèque Nationale de France, Paris.*

Plate 3. Der Kramer, *German, late 16th or early 17th century. Bibliothèque Nationale de France, Paris.*

> il a été écroué; en quoi il a recu l'insulte la plus cruelle qui puisse être faite à un Marchand, dont la réputation est de la derniere délicatesse; en sorte que cette violence seroit capable de luy faire perdre son honneur et son crédit . . .[19]

The mercers' ability to identify themselves with the nobility of commerce and civic ceremony was reinforced by their early origins within the history of the incorporation of merchant and artisanal groups. The genealogy of the corporation of mercers was long and distinguished. First mentioned in 1137, the mercers were amongst the earliest recorded merchant bodies in Paris, along with the *marchands drapiers* and the *marchands d'eau.*[20] In 1268 the first statutes of the mercers were listed by Boileau under *Le Tiltre du mestier des Merciers de Paris.* The fourteen articles indicate that at this date the mercers were trading in toilet articles, clothing, accessories, and textiles.[21] The regulations did not distinguish between making and selling, being preoccupied, rather, with distinctions between old and new goods and the genuine article in relation to imitations (pearls). Cleret's thesis describes their trade as dominated from the fourteenth century by textiles, especially silks.[22] In 1324, new statutes added, under article 30, *objets de provenance orientale.*

The letters patent granted in 1413 gave the mercers the clear prerogative to trade in multiple markets 'en raison de ce que leur négoce est le profit de tout la gloire

Plate 4. Le Mercier, *French, late 17th/early 18th century, Jean-Baptiste Bonnart. Bibliothèque Nationale de France, Paris.*

Plate 5. Le Marchand de frange, *French, late 17th century. Bibliothèque Nationale de France, Paris.*

de la capitale'.[23] However, the dramatic increase recorded in this document in the scope of their activities may have been driven by the need to specify formally and precisely the rights of the mercers in the light of growing inter-corporate conflict and the 'fine-tuning' of the rights of one corps in relation to another. The need for the corporate regulations to respond to changes in the market and trading practice are strongly invoked in the text of the letters patent of 1558 (confirmed in 1570), which stated that the old regulations were insufficient to regulate complex and diverse trading practices.

Contiguous with the expansion in trading rights was the increase in size of the corporation from several hundred to over three thousand by 1775 (fig. 4). Few records seem to have survived, and are lamentably scarce for the period between 1300, when several hundred members were recorded, and the mid-sixteenth century, by which it had seemingly expanded to three thousand. Even allowing for inaccuracies in these estimates, it is possible to imagine that the major expansion in the numbers of mercers either motivated or in some other way coincided with the revised statutes of 1413.

DATE	NUMBER	SOURCE
1292	200	*taille*[24]
1300	176	*taille*[25]
1557	3000	Félibien[26]
1570	2000	*procès*[27]
1642	2400/2500	Sauval[28]
1725	2167	Marion[29]
1754	2184	Abbé le Boeuf[30]
1775	3207	Delacroix[31]

Fig 4. Membership of the corporation of mercers, 13th–18th century.

Plate 6. Le Marchand de rubans, *French,* c. *1700. Bibliothèque Nationale de France, Paris.*

The statutes registered at the *parlement* in 1613 governed its membership until the late eighteenth century. To become a mercer required French nationality and three years' continuous apprenticeship, followed by a further three years' work.[32] The *maîtrise* cost 1000 *livres*. Thirty-three articles laid down regulations which gave the mercers full rights to trade 'acheter, troquer ou échanger . . . toutes sortes de marchandises' originating in many countries. The list of goods, from article 12, is reproduced in full in appendix 1.

Lespinasse states that during the thirteenth century the mercers were already distinguishable as either wholesalers or retailers.[33] In 1601, the first three categories of six were described as wholesalers (fig. 5). By 1675, Jacques Savary classified all the merchants of the Six Corps in six groups (three wholesalers, three retailers), and his son, Savary des Bruslons, listed twenty specialist branches of the mercers' commerce (fig. 6).

1. Wholesalers
2. Wholesalers of fabrics of gold, silver and silk
3. Wholesalers of serges and cottons
4. Tapestries/upholstery
5. Small items of mercery
6. Jewellery

Fig 5. Classification of mercers by statutes, 1601.[34]

1. Wholesalers
2. Gold, silver, silk fabrics
3. Gold & silver braid, lace, buttons, fringes
4. Wool-based cloth, muslin, camlet, serge
5. Jewellery (gold, silver, precious stones)
6. Linens/calicoes, fustians, ticking
7. Lace, cambric, lawn
8. Raw silk
9. Animal skins
10. Tapestries, carpets, textiles for furniture
11. Iron/metalwork
12. Hardware (cutlery, tools, & locks)
13. Paintings, bronzes, furniture, clocks etc for furnishing
14. Mirrors
15. Gold, silver & silk ribbons, fans & fashion accessories
16. Paper, ink, sealing wax, penknives
17. Tin/copper work
18. Waxed cloth, umbrellas, hats
19. Mercery
20. Toys, snuff boxes, devotional items

Fig 6. Twenty subdivisions of mercers' corporation after Savary des Bruslons, 1723.[35]

Until 1776 (when all the Parisian corporations were restructured), the regulations of 1613 remained more or less valid. During the seventeenth century the corporation was involved less in redefining its statutes than in the business of negotiating existing rights, trading with the king for further privileges, and building its visual identity. Some reorientation of the corporation took place during the seventeenth and eighteenth centuries which reinforced their noble statutes. For example, in 1723, the upholsterers (*tapissiers*) left the corporation of mercers, which considered the *tapissiers* 'que des artisans'.[36]

The statutes allowed them to sell the products of almost any workshop, but prohibited them from stocking tools for manufacturing, allowing them only to finish goods. The mercers, explained Jacques Savary in 1675

> ne travaillent point, et ne font aucuns ouvrages de la main, si ce n'est pour enjoliver les choses qui sont déjà fabriquées et manufacturées, comme de garnir des gants, attacher à des habits et autres vestemens des rubans, et autres sortes de galenteries, et generalement toutes sortes d'enjolivements.[37]

Given the importance of finishing work within the luxury trades, this right to *enjoliver* offered the mercers considerable commercial advantage.[38] In particular, it gave the mercers the possibility of allowing clients to choose the exact finish of their purchases at the point of sale. This practice was considered by other trades to impinge upon their corporate rights and privileges. The 1613 statutes were invoked by the mercers in 1699, when, as a result of a dispute with the paper-makers, they were accorded the right

> de se servir d'un marteau, un couteau attaché sur son fust, une presse et un coussoir, pour parer et enjoliver leur papier suivant l'article quatorze de leurs statutes.[39]

This decision was reached only after independent experts (two *maîtres écrivains*) were called in to advise on the difference between tools for embellishing, and tools and materials for manufacturing.

The mercers' statutes allowed them to sell any kind of object. In general, the statutes of the artisanal corporations stated that they were not to act as dealers, but to sell only the products of their workshops, in many cases bearing the mark which was used by the corporation to police production and distribution.[40] Perhaps more than any other group, the mercers' commerce touched or crossed the boundaries of other corporations' products. Frequent arguments broke out over the right to trade a particular good, or stock a particular tool for assembling or finishing goods, or of one corporation to visit the premises of another's members.[41] These were part of a continuous argument both about the control of highly lucrative markets, and about rights and freedom within a perceived hierarchy of the trades.[42] Freedom was expressed in terms of the right to be protected from interference from other corporations, which was manifested in the inspection (*visites*) and confiscation (*saisies*) of goods. In the statutes of 1613 the mercers' rights seemed absolute – 'les Jurés des autres gardes ne peuvent faire de visite chez les Merciers'.[43]

The mercers shared the trade in woollen cloth, which at times was contentious. In 1680, a proposal had been made to transfer in a single act one hundred mercers to the corporation of drapers.[44] Such an idea appears to have been without precedent, and represents a pragmatic solution to the problem of regular battles between the two corporations over the trade in woollen goods. Both corporations' statutes could be interpreted as permitting individuals to stock such goods. This branch of commerce was highly developed, and extremely lucrative, and the one hundred mercers were specialists in this branch of trade. The move did not take place, and Colbert authorized the mercers to continue selling wool-based cloth. The tension remained unresolved until 1776, when the two bodies were merged into the corporation of draper-mercers.[45]

The policing of the trades and the administration of the corporation fell to the six *gardes* and one *grand garde*. The mercers met annually, in July, for the purpose of electing each year a new *grand garde* and two *petits gardes*.[46] For three years, in rotation, they acted as experts by virtue of their status as leaders of the corps, rather than expertise in a certain product area. Their duties ranged from internal policing to participating in the legislative processes involved in inter-corporate disputes. The mercers shared with the drapers the right and responsibility for monitoring cloth imported into Paris at the Halle aux Draps (the customs point for cloth). This duty fell to the six *gardes* of the corporation of mercers, although some of these individuals had no specialist knowledge of cloth – corporate duty in this instance outweighed personal expertise. The policing of the city's commerce involved regular checks throughout the streets of Paris as well as inspections of goods coming into Paris for the fairs. A record of the mercers' route around the city looking for illicit traders, and the individuals whom they arrested on various expeditions during 1774–5 are described in the papers of the *commissaires de police*.[47] In cases of serious contravention, or when the case might set a useful precedent, the allegations might be pursued through the courts. (Appendix 2 lists disputes between the mercers and other corporations in the seventeenth and eighteenth centuries.)

ARCHITECTURAL AND ARTISTIC COMMISSIONS

Alongside the statutes and ongoing administration and hostilities, the corporation established and expanded its headquarters, and invested considerable sums in the commissioning of art. The *bureau* of the corporation was in the rue Quincampoix, which runs parallel to and between the rues St Martin and St Denis. According to Hilairet, it was, until the fifteenth century, populated by well-known mercers.[48] In 1904, an inscription on the buildings at numbers 38 and 40, rue Quincampoix stated that they had been the premises of the mercers from the sixteenth to eighteenth centuries.[49] In 1660, the premises were enlarged by the acquisition of neighbouring property.[50] The building no longer survives, but it was reputed to have been as impressive as that of the merchant drapers in the rue des Déchargeurs designed by Bruant (plate 7). Sauval said of the mercers in 1724

> ils tiennent leur bureau à la rue Quincampoix, dans une maison . . . plus spacieuse que beaucoup, & non moins superbe que celle des Drapiers.[51]

Plate 7. Façade of the headquarters of the corporation of merchant drapers, c. 1655–60, by Jacques Bruant. Bibliothèque Nationale de France, Paris.

The Bruant façade presents the armorial of the corporation at its centre, flanked by caryatids in relief and framed by Ionic pilasters and a broken entablature. In its architectural scale and detail the façade represents an imposing statement of the corporation's power and identity. It would not be surprising that the mercers, peers and rivals of the drapers, would construct an edifice of comparable ambition.

Like other *confréries*, the mercers' artistic commissions also include painting.[52] In 1674 the corporation ordered from Charles Lebrun a painting of the Resurrection of Christ to be placed above the altar at the church of Saint Sépulchre (colour plate 1).[53] In 1470 the *confrérie* had been established under the patronage of Saint Louis at the Church of Saint-Innocents, and later moved to the church of St Sépulchre in the rue St Denis. The mercers had made a gift to the king of 50,000 *livres* towards his war expenses, and when he returned this sum, he contributed an additional sum which was to be spent on embellishing their chapel (Saint Voult), and on prayers for the king.[54]

Part of the mercers' gift from the king was spent on a large altar painting to be placed, surmounted by cherabims, prominently over the main altar of the church.[55] The corporation had drawn up a contract with the church administration in 1666 agreeing that the services on the days of Saint Louis and Sainte Croix would take place at this main altar, which was in the choir, rather than in the chapel. They had occupied the chapel until 1673 and had commissioned a series of ten paintings depicting the life of St Louis.[56] A missal of 1749 which was used for the mercers' services has as its frontispiece a print after a painting of St Louis also by Lebrun (plate 8).

Now in the Musée des Beaux Arts in Lyon, the

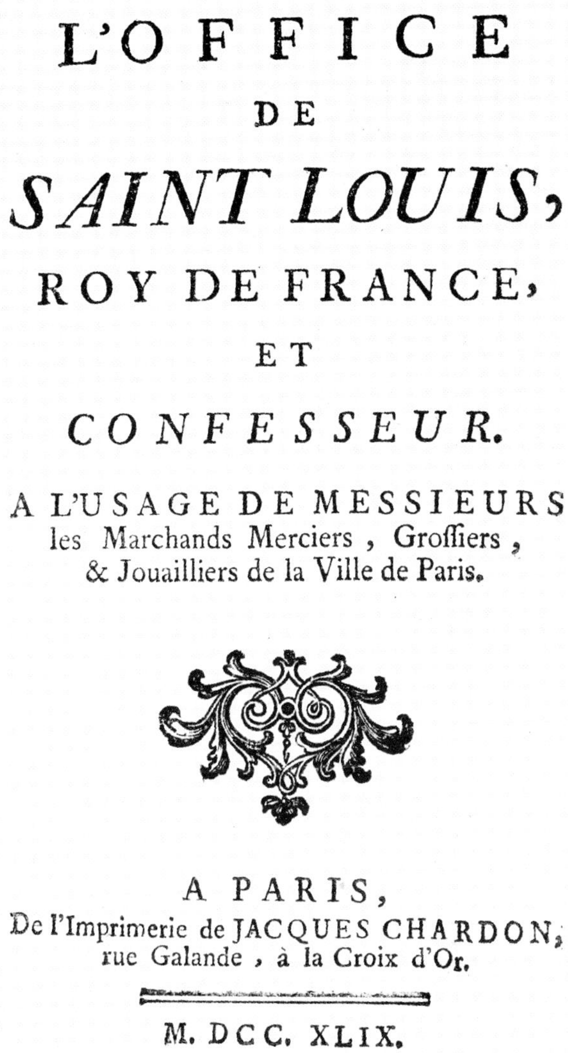

L'OFFICE
DE
SAINT LOUIS,
ROY DE FRANCE,
ET
CONFESSEUR.
A L'USAGE DE MESSIEURS
les Marchands Merciers, Groſſiers,
& Jouailliers de la Ville de Paris.

A PARIS,
De l'Imprimerie de JACQUES CHARDON,
rue Galande, à la Croix d'Or.

M. DCC. XLIX.

Plate 8. Frontispiece and title page L'Office de Saint Louis, Roy de France et Confesseur, *Paris 1749. Victoria and Albert Museum, London.*

painting shows St Louis, patron saint of the corporation, with Louis XIV who is presenting his armour to Christ. Colbert stands to the right of the composition nearby an array of luxury objects, and the coat of arms of the corporation and their device are depicted at the lower left corner. According to de Montgolfier, the corporation had included Colbert as a tribute both to his role as protector of commerce and the arts, and indeed as the dispenser of privilege to the mercers who traded their contribution of 50,000 *livres* against the freedom to trade in wool and thread without interference from the drapers.

It is clear that by the seventeenth century the corporation was well-established, with a long-held reputation for its strength in numbers, trade and wealth. This strength was in part due to the collective trading successes and repute of its members, and to the corporation's ability to secure both privileges from the king and control of markets which other corporations sought to annex. Perhaps most importantly, it was firmly established on an accumulation of trading rights accorded to the mercers by statutes which gave them extraordinary rights and freedoms (in relation to the other corps) to trade in many branches of commerce. The following chapter looks at the way in which individual mercers used these trading rights, and at the activities which formed the day-to-day business of the members of the corporation.

NOTES

1. *Dictionnaire du citoyen ou abregé historique, théorique et pratique du commerce*, Paris 1762, 55.
2. The papers of the corporations were destroyed by fire at the Hôtel de Ville in 1871. A number of printed papers survive, sometimes in the form of compilations assembled during the eighteenth and nineteenth centuries. These papers include statutes, acts granting privileges or amending statutes, and records of disputes between various corporations (appendix 2). The accounts of the corporation of mercers in 1791 are reported as 93,805 *livres* in assets and 178,573 in debts, some 54,000 of which were owed to individuals since 1782, when the mercers collected money to contribute to the 1,500,000 *livres* given by the Parisian corporations to the king for the purpose of building a ship (Vidal and Duru 1911, 326).
3. See Sonenscher 1989, 1–6.
4. Gaston 1910, Franklin 1968, 194–6, and Musée Carnavalet 1991–2.
5. Marion 1989, Franklin 1968, 645–647, Lavergne 1879.
6. Franklin records that the mercers' ceremonial robes were as follows:

1505, entrée d'Anne de Bretagne	satin tanné (brown/tan)
1517, entrée de Claide de France	velours noir
1531, entrée d'Eléonore d'Autriche	velours pers (blue)
1540, entrée de Charles Quint	velours pers
1571, entrées de Henri II et de Charles IX	velours violet
1660, entrée de Louis XIV	velours violet

   When the wine merchants finally opposed the resistance from the other corps and took their place as seventh in rank (a right originally accorded to them by Henri III) they wore caps trimmed with silver, rather than gold like the other Six Corps. (Franklin 1968, 771).
7. Franklin 1968, 645–647. Before 1531, the mercers occupied either fourth or fifth rank, but there ensued a 'violente animosité entre les pelletiers et les merciers, qui se disputeraient le troisième rang', Franklin 1968, 645.
8. Marion 1989, 152.
9. *Dictionnaire portatif du commerce* Paris 1776.
10. De Bruslons 1723.
11. Savary 1675, 44.
12. *Arrêt du Conseil d'état du Roi, concernant la nomination d'un Député pour le Commerce, réprésentant les Six Corps de marchands de la Ville de Paris, 27 avril 1785*.
13. See Bien 1995 and Bossenga 1988.
14. Sauval 1724 vol. 2, 475.
15. *Lettres patentes du roi*, 26 February 1762, which authorized the mercers to raise 340,000 of this sum through selling annuities (*rentes*).
16. Text reproduced in Vidal and Duru 1911, 352.
17. Sauval 1724, 476. Although he states that neither the *pelletiers* nor the *orfèvres* used the new armorials, Franklin does not mention the mercers (Franklin 1968, 647).
18. See Choux 1980, La Fontaine 1993 and Taubert 1966.
19. *Arrest du Conseil Privé du Roy* 5 October 1691 (AN AD XI/22).
20. The mercers were granted the right to trade at the market of the Halles of Charles X in return for a payment of 5 *sous* per annum payable by the *communauté*. The earliest record of a body of merchants as 1121, when the *marchands d'eau* were accorded privileges, promulgated in 1170 by Louis VII. The merchant drapers as a body were granted property in 1181, in return for a payment to the King of 100 *livres* per annum (Boileau 1268).
21. Boileau 1268.
22. Cleret 1941. She characterizes their specialist markets as follows:
   1. Silks imported from the Orient and from Italy, at first those woven with gold and silver thread but later including lighter weight silks such as velvets, damasks, satins and taffetas.
   2. Serges, especially the silk serges made in Florence.
   3. Cottons from Reims, Compiègne and Marigny, and from the fifteenth century, from Holland.
   4. Tapestry, mainly hangings but from the sixteenth century, bedding.
   5. Trimmings (*passementerie*).
   6. Mercery (*la menue mercerie*).
   7. Jewellery, more valuable for its making (*façon*) than for its material value.
   8. Metal wares (*quincaillerie*) including tools.

23. *Lettres patentes* Paris, 1413.
24. *Livre de taille de Paris*, in Franklin 1968, 43, Lespinasse 1897, 233, Vidal and Duru 1911, 87. Vidal and Duru break this figure down as follows: 70 mercers, 129 *mercières* and 1 valet mercer.
25. 152 mercers, 23 *mercières* and 1 valet mercer.
26. Félibien 1725.
27. Between the mercers and hatters, 1570, cited in Franklin, 479 and Vidal and Duru 1911, 87. The figure represented *merciers tenant boutique, sans colporteurs*.
28. Sauval 1724 vol. 2, 475, gives this figure for the number of heads of mercers' families.
29. Marion 1989, 152.
30. Cited in Vidal and Duru 1911, 87.
31. Maître Delacroix used this figure to demonstrate an increase in numbers by a third since 1750, cited in Vidal and Duru 1911, 87.
32. The *brevet d'apprentissage* cost 90 *livres* and had to be registered by a notary. The duties of the apprentice were as follows:

    Le devoir de l'apprenti marchand, était d'ouvrir la boutique le matin, le fermer le soir, la bien nettoyer, y mettre les tapis et autres étalages, bien ballayer devant la porte, à aller promptement porter ou quérir les marchandises; s'étudier à bien connaître la marque du marchand, les prix et les numéros des marchandises afin qu'en son absence et des garçons il puisse vendre.

    Prendre garde de ne point se tromper sur la qualité et valeur d'icelle. Savoir écrire, jetter, compter, calculer, tant é la plume qu'au jetons. Se faire aimer de son maître et de sa femme. Il faut qu'il soit fidèle, civil, honnête et si il veut faire tort à son maître, lui en donner aussitôt avis de peur d'être accusé lui-même; prendre bien garde à la boutique lorsque les garçons sont occupés à vendre, afin que ceux qui viennent pour acheter ne volent rien. Il doit apprendre à bien auner, mesurer et peser, bien vendre et bien livrer.

    Ne point faire des bassesses, comme de laver la vaiselle, promener et amuser les enfants, nettoyer les souliers et autres vilénies qu'on pourrait lui faire faire. Le marchand même ne doit pas le souffrir.

    (*Extrait de la maison reglée*, by Audiger, 1692, cited by Vidal and Duru 1911, 175.)
33. Lespinasse 1886–94, 232.
34. Franklin 1968, 475.
35. Des Bruslons 1723.
36. Sauval 1724, 476. The *tapissiers* were prohibited from living and trading with the mercers, and the fine set at 300 *livres*, *Arrest de la Cour de Parlement qui omologue une Délibération de la Communauté des Mes et Mds Tapissiers, 31 aout 1723* (AD XI, 27).
37. Savary 1675, 45. Cleret argues that the mercers did not achieve a monopoly on the sale of non-Parisian goods until the late sixteenth century, by which point the artisanal groups had reserved the right to manufacture, a right prohibited from the mercers who maintained the right to finish. She maintains that this was the resolution of some two centuries of dispute.
38. On flexibility in production methods in fashion markets, see especially Sabel and Zeitlin 1985.
39. *Arrest de la Cour rendu en faveur des Marchands Merciers, Grossiers, Jouailliers à Paris* . . . 31 March 1699 (AN AD XI/22).
40. For example, in the case of the cabinet-makers or goldsmiths.
41. The nature of this inter-corporate conflict is to some extent documented in the *mémoires* and *précis* which, though incomplete in their survival, record official disputes between corporations (appendix 2). The mercers exploited their position within the hierarchy of merchants and artisan corporations as a justification for maintaining or claiming anew their rights to trade in specific types of goods, and to control the process of finishing.
42. See Sonenscher 1989.
43. *Guide des Corps des Marchands* Paris, 1766.
44. Saint Joanny, 145–54.
45. Franklin 1968, 292–6.
46. An equivalent of a guard, a *roy des merciers*, had apparently existed until 1597, in part to control the wholesale commerce within the French borders, but the office was suppressed by royal edict because its holders had become unmanageable (Franklin 1968, 480–81).
47. Y11990, *procès verbaux*, 22 August 1775.
48. In 1313, of 122 merchants (*commerçants*) in the Rue Quincampoix, 36 were mercers. From 1719, Law's bank was at number 65, in the old Hôtel de Beaufort, see Hillairet 1956, 95–6.
49. The building was sold during the Revolution as *bien national* (Hillairet 1956, 96).
50. Franklin 1968, 480.
51. Sauval 1724 vol. 2, 476.
52. See for prints of the *confréries* Gaston 1910 and Bibliothèque Historique de la Ville de Paris, 1991–2.
53. De Montgolfier 1960.
54. Described in Piganiol de la Force, *Description de Paris* Paris, 1765, vol. 2, 145–7, cited in De Montgolfier 1960, 197.
55. The altar was carved in wood and highly ornate, and was framed with sculptural elements. An inventory of the church of 1790, describes the altar, (AN S922, cited in De Montgolfier 1960, fn. 21, 206).
56. De Montgolfier 1960, 108–9.

2 BUSINESS ORGANIZATION

'Trade is a straight and direct road, but there are many turnings and openings in it, both to the right and to the left, in which, if a tradesman but once ventures to step awry, it is ten thousand to one but he loses himself, and very rarely finds his way back again'.[1]

'. . . on peut commencer la négoce par cent écus, et la faire dans la suite avec des millions'.[2]

The mercers, like many others, were involved in the complexities and uncertainties of eighteenth-century commercial life. Their businesses ranged from small-scale trading to large wholesale and retail enterprises, and encompassed a range of practices involving capital financing and credit.

In contrast to the preceding discussion of the mercers' institutional identity as a corporation, this chapter turns to the subject of the business organization of individual mercers. Little has been written about the economy of luxury enterprises either in the sense of its part in the gross national product of a nation, or at the level of individual enterprises.[3] Although the inventories present only a snapshot view of a business, they yield much detail about the stock, assets and credit of the mercers. The evidence of a collection of inventories is used here to establish the common patterns of business practice within a group of mercers trading in the rue St Honoré between about 1720 and 1780.[4]

The concept of specialist traders settling in a particular district was neither new to the eighteenth century nor restricted to Paris. A number of studies have documented the way in which certain streets or neighbourhoods in Paris became known for their clusters of workshops, factories or shops specializing in various branches of production.[5] The Quay des Orfèvres and the Place Dauphine were known for their jewellery and goldsmiths' shops.[6] When the mercer Charles-Raymond Granchez set up his business just opposite, on the Quai de Conti, he was choosing an area which had a long-established reputation for its metal wares, jewellery and trinkets (see chapter 6). The rues St Denis and St Martin were in part inhabited by mercers wholesaling fabric, and the Quai de la Mégisserie was known during the *ancien régime*, after its population of hardware merchants, as the Quai de la Féraille. It was along this quayside that many of the mercers who specialized in non-precious metal wares, tools and imported metal goods had their shops (plate 9).

THE RUE ST HONORE

The establishment of luxury shops along the rue St Honoré appears to have been an eighteenth-century phenomenon. In 1761, the rues St Martin and St Honoré were deemed by the Six Corps to be the 'grandes rues de commerce' of the city.[7] Of the mercers who sent their details to the editors of commercial almanacs during the second half of the eighteenth century,[8] over half the mercers listed were based in the first two areas, and between 27 and 29% of mercers had shops around the rue St Honoré area (figure 7). Of all the mercers specializing in furniture, jewellery, hardware, fabrics and fashionable clothing in 1769, nearly half had shops in the rue St Honoré area (figure 8).

Plate 9. Trade card of Perrier, 1767, Gabriel de St Aubin. Metropolitan Museum of Art, New York.

DATE	MERCERS	A	B	C	D	E
1770	173	48	40	5	77	3
%	100	28	23	3	44	2
1774	379	104	139	11	119	6
%	100	27	37	3	31	2
Dauphin	245	71	68	9	92	5
%	100	29	28	3.5	37.5	2

Fig 7. Mercers by area, after commercial almanacs 1770–1774.

DATE	MERCERS	A	B	C	D	E
1769	67	31	25	2	9	–
%	100	46	37	3	14	–

Fig 8. Specialist mercers by area, after commercial almanac of 1769.

A. From the rue St Honoré to the area around St Germain l'Auxerrois
B. The area around and between the rues St Denis and St Martin
C. The Quai de la Mégisserie
D. The Palais (the galleries in the Palais de Justice)
E. All other areas, including the faubourgs St Antoine, St Marceau and St Germain.

Key to Figures 7 and 8

The building of the road had begun in 1135 (following the construction of the market at Les Halles) and it became a principal east–west artery passing the Tuileries, the Louvre and the Palais Royal. According to Albert Babeau, the rue St Honoré was populated during the reign of Louis XIV by *jardiniers, maraîches et le menu peuple*.[9] Hilairet describes the street during the early seventeenth century as partly 'plébéienne' (the section between the rue de la Féronnerie and the Oratoire inhabited by merchants of the Six Corps, (*bonnetiers*, *drapiers* and *merciers*) and partly 'patricienne' (the section beyond, with its private *hôtels*).[10] Land records document an increase in the number of mercers buying or renting property in the street. The land in the rue St Honoré was owned partly by the church, partly by the king. In 1700, the *Terrier du Roi* listed only four merchants or artisans and a doctor in the street.[11] The *Terrier de l'archevêché* listed twenty-two mercers who owned property there, mainly during the second half of the eighteenth century.[12] Even more rented shop and living space in the street.[13]

From the early eighteenth century, commentators and historians of the city observed the increasing merchant presence in the rue St Honoré. Of the illicit trade in printed cottons during the period 1715–1723, Henard states that in the rue St Honoré 'une espèce de guerre éclata entre les manufacturiers favorisés par la loi et les marchands recaltricants'.[14] Sauval said of the street in 1724

> . . . c'est un des plus marchandes de Paris . . . non pas toujours des deux côtés à la fois, mais alternativement et avec interruption tantôt d'un côté, tantôt de l'autre. Et de fait depuis la rue des Déchargeurs jusqu'à la rue Tirechappe, ses maisons sont habituées de ce côté-là par des riches drapiers qui les louent bien cherement, et dont les boutiques et magazins sont pleins de marchandises et de draps de toutes les sortes. De l'autre côté vis-à-vis, elle n'est occupée que par des Fripiers mal fournis, et autres semblables Artisans qui ne font pas grand trafic, et qui louent peu leurs logis.[15]

The identity of the street as *marchande* was clearly dependant on a mix of luxury shops. As Sauval indicated, the mercers were but one consituent group within the street. Its residents, according to Robert Henard in an early twentieth-century history of the street, included the nobility, several clergy, notaries, a range of merchants and artisan shopkeepers, prostitutes and at least one dentist. It also housed the salerooms used for auctions at the Hôtel d'Aligre[16] and six cafés.[17] Amongst its occupants were mercers specializing in a range of branches of commerce. These were predominantly silk dealers and milliners (*marchands d'étoffes de soie* and *marchand(e)s de modes*, see chapter 5), furniture and porcelain dealers (sometimes referred to as *bijoutiers*)[18] and luxury hardware merchants (*quincailliers*).[19] Also, a number of merchant drapers' businesses were established in the street, including the Cavillier family, Martin Mathieu Doré, Foucart, Boucher, the Nau family and others.[20] Other traders included Odiot, goldsmith to the King, Macret, cabinet maker to the Menus-Plaisirs, the clock-makers. Furet and Lenoir, Hannong's depôt for Strasbourg porcelain, the perfumers Montclar, de Tremblay and Rousselot-Clousseau,[21] and up-holsterers Jean-Baptiste Delaporte (who rented his shop from Thomas-Joachim Hebert), François Bonastre, and others.[22]

Some of these sold from shops at street level, with several rooms of stock behind and above the entrance. Thomas-Joachim Hebert owned three houses, and rented most of the space in them to others.[23] Others traded from rooms in the upper stories and others traded from stalls (*échoppes*) set up in the street, some on a relatively long-term basis. A document of 1780, disputing the right to light these stalls at night, describes one Victor Bruer's stall, at the corner of the rue des Vieilles Etuves 'ou'il n'a jamais gené depuis 4 ans'.[24] The shopkeepers and stall holders in the rue St Honoré offered the finest luxury products and novelties from Parisian workshops and abroad, and constituted, collectively, a luxury market place within which traders both competed with and complemented each other. Through such diversity of skills, products and business enterprise, the street was able to develop and sustain its reputation as the most fashionable quarter in Paris.

The distinction between maker and merchant was in theory very clear at the corporate level. However, in practice, the terminology used to differentiate maker and merchant was rather blurred. Many mercers were merely styled *marchand bourgeois* in the inventories, and commercial almanacs often listed individuals according to their specialization, so that a mercer specializing in furniture (such as Dominique Daguerre) might be listed along with *ébénistes*.

The differences between these individuals can often only be clarified through an examination of the inventories and the corporate statutes. A *marchand de soie* was invariably a mercer, often specializing in silks with gold and silver thread, *étoffes de soie, d'or et d'argent*, and was distinguishable from the silk manufacturers who were usually described as *fabricants d'étoffes des soie* or *marchands fabricants*. Within the furniture market, a number of artisans and merchants competed and overlapped. A *marchand de meubles* was more often a cabinet-maker (*menuisier-ébéniste*) than a mercer, who would have traded in a wider range of goods than furniture. Sometimes this term seems to have been used to designate a cabinet-maker who ran a middle-sized or large enterprise involving considerable sub-contracting. As a *maître ébéniste*, his stamp would be used for furniture leaving the workshop, though in no way acted as a guarantee that he manufactured it himself. The upholsterers also traded in a range of furniture, selling and renting upholstered seat furniture and bedding, tapestries and wall hangings, and in some cases they hired out furnished apartments or were employed as a *valet de chambre*. The second-hand trade in furniture was hotly disputed between mercers, upholsterers, mirror-makers and the *fripiers* (second-hand dealers).[25] The upholsterers and mercers also sold a range of new framed mirrors, thereby providing retail outlets for the mirror factory at St Gobain and the silverers and frame-makers in Paris. Both the mercer and the mirror-maker bought mirror glass direct from the St Gobain factory, and organized the production of carved and gilt frames by the Parisian joiners (*menuisiers*) and gilders (*doreurs*).[26] Alongside a trade in mirrors, the mercer was likely to be retailing all sorts of other goods, including veneered and sculpted furniture, porcelain, bronzes, clocks, crystal and bronze chandeliers, small statuary and paintings. The mercer retailed from a shop, the upholsterer and mirror-maker, though they may well have had premises for display, employed journeymen and others to work in their workshops.[27]

A mercer specializing in mirrors had much in common with a master mirror-maker (*miroitier*) or an upholsterer (*tapissier*), who also had the right to trade in mirrors.[28] The example of the Darnault family illustrates the way in which a family developed a business from a single product business to a luxury shop selling a wide range of wares by joining the corporation of mercers. François Darnault started trading as a mirror-maker, a *maître et marchand miroitier*, in the rue Grenier St Lazare. An inventory of 1731 describes his 'lettre de reception à la maîtrise de miroitier et lunetier bimblottier, doreur sur cuivre et enjoliveur', registered at the Châtelet on 27 March 1715.[29] The inventory listed small mirrors, large mirrors with carved giltwood frames, and components (glasses, mercury for silvering, mouldings, frames etc.) at various stages of finishing and assembly, including glasses for carriages. The mirrors were silvered in one of the *magasins*, where fifteen pounds of mercury, two work tables and tools are inventoried. The business owed 2,332 *livres* to the manufacture des glaces, and 150 to the widow Lejeune, *marchande d'étain*.

Over a twenty-year period Darnault developed the capital and clientele to expand the product range from mirrors to a much wider range of furnishings including furniture veneered with exotic woods and lacquer (oriental and French), paintings, clocks and bronzes. Father and son combined resources and moved the business entirely from the rue Grenier St Lazare (where Darnault *fils* had commenced trading)

Plate 10. Trumeau *with two* parcloses, *French, 1745–1753, François-Charles Darnault. J. Paul Getty Museum, Malibu, California.*

to the business premises of Darnault *père* in the rue de la Monnoie (in the same neighbourhood as the rue St Honoré). The father's business premises just off the rue St Honoré would have been infinitely preferable to his son's address in rue du Grenier St Lazare, more of a manufacturing than a retailing area. In 1753 Darnault *père's* inventory listed 542 items in stock, comprising many types of veneered furniture, porcelain, bronze lighting fixtures, lacquer, crystal and numerous mirrors.[30] The stock included models for furniture and clock mounts but no workbenches for *étamage*. They sent their mirrors out to one Audot for silvering, and sub-contracted work to bronze and furniture makers.[31] To expand his product line, Darnault was obliged to join the corporation of mercers, since the mirror-makers were not permitted to sell anything other than the products of their workshops.[32] No longer were the Darnaults running a manufacturing concern. Mirrors still formed the largest single product group, but the trade cards also emphasized oriental lacquer goods and *chinoiseries* and a wide range of furniture and gilt bronze (plates 10 and 11 and colour plate 2).

The mercers and artisans were distinguishable by the contrast in their stock and their work as merchants and manufacturers. A further category of traders is discernible, which blurs the distinctions between the first two groups. Present in the rue St Honoré were a number of artisans and mercers who held privileged titles of some description and who were exempt from certain corporate regulations.[33] These mercers included Lazare Duvaux, in the rue de la Monnaie, *marchand bijoutier ordinaire du roi* and later Madame Blakey, of the rue des Prouvaires, *mercière priviligée du roi*. These privileges allowed an individual to style him/herself as a supplier to specific aristcratic or royal families, and to display the coat of arms of that family as part of the presentation of the shop. These titles were distinct from that of *marchand mercier suivant la cour* which was held by twenty-six mercers at any given moment, and which gave them freedom to trade outside corporate legislation.[34]

The extent to which the corporate allegiance of any shopkeeper mattered to those outside the world of the trades is debatable. The question was the subject of a dispute over the usefulness of corporate emblems or attributes in identifying to the public the merchandise available in a particular shop. In 1778, the inlay-workers (*tablettiers*) attempted to prosecute the mercer Bierne for displaying attributes of their trade outside his shop.[35] The inlay-workers demanded that he use the inscription *magasin de mercerie* in place of *magasin de tabletterie*, and that he remove their attributes, the gaming boards. The mercers deemed this ultimatum 'absurde' and 'ridicule', and demanded to know the sense in using their own attributes of combs and ribbons (mercery in its most traditional sense) to signify their specialist trade.[36] A compromise was proposed by the mercers in the wording 'marchand mercier tenant magasin de tabletterie'.[37]

Privilege-holders or not, those mercers who operated as retailers in the rue St Honoré shared some of the patterns of business operations common across the luxury economy of the neighbourhood and the city. In part, a mercers' business followed similar patterns of close coordination and financial management of production by a number of specialized parties.[38] Skilled labour was readily available in Paris, and the mercers' inventories list payments made to individuals for specific, apparently short-term work, as well as, in some cases, regular payments to *ouvriers* over periods of several months or years. Like any artisanal business, the balancing of credit given and taken (i.e. cashflow) was a crucial part of the mercers' business practice. In this sense, they had something in common with a very large artisanal workshop.

As more is understood of the extensive subcontracting systems used by some of the largest workshops, it becomes clear that, for example, the wealthier master cabinet-makers or bronze workers were likely to spend as much time coordinating production and cashflow as they were engaged in skilled manual work.[39] Their ability to survive and prosper depended on an ability to control the acquisition and sale of stock, and to use credit to extend their business operations beyond the boundaries imposed by the availability of hard cash. The mercers' skills lay in sound business practice rather than manufacturing.

These practices revolved around the movement of raw materials, part-finished and finished goods between the mercers' premises and local workshops, employing many different types of skilled labour to complete each item.

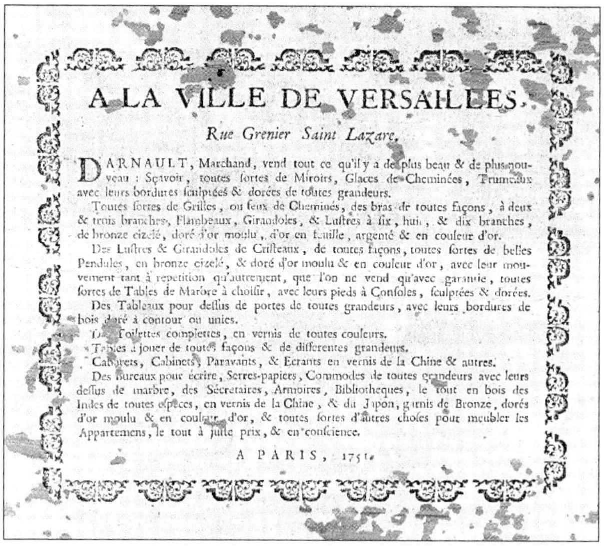

A LA VILLE DE VERSAILLES.

Rue Grenier Saint Lazare.

DARNAULT, Marchand, vend tout ce qu'il y a de plus beau & de plus nouveau : Sçavoir, toutes sortes de Miroirs, Glaces de Cheminées, Trumeaux avec leurs bordures sculptées & dorées de toutes grandeurs.

Toutes sortes de Grilles, ou feux de Cheminés, des bras de toutes façons, à deux & trois branches, Flambeaux, Girandoles, & Lustres à six, huit, & dix branches, de bronze cizelé, doré d'or moulu, d'or en feuille, argenté & en couleur d'or.

Des Lustres & Girandoles de Cristeaux, de toutes façons, toutes sortes de belles Pendules, en bronze cizelé, & doré d'or moulu & en couleur d'or, avec leur mouvement tant à repetition qu'autrement, que l'on ne vend qu'avec garantie, toutes sortes de Tables de Marbre à choisir, avec leurs pieds à Consoles, sculptées & dorées.

Des Tableaux pour dessus de portes de toutes grandeurs, avec leurs bordures de bois doré à contour ou unies.

Des Toilettes complettes, en vernis de toutes couleurs.

Tables à jouer de toutes façons & de differentes grandeurs.

Cabarets, Cabinets, Paravants, & Ecrants en vernis de la Chine & autres.

Des Bureaux pour écrire, Serres-papiers, Commodes de toutes grandeurs avec leurs dessus de marbre, des Sécretaires, Armoires, Bibliotheques, le tout en bois des Indes de toutes espéces, en vernis de la Chine, & du Japon, garnis de Bronze, dorés d'or moulu & en couleur d'or, & toutes sortes d'autres choses pour meubler les Appartemens, le tout à juste prix, & en conscience.

A PARIS, 1751.

Plate 11. Trade card of François-Charles Darnault, 1751. J. Paul Getty Museum, Malibu, California.

STOCK PROFILES

Within a group of mercers in the rue St Honoré who dealt in furnishings and porcelain (Savary des Bruslons' thirteenth category, see chapter 1, figure 6), this was a representative pattern.[40] Each stocked several hundred items comprising bronze items, clocks, furniture, lacquer, porcelain, rock crystal, sculpture and paintings.[41] Bronze items invariably fell into two categories – lighting (chandeliers, girandoles and branches) and fire irons of various designs. Each furniture group included a combination of marble console tables, furniture veneered with wood and marquetry, and furniture veneered with oriental and European lacquer. Each mercer's porcelain stock included a high proportion of oriental items, and in some instances (notably Delahoguette 1768 and Duvaux 1753) Sèvres, Chantilly and other French porcelain. Hennebert 1770 and Delahoguette sold Meissen wares. All except Delahoguette (1768) stocked mirrors. Claude-Antoine Julliot (1736 and 1760), Delahoguette and Hennebert stocked marble vases.

The stock consisted of goods at various stages of manufacture and completion. Some mercers stocked raw materials, mostly bronze.[42] All of them stocked part-finished items, or components, which ranged from clock cases and table legs to uncut precious stones for jewellery and separate fan sticks and leaves. Small bronze mouldings such as masks, medals and drawer handles were kept in stock to finish and repair furniture. The porcelain is slightly more difficult to classify in terms of its readiness for sale, mainly because items set in gilt bronze mounts (such as vases and urns) did not differ much in description from those which were sold unmounted (see chapter 4). It is possible, therefore, that some of the porcelain listed in stock might have been destined for the bronze workshops.[43]

Of the furniture in stock, the components represented between 1% and 11% of the total furniture value. The component items included table legs, pieces of marble and bronze mounts. Julliot (1777) had a particularly impressive range of bronze mounts: *modeles dornements d'après Boule propres pour bibliotheques*, and others for commodes and cupboards. Other descriptions were less specific: *ornements de bronze dorés* (Hennebert) or 7 *onces de cuivre doré* (Delahoguette). Lacquer furniture was commonly veneered with new *vernis de Paris* and *vernis Martin*, or old lacquer stripped from imported oriental cabinets (often described as *bahuts*) and screens.[44] Each inventory lists a combination of these cabinets and screens. Often the lacquer in stock had been removed from its original chassis and was waiting to be reused, either in large pieces as panels for commodes, desks, tables and cabinets or for boxes (the inventories list drawers full of smaller pieces of lacquer for this purpose). The lacquer tended to be from China or Japan, often red, or black with gold, sometimes *en relief*. The Chinese lacquer included a few pieces of Coromandel.

Some items were specified as old (such as Delahoguette's '18 vieux pieds de table . . . prisés 72 livres' or Daguerre's 'vielle table de jeu . . . 20 livres'). A small part of the stock (less than 1% in any case) consisted of broken items. These were mainly various pieces of porcelain. The items described as *cassé* or *felé* were sometimes valued highly in the inventories, and some were described as *recolé*. Depending on the nature of the damage, some of the broken items would have been set in gilt bronze mounts (see chapter 4).

A few items of porcelain were described as *defectueux*, and were for the most part valued at only a few *livres*. Two slabs of marble in Daguerre's stock were 'd'epaisseur inegale et imparfaite' but were still valued at 200 *livres*, perhaps because they could be reused. In some cases, a damaged or imperfect item may not have been greatly devalued by the flaw. Claude-Francois Julliot said of a pair of green porphyry vases fitted with gilt bronze branches and mounts that 'ces vases . . . a eu quelques éclats en le travaillant . . . l'artiste qui les a faits a su si habilement reparés, qu'il seroit difficiles de s'en apercevoir si l'on n'en étoit averti'.[45] Julliot commented on the rarity of the material 'de très difficile travail' which was 'd'autant plus interessante lorsqu'elle réunit une égale variété d'accidents comme les deux vases suivants'. These vases were sold for 2,050 *livres*.[46]

The mercers' stock was composed mainly of finished items, ready for sale. Most of the mercers spread their capital fairly evenly across more than one group of products, though Hebert and Hennebert each focussed markedly on a single group – in Hebert's case porcelain (42% of the total stock value), in Hennebert's, furniture (34%). In all cases except Julliot (1760) and Hennebert, porcelain was the largest single group in terms of value. Other groups representing over 20% of the total stock value were furniture in the cases of Julliot (1736), Hennebert and Julliot (1777), sculpture for Delahoguette and rock crystal for Julliot in 1777. As a proportion of the total stock value, bronze items varied from 4 and 5% (Hebert and Julliot 1736) to 7% (Delahoguette), 14% (Hennebert) and 10% (Julliot 1777).

The value of individual items in stock varied from a few *livres* to several hundred. Items valued at over a thousand *livres* appear in very low numbers in all cases, although the proportion of total stock value accounted for by this range of goods varied – 3% for Hebert, 10% for Hennebert and 50% for Julliot in

Mercer	Lowest value		Highest value	
Hebert 1724	under 1 *livre*	single cups and saucers	233 *livres*	Chinese urn
Julliot 1736	under 1 *livre*	single cups and saucers	150 *livres*	Japanese dish
Julliot 1760	under 1 *livre*	single cups and saucers	80 *livres*	garniture of 3 mounted pots pourris
Delahoguette 1768	under 1 *livre*	single cups and saucers	240 *livres*	garniture of 3 urns, celadon, 5 feet high
Hennebert 1770	under 1 *livre*	single cups and saucers	500 *livres*	garniture of 5 Persian vases, mounted

Fig 9. Values for porcelain 1724–1770.

1760 (see appendix 3). All mercers had more items in stock with a unit value of between 1 and 10 *livres* than in any other range. 50% of Delahoguette's stock was comprised of objects each valued at under 50 *livres*. For Hebert and Hennebert, the equivalent figure was 40%, for Julliot in 1760 only 7%.[47] This can be largely accounted for by high volumes of low-value porcelain. Most mercers stocked large quantities of tableware, and lower volumes of expensive porcelain which usually comprised vases and urns, sometimes set in gilt bronze mounts, and often listed as garnitures (figure 9).[48]

The average values for each product group show some variation. Rock crystal items represented relatively high unit values in the cases of both Claude-Antoine Julliot and Hennebert.[49] Clocks were consistently high in value – 432 *livres* (Hebert), 400 (Julliot 1736), 272 (Hennebert) and 170 (Hennebert). Mirrors averaged over 100 *livres* in several cases (193 *livres*, Hebert, 113 and 100 *livres*, Julliot 1736 and 1760 and 196 *livres* Hennebert).

The stock tended to be highly individualized – apart from small items of porcelain, items were rarely listed in identical groups of more than two or three, and often these were defined as pairs (of vases, *girandoles*, *commodes* etc) or *garnitures* (of porcelain vases or urns). The descriptions of items were relatively similar, rather than identical, which suggests that they were stocked in series with variations in size and finish (see chapter 3).

A number of items were stocked in several sizes – particularly porcelain and sculpture. For example, Julliot (1777) stocked bronze figures of *Lantin et Venus pudique* in small, medium or large sizes (valued at 48, 84 and 150 *livres*). Fire dogs were stocked in a number of different patterns, including vases, horses, flying dragons, female heads, pyramids, sphinx, Vulcan and plain (Hebert 1724). In most cases, the clocks differed in terms of material (veneered, marquetry, lacquer or bronze case), movement (maker and type of mechanism), size and function (wall, desk, long case). Furniture types were very varied, which indicates that the mercers were selling furniture for different purposes and places – from large, heavy marble console tables which stood permanently at the base of a pier glass (*trumeau*) to small, movable games tables.[50] Within the category of tables used for writing were both small writing tables (*tables à écrire*) and larger *bureaux*. The bureaux ranged in value, within inventories and between mercers. Hebert's *bureaux de cabinet* ranged in value from 200 *livres* for stained pearwood (*poirier*) to 1,000 *livres* for Boulle marquetry with bronze mounts and *pieds de biche*, covered with Morocco leather.[51] Delahoguette had in 1768 a bureau, seven feet long, of ebonized wood with bronze mounts (ungilded), valued at only 96 *livres*.

The figures given here offer an impression of the range of items stocked within one specialist branch of the mercers' trade, and their relative unit values.

The prices paid by the Garde Meuble du Roi for furniture and bronzes supplied by mercers and artisans were frequently considerably higher than those values cited here.[52] This raises the question of special commissions, which do not appear in the mercers' inventories, and for which special financial arrangements may have been made. Hebert's commission of November 1723 from the Boulle workshops, for example, of copies of the king's commodes originally made for the Trianon, and of a model of a clock probably represented a specific commission rather than the order of items for stock.[53]

Some of the less valuable stock also appears to have been made to order. For example, the carcases of several pieces of furniture made for the mercer Simon-Philippe Poirier were marked with his name, and sometimes with instructions to the makers which relate to the form of decoration and finishing of the piece. One of the drawers of a small marquetry *sécretaire en pente* bears the inscription 'Poirier 3 pieces argentées', to indicate that three containers for ink etc. should be silvered and fitted into this drawer (colour plate 3).[54]

SOURCES OF CAPITAL

The financing of this volume and assortment of stock was achieved in a number of ways which involved both the use of capital and credit. Short-term, renewable business partnerships were a means of raising capital sums.

Personal and business finances were inseparable in the eighteenth century and the family was an extremely important source for capital. It provided inherited wealth, dowries and gifts on marriage, and sometimes loans or advancements on an inheritance. It seems that these types of capital were particularly useful to a mercer early on in his or her business life. For example, Claude-François Julliot became a member of the mercers' corporation in 1753, after inheriting over 6,000 *livres* from his mother's estate in 1752, marrying in 1753, and borrowing about 11,000 *livres* from his father during 1754.[55] From then on, he seems to have been financially independent, until he inherited part of an estate of over 200,000 *livres* after his father's death in 1760.

The timing of a marriage was also significant in relation to a business career, since a dowry often doubled the estate. Lazare Duvaux' assets were worth 16,000 *livres* when he married in 1741, and his wife's dowry 15,000. When Delaplanche married the widow of a mercer in 1774, she brought 40,000 *livres* – given that his entire business assets at that date were estimated at 10,000 *livres*, the marriage injected a major capital sum.[56] When Dominique Daguerre married, his wife's dowry was worth 31,600 *livres*. The marriage also occasioned a gift of 20,000 *livres* by his guardians and business partners, the Poirier family, and promises of a further 30,000 *livres* from the Poiriers' joint estate.[57]

As well as providing a direct source of cash, the family often represented an extensive network of commercial contacts. The Legras family, themselves very successful mercers dealing in textiles, married into some of the wealthiest merchant families in the rue St Honoré – the drapers Nau, and merchant hosiers Delacroix.[58] Through such family connections, a mercer might not only have access to funds but also ready-made links with networks of artisans and merchants, and an established clientele. Claude-Antoine Julliot's marriage contract also shows the extent of the network of his immediate family and friends. His relatives by marriage included a number of major families of merchants – the Heberts, Legras and Daustel were all wealthy and successful mercers. He was also distantly related to the family of Lazare Duvaux (via the Legras family), to the Poiriers (Simon-Philippe, mercer, was married to the daughter of Thomas-Joachim Hebert's niece), and thereby to Daguerre, Simon-Philippe Poirier's cousin.[59] Poirier and Daguerre were in partnership during the 1770s and 1780s, and were known for their sales of Sèvres porcelain, clocks, bronzes, marble vases and furniture.

A further means of raising capital was to go into

partnership. This sometimes happened within the family, particularly at the time of a marriage, but often outside it. A partnership was commonly established for a period of nine years, sometimes renewed for a longer period, and sometimes dissolved early, on the death of a partner, or when one of them wished to withdraw from the arrangement. Partnerships within the family were another example of the family's support of their offspring's enterprises, and also reflected the drive to ensure the future of the dynasty. When in 1738 Raphael Boscheron, son of the chief guard of the mercers' corporation married Angelique Julie Bauvin, daughter of Pierre Joseph, also a guard of the corporation, her parents gave their son-in-law a quarter share in the business.[60] They stated that they would do the same for their only son, when he came of age. They were in the cottons and lace trade, and the business assets amounted to nearly 700,000 *livres*.[61] The fortunate couple also received a gift from his parents of 30,000 *livres*, and a dowry from hers of 40,000.

The sums involved were often considerable. For example, three mercers, all from the rue des Bourdonnais, a street well known for its textile shops, combined their capital in a nine-year partnership established in 1752. Each contributed 75,000 *livres*, either in cash or in goods, bringing the total assets of the partnership to 225,000.[62] When one of the partners, Henri Maximilien Gaucherel, died, his son took over his interest in the business.[63] Merchants from within the family and acquaintances who included a number of office holders were present at a marriage which linked in family and business partnership the silk dealers Boscheron and Bauvin.[64]

Another major textiles partnership, in this case based on unequal shares, was set up between Jean-François Bentabole and the brothers Rohault, from the rue St Honoré. In 1748, the partnership was dissolved – Bentabole was pulling out of the business.[65] Their assets at this date totalled 234,626 *livres*. They owed over 170,000 to suppliers, and their profit amounted to 62,000. Jean-François Rohault held the controlling interest in the company. He was allocated just over 44,000 *livres* from the total profit, whereas Bentabole received only 12,200 *livres*, after a deduction of 2,000 which he owed the partnership. The second Rohault brother took only 2,400 *livres*, which represented his part of the profits, but no capital share in the business. Bentabole's final payment amounted to just under 27,000 *livres*, which represented the repayment of his capital, rent on the house which he owned from which the business was run, plus over 14,000 *livres* as a *pot de vin* and for the shop sign, La Toison d'Or. The *pot de vin* was a goodwill payment.[66]

Other partnerships were set up with sleeping partners. When Omont and Guérin (both mercers) established a company dealing in textiles for furnishing in 1737, Guérin stated that he wanted to retire from retailing.[67] He invested 6,000 *livres* in the new partnership, and lent a further 24,000, at 5% interest. Omont contributed no money at all, just his hard work and experience.[68] The new partnership was to trade under the name *Omont et Compagnie* and in this case the profits were to be shared equally.

Partnerships were frequently renewed by the original partners for a further term. However, changing circumstances and demands for capital might impose a need for a new contract with new individuals, or different terms, to be drawn up. A number of mercers exploited the flexibility of the system by changing partners and premises fairly regularly. For example, Dominique Daguerre formed a series of partnerships to finance his shop, A la Couronne d'Or, in the rue St Honoré, between the 1770s and the 1790s.[69] He finally went into partnership with Martin Eloi Lignereux in 1789; each contributed 17,500 *francs*. Daguerre also brought his stock of furniture, porcelain and bronzes (from his continuing business) worth just under 300,000 *livres*. The value of the furniture was treated as a loan to the business, with a return of 5%. Daguerre retained the controlling interest in the new partnership – his share was nine sixteenths,

Lignereux' seven sixteenths and the profits were divided on that basis.[70]

Other partnerships were set up to finance large-scale production, particularly for printed cottons. For example, François Rozelet, a mercer, formed a partnership in 1775 with one Louis François Desmarest, referred to as a *bourgeois de Paris*.[71] Presumably, cashflow problems or a new venture requiring more capital forced them to take a third shareholder, another 'bourgeois' called Durand, three years later. The latter invested 36,000 *livres* in the manufacture for printed cotton outside Paris.

A shareholder might be taken into a business if the business was having difficulty paying its debts, or needed a replenishment of stock. If its creditors were not being paid, or they perceived that the business was not doing well, they were extremely unlikely to offer favourable credit terms which would allow the mercers to restock the shop without any outlay of hard currency. Claude Carelu, whose daybook survives, bought new stock with the capital raised from taking on a partner.[72] The latter, Malezieu, was not a mercer; rather he was described as 'interessé dans les affaires du roi'. He agreed to pay 30,000 *livres* into the business, and Carelu states that it was to be used to pay the journeymen and to buy new goods. Unfortunately for Carelu, Malezieu then reduced the sum to 20,000 *livres*, the result of a private agreement being made, rather than drawn up by a notary as legally binding. During the period of several months immediately following the partnership agreement, Carelu used much of the capital to restock the shop and refit the interior. The new stock included furniture, porcelain and seventy-eight tortoiseshell and silver snuff boxes. He went to Rouen to buy the latter items, equipped with letters of exchange from his partner. Frequent notes in the day book testify to the fact that Malezieu held considerable authority over the outlay of the capital, giving it to Carelu bit by bit over the following months. Carelu continued to be responsible for purchasing and book-keeping.

A mercer might pay for goods in a number of ways: by current account, by promissory note, by bill of exchange, in cash, or in kind.[73] The first three types of transaction, essentially credit-based, were the most common, though the terms varied from one business to another. Most mercers' inventories show a combination of these forms of exchange. Payment was sometimes made in kind – for example, Carelu bought two clock movements for 270 *livres* from a clockmaker named Grebet. The transaction was agreed on February 23 1724, when Carelu paid Grebet 206 *livres*, 96 in cash, and 110 in the form of a metal watch. He received one of the movements on March 5th, and paid him a further 30 *livres* on the 12th. The account was finally settled on April 8th.

Perhaps credit was the most fundamental element within the mercers' business relationships. The market itself was defined by credit links, between suppliers, intermediaries and clients. Credit linked the participants in the market over both space and time. The type of credit agreement made by a mercer reflected his or her relationship with either supplier or client, and his or her ability within that relationship to drive a hard bargain. Whilst the capital sums discussed earlier were critical for establishing or rapidly expanding a business, or for any new enterprise, most businesses were based on a variety of credit agreements which extended the business assets at any one time to represent more than the cash in the till and the goods in stock.

Credit cycles in large businesses were usually long – the inventories include some promissory notes fixing the date of payment over a year after the agreement took place. For example, the 37,953 *livres* owed by Porlier to Bentabole was transacted in March 1753, in eleven promissory notes payable at regular intervals between the subsequent December, and the end of January 1754. His credit to others was similar, most payments being due monthly, over a period of several months to a year. Mercers in other types of commerce also used promissory notes to acquire stock on credit.

Carelu's daybook shows that his credit cycle was much shorter – often only weeks, sometimes a month. He frequently paid for goods in cash – not, presumably, from preference but because his credit rating was low. His father-in-law was one of the few individuals offering him credit. He was buying in very small volumes, on a daily basis, in contrast to those textile houses which were buying large volumes of goods infrequently. Most of Carelu's transactions were under 100 *livres* – and were distinct from the longer credit cycles exemplified by the terms negotiated by mercers such as Hebert, Daguerre, Porlier, or Bentabole who dealt with some suppliers in thousands, or tens of thousands of *livres* per deal. Carelu's daybook charts a steady decline into severe cashflow problems, and later documents reveal that his career ended in prison, much to the chagrin of his wife who had to collect his debts.[74] The mercers were dependant on credit not only to acquire the necessary range and quality of stock to attract clients, but also to absorb the cash flow problems exacerbated by their clients' unwillingness to settle their bills. Hence they paid as little up front to their suppliers as possible, and often managed payments to them by using current accounts. For example, when Hebert ordered from Pierre I Migeon a *sécretaire*, or *commode*, he would not pay for it for some time.[75] At the end of 1731, Hebert owed Migeon 360 *livres* outstanding from six items together worth 650 *livres*.[76] He paid 192 *livres* at this point, and continued to be supplied by Migeon in 1732, without having cleared his debt. A day-book recording Migeon's business in the 1740s and 50s shows that he too built up credit with his journeymen. For example, Letellier supplied Migeon with chairs throughout 1758, and was owed 1,048 *livres* by the end of the year, of which Migeon had only paid him 674.[77]

Migeon's suppliers were local artisanal workshops, within easy reach. The management of long-distance business transactions was complex, and carried considerable risks. Jacques Savary points out that such trade was often based on high capital transactions and generated difficulties in controlling credit and quality of goods overseas. Many of the mercers were involved with a combination of long distance and local suppliers. The furthest away were based in China, the closest in the same street in Paris. Similarly, a mercer's clientele might extend from Paris to other European cities and as far as the colonies.

It seems that a Paris-based mercer was likely to communicate with overseas producers via a chain of intermediaries. These included individual agents and larger organizations. For example, the East India Company was probably the largest such intermediary, importing textiles, porcelain, furniture and other items into Europe. In 1768, Antoine Porlier, who sold silks, velvets, satins, taffetas and damasks from his shop in the rue St Honoré, was owed nearly 7,000 *livres* by customers in Guadeloupe. He was represented there by a man named Rousseau, who acted as his agent in recovering these debts.[78] Madame Blakey, who had a *magasin anglais* in the rue des Prouvaires, just off the rue St Honoré, imported many goods from England including furniture, clocks, cabinet makers' and clockmakers' tools, saddlery and metalwork.[79] She had agents in both Dunkirk and London. The London connections also seem to have supplied her with German products – for example, she received a bill from Jacques Granges in London for goods bought from Thomas Clark in Hamburg.[80] She sold goods worth over 38,000 *livres* in St Domingo through an intermediary called Tardivy. Her customs bills alone were estimated at 34,000 *livres* when she went bankrupt in 1772.[81] Baudouin, who sold *chapeaux anglais* to the English, listed amongst his business expenses insurance, commission, packaging and customs bills.[82]

Both Porlier and Madame Blakey also used suppliers rather closer to home. She bought goods from Sheffield, Birmingham, Edinburgh, London, Cadiz, Seville, Geneva and Flanders. In France she owed money to individuals in Bordeaux, Calais, Caen, Coutray, Orleans, Versailles and Lyon. It would seem that she was exploiting the cheaper labour outside Paris by using clockmakers from Bordeaux, Caen and

Coutray. She was supplied with clock cases from England.[83] She, like Granchez who was in a similar line of business, also bought metal goods from England and Germany.[84] Granchez' creditors extended from Paris to Frankfurt, London, Sheffield and Birmingham, from whom he presumably bought metal items such as snuffboxes and tableware rather cheaper and of better quality than Parisian wares.[85]

Porlier imported textiles into Paris from several manufacturing areas of France. He owed 36,531 *livres* to three suppliers in Lyon, three in Tours and eleven in Paris. Five of the Parisian creditors were mercers themselves, including Baillet who had a shop in the rue St Honoré, to whom Porlier owed nearly 20,000 *livres*. He sold his goods to other merchants, to various tailors and to a *marchande de mode*.[86] Textiles were imported by other mercers into Paris from all over Europe – Pierre Bourgeois, who half-owned a textiles factory at Crépy, also bought fabric from Zurich, Tours, Nîmes, Paris and Alençon, and from twenty-three suppliers in Lyon.[87] Jean-François Barbier, a mercer specializing in woven silks at the sign of the Barbe d'Or, rue des Bourdonnais, was supplied by over eighty Lyonnais merchants. When he went bankrupt in 1762, his stock was valued at over a million *livres*. His debts outweighed his assets, both of which amounted to over four million *livres*. He was supplier to the king and some 200 high-ranking clients – his business was so extensive, and so many other enterprises depended upon it, that the king and the Lyonnais appointed a syndicate to run the business. They agreed to keep the shop well-stocked so that turnover remained healthy, and the Lyonnais supplied him with over 1,300,000 *livres'* worth of silk between January 1762 and May 1763. Once in Paris, they were sold either to individual customers, upholsterers, mercers (including *marchand(e)s de modes*) or any number of skilled workers, such as the tailors and couturiers.

The pattern of supply of goods and labour within Paris was equally complex, though perhaps more flexible by virtue of proximity to the mercers and also the specific character of the Parisian workshop economy for luxury goods. Markets for skilled labour, raw materials and part-finished goods were extremely fluid. Some mercers bought almost all of their stock within the city boundaries – particularly furniture and bronze items. A mercer like Claude Carelu, selling furniture, porcelain and other *objets d'art* represents a common pattern. He used a number of different specialist sources for furniture. These included the cabinet-makers Criard, Boulle, Gisquier, Garnier, and Bellanger. He patronized two marble sellers, three sculptors, two gilders, several bronze workers, and various individuals for porcelain goods and other skilled labour. His daybook shows that he co-ordinated the production of most objects individually or in very small numbers, and that almost every day materials and part-finished goods were passing through his shop, to and from the workshops.[88]

Similarly, Nicolas Guillaume Daustel used three cabinet makers (*ébenistes*), two sculptors, a mirror-finisher (*miroitier metteur au teint*), a clockmaker, gilder and marble seller. He also owed the glass factory 6,261 *livres*.[89] Hebert was supplied by seven unspecified merchants (one of whom was based in Amsterdam), two cabinet-makers (*ébenistes*), two joiners (*menuisiers*), two mirror-finishers (*miroitier* and *miroitier-garnisseur*), two gilders (*doreurs*), a goldsmith (*orphevre*), a box-maker (*layetier*), a tool-maker (*taillandier*), a marble seller (*marbrier*) and an inlay worker (*tablettier*).[90] A mercer selling luxury hardware and iron goods, Etienne Guillaume Disnematin, used six bronze workers (*fondeurs*), five silverers and gilders (*doreurs* and *doreurs-argenteurs*), and a locksmith.[91] He also owed money to Joseph Oppenheim – possibly the same Oppenheim of Birmingham who supplied Madame Blakey. Michel Delahaye *bijoutier* (mercer) was supplied by sixty individuals, most of whom had addresses in Paris.[92]

The number of instances recorded in the inventories of mercers exchanging goods with each other is notable. By no means did the mercers act only as the intermediary between manufacturer and private customer. Their customers were also sometimes artisans (buying raw materials and tools), and frequently other mercers. Three examples from different branches of commerce illustrate the pattern. Dubuisson, who specialized in porcelain, bought much of his stock from Parisian merchants. His Chinese porcelain came from Bouffée, or Jacquet and Tixier in the rue Bertin Poirée, and Chantilly porcelain from Dutfois. He also bought directly from the Sèvres factory.[93] He bought drinking glasses elsewhere, from merchants such as Noblin, in the rue St Antoine, whom he supplied with porcelain. Dubuisson supplied other mercers himself – Tesniere, Tuart, D'Avie, Bailly and Poirier, all in the rue St Honoré.[94] Many of these transactions were on a sale or return basis. In the case of a mercer named Bossuet, who specialized in mirrors and furnishings, although most of his suppliers were artisans, he seems to have specialized in supplying merchants.[95]

In the market for silks, a similar pattern of distribution amongst mercers can be discerned. Porlier bought textiles worth over 37,000 *livres* from Jean-François Bentabole, worth 6,316 *livres* from Clement, 1076 *livres* from Jean-François Barbier and 5,990 from Jean Gaston Doucet, all of whose shops were in the same street. He was also supplied by the widow Chauvin and Delarue of the rue St Denis, (15,843 *livres*), Lhorloger et Cuvillier, rue de la Limace (5,116 *livres*), and a number of other suppliers in Paris. A mercer named Doucet (of the rue St Honoré) appears both as his creditor and debtor – unfortunately information about the nature of the exchange is no more precise than that.[96]

Carelu bought small volumes of goods from the mercers Julliot and Hebert. They appear infrequently in his day book. He bought a tric-trac table from Hebert in May 1724, which he paid for in cash (95 *livres*). Julliot supplied him with porcelain goblets and a Chinese cabaret, for 26 *livres* 10 *sols*, for which he also paid cash. In October 1724, he paid Julliot 22 *livres* cash for two paper screens.[97] Since all of Carelu's transactions were for relatively small volumes of goods at low prices, perhaps it is no great surprise that his purchases from Julliot and Hebert followed the same pattern as the rest of his daily business. It is possible that these transactions represent a sort of 'top down' distribution system, whereby the most fashionable goods in Paris, from the most wealthy and reputable mercers, were circulated to lesser retailers in other parts of the city. (Carelu's shop *au Cabinet d'Italie* was in the faubourg St Germain, in the rue St André des Arts.)

These exchanges demonstrate very clearly the degree of dependence and cooperation between local mercers, and the fluidity of the circulation of goods within the city after they have left the workshops. A fashion-driven economy put certain pressures on mercers. Their customers were unpredictable in their demands, and a mercer may not have had the precise combination of stock required to satisfy them. He or she could presumably fulfil some orders by buying the item(s) from a local mercer. For example, it would take much longer to order silk lengths from Lyon than to buy them from a local mercer in the rue St Honoré or des Bourdonnais. Mercers might agree a reciprocal arrangement, benefiting both parties. If this were to be the case, though, one would expect individual transactions to be fairly minor – whilst this might explain Carelu's purchases from Julliot and Hebert, the scale of Bentabole's transaction with Porlier is too large to fit the model of small occasional exchanges to supplement the less flexible supply of goods from outside Paris and suggests a different role.

Some mercers performed the function of distributor for certain goods imported from outside Paris. Unfortunately, the inventories do not relate the exact goods sold in each individual transaction, so it is difficult to demonstrate conclusively that this was the case. It is possible that Bentabole could buy in bulk at favourable rates – indeed, the weavers may have preferred larger orders, as they could schedule weaving work accordingly. Bentabole was not acting solely as a wholesale distributor within the Parisian market – his customers include many private individuals, including a number of Comte(sse)s,

Marquis(e)s, Ducs, Chevaliers and others. However, he may well have been the only importer of certain product lines which he then distributed to other Parisian retailers.[98] Whilst it is impossible to be certain whether this was the case for silk mercers, others, such as Granchez, acted as sole outlets for certain goods. In his case, an almanac advertized that the Manufacture de Porcelaine de la Reine had established its dépôt at his shop, au Petit Dunkerque on the Quay de Conti,[99] and Dominique Daguerre was in the 1770s the sole distributor in Paris for Wedgewood.[100] However, the distribution rights were not always perceived by suppliers to represent the most profitable form of marketing. In 1790, the Manufacture Royale de Faience et Porcelaine used multiple outlets in Paris for its wares, not surprising given the difficulties of selling luxury goods at this time. The factory was established at Bourg la Reine and is documented in an inventory of 1790 after the death of the wife of its *entrepreneur* Charles Symphorien Jacques.[101] The products included tablewares and objects for display in three categories: coloured porcelain,[102] white faience,[103] and gilded porcelain.[104] The fourth product group, biscuit porcelain, comprised vases, pedestals, figures, glasses (*verres*, which may have been for ices, like the *verres à glaces* listed under coloured porcelain), and medallions. The latter may well have competed with both Sèvres and Wedgwood. Under *rebut* (rejects) were listed objects of white porcelain and coloured faience. Twenty-eight merchants were listed in the inventory as debtors.[105]

SECOND-HAND AND RECYCLED GOODS

Second-hand goods were a useful source of stock for the mercers. The few surviving daybooks show that the mercers were buying regularly at household sales, as a means of acquiring stock cheaply. Some reconditioning would often take place subsequently. In the 1730s, for example, Claude Carelu bought at sales several times a month, five to ten items at a time, sending the goods out to specialist workshops before reselling them. For the supply of new goods he went to cabinet-makers Criard, Boulle, Gisquier and Garbier and for repairs he used Bellanger. The sales were an obvious way to build up stock relatively cheaply – great savings could sometimes be made, though do not seem to be typical. For example, Claude-Antoine Julliot bought two rock crystal chandeliers and a girandole at a sale in 1747, paying only 10,000 *livres* against an inventory value of 17,625.[106]

The trade in used goods also represented a part of the credit and cashflow arrangements of clients and merchants. Payment in kind was one option, and at least avoided the common problem of trying to persuade clients, particularly the aristocracy, to pay up. Valued clients tended to keep current accounts with their regular suppliers, and chasing the settlement of outstanding sums was an ever-present problem for the merchant, who at the same time was keen to continue to shift stock. Exchanges with customers of old for new goods were relatively common. François Boucher exchanged two porcelain urns in gilt bronze mounts for two Chinese figures from the porcelain dealer Dubuisson in the 1750s.[107] Dubuisson's daybooks record other similar arrangements with clients. In February 1724, Carelu accepted an old bookcase from the Marquis de Chartre, with one glass door broken, in part payment for new goods. On October 29th 1723, Carelu bought a large framed mirror, from the king's procurer at Versailles for which he paid 530 *livres* in cash, and a pier glass worth 90 *livres*. Delahoguette accepted 3,000 *livres*'s worth of *effets* from De Suoyere for two large girandoles with three branches and a gilt bronze statue.[108]

To service the used goods, the merchants had ready access to a complex network of specialist workshops offering a range of repair services. Some acted as specialist restorers, for example, Madame Kumpff, who advertised that she possessed 'le secret de raccomoder très proprement, avec une fondure au feu, les porcelaines cassées, de même que le crystal, les tables de marbre, figures de porcelaine, tabatieres etc'.[109] Her premises were in the rue des Canettes, in the house of a wig-maker. Other artisans provided a restoration service as part of their provision of goods and services. For example, at the sign of the Château de Bellevue, rue St Honoré, the merchant Tuart advertized a stock of veneered furniture, mirrored goods and bronzework. At the end of the text, he stated that he restored to new old furniture and bronzes. The cabinet-maker Montigny is now best known for his pastiches of Boulle furniture made in the 1770s, including cabinets with new carcases veneered with late seventeenth and early eighteenth-century marquetry panels. He also promoted himself as the only craftsman in Paris who should be trusted with the cleaning and repair of old Boulle furniture.[110]

Maintenance services available to clients seem to have been very much part of the merchants' activities, and are particularly well documented in the daybook of Lazare Duvaux (1748 to 1758). The relationship in business terms between outright sale and services is clear from the daily entries. He sold a wide range of fashionable and novelty furniture, rock crystal, porcelain and bronzework and dealt in some antiques in the 1750's. He also serviced goods after the point of sale. He arranged for rock crystal chandeliers to be cleaned – a task not to be underestimated as they were fragile and complex in construction and needed to be completely dismantled for cleaning. When the Marquise de Pompadour had all the gilt decorations, porcelain, lighting and furniture at Bellevue moved and cleaned, Duvaux sent a team of specialists to work on site and at other times he worked on the redisplay of her collection.

Candlesticks were repainted, wallpapers refreshed, and lacquer surfaces revarnished. In 1751, Duvaux had the veneer removed from a table before reconditioning and repolishing it. Items and decoration in bronze required regular attention, and the day book is littered with entries recording the cleaning and relacquering of bronze, gilt or lacquered, for clocks and candlesticks or furniture mounts. For example, the Princesse of Turenne had a porcelain clock dismantled and cleaned, and the bronzes refurbished 'as good as new'. Watches and clocks might need repair, hinges on boxes and pots replacing, and objects could be brought in for embellishment. An old snuff box was given a new tortoiseshell finish. Porcelain, for example, could be repainted, gilded, or provided with a new and fashionable gilt bronze stand. This might involve structural alteration, such as the cutting down of four large porcelain vases to fit gilt bronze mounts for the collector de Jullienne. In December 1750, Duvaux fitted an old gilt bronze stand which he had regilded to a new porcelain pot and a few months later he fitted new gilt bronze mounts to a *serre-papier* – a filing cabinet normally used with a desk. He also altered the carcase of a cedarwood cupboard by fitting it with an oak carcase.

All these transactions appear on a daily or weekly basis, alongside recorded sales and exchanges of goods. However, the revenue from these activities was low compared with the turnover of new goods, and the commercial advantage of these activities probably lay in locking a client into a particular house, developing an ongoing relationship with that client around the object, and providing convenient and flexible credit arrangements.

TURNOVER, PROFIT AND PRICING

In only a few cases is it possible to get a sense of the running of a mercers' business, and particularly of the rate of turnover of money and goods. A rare instance of an inventory which lists the sales of goods over a short, fixed period alongside an inventory of the total stock allows a calculation of the average figure for the annual turnover to be made (figure 10). Between the date of his wife's death on 12 February 1774 and the date from which the inventory was drawn up (26 June 1775), the mercer Delaplanche sold 192 items worth 29,578 *livres*.[111] (The average item value was therefore 154 *livres*.) The objects sold are listed in a separate *état* at the end of the inventory.

Sales Feb 1774–June 1775	29,578 *livres*
Average monthly turnover	2,113 *livres*
Average annual turnover	25,356 *livres*
Value of total stock 1774	57,904 *livres*
Ratio of turnover to stock value	43%

Fig 10. Stock of Jean Rachinel Delaplanche, 1774–1775.

This shows that in this particular case an item was in stock for an average of 2.28 years (about 27 months). No doubt this figure, as an average, may well obscure the more subtle relationship between turnover and stock – cheaper items may have remained in stock for shorter periods. Or indeed, the cycle may have been affected most by the degree to which the object was fashionable, regardless of size or value.

The pattern of sales on a daily, monthly or annual basis is recorded in Lazare Duvaux' daybook which records the daily sales from his shop 'Au Chagrin de Turquie' in the rue de la Monnaie, near the rue St Honoré. The entries for the year 1750 have been analyzed to show the rate and value of his turnover (appendix 3). Entries were made every few days[112] – some customers buying a single item, others buying many. During 1750, he sold goods worth 137,721 *livres*. On average, he sold 11,477 *livres'* worth of stock per month, but the chart shows that during November and December, his turnover was particularly high. This can be accounted for largely by purchases made by Madame de Pompadour, who bought a large volume of items which tended to be of above average value.

The inventories give little information about profit rates. Duvaux' daybook gives some information, at least about a particular way of calculating profit. For a few items, a percentage rate is given. For example:

> '6. Du 24. – M. de SONNING : Posé à Neuilly trois glaces de cheminée, dont une de 30 pouces sur 30, 64l.; une de 20 pouces sur 30, 34l.; une de 12 pouces sur 30, 19 l. – Les tains, 15l. – Profit à deux sols pour livre, 13l. – Frise, vis et clous, 3l.'[113]

This represents a typical profit of 10% on the mirrors. In some cases, the discount or commission appears to have represented the mercer's profit. Duvaux seems to have sold Sèvres porcelain at the same price as the factory.[114] The Sèvres sales registers document the rate of discount allocated to each mercer, or agent, who bought wholesale from the factory. These were fairly consistent at 9% for a sale or return transaction (figure 11).

MERCHANT/AGENT	DISCOUNT
Bachelier	12%
Bailly	9%
Bréant Vve	9%
Dulac	9%
Dumoulin	9%
Lair Mme	9%
Poirier et Daguerre	9%
Sayde	9%
Sprote	9%
Tesniere	9%

Fig 11. Sèvres sales registers Ventes des marchands, *1772.*[115]

Bachelier was given a higher percentage discount, either because he bought the goods outright, or because the factory wanted to give him a competitive advantage in his pricing – his shop was the factory's official depot. Occasionally other merchants (listed in the purchases by individuals rather than the *ventes aux marchands* section of the registers) were offered a higher discount. For example, a Lefebvre of Amsterdam was given a 12% discount, and a M. Picaluya 10%. These cannot have represented a discount rate for outright sale because Lefebvre sometimes returned items to the factory.[116] It is much more difficult to find out about discount or commission rates for goods purchased from smaller workshops. Hebert, *maitre de la manufacture de faience*, rue de la Roquette, offered a 20% discount to merchants.[117] The retailer Bailly[118] was listed amongst his customers.

The profit rate per item, or in relation to capital investment cannot easily be calculated. However, other data on profit survives, though it is fragmentary. When a business partnership was dissolved, the profit was sometimes listed in the notarial act. For example, the following table shows the profit rate for a large textile business. The partners – Jean-Baptiste Buffault, Robert Lenormand, Prosper Leduc and André Gilles – were trading in *étoffes de soye or et argent* from a shop in the rue St Honoré, Au Grand Turc.[119] Buffault was the principal financier and partner.[120] The stock (at the beginning of the partnership) was valued at 567,778 *livres*. The profit represented over a third of the value of the stock for the year 1772 (figure 12).

YEAR	PROFIT	BUFFAULT'S SHARE
1773	165,350	77,510
1774	275,400	121,093
1775	95,511	44,770
1776	56,687	32,449
1777	220,012	123,757
1778	32,191	18,107
TOTAL	845,151	417,686

Fig 12. Profits Buffault partnership, 1772–1778.

Other figures for profit were less impressive. Claude Carelu's case makes an interesting comparison with the more successful mercers trading around the rue St Honoré. He went into partnership on 1st January 1735 with Augustin de Malezieu. His business expenditure for 1736 amounted to 7,931 *livres*.[121] His profit of 1,573 *livres* represents a return of 20%.

DATE	PROFIT	ANNUAL PROFIT
1735	1002	1,002
1736		
2 Jan – 27 Mar	430	
10 Apr – 7 June	407	
3 July – 30 Sept	390	
2 Oct – 26 Dec	346	1,573
1737		
3 Jan – 20 June	626	
20 July – 28 Sept	495	
2 Oct – 31 Dec	375	1,496
1738		
2 Jan – 27 June	754	
3 Jul – 30 Sept	73	
6 Oct – 22 Dec	309	1,136
1739		
12 Jan – 25 Mar	201	
4 Apr – 30 Jun	142	
2 Jul – 27 Sept	283	
2 Oct – 21 Dec	271	897

Fig 13. Profits Carelu/Malezieu partnership 1735–1739.

INVESTMENTS

The wealthier mercers extended their activities into financial investment, converting any available capital into annuities. They also sought to enter the realms of the elite office holders, increasing their status towards that of a successful financier. Thomas-Joachim Hebert is a prime example of this sort of activity. A survey of his career (from mercer to *sécretaire du roi*) shows the way in which a mercer's social and financial success could augment the family's wealth and status over time, increasing the possibilities of a good marriage for the offspring. At the highest level, it seems that the aspirations of a mercer were to retire from retailing or wholesaling and into higher social and financial spheres.

Appendix 5 shows a brief history of Hebert's marriages and financial transactions relating to capital sums.[122] He first married (in 1714) the widow of another mercer, Nicolas Guillaume Daustel. Hebert took over the business, which specialized in mirrors, furniture veneered with various types of marquetry, clocks, console tables with marble slabs, and the suppliers numbered fourteen individuals, and the Manufacture des Glaces. She died ten years later, by which time the stock was estimated to be worth about three times as much as it had when he took over the business. At this point, he had built up a wealthy clientele, including the king, the court and various financiers. When he remarried in 1730, his assets were valued at nearly a quarter of a million *livres*. His wife's dowry was set at 30,000 *livres*, twice the dowry brought by his first wife.

It is interesting to note the timing and circumstances of his daughter's marriage. She married one Pierre Dufour, *écuyer* and member of the royal household,[123] who had at one time been a *ministre du roy* based in Germany. Hebert offered a dowry of up to 200,000 *livres*, more than ten times his first wife's dowry. This sum is extremely high relative to Hebert's total estate. The terms were thus:

> le Sr et De Hebert ont constitué en dot a ladite De Dufour en avancement d'hoirie de leurs successions futures également et par moitié 200,000 *livres* quils ont promis a payer auxdits Sr et De lors futurs epoux lorsquils se presenteroit loccasion den faire employ.[124]

Until that moment, the Heberts committed to paying interest on the capital sum (at *denier 20,* 5%) which represented an annual income for their daughter and son-in-law of 4,000 *livres*. Hebert's use of the promise of such a large dowry ensured a good marriage for his daughter, and appears to have been part of a dynastic strategy.

His financial strategies are equally interesting. After his second marriage, Hebert began to invest large sums of money in three ways. First, the *rentes*, or annuities, in which he invested between 1724 and 1761. Notes in the inventory drawn up after his second wife died suggest that some, if not all, of these *rentes* may have originated in sales of goods. For example the Prince de Soubise bought goods from Hebert in 1746 worth 22,000 *livres*, and the Prince seems to have opted to pay this in the form of an annuity, fixed at an annual payment. The inventories include many references to payments of the interest falling behind (*arrerages*), though Hebert was able to pursue the debts through legal proceedings. By 1763, the date of his second wife's death, Hebert was no longer trading in goods, living off the income generated by capital investments of a quarter of a million *livres*.

A number of other mercers also invested in *rentes*, though none as heavily as Hebert.[125] Despite the problems of collecting the income from annuities, the *rentes* must have represented a reliable, predictable, source of revenue for a mercer. If significant capital sums could be made from a business, they could then be invested in diverse ways to provide a regular income. These sorts of capital sums, though far removed from the capital used for setting up a business, perhaps demonstrate the way in which financial security could be established, financial and social status increased, and a means of leaving the trading world altogether could be effected.

Secondly, Hebert invested in property. He bought five houses, at a total cost of 222,050 *livres*, and rented them out to provide an annual income of 17,000 *livres*.[126] Thirdly, he became a shareholder in the Compagnie des Indes, buying shares worth 35,000 *livres* in 1774.[127] Perhaps the most significant mark of his shift from retailing into investments was the office which he purchased in 1752, of *sécretaire du roy*.[128] This cost him 110,000 *livres*, and conferred noble status on his children.

The status attained by Hebert was not unusual for the more successful mercers, and there were others who pursued careers leading to influential positions outside the world of goods. A number of mercers bought, like Hebert, the office of *sécretaire du roi* during the eighteenth century: Guillaume Scourjon, Marc François Lay (Seigneur de Gibercourt), Pierre Chauvin, Estienne Laurent, Philippe Legras, Pierre-

Julie Darlu, Pierre Bellet and Jean-François Brallet. They were all *échevins*, and some were also elected *quartiniers*. Charles-Pierre Huet became an *écuyer*. For example, Philippe Legras, one of the guards in charge of the corporation of mercers, was a *consul* and *échevin* of the city, was a *marguiller*, *commissaire des pauvres* and also a *doyen de messieurs les conseillers du roi*.[129]

The development of the *commerce de luxe* in the area of the rue St Honoré no doubt depended in part on the entrepreneurship of the mercers whose business practices have been discussed in this chapter. The mercers' activities within this market place were multi-faceted, and extended beyond the straightforward definitions of retailing or wholesaling to the exchange of goods between mercers and in some cases the establishment of monopolies through exclusive access to certain factories and suppliers. Each business was likely to perform some of each function, circulating a range of goods through the Parisian economy at a number of levels. As individuals, some of the mercers made considerable progress despite the pitfalls of commerce. As a group, their trade formed an important part of the movement of luxury goods into and around the capital. Although they were dependant on the shrewd management of finance, their activities were by no means restricted to this area. Their business relationships and financial strength, combined with the trading rights accorded to them by their corporation, positioned them to influence design and production.

NOTES

1. Daniel DeFoe 1745, p. 65.
2. Savary 1675, 45.
3. For the latter, see Sonenscher 1995 and Sturmer 1978.
4. The inventories were collected by searching through the papers of notaries with addresses in or near the rue St Honoré, or those who seem to have specialized in the legal requirements of large merchant enterprises. Various historians have attempted to extract from the immense catalogue of the *Minutier Central* some kind of representative sample of inventories (Chatelus 1973, Roche 1981 and 1989, Pardailhé-Galabrun 1988, Rimbaud 1964–71 and Wildenstein 1956). Fairchilds sampled the papers of notaries with addresses in the rue St Honoré in 1725 and 1785 in order to compare the belongings listed in the inventories over time. For further discussions on the representativeness of such inventories, especially as evidence for measuring changes in consumption, see Baulant, Schuurman and Gervais, 1988. It remains difficult to establish the degree to which inventories collected in these ways are representative of the typical circumstances of social and economic life of a group of people, a period of time or geographical area.
5. Historians of Paris and of the artisanal trades have looked at geographical patterns and workshop organization for specific trades. See, for example, Garrioch 1986 and Burstin 1977.
6. See Nocq 1926–31 for a list of the goldsmiths' signs at nos. 1–28, Place Dauphine. Other goldsmiths had shops on the Pont au Change, according to Nocq, on the 'downstream side' only, whereas the opposite side was inhabited by a mix of trades.
7. *Mémoire* . . . 1761.
8. See Grand-Carteret 1896.
9. Babeau 1907, 1.
10. Noteable architectural developments during the eighteenth century included the building of *hôtels particuliers* such as the Hôtel des Ambassadeurs, the Hôtel d'Evreux (1718), the Hôtel of the Duc de Béthune Charost (much later to become the English embassy) and the residences of a number of *fermiers* (farmers general) such as Chevalier and Legendre.
11. At La Place aux Chats, the Tourneuf family of drapers, at L'Image de Notre Dame, Renault, paver to the King, at La Grande Barbe Grignon, hatter, and Brochand, merchant, listed with no sign (*Terrier du Roi*, vol. 1, 1700, AN Q1^{1}099^{3}).
12. *Terrier de l'Archevêche de Paris*, AN S1302.
13. These are more difficult to quantify, since they are individually recorded as *bails* in the notarial records.
14. Henard 1908–9, 394. Mercers who dealt in printed cottons in the rue St Honoré included Baron et Cie, and François Rozelet (see Chassagne and Chapman 1981, and Chassagne 1980). The inventory of Baron's business describes his factory at Corbeil and shop in the rue St Honoré, which stocked both the products of the factory and other accessories.
15. Sauval 1724, vol. 2, 142.
16. The Hôtel d'Aligre was one of the venues used by the mercers for auctions, especially during the latter part of the eighteenth century. The salerooms were reconstructed by Mercier for the paintings dealer and auctioneer Paillet in 1776 (Henard 1908–9, 532).
17. The Cafés de la Régence, de l'Impasse de l'Opéra, Dupuis, du Prophète Elie, Militaire and du Danemark.
18. Including Jean-Baptiste Tuart, mercer, recorded as the owner of

three properties, in 1764, 1777 and 1792 (*Terrier de l'Archevêche de Paris*, AN S1302). Michel Delahaye, *marchand bijoutier*, rue St Honoré, sold gold boxes and jewellery, clocks and bronzes (AVP D^4B^6 *carton* 40, *dossier* 2224).

19. Such as Jacques Davollé *marchand clincaillier*, rue St Honoré, who sold furniture mounts, metal goods such as buckles, cafetières, chandeliers and lanterns, tools and nails for upholsterers and shoemakers, ticking and stuffing for bedding for upholsterers, and whose inventory gives the name of François Dumontier, also of the rue St Honoré, mercer specializing in the same branch of commerce (AN MC LXXXIX, 36, 23 May 1742, Davollé). His brother was Pierre Davollé, *marchand clincaillier*, rue St Honoré (AN MC CXVII, 800, 23 May 1755, Davollé). Several others in the family were styled *marchands de fer*.
20. Emmanuel Louis and Emmanuel Jacques Cavillier are listed in 1778 as co-owners of Le Louis d'Or with Boucher, *drapier*, and owners of Le Lion d'Argent (*Terrier de l'Archevêche de Paris*, AN S1302), and see also AN MC VI, 892, 22 brumaire an III, *dissolution de société les cit Cavillier*, in which the Cavillier partners of 321, rue St Honoré, agreed to discontinue their partnership from the coming month (*prairial*) , and until then to stop trading as wholesalers and continue only with retailing. Doré owned two houses, including 'La Croix d'Or' in 1770 (*Terrier de l'Archevêche de Paris*, AN S1302).
21. Jean-Baptiste Roux de Monclar, mercer, recorded in 1781, (*Terrier de l'Archevêche de Paris*, AN S1302).
22. AN MC XXIX, 472, Jean-Baptiste Delaporte, *tapissier ordinaire du roi*, rue St Honoré, paroisse St Eustache. In the area were trading Jean-François Dumont, *tapissier*, rue Neuve des Petits Champs, paroisse St Roch (AN MC LIII,492, 22 December 1772), who sold Brussels and Gobelins tapestries, Turkish carpets, mirrors, bronzes, a range of clocks and furniture (carcase and upholstered) which included two dog kennels upholstered in Utrecht velvet. A further list in his inventory itemized beds and bedding for rent. Aside from his shop he had three rooms (*magasins*) for storage and kept three carriages. François Noblin, *marchand tapissier et tapissier valet de chambre de Monsieur le Duc de Levy* resided in the rue de Richelieu, but had no stock when he died (AN MC LIII, 243, 31 October 1727, Noblin). As well as selling a range of carcase furniture, Jean-Baptiste Briant ran a considerable upholstering business in the rue Neuve St Roch, from a hangar between the shop entrance and the courtyard (AN MC LII, 361, 23 June 1759, Briant). He was supplied by a number of neighbouring tradesmen including Barbier, *marchand d'étoffes*, Nau, *drapier* and Dehenin, *marchand*.

    Other *tapissiers* worked in the rue St Antoine area, centre of the furniture industry, for example, AN MC XXVIII, 4111, 7 October 1768, Garnier (wife of Pierre Bobée, *tapissier*, grande rue du Faubourg St Antoine). A Pierre Bobée is listed as a property owner in the rue St Honoré, between the rue des Frondeurs and the rue St Roch in 1756.
23. Hebert owned La Toison d'Or, part of which was rented to Martin Paillard Delorme, mercer and his wife.
24. *Mémoire pour les Srs Marchand, Fouquet, Derault, Moulins, Lefevre, Degamaches, Tiphaine, Lizeret, Onfroy, Villegoulet, Cheron, Lemoine, Brousse, Dilieu, Dubois, Magu, Baron, Roussel, Quignon, Boucherelle, Legay, Boucheri, Isselot, Manson, Lefevre, mds merciers, étalans dans les rues, places et marchés, intervenans dans la caused'entre M. le procureur général et le Sr Bruer*, Paris 1780, BN MSS Mss Joly de Fleury 515, fo. 265–274.

    The document refers to an *Arrêt* of 1776 which allowed the poor master artisans and their widows to have 'une échope ou étalage couverte' in certain fixed positions in streets, places and markets, and another dated 16 December 1769 stating that these positions must be authorized by the Lieutenant Général de Police. A debate ensued about the need for the stalls or shops to be set up in positions which were commercially advantagous, rather than according to the public interest (ie without blocking access and views): 'l'arrangement de létallage peut occassioner la ruine complete d'un marchand, ou l'en guarentir'. Claiming danger from hungry horses and inclement weather, the claimants demanded the right of two or three thousand of these 'infortunes marchands' to maintain their stalls and shops and to illuminate them when necessary.
25. See Sargentson 1994.
26. The inventories show this to be the case. However, the rights to practice these skills and to sell framed mirrors were the subject of some dispute. The links between the mercers and the *miroitiers* were close, in that several wealthier *miroitiers* joined the corporation of mercers and extended their commerce to include other items for furnishing.

    Specialist framers such as Tremblin also offered their services within the market place. André Tremblin/Tramblin had an extensive framing business on the Quai de Gèvres (AN MC CIX, 537, 5 July 1742, cited in Sonescher 1989, 222). This included mirrors as well as paintings, and other items of carved wood such as giltwood stands for clocks and stands, also giltwood, for marble table tops. On his son Charles-Andre Tremblin and his partnership with Pierre de Deneumaison, see Sonenscher 1989, 222–3.
27. Other mercers specializing in mirrors included Laurent Malencourt, *marchand mercier miroitier* who stocked furniture, mirrors and components in the rue Bourglabbé, paroisse St Leu St Gilles (AN MC X, 788, 22 October 1790, Malencourt). His debts to the Manufacture des Glaces totalled 35,299 *livres* in 1790. He was related by marriage to Edme Thereze Bourdon, thereby linking Malencourt to two families also engaged in the commerce in mirrors. Jacques Honnez and Jean-Jacques Bourdon were both *marchands merciers miroitiers*, and Jean-Jacques' sister was married to Honnez. Honnez resided in the rue Bourglabbé,

Bourdon in the rue Greneta. Honnez stocked an extensive range of frames, mirrors and paintings, and owed the Manufacture des Glaces 16,463 *livres*. He became a mercer in 1768, and a *miroitier* in 1773 (AN MC X, 652). Honnez was in partnership with Vatinelle and Dufrayer for the *commerce de la grande miroiterie* (the capital sums invested were 4,000 *livres* each), and Honnez, independantly of the partnership, also sold toys, including 500 dolls and dolls' heads (AN MC X, 655, 23 July 1776, Martin). Nicolas Merre, Martin's first husband, was also a mercer, in the rue St Denis (AN MC LIV, 927, 14 March 1768, Merre).

28. See Pallot 1987 and Munger 1987 on the *tapissiers* and Melchior-Bonnet 1995 on the *miroitiers*.

29. AN, MC, LII, 249, 20 November 1731, Ziegler. On 14 April 1731 Catherine Antoinette Ziegler, wife of Darnault père, died. The premises were rented from a Dame de Berlize. At this time they had three children, François-Charles (thirteen years old), Jacques (seven) and Louise (three). Ziegler's brother was a *fondeur*, living in the Cloître et paroisse St Jean de Latran. Her father was an *ébéniste*, as was her mother's first husband (she had three).

30. The stock was valued by experts Denis-Louis Beroin de Villeroy and Leger Bertin, *marchands du meme commerce que Darnault*, both in the rue St Honoré. On 8 October, 1753, a partnership agreement (*acte de société*) was drawn up whereby Darnault *père* et *fils* enter into partnership for the 'commerce de glaces, meubles et autres' at Le Roy d'Espagne, the shop in the rue de la Monnaie rented from M et Mme Calley, for four years from 12 September 1753 (AN, MC, LXXXVIII, 630, 8 October, 1753). François had been until June of 1753 in partnership with Sieurs Glavet and Vallée, the partnership when wound up was worth 58,614 *livres*, and François put his share, 29,656 *livres* into the next agreement with his son, and Glavet and Vallée also put in an almost equivalent sum from the dissolution of the previous partnership. Presumably this new contract was drawn up in order to ensure the survival of the family business after the impending death of François. François-Charles Darnault contributed 17,541 *livres* in cash to the partnership, and the rest in goods worth 12,115 *livres* from the business which he had previously run from rue Grenier St Lazare. In fact, due to *père's* ill health (he died shortly after this), the partnership was never formalized, and clauses were added explaining that *fils* alone would continue the business.

31. In 1753, debts included 1,050 *livres* to the Manufacture des Glaces, 64 to an *ébéniste* named Hubert, 113 to a *menuisier* named Gaultier, and 174 to a sculptor, L'heureux. 260 *livres* were paid to Audot for *étamage*.

32. He continued trading with membership of both the corporations of *miroitiers* and *marchands merciers*, and so paid both dues. He paid in *capitation* (a tax paid to the corporation in addition to the sum paid for membership to the corporation) 56 *livres* per annum for the *miroitiers*, and 228 for the *merciers*.

33. See Sturmer (1979) for the argument that the system of royal privilege which exempted artisans from corporate restrictions was designed to facilitate supplies to the court.

34. This title was established originally in order to supply the court as it moved from place to place.

35. *Précis servant de réponse a précis pour le corps des Marchands-Drapiers-merciers . . . contre la Communauté des Maître Tabletiers-Luthiers-Evantaillistes . . . en présence du sieur Bierne, Marchand mercier à Paris, aussi appellant et demandeur*, Paris 1781, BHVP 132256. The mercers claimed a 'droit naturel' to state the precise contents of a shop, through words and images.

36. One of the mercers' objections read as follows:
'On cite deux prétendus Arrêts de 1682 et 1684: le premier a, dit-on, confirmé une Sentence de Police, qui ordonnait à un marchand Mercier de reformer son étalage, d'y avoir *quatre cordons*, garnies chacune *de deux peignes*, entremêlés d'autres marchandises de mercerie; avec défenses d'étaler des morceau de bois &c. L'autre défendoit, dit-on, aux marchands Merciers d'étaler *ni échiquiers, ni cartons peints & taillés en forme d'échiquiers*, parce que c'étoient les attributs de la profession de tablettier. Il faut, dit-on, que le marchand Mercier entremêle plusieurs objets à la branche de commerce qu'il adoptera.'
The mercers' response was 'N'est-il pas, encore une fois, absurde de forcer un marchand qui ne fait pas de commerce de *rubans*, ni de *peignes*, ni de *cordons*, d'en mêler à sa branche de commerce?'.

37. Given that the corporations had been abolished and reconsituted only two years earlier than the visit to Bierne's shop, it would seem likely that this was an expression of uncertainty over how the mercers and other trade groups related to each other.

38. The mercers claimed that over fifty families of mercers were trading, like the tailors, in ready-made clothing (and claimed that they had initiated the trade [mémoire 1766, BHVP 13 2 24 3]).

39. Hugh Roberts 1972, and Eriksen 1968. The daybook of Pierre Migeon shows that much of his workshop practice was based on sub-contracting work out to cabinet-makers and bronze workers amongst others.

40. The data presented here was taken from the following inventories: AN MC CXVI, 439, 23 December 1768, Delahoguette, AN MC LIII, 226, 22 May 1724, Desgodets, AN MC, XCIV, 290, 29 November 1758, Duvaux, AN MC XXXIX, 353, 7 December 1736, Fevrier, AN MC XLII, 521, 24 October 1770, Hennebert, AN MC X, 540, 20 Mar 1760, Julliot, AN MC XXIII, 654, 26 Aug 1763 Legras, and AN MC IX, 666, 5 November 1777, Martin.

41. Although Claude-Antoine Julliot did not stock lacquer or sculpture items in the inventory drawn up after his death in 1760, each of these groups is listed in the inventory of his stock taken in 1736, when his wife died. Rather than assume that his business patterns had changed in relation to market changes, it seems probable that the business had been run down towards the end of his life.

42. *Bronze brute*, valued by the pound weight, used to manufacture mouldings for furniture, clocks etc. For example, Delahoguette

had 38 lbs of bronze, valued at 20 *sols* the pound (AN MC CXVI, 439, 23 December 1768, Delahoguette).

43. It is also possible that a client choosing a piece of porcelain from a shop might select a piece but ask for it to be mounted in gilt bronze – entries in Duvaux' daybook suggest this possibility.

44. Roubo's directory of cabinet-making describes the process of removing the lacquer and applying it to new carcases – particularly difficult technically when the new carcass was convex in profile (eg. a *commode bombée*, *chantournée,* see appendix 7).

45. *Catalogue des Marbres, Bronzes, Agates, Porcelaines* . . . composant le Magasin de JULLIOT, Marchand rue S. Honoré, attenant celle du Four, Paris, 1777. The auction of his stock following his wife's death, was held from 20 November, 1777. (Annotated copy with prices in the collection of the Bibliothèque Doucet.)

46. At the auction (see footnote above).

47. This was an inventory taken when the mercer Julliot, rather than his spouse, died. Perhaps the more expensive items had remained in stock longer.

48. i.e. sets of vases for display, for example above a fireplace in front of a pier glass. These sets usually consisted of a central, taller, piece flanked by a pair of smaller matching vases, although sometimes the set was made up of five or seven pieces. Items of porcelain set in gilt bronze mounts were often of higher value than unembellished pieces.

49. And for Claude-Francois Julliot who stocked rock crystal chandeliers valued up to 16,000 *livres* in 1777.

50. For example, the following chart shows the types of furniture stocked by three mercers.

Hebert 1724	Julliot 1736	Delahoguette 1768
armoire	*armoire*	*armoire*
bahut	*bahut*	*bibliothèque*
bas d'armoire	*bas d'armoire*	*bureau*
bureau	*bibliothèque*	*cabinet*
bureau de cabinet	*bureau*	*coffre*
cabinet	*cabinet*	*coin d'appui*
coffret	*coffre*	*commode*
commode	*écran*	*écran*
écran	*encoignure*	*gradin*
table	*gueridon*	*gueridon*
table à écrire	*serrepapier*	*table*
*table de marbre**	*table*	*table à cadrille*
table de nuit	*table à écrire*	*table a trictrac*
tablette	*table de marbre**	*table de marbre**
	table de nuit	*table de picquet*
	tablette	

* in all cases, the variety of marble types was notable but has not been included here.

51. The stained pearwood imitated the more expensive ebony veneer.

52. See especially Verlet 1990–4.

53. Although the agreement does not specify Hebert's client. The inventory includes the following record of a contract made between Hebert and the Boulle brothers:

'signé Boulle et Boulle pour lequel les soussignés reconnoissent avoir compté avec ledit Hebert pour tous les ouvrages qu'ils estoient obligez de luy fournir por plusieurs marchés faits ensemble par comts(?) tant doubles que simples et qu'ils se sont trouvés redevables envers luy d'une boeste de pendulle avec des figures couchées à costé du cadran d'apres Michel ange et d'une commode de marqueterie garnie de bronzes doréz dor moulu laquel commode doit estre pareil a celle du Roy a Trianon. Lesdits ouvrages ensemble de prix fait a la somme de 3000 *livres* sur laquelle somme lesdits Srs Boulle ont reconnu avoir recu la somme de 1500 *livres*, et que portant ne restant plus a leur payer que la somme de 1500 *livres* en livrant lesdits ouvrages et ce pour demeurer quittes de part et d'autre generallement jusqu'au jour dudit ecrit.' (AN MC LIII, 226, 22 May 1724 Desgodets, *papiers*, item 52, see Sargentson 1992).

54. I am very grateful to Lucy Wood for passing on information about this piece.

55. AN MC X, 540, 20 Mar 1760, Julliot.

56. She was previously married to Martin Hennebert, mercer.

57. AN CXVIII, 857, 15 April 1772, marriage contract cited by Geoffrey de Bellaigue 1974, 858.

58. I would like to thank Monsieur Claude Jollin for giving me this information about the Legras and Delacroix families.

59. Marriage contracts cited by Geoffrey de Bellaigue 1974, 858–862.

60. AN LXXXIII, 363, 4 August 1738 Boscheron Bauvin *Mariage*. Another document (same *étude*) recorded that Pierre Joseph Bauvin was legally in partnership with his sister, Anne Françoise until 23 September 1738. He was to pay her the 142,353 *livres* owed to her for her share in the business within a year of the act. She had entered the business after the death of her husband, Joachim Aubertin (*marchand bourgeois*, rue des Deux Ecus). Effectively, it seems that Boscheron replaced her in the business.

61. The stock was worth 284,707 *livres* and the assets in the form of outstanding debts by customers amounted to 402,916 *livres* (AN MC LXXXIII, 363, 29 September 1738, *Bauvin Aubertin*).

62. AN XCVIII, 517, 8 Jan 1752, Gaucherel, Corvoisier and Richer.

63. AN MC XCVIII 8 January 1752, Gaucherel, 8 January 1752 AN MC XCVIII.

64. Including members of the merchant families Coucicault, Boutillier, Delamotte and Frion, a doctor, *officier de la maison du roy*, an *échevin* and several *ecuyers*.

65. AN MC CXVIII, 454, 18 Dec 1748 Bentabole and Rohault.

66. A similar payment formed part of the sale of Madame Blakey's *magasin anglais* to Jean René Jousset de Lizy, merchant draper and mercer in 1776. The *pot de vin* was set at 10,000 *livres*, the goods at 36,579 *livres*, AN LXXVIII, 786, 29 Dec 1776. Blakey to Jousset de Lizy. Another *pot de vin* of 18,000 *livres* was added to

the sale of stock (valued at 23,336 *livres*) by Pierre Davollé to Claude Moreau, *marchand bourgeois*, in 1755 (AN MC CXVII, 800, 23 May 1755 Davollé).

67. AN MC CXVII, 930, 17 Feb 1737 Guerin and Ormont. 'Guerin, ne voulant plus s'occuper du commerce en détail, rélatif aux meubles et desirant procurer au Sr. Omont son commis les moyens de s'etablir avantageusement, il lui a proposé un société, de la maniere quelle sera reglée cy apres . . .'
68. *Société entre M. Guérin at M. Omont*, AN MC CXVII, 930, 17 Feb 1737.
69. See especially de Bellaigue 1974 and 1995.
70. AN MC XXVI, 633, 15 Frimaire an V, and 21 Pluviose an V Daguerre.
71. AN MC XCIV, 429, 11 January 1778. Rozelet-Desmaret-Durand.
72. *Livre journal de Claude Carelu*, AVP D^5B^6 *régistre* 2464, 17. The partnership was *sous seing privé*, and the terms written in the day-book.
73. McCusker 1978, and for description of these methods of payment, Savary 1675 and de Bruslons 1723.
74. AVP D^5B^6 *régistre* 2464, Carelu.
75. Migeon supplied Hebert on account.
76. *Livre de Commerce 1730–1736*, BN, mss. Nouvelles acquisitions français 4765.
77. *Livre des Ouvriers*. AVP D^5B^6 *régistre* 5491 Migeon.
78. AVP D^4B^6 *carton* 12 *dossier* 560. Porlier.
79. AVP D^4B^6 *carton* 44 *dossier* 2490, Blakey.
80. AN Y13701, Blakey papers.
81. AVP D^4B^6 *carton* 44 *dossier* 2490, Blakey.
82. AVP D^5B^6 *régistre* 2813, *Baudeuin* 1772–1776, Blakey.
83. From Oppenheim in Birmingham: '16 boetes vides grandes et moyennes 1600 *livres*', 8 Nov 1768, AN Y 13702, Blakey. She also bought some finished clocks and watches from the same supplier.
84. It is difficult to find out exactly how these long range agreements were made. Madame Blakey's bankruptcy accounts record that she travelled to England, and a supplier's bill includes the comment 'to the pattern which you left when at Sheffield'. A Mr. Craw of Covent Garden received a letter from her with a pattern, and Hanscombe wrote a letter stating that he had sent the goods according to the design which she had commissioned when she was in London, and giving her six months to pay. (AN Y13701 and Y13702, Blakey.)
85. AN MC IX, 795, 4 Oct 1784, Granchez and AVP D^4B^6 *carton* 91 *dossier* 6280. Granchez.
86. AVP D^4B^6 *carton* 12 *dossier* 560, Porlier.
87. AVP D^4B^6, *carton* 32 *dossier* 1696, Bourgeois.
88. AVP D^5B^6 *régistre* 2464, *Livre Journal*.
89. AN XXXIX, 271, 26 Sept 1713, Daustel.
90. AN LIII, 226, 22 May 1724 Degodets.
91. AN MC XI, 590, 10 Dec 1765, Disnematin.
92. AVP D^4B^6 *carton* 91 *dossier* 6280, Michel Delahaye.
93. 6 December 1767, 'payé a Monsieur Chouen, caissier de la manufacture royalle des porcelaines de france etablie a Sevres 329 livres pour fournitures de trois figures de biscuit de la manufacture'. ADVP D^5B^6 *régistre* 1967, *Brouillon, 1767, Dubuisson*.
94. Most of these names appear in the Sèvres registers of sales to *marchands*.
95. Mr Cousin md

rue des mauvaises paroles memoire	41 *livres* 10 *sols*
Mr Dufour marchand au palais memoire	4 *livres*
Mr Imbert au palais royal memoire	425 *livres*
Mr Lafrenaye a la tabatiere d'or memoire	15 *livres*
Mr Legendre, md au Palais	
sa reconnaissance du 24 juillet 1724	20 *livres*
Mr Morandet md au Palais memoire	30 *livres*
Mr Mercier md confiturier rue St Benoist	
memoire	16 *livres*
Mr Richelet au palais royal memoire	17 *livres*
Mr Robbert Limonadier	
pour reste de son billet du 6 mars 1725	50 *livres*

DEBTORS, BOURG LA REINE, 1790

Bertin	rue Jacob	585 *livres* 8 *sol*
Duhamel	pont Notre Dame	195 *livres* 9 *sol*
Ducis	de Versailles	175 *livres* 18 *sol*
Aclogue	marché neuf	40 *livres* 13 *sol*
Bailleux	rue du Four	201 *livres*
Chambeau	de Versailles	8 *livres* 8 *sol*
Chocadel	rue des Fossés St Germain des Pres	199 *livres* 19 *sol*
Chentin	vieille rue du Temple	50 *livres* 12 *sol*
Dubois	rue de Richelieu	389 *livres*
Deux	pres la Comedie Italienne	102 *livres* 17 *sol*
Girard Lé	butte St Roch	40 *livres* 8 *sol*
Girand	marché neuf	35 *livres*
Gilbert	rue des petits carreaux	315 *livres* 3 *sol*
Lheullier	pres la Bastille	28 *livres* 18 *sol*
Le Bie	cour St Martin	239 *livres* 12 *sol*
Lestre	rue St Paul	331 *livres* 4 *sol*
Vve Lepreux	rue Beauregard	89 *livres* 12 *sol*
Laforest	vielle rue du Temple	199 *livres* 19 *sol*
Montvoise	marché St Germain	80 *livres* 3 *sol*
Marcotel	rue St Martin	191 *livres* 16 *sol*
Pillot	rue Aubry le Boucher	227 *livres* 5 *sol*
Petit Lé	porte de Paris	68 *livres* 17 *sol*
Vve Petit	rue de la Verrerie	187 *livres* 8 *sol*
Petit	rue St Martin	28 *livres* 18 *sol*
Simon	rue du fbg St Denis	103 *livres* 17 *sol*
Victor Lheullier	rue du fbg St Antoine	84 *livres* 12 *sol*
Lutoz	rue de Bussy	67 *livres* 19 *sol*
Mignard	rue Montorgueil	139 *livres* 15 *sol*

Mr Thevenet md pour un memoire	86 *livres*
pour son billet du 14 juillet 1721	130 *livres*
Mr Teniere md au palais memoire	10 *livres*

Few business debts were outstanding on Bosseux' death – his creditors included one Sr Jossin, *marchand* who was owed 600 *livres*, and was evidently a tenant of Bosseux, since the debt was reduced by 250 *livres* which represented a quarter's rent. A *menuisier* named Crele was also listed, to whom was owed about 60 *livres*. A Sr Petit, *metteur au tein* was owed about 100 *livres*, presumably for silvering. 800 *livres* were owed to Bosseux' son-in-law, Rousselot. (AN MC, CXV, 447, 6 June 1726 Bosseux.)

96. AVP D4B6 *carton* 12 *dossier* 560, Porlier, 1753.
97. Courajod 1874 10, 44, 60.
98. Certainly the Sèvres sales ledgers show that the factory sold at discount to a small number of mercers – usually under ten, at a discount of 9% for sale or return, 12% for outright sale.
99. *Almanac des marchands . . .*, Paris 1779, BN 8oV58825.
100. See Dawson 1989 and de Bellaigue 1995.
101. AN MC XXVII, 499, 30 avril 1790, Adam.
102. *Assiettes, sceaux, plats, saladiers, tasses, theyeres, pot pourris, pots, tasses, soucouppes, verres à glaces, pots, theyeres, plateaux d'ecuelles, plats, bassins* etc.
103. *Plats, pots, ecritoires, pots de chambre, soupieres, moutardiers, assiettes* etc.
104. *Theyeres, pots (a lait, a confiture), boetes a savonette, moutardiers, dejeuners, vases, urnes, plateaux d'ecuelles, cuilleres, pots pourris, pedestals* etc.
105. 'Du par comte courant et par solde des marchandises'.
106. AN MC III, 928 28 March 1747, Pator to Julliot, and Klappenbach 1995.
107. 8 Jan 1767, AVP D5B6 *régistre* 2464, Dubuisson. Also see 16 Jan 1768 in AVP D5B6 *régistre* 1967 Dubuisson.
108. AN CXVI, 439, 23 Dec 1768, Delahoguette.
109. *1er Trimestre des Tablettes Royales* 1775. 'Madame Kumpff, rue des Canettes, chez le Perruquier'.
110. See Pradère 1987 and 1989.
111. AN MC XLII, 543, 26 June 1775, Delaplanche. This inventory is likely to represent fairly normal trading patterns since it was Delaplanche's wife who died – the business was unlikely to be run down before her death (presuming that Delaplanche was in reasonable health).
112. This does not necessarily mean that sales were not made daily – according to Courajod (who edited the daybook), the entries are all in Duvaux' own hand.(The original daybooks seem to have disappeared from the archives.) Since Duvaux was regularly absent from the shop, visiting clients and presumably suppliers, he probably only updated his accounts every few days.
113. Courajod 1874, entry no. 6, 24 September 1748.
114. According to Rosalind Savill at the Wallace Collection, London.
115. MNS *régistre de vente*, 54 AQ 5.
116. For example, in March 1786 he bought 3,169 *livres'* worth of goods, from which sum was deducted 906 *livres* for items returned from a previous sale. (MNS *régistre de vente*, 54 AQ 10.)
117. Account book, AVP D5B6 *régistre* 326, 29 April–Oct 1754. I would like to thank M. Bernard Dragesco for drawing this document to my attention.
118. Bailly also appears in the Sèvres registers and is listed in the almanac of 1770 as 'marchand faiencier bijoutier, au Roi de France, rue St Honoré . . . vend plateaux pour les desserts, lustres, lanternes à reverbes et autres . . . porcelaines . . . cristaux et verrerie'.
119. AN LII, 535, 30 November 1777, Buffault. The partnership was established on 30 August 1772, and a new act changing the terms of the partnership was drawn up on 31 August 1778.
The trade card for the shop reads:
AU GRAND TURC
BUFFAULT
marchand de toutes sortes d'etoffes de soie, d'or et d'argent, rue St Honoré au coin de celle des Frondeurs, vis-à-vis la rue de l'Echelle. A Paris.
(Bill dated 1765 for damask sold to the Marquise de Janson, ADVP 6AZ 440.) A Lenormand was still trading in silks at the same shop in 1851, according to a trade card in the same collection.
120. Of the value of the stock and shop fittings, totalling 573,221 *livres*, he contributed 100,000 *livres* as his share of the capital, plus 300,000 as a loan. The 173,221 was to be paid back over one year.
121. This expenditure comprised:

253 items of stock (average 28 *livres*)	7046
taxes, rent, clothing expenses etc	885
Total	7931

122. This was complied from information in the following inventories: AN MC XXXIX, 271, Daustel, AN MC LIII, 226, 22 May 1724, Desgodets, AN MC XXIII, 654, 26 Aug 1763, Legras, and AN MC LII, 502, 15 Jan 1774, Hebert.
123. *Ecuyer gentilhomme ordinaire et Maitre d'hotel du Roy et de la reine.*
124. AN MC LIII, 502, 15 Jan 1774, Hebert.
125. The inventories of the following include references to *rentes*: Claude-Antoine Julliot, Claude-François Julliot, Pierre Davollé, Jean Antoine Cresson, Jean Rachinel Delaplanche, Simon Henri Delahoguette and Etienne Guillaume Disnematin.
126. As the early part of this chapter showed, investing in property was not uncommon amongst the wealthier mercers. Several (Thomas-Joachim Hebert, Jean-Baptiste Tuart, Jean Renard and Jean-Baptiste Buffault) owned more than one house in the street.

Rents provided a guaranteed income. Some mercers purchased land or houses outside Paris, including Charles-Raymond Granchez who owned a country house at Clignancourt.

127. Louis-François Baillet, mercer, rue St Honoré, was also a minor shareholder in the Compagnie des Indes (AVP D^4B^6 *carton* 14, *dossier* 654, Baillet.

128. See Doyle, 1984, on the price of offices in eighteenth-century France. Other examples of the purchase of offices by mercers include Claude-Antoine Julliot who bought an office for 9,600 *livres* (*juré porteur de grains et farines*) which gave him an income of 347 *livres*.

129. Listed in Vidal and Duru 1911, 417–420.

3 The Mercers' Role in Design

The mercers' business practices meant that they operated across various borderlines. Their complex business relationships, and the way in which they exploited opportunities to combine the products of different trades gave them an intriguing set of roles in the design of luxury objects. This chapter is concerned with the ways in which the mercers intervened in the design process, in particular their use of design prints, drawing and models, but also the broader context within which they were able to influence the look and quality of the objects which they sold.

This is a problematic subject for several reasons. As the previous chapters indicated, the mercers' business interests intersected with those of a wide range of manufacturers and suppliers. Within these various trades a diverse range of design practices was adopted. Design decisions may have been conveyed through images, models, text and verbal communication, or a combination of these. In only some branches was the drawing or print of fundamental importance.[1] Also, a number of individuals may have been involved in these processes – design may have been the responsibility of a draughtsman, a master artisan running a large workshop and extensive system of sub-contraction, an architect or another intermediary. In some cases, design decisions lay largely in the hands of a client. The existence of a drawing may prove that this was a necessary stage in the preparation of a particular model, but it may not necessarily be used as the basis for attributing authorship of a design. Finally, the inventories of the mercers are by no means an ideal source for investigating the mercers' role in the design process, since they give little sense of process and were rarely concerned with describing design methods.

The mercers were involved in such a wide range of merchandise that no consistency may be discerned. However, the corporation did take a formal interest in design training in the form of the newly emerging design schools. Various schools of design were established in Paris in the eighteenth century, notably the Ecole Royale Gratuite de Dessein, set up by Jean-Jacques Bachelier in 1766.[2] Bachelier and his supporters established the school as a response to the need for improved drawing skills in the luxury trades. The school taught decorative drawing skills rather than fine art, and intended tuition to form part of an education which included apprenticeship within a trade.

The corporation of mercers was amongst the Ecole's first subscribers, a rare example of the mercers' interest in gaining and promoting drawing skills at both corporate and individual level. The corporation bought twenty places at an annual cost of 4,000 *livres*.[3] Other corporate subscriptions included five places each for the goldsmiths and tailors, and four places for the *corps des marchands de Paris*. Individual mercers and *négotiants* bought a further fourteen places,[4] one of whom was the mercer Jean-François Barbier, a renowned silk dealer in the rue des Bourdonnais who had extensive business and design links with Lyonnais weavers. A number of the individual subscribers were from the port cities rather than Paris, and their subscriptions may represent an attempt both to acquire skills in decorative drawing and to gain access to the Parisian design vocabulary. Whilst the subscriptions from the merchant bodies may have been motivated by a straightforward interest in training their own members in design, it is equally possible that this commitment represented a financial and symbolic act of encouragement to the newly-established school.

Despite the evidence of these subscriptions, the extent to which an individual mercer was skilled in design is highly debatable. After all, the apprenticeship agreements do not mention drawing skills, emphasising rather the trainee's need to learn book-keeping.[5] By the 1760's, Jean-François Barbier was managing a business with assets of several million *livres*, and it seems highly unlikely that he would have intended to personally use his place at the Ecole Gratuite. It is possible that some of Barbier's contacts in Lyon might have benefited from access to such training.[6] Alternatively, the employees of his shop might have required drawing skills either for tracing patterns or preparing them for printing. The Lyonnais silk designer Joubert de l'Hiberderie described in 1765 two Parisian silk merchants from whom copies of silk patterns on paper could be purchased

> qui levent au papier verni, tous les beaux desseins qui parroissent, & que l'on a la facilité d'acheter.

Students of the Ecole Gratuite were often engaged in designing patterns which could be printed or easily transferred. Perhaps such procedures were relevant to those mercers who were concerned to some degree with both the production of and commerce in printed designs. The mercer Louis Bonaventure du Bois, for example, was evidently involved in the production of prints for twelve screens engraved by Aveline and Tardieu which were granted a privilège du roi in 1736.[7] The screens were described as 'dessignez par Bonaventure du Bois, Marchand Mercier'. Whether or not he drew the designs himself, he both styled himself as designer and was involved in the process of marketing them as prints. Some direct involvement with design is also suggested by Joubert's recommendation that Lyonnais designers should go to Paris to buy designs from mercers specializing in patterned silks.[8] In the case of the chinoiserie prints by the designer Jean Pillement, on the other hand, the mercer's role was solely that of vendor, since the frontispiece of the collection advertises their availability from a silk mercer's shop (plate 12).

Plate 12. Frontispiece of Recœil de Fleurs de Caprice inventé et dessiné par Jean Pillement. *Victoria and Albert Museum, London.*

THE USE OF SKILLED DESIGNERS

Very few drawings or designs survive which can be associated closely with an individual mercer and the role of the few remaining designs which are marked with a mercer's name is unclear. The only drawing found amongst the mercers' inventories was a sketch, of dubious quality, for the frame of a screen (*écran*), in the bankruptcy papers of Madame Blakey (plate 13).[9] Her *magasin anglais* was stocked with many goods, particularly from England and there is some evidence that she used drawings to communicate the design requirements for her orders. A Mr. Craw of Covent Garden received a letter from her with a pattern,

Plate 13. Drawing of a screen, 1760s.
Archives de la Ville de Paris.

and another supplier's bill includes the comment 'to the pattern which you left when at Sheffield'.[10]

This sketch for the screen was perhaps in Madame Blakey's hand. However, for certain objects whose successful manufacture depended on the accuracy of drawn detail, the mercers were better served by employing specialist designers. In the mercer Poirier's case, he is known to have commissioned designs, as recorded by the payment for a design of a bronze candelabrum 'que J'ai fait faire'.[11] A drawing dated 7 September 1784 and bearing the name of the mercer Philippe-François Julliot specifies that the drawing was made 'sous la direction de P.F. Julliot fils' (colour plate 4).[12] Julliot obviously employed a skilled designer, though the function of this drawing remains uncertain. A possible interpretation of some of these drawings is that they were used as proposals to potential clients. As in the case of sculptors' presentation drawings, they were thus part of the marketing process rather than the design process.[13] This may well have been the case with the Julliot drawing. The subtle colouring and attention to detail (of the plaques particularly) would hardly have been necessary to convey information to the maker, particularly since Julliot himself is likely to have supplied the *pietre dure* plaques for such a piece.[14] On the other hand, its high finish would presumably have been appealing to a potential buyer. It is intriguing that no cabinet of this pattern survives, though Setterwall has demonstrated that the *pietre dure* plaques appear on a number of pieces of cabinet furniture now in the British and Swedish Royal Collections.[15] It is possible that the drawing represents a proposal by Julliot to a potential client who then rejected it and that the plaques were then used on other pieces.

DESIGNING AROUND VENEERS

The production of design drawings was not the only way of playing a role in the design process, and the other means used by the mercers are apparent in another important area of their activities. The mercers' control over finishing (*enjolivement*) and their practice of stocking part-finished goods meant that they were in a position both to assemble goods to their own specification and to offer their clients considerable choice in the final configuration of goods.[16] This necessarily meant some involvement in the formulation of designs even if the extent and nature of this are difficult to establish. Some notion of the mercers' role may be formed by examining the detailed descriptions of unmounted goods in mercers' inventories and deducing from them what design procedures may have been required in order to assemble them in the form of marketable and finished luxury objects. The inventory of Dominique Daguerre, for example, included oriental lacquer and *pietre dure* panels that were

Plate 14. Commode, French and Italian, c. 1785, attr. A. Weisweiler. J. Paul Getty Museum, Malibu, California.

intended for mounting on furniture and boxes.[17] Typical of the *pietre dure* panels were the 'moyen tableau quarré en pierre de rapport ouvrage de florence représentant un centaure avec cadre de cuivre doré' valued at 60 *livres* and the 'vingt six petits & moyens panneaux de pierre de rapport sujets de fruits & d'oiseaux ouvrages de florence, Dix autres de même genre un peu plus grande' valued at 108 *livres*.[18] A commode attributed stylistically to Adam Weisweiler, one of Daguerre's suppliers, is mounted with such plaques (plate 14).

Such descriptions not only illustrate vividly the stock of part-finished goods such as a mercer carried, but also suggest, by implication at least, the degree to which the design of the objects of which they were to form a prominent part was determined by the form and pattern of these constituent elements. To some extent, the shape of a carcase of a piece of furniture was dictated by the dimensions of the panels as supplied by the mercers to the cabinet makers. In the case of a commode with veneers of Japanese lacquer, the front of the commode was designed around a single piece of lacquer (colour plate 5). The design of this piece is dominated by the Japanese landscape scene. The bronze cartouche appears to run continuously around the panel, framing both drawers without breaking into the landscape composition.[19] Whilst design drawings as such were not necessarily required for the assembly of such objects, there is some evidence to indicate that the interventions of the mercers was significant, albeit by other means.

DAGUERRE,
MARCHAND,
Rue St-Honoré, vis-à-vis l'Hôtel d'Aligre.
TIENT Magasin de Porcelaines, Bronzes, Ebénisterie, Glaces, Curiosités, & autres Marchandises.
A PARIS.

Plate 15. Trade card of Dominique Daguerre. J. Paul Getty Museum, Malibu, California.

Plate 16. Detail Sèvres *porcelain plaque, 1778. J. Paul Getty Museum, Malibu, California.*

Plate 17. Detail lacquer panel, Japanese, late 17th century. Victoria and Albert Museum, London.

In the case of the porcelain plaques supplied by the Sèvres factory from the 1750s, several mercers have been credited with both the design of the plaques and the forms of furniture and other items into which they were incorporated.[20] For example, in 1770 five plaques, *bleu celeste* were described in the factory's sales registers as 'pour coffre Daguerre'.[21] In the case of two bureau plats stamped by Martin Carlin, the overall form of the bureau was presumably first established in order to carry the fourteen plaques (colour plates 6 and 7). The trade card of Daguerre is fixed to the underside of the piece (plate 15). Some of the plaques are dated for 1778, but were not bought until May 1784 by the Grand Duke Paul (later Tzar Paul I) of Russia and the Grand Duchess Maria Feodorovna for Pavlovsk.[22] The lacquer version is mounted with an assortment of Japanese lacquer panels cut to match the shape of the Sèvres plaques (plates 16 and 17). On the Getty piece (but not the V&A bureau which is stamped three times), the stamp of the cabinet-maker Carlin has been obliterated, possibly by Daguerre. Another lacquer bureau (unstamped) survives, as does a drawing of a similar version with porcelain plaques, both of different proportions but sharing the same apron-shaped swags of the Getty and V&A bureaux (plates 18 and 19). Although the two large curved plaques of porcelain on the Getty bureau are the only two surviving examples of this form of plaque produced at Sèvres, it appears that the design of the bureau was used and adapted for use with small lacquer panels.

Both Simon-Philippe Poirier and Dominique Daguerre sold a range of small tables of incorporating plaques of various shapes (plates 20 and 21) and small pieces of furniture with Sèvres plaques were made in series over a period of some years. Ten almost identical *bonheurs du jour* survive in public collections, each mounted with seventeen small plaques (plate 22).[23] The placques were dated by the factory from 1766 to 1774. Savill attributes the design of the early porcelain plaques at least in part to Poirier, who was the first to co-ordinate on any scale the mounting of the plaques onto tables and other forms of furniture. Eriksen calculated that Poirier had purchased 1,400 plaques by 1770.[24] From the 1770's, Daguerre became the principal purchaser, and he seems likely to have designed and been exclusively associated with various forms of object inset with plaques of porcelain. Some of the furniture plaques were decorated expressly for him,[25] and he was also involved in the design of vases. In 1782–3, the factory produced seven 'vases à monter Daguerre', of a form copied from a wooden model supplied by him.[26] Other variations were produced during subsequent years, including oval and round vases of cassolette form (plates 23 and 24).[27]

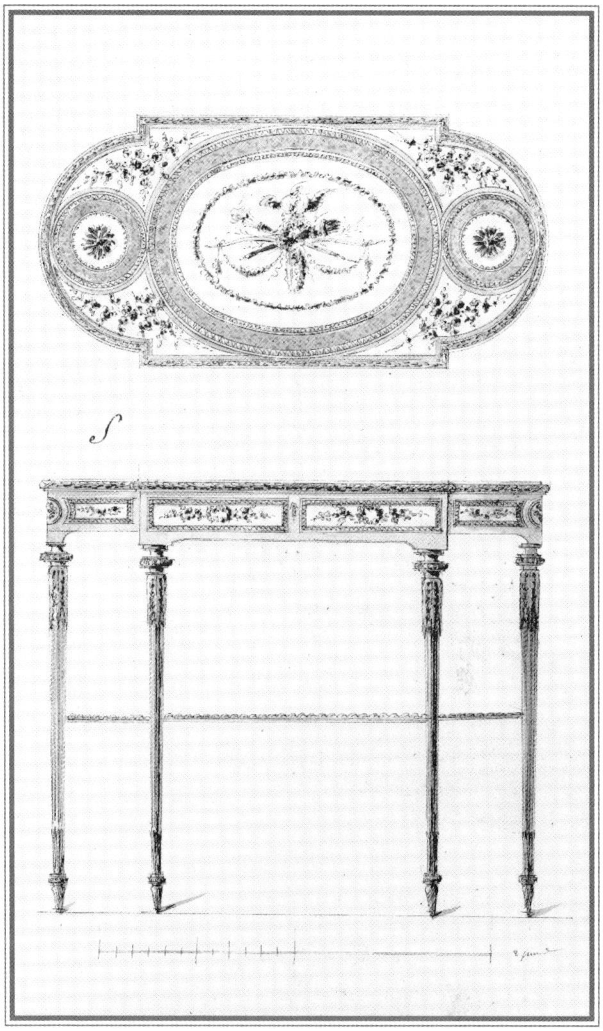

Plate 18. Coloured drawing of a table, 1770–85. Metropolitan Museum of Art, New York.

Plate 19. Detail of table, 1770–80, attr. Martin Carlin. Photo Sotheby's.

Plate 20. Table, French, c. 1773, stamped by Martin Carlin. J. Paul Getty Museum, Malibu, California.

Plate 21. Table, French, c. 1785, stamped by Martin Carlin. Victoria and Albert Museum, London.

Many objects were stocked in small groups or series within which there were small differences. The stock tended to be highly individualized – apart from small items of porcelain, items were rarely listed in identical groups of more than two or three, and often these were defined as pairs (of vases, *girandoles*, *commodes* etc) or *garnitures* (of porcelain vases or urns). Such a pattern of production in small series with some differentiation seems typical within the luxury trades. For example, Claude-Antoine Julliot's inventory of 1736 listed ten different commodes of violet-wood (*bois de violette*). They differed in size (from three to four-and-a-half feet wide), in the number of drawers and shape. Some had bronze mounts and feet (*pieds de biche*), some had marble tops, one top was made of purplewood (*palissandre*) and one commode was *sans dessous*. Each was itemised separately, valued at between 70 and 150 *livres*.[28]

One case in which particular designs may be closely associated with an individual mercer is that of the mounts used to frame a series of Sèvres porcelain vases (plate 25).[29] These vases apparently served as both pot pourri vases and candelabra since on some pairs, such as the examples at Fontainebleau, each has a lid that can be reversed so as then to be surmounted by a three-light candelabra. The mounts were therefore rather elaborate. More significant in the context of this argument, however, is the distinctiveness of their decorative features, especially the lion's heads. As Verlet has remarked, since the cover of one of a pair of blue Sèvres vases of this model in a Polish collection has on its underside an inscription recording the name and

Plate 22. Bonheur du jour, French, c. 1765, stamped by Martin Carlin. Bowes Museum, Barnard Castle, Co. Durham.

Plate 23. Vase, Sèvres, with gilt bronze mounts c. 1785. J. Paul Getty Museum, Malibu, California.

address of the mercer Dulac, and includes the word *invenit* it would seem that Dulac was here presenting himself as author of the model.[30] This does not mean that he designed the bronzes himself, but it suggests that he considered that he owned the model and that its use was restricted to vases that he supplied.

Another example of distinctive bronzes being used by a mercer Martin-Eloi Lignereux, Daguerre's last business partner towards the end of the eighteenth century, has been considered by Geoffrey de Bellaigue.[31] In discussing the puzzle of Lignereux' precise role in the design of a series of very similar clocks, he observes that the bronze ornaments, comparable to those used on other objects which he is known to have sold, may constitute a model specific to Lignereux. Such evidence, along with other mercers' ownership of bronze models, might indicate some direct intervention in the design of

Plate 24. Vase, Sèvres, with gilt bronze mounts c. 1785. Wallace Collection, London.

Plate 25. Vase and candelabra, c. *1765.*

Photo Christie's Images.

mounts. But the attribution of bronzes remains highly problematic. As de Bellaigue remarks, the connection observed may be 'fortuitous; it could merely indicate the popularity of the particular neo-classical motif'.[32]

Nevertheless, the inventories suggest that certain models for bronzes were exclusive to individual mercers. Whether or not they designed them, they were able to maintain effective copyright through commissioning and preserving the lead models from which the bronzes were cast. Models for bronzes were given by Simon-Philippe Poirier to Dominique Daguerre on the occasion of the latter's marriage in 1772.[33] Claude-François Julliot stocked a range of bronze mounts for furniture, both gilded and not gilded.[34] Julliot also kept the bronze models for casting, as his inventory of 1777 shows.[35] Although the mercer Lazare Duvaux commissioned bronze mounts for porcelain 'modèles fait exprès', there is no evidence that he kept the models himself.[36] Like Julliot, Martin Hennebert's stock included *ornements de bronze dorés* though no models were listed, and most mercers who stocked furniture also kept an assortment of bronze mounts and locks in stock.[37] Those mercers whose inventories described only the cast bronze mounts were presumably buying them on the open market. The mercers' role in holding their own models, and also in copying or imitating bronzes was a subject for debate within the corporations. Following legislation drawn up in 1766, a bronze model and/or drawing for each pattern was to be registered in an attempt to prevent its use by any other bronze worker.[38] The legislation does not appear to have allowed for the registration of designs by any individual, such as a mercer, outside the corporation of *bronziers*. Indeed, the document expressly forbade the members of the mercers' corporation from plagiarizing models.

DESIGN THROUGH ASSEMBLY

No category of work illustrates more strikingly the mercers' involvement in design – and the difficulties in understanding this – than the clocks

Plate 26. French clock, mid 18th-century, with Meissen figures and Vincennes porcelain flowers.

The National Trust, Waddesdon Manor.

Colour Plate 1. La Résurrection de Christ, *1676, Charles Lebrun. Musée des Beaux Arts, Lyon.*

Colour Plate 2. Commode c. *1750, attr. Joseph Baumhauer. J. Paul Getty Museum, Malibu, California.*

Colour Plate 3. Sécretaire à dos d'âne, *stamped RVLC (Roger van der Cruse or Lacroix), Konrad O. Bernheimer Ltd, London.*

Colour Plate 4. Coloured drawing, dated 7 September 1784. Musée des Arts Décoratifs, Paris.

Colour Plate 5. Commode, c. 1750, stamped by BVRB II. Victoria and Albert Museum, London.

Colour Plate 6. Bureau plat, 1778–84, stamped by Martin Carlin. J. Paul Getty Museum, Malibu, California.

Colour Plate 7. Bureau plat, c. 1780, stamped by Martin Carlin. Victoria and Albert Museum, London.

Plate 27. Clock, mid 18th-century, with blanc de Chine *figures c. 1700. Photo Christie's Images.*

Plate 28. Group of blanc de Chine *figures of a Dutch family, Dehua, c. 1700. Victoria and Albert Museum, London.*

and ornaments combining a number of materials. The mercers' corporate statutes gave them the right to stock such a range, and they produced new models through combining imported and domestically produced porcelain, bronze and other materials such as clocks or mechanisms. From about the 1740s, a range of new objects was sold by mercers such as Lair, Duvaux, Dubuisson and Delahoguette. Clocks and ornaments combining bronze, porcelain and other materials and mechanisms in extravagant configurations were highly valued in inventories. The mercers were uniquely placed to create such confections – they had access to imported porcelain, to the bronze workshops and clockmakers. Moreover, their statutes gave them the right to trade in all of the materials and items. Each was probably slightly different, and it is possible that design drawings were not necessary for their assembly. Michel Joseph Lair, for example, had in stock in 1759 the following clock, valued at 2,000 *livres*

> Une grande pendule en chef doeuvre garnie de jeu dorgue, montée en cuivre doré et ornement de fleurs de porcelaine de Saxe prisé avec seize figures aussy de porcelaine de Saxe faisant partie de son ornement.[39]

Several clocks with such organ movements and figures survive.[40] Whilst Lair's was a highly individual, and

Plate 29. Clock, mid 18th-century, elephant of Meissen porcelain. The National Trust, Waddesdon Manor.

Plate 30. Detail of base of clock, c. *1750. Waddesdon Manor, National Trust.*

valuable, piece, other inventory descriptions record more standard objects, varying in terms of their individual parts, but broadly similar (plate 26). The descriptions do not give enough information to differentiate between the designs or patterns sold in one shop from those in a neighbouring mercer's stock. No longer were the products from the Orient unusual or inaccessible, and within the Parisian marketplace around the mid-century, the mercers appear to have had access to a similar range of skills and materials. Simon Henri Delahoguette's inventory of 1768 included less valuable pieces, such as

> Une pendule composée de cinq chinois et d'un tambour de porcelaine de la Chine letout richement garni en bronze doré d'or moulu le mouvement fait par Gudin.[41]

The clock was valued at 288 *livres*, and is similar to a surviving model which remains anonymous (plate 27). The figures of Chinese porcelain were made for export in Dehua (plate 28).

Delahoguette also had in stock a figure of a elephant supporting a clock case without its movement, (plates 29 and 30), and other clock cases awaiting gilding.[42] The fact that he owed money to one *sculpteur en bronze*, a *maître fondeur cizeleur* and a *maître doreur argenteur et cizeleur sur métaux*, as well as two clockmakers, strongly suggests that he was employing skilled modellers and chasers to supply the bronzes for his confections.[43]

The Use of Models and Presentation Drawings

Other forms of pre-production models were used by the mercers, but these were apparently employed for marketing rather than manufacturing purposes. A few such small-scale models from the eighteenth century survive, particularly for upholstered furniture such as beds and chairs, for porcelain objects and, in a rare instance, for a clock.[44] Whilst the plaster models for Sèvres porcelain were made as part of the design and production processes and remained the property of the factory, other models were used for marketing new designs. In the case of imports of oriental porcelain, *modèles* were supplied to retailers by the East India companies, from which, presumably, the mercers could order supplies in higher volumes.

The mercers also had access to models made in Paris which were able to convey the perhaps unfamiliar form of certain types of goods to foreign clients. For example, a model chair which is strongly associated with Lord Coventry's purchases of French furnishings in the 1760's may have been supplied by the mercer Simon-Philippe Poirier (plate 31). The chair, re-upholstered and painted in imitation of wood grain in the nineteenth century, is an example of the advanced neo-classical taste developed in Paris during the early 1760's.[45] The model is stamped by the chair-maker (*menuisier*) Tilliard and marked in ink on the underside with the upholsterer's name, Petrus.[46] Poirier is known to have supplied other items of furniture for Croome Court.[47] Coventry bought a suite of tapestries direct from the Manufacture Royale des Gobelins in the mid-1760s and the *gout grec* chair is assumed to have been intended to match the hangings.[48] The factory also supplied the tapestry panels for upholstering the seat furniture. This was undertaken by the chair-makers Mayhew and Ince, who also made the frames, and though they are unmistakeably English, the chairs retain their French-style oval backs. Should this speculative link with Poirier be proven, it would be consistent with other examples of the mercers' use of design material for marketing purposes.

Other than Madame Blakey's drawing, many of the examples cited earlier in this chapter were related to the mercers' relationships with local suppliers. An example of the mercers' exploitation of drawings in long range marketing may be seen in the case of a collection of drawings in the Metropolitan Museum of Art.[49] Drawn and sometimes coloured in a number of different hands, these depictions of furniture, clocks and porcelain are dated to the early 1780s and are linked with the decoration of the palace at Laeken, residence of Albert, Duke of Saxe-Teschen and the Archduchess Maria Christina, governors of the Netherlands and now the Belgian Royal Palace.

The collection has long been assumed to be associated with Dominique Daguerre, from whom the Duke and Archduchess are assumed to have ordered furnishings for the palace.[50] Reputed to have sunk en route from Paris, the objects themselves no longer survive. The association with Daguerre is plausible. His shop, A la Couronne d'Or in the rue St Honoré, was stocked with similar objects.[51] In some cases, surviving pieces can also be linked with the Esmerion drawings (plates 32 and 33). The function of the drawings as aids to selling is made clear by

Plate 31. Model armchair, French, 1763–1768, stamped Tilliard and marked petrus. *Photo Christie's Images.*

Plate 32. Coloured drawing of a mounted vase, French, 1770–80. Metropolitan Museum of Art, New York.

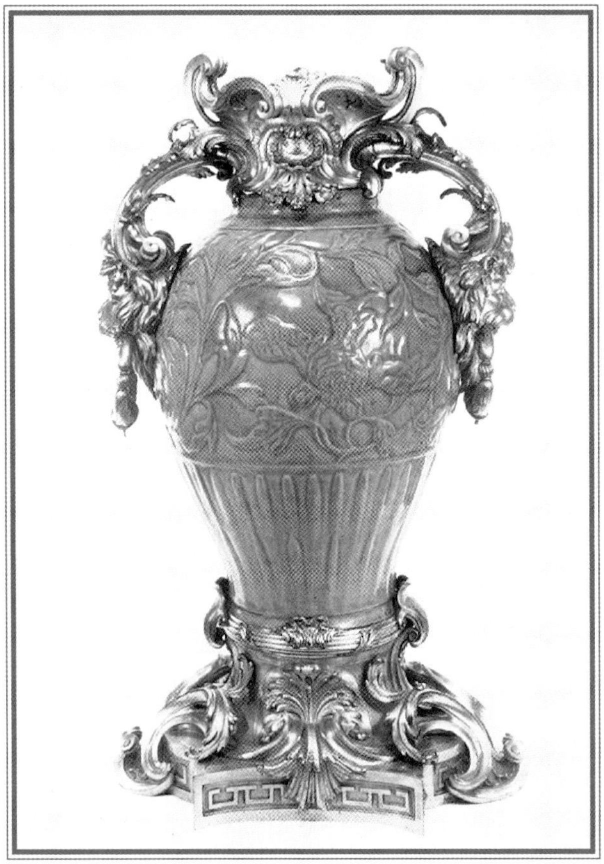

Plate 33. Vase, Chinese celadon porcelain with French mounts, c. 1750. Photo Sotheby's.

manuscript explanations which further describe the qualities and scale of the objects. The coloured drawing of the sécretaire mounted with plaques of Sèvres biscuit porcelain (colour plate 8) is annotated thus:

> C'est encore imparfaitement que le dessin rend l'effet de la bauté de la secretaire qui est orné de 4 bas reliefs en porcelaine de franc biscuit sur un fond petit bleu et bronze doré au mat.[52]

Other inscriptions describe the nuances of colour (sometimes on the interior as well as the exterior), the relative sizes (of pieces in a garniture) or the origin of items. The collection has never been fully researched, but it is certain that a number of different draughtsmen are represented. Some sheets are signed, others attributed. For long-distance marketing, then, the employment of draughtsmen and colourists was one response to the problem of describing, tempting and selling.

The role of the mercers in design evidently varied but seems to have been significant. Their interventions in the design process ranged from employing designers to produce drawings for manufacturing and marketing purposes to supplying materials such as *pietre dure* around which a piece of furniture might be built. They appear also to have been involved in designing, or creating new models, from combining a number of different materials which only they held the right to trade. In addition they also reserved the exclusive use of certain patterns by safeguarding the models from which bronzes were cast. The mercers' exploitation of designs needs to be seen in the widest context, extending beyond the documentation and attribution of drawn or printed designs. Their complex business relationships, and ability to finance the production of certain goods, enabled them to exercise considerable design control within the commissioning process, and indeed gave them the opportunity to create products unique to their individual businesses.

NOTES

1. For example, the motifs used by Parisian lacquerers (*vernisseurs*) are frequently traceable to engraved sources (see Huth 1971 and Grosheide 1986). The goldsmiths, with their close links with the engraving trades, appear to have used drawn designs for a large proportion of their work. At Sèvres, the preparatory drawings and plaster models conserved in the factory's museum demonstrate the careful planning process which preceded the launch of a new vessel (see especially Savill 1988). In the case of patterned silks, the well-documented design process involved the transfer of a painted design or pattern to point paper which, along with written instructions, made possible the setting up of the loom and the weaving of the pattern to the correct scale, in the right colours and with the intended texture (Miller 1996).
2. See Benhamou 1993, Leben 1994 and 1995 [2].
3. AN MC XXXIII, 641. I would like to thank Lesley Miller for providing this reference.
4. Priced at 375 *livres* per annum.
5. See note 32, page 17.
6. Though design training was available in Lyon, the designers working within the silk industry were encouraged to study Parisian designs.
7. Fuhring 1986[2], 27.
8. De l'Hiberderie, 1765.
9. ADVP D[5]B[6] *régistre* 2813.
10. AN Y13701 and Y13702.
11. Croome Court Archives, Bill no. 53, cited in Eriksen 1974, 135.
12. See Arts Council, Great Britain, London 1960, 22 and Lemonnier 1986.
13. For presentation drawings executed by specialist draughtsman for a French-trained sculpture working in England see Baker 1992.
14. The plaques were made available from the holdings of the Garde Meuble (Setterwall 1959).
15. Setterwall 1959, 425.
16. All mercers stocked part finished items, or components, which ranged from clock cases and table legs to uncut precious stones for jewellery and separate fan sticks and leaves. The proportion of each mercer's stock comprising components varied from 3% to 30% of the total value of the stock. Claude-Antoine Julliot's 30% is largely accounted for by the pieces of rock crystal used to build and repair chandeliers. (The chandeliers themselves were valuable items – the most highly valued in 1760 was worth 6,500 *livres*.) In the case of mercers dealing in furniture, the components represented between 1% and 11% of the value of the total furniture value. The component items included table legs, pieces of marble and bronze mounts.

    A number of inventories listed components of fans, and the bankruptcy papers of Simon-Henri Delahoguette included 270 fan sticks, lacquered red, worth 125 *livres* (ADP D[4]B[6] *carton* 14, *dossier* 677, 2 April 1755). The rights to assembling these formed the subject of intense debate in the eighteenth century, as the fan-makers (*eventaillistes*), inlay-workers (*peigniers-tablettiers*) and painters (*peintres*) disputed with the mercers over the trade in and assembly of fans. Apparently 200 mercers were specializing in the wholesale and retail trade in fans, both imported and made in Paris. They maintained the right to stock the component parts, and to assemble them. The sticks were supplied by the inlay-workers and the leaves by the painters, and the fan-makers were attempting to reserve the right of assembly. However the mercers proved too important a market for the other two corporations, who refused to acquiesce. The fan-makers' strategy, had it worked, was probably aimed at preventing the mercers from getting the sticks directly from the inlay-workers, rather than being compelled to buy them from the fan-makers. (The debate involved much paperwork and many corporations over time, see for example BN MSS Mss Joly de Fleury 2018, fo 245.)
17. AN XXXXVI, 633, 15 Frimaire an 5, Daguerre, first published by Lemonnier 1986.
18. Listed under *Objets divers lestout du magazin destinés à l'establissement de meubles à faire ou provenant de meubles défauts*.
19. The bronzes are arranged *sans traverse*, that is without horizontal borders along the length of each drawer front. The lower drawer opens by means of the scrolls which project from the bronze surround at lower left and right, and the upper drawer has no handles and opens using the key.
20. The mercers Simon-Philippe Poirier and Dominique Daguerre are credited with the design of various small pieces of furniture inset with Sèvres porcelain plaques. They were in partnership between 1772 and 1785, when Poirier died (see chapter 2). Savill documents the history of the production of the plaques for furniture and snuff boxes, stating that though plaques for furniture were made only in small volumes from 1752, their production in any quantity depended on Poirier's orders, which dated from the end of 1758. Several authors have pointed out that a small number of mercers had a virtual monopoly on the purchase of these plaques, and may have been involved in their design, as well as in the design of the forms of boxes and furniture onto which they were mounted. For example, all snuff box plaques made before 1759 were purchased by Duvaux. Duvaux is also credited by Francis Watson as the originator of a range of snuff boxes fitted with porcelain plaques (See Grandjean 1959 and Watson 1966, vol. 3, 104).
21. Savill 1988, 843.
22. Wilson 1981.
23. New York, Metropolitan Museum of Art (Jack and Belle Linsky collection, 2, Kress collection, 2), San Marino, Huntingdon Art

Gallery (2), Britain, Waddesdon Manor (2), Northamptonshire, Boughton House, (1), Paris, Musée Nissim de Camondo (1). See Medlam 1992 for a discussion of the presumed prototype now in the Bowes Museum.

24. Eriksen 1974, 215.
25. Savill 1988, 976.
26. See Savill 1988, 468–480. Eriksen states that vases made at Sèvres for the purpose of setting in bronze mounts were not generally available, but specially made for the mercers (Eriksen 1974, 135). In the 1750's, a range of porcelain forms made at Sèvres was named after each of two mercers, Lazare Duvaux and Thomas-Joachim Hebert. No evidence survives that they were involved in the design of these objects – the pieces so named were amongst a number of forms named after shareholders and dealers associated with the factory (Savill 1988, 961–90).
27. The Wallace piece is the only known example with a cover and stem of gilt bronze rather than porcelain.
28. 1 at 70 *livres*, 3 at 75 *livres*, 1 at 80 *livres*, 3 at 100 *livres*, 1 at 110 *livres*, 1 at 150 *livres*.
29. For a pair using Sèvres vases in apple green see Christie's, London, 4 December 1975, lot 51 (ill.), and Christie's, London, 19 March 1964, lot 59 (ex-Ashburton collection).
30. Lazienski Palace, Warsaw. See Verlet 1987, 73 and 263, ill. 66 and 67. In this example, the porcelain may well be of later date.
31. De Bellaigue 1968.
32. De Bellaigue 1968, 291. Ottomeyer and Pröschel (1986), Baulez (1986 and 1995) and Verlet (1987) discuss the mercers' suppliers of bronzework, particularly for the later eighteenth century (Omont, Remond and Gouthière).
33. Eriksen, 1974, 135 and de Bellaigue 1974.
34. The list comprised *ornements de bronze non dorés*, items 811–814 (furniture mounts), *bronzes doré* items 815–822 (more mounts including some for porcelain, edging for drawers, and paperweights) (AN MC IX,666, 5 November 1777, Julliot).
35. *Modeles dornements d'après Boule propre pour Bibliotheques* item 828, *modeles de commode* item 829, *modeles d'armoire*, items 829–835.
36. These cost 960 *livres* and were designed by Duplessis as mounts for two celadon urns, (Courajod 1874, 15 June 1754, 1810). Nine other examples of mounts by Duplessis are listed in the daybook (entries 601, 1021, 1124, 1493, 1713, 1738, 1810, 2420, 2806, 2999).
37. AN MC LXII, 521, 24 October 1770. Nicolas Guignard, *marchand bourgeois faisant commerce de cabinets, bureaux et armoires d'ebenne*, at the sign Au Nom de Jesus on the Pont Notre Dame. His stock of mounts included keyholes or escutcheons for drawers (*serrures de tiroir*), bronze rings (presumably for drawer handles), and 6,000 brass nails. Thirty-two keyholes of lacquered bronze (*cuivre en couleurs*) were specifically 'pour servir dornemens a des bureaux (8 livres), quatre tetes de cuivre en couleur acompagné de leurs chuttes et deux pieds de biche aussi de cuivre en couleur' valued together at 100 *sols* and *quatre griffes de lion de cuivre en couleur 6 livres*. (AN MC XXXVIII,130, 19 July 1714 Guignard).
38. See Eriksen 1974, 271–6 for a full transcription and translation of this document, and a translation, and Verlet 1988 for further discussion of models.
39. AN MC LX, 481, 17 January 1759.
40. For a clock with soft-paste porcelain flowers and a group of four figures of *blanc de Chine*, mounted in bronze, the clock movement by Noel Balthazar, see Christie's Monaco, 2 December 1994, lot 23 (ill). For a later automaton clock with organ, with a tree and automated bird which flaps its wings, the clock movement by Ardiot, set on a neo-classical base, see Christie's London, 13 June 1991, lot 20.
41. AN MC CXVI, 439, 23 December 1768, Delahoguette, item 295.
42. 'Un elephan portant une boete de pendule', valued at 120 *livres*. A similar clock, also without its movement was described both in the inventory of Alexandre Lefaucheur in February 1750 and a model formed part of Caffieri's assets on the occasion of his marriage in 1747 (de Bellaigue 1974 vol. 1, 102). The V&A has an example of this model, with a clock movement by Martinot, marked with the inscription 'fait par Caffieri' (252–1882, Jones Collection, see Verlet 1987, 201). Lazare Duvaux also stocked a model of an elephant clock, with a movement by Moisy (de Bellaigue 1974 vol. 1, 102). Duvaux owed money to three clockmakers (Moisy, Lenoir et Masson), a sculptor, six bronze founders and a gilder on his death in 1758 (AN MC XC 290, 29 November 1758, Duvaux).
43. As Verlet points out, a number of clockmakers were involved in commissioning bronzes, but in this case it appears that Delahoguette was controlling the manufacture and assembly of his clocks (Verlet 1987).
44. Drawings were sometimes followed by models made in wax, wood or terracotta, usually about one seventh of the full size, and then a model around one third of the full size might be made. For example, models for the Royal Palace at Warsaw, after drawings by J-L Prieur in 1765–6, included a bed and two chairs. The model bed was gilded, and may have been a full mock-up, including hangings, and the chairs were modelled first in wax to a small-scale, then in larger size in terracotta. However, none of these models survive. Extant French chair models dating from the eighteenth century include a wax model of an armchair showing variations in the legs etc, in a private collection. Models in public collections include a full-size model in terracotta for a clock, in the J. Paul Getty Museum, and the model for Marie-Antoinette's jewel cabinet, at the Baltimore Museum of Art.

45. The model is an interesting document of the emerging *gout-grec* in France. Most surviving French neoclassical chairs for which a date of manufacture can be established date from 1768 (Eriksen, 1974, 337). The Tilliard model is very close in design to a chair stamped by Louis Delanois which Eriksen dates to 1768–70 and describes as 'an early essay in neoclassicism'. Eriksen points to the heaviness of the garland of bay leaves which surrounds the back, which is very close to the design of the Tilliard model.

46. Jean-Baptiste Tilliard (1686–1766), who from 1752 was working with his son Jacques-Jean Tilliard (1723–1798), both *menuisiers* from a family of specialist chair-makers of the first rank. Jean-Baptiste became *Menuisier du Garde Meuble du Roi* in 1728 and his son took over the position in 1766. The inscription PETRUS on the webbing provides very rare evidence of the involvement of an upholsterer. The *marchands tapissiers* acted as intermediaries between the skilled upholstery trades and clients in *ancien régime* Paris. A chair in the Camille Lelong sale (Paris, 1903) bears an ink inscription for Petrus, and forms part of a set assumed to have been bought in Paris by Louise-Elizabeth (daughter of Louis XV) for the royal palace of Parma. Bill Pallot attributes the Parma chairs to N-Q Foliot. Petrus is known to have been part of a network of craftsmen working in Parma for the Duchess of Parma, which included another *marchand tapissier*, and three *menuisier-ébénistes*. In 1754, a Baptiste Petrus is listed with Nicolas Yon, who jointly signed a valuation in French currency of items of furniture for the Parma court, and in 1765, J. Baptiste Petrus co-signed another estimate for furniture, in Spanish currency. It is interesting to note that Tilliard also appears in archives relating to Parma as a supplier of chairs (caned) in 1755.

47. See the accounts published by Beard 1993.

48. Coventry was the first of the British purchasers. He saw the prospectus in August/September 1763 and ordered in 1764. The bulk of the order was ready for shipment in 1767 and the chairs were being completed (upholstered) in 1771. When looking at the cartoons for tapestry chair covers by Tessier, Coventry would have been looking at cartouche-shaped backs. A painting by Maurice Jacques recorded at the Gobelins in 1762 is said to have shown oval-backed chairs. A gouache by P-A Baudouin *Le Lever*, dated 1765 and exhibited in the Salon that year (and engraved thereafter) is always claimed as the earliest illustration of oval-backed chairs. Though the Croome Court chairs as supplied are much less strongly architectural, it is possible to see influences from the model, though by 1771 other sources, such as the Baudouin engraving, would have been available. See Harris 1962, 100–116.

49. The Esmerion collection, 59.611 1–10, 60.692 1–10, 61.680 1–36. See Myers, 1981 for an all-too-brief discussion of these drawings and watercolours.

50. They bought from London, Paris and Vienna. The Esmerion collection appears to include items purchased outside Paris. In 61.680, folio 1, a coloured drawing of a vase bears a note in French stating that the pair was bought for 100 guineas.

51. For example, two tables with Sèvres plaques in the V&A collection were sold by Daguerre in the 1780's. Daguerre was one of the few mercers to buy the furniture plaques from the manufactury. For further details on Daguerre's enterprise, see de Bellaigue 1974 and 1995, and Lemonnier 1986.

52. Pen, black ink and watercolour, MMA 59.611.10.

4 Importation and Imitation

The European market for oriental goods in the late seventeenth and eighteenth centuries generated a sizeable revenue for the Canton merchants and the trading companies which shipped merchandise into Europe. Traded in the luxury market places of large European cities, the cargoes consisted of oriental goods manufactured in the east, particularly in China and Japan, explicitly for export. These novelties were a highly important stimulus and point of reference for the development of *chinoiserie* styles in Europe, and several types of oriental porcelain and lacquer became part of the French canon of good design and craftsmanship.

The ways in which the Europeans traded with and communicated design requirements to the merchants based in the Far East have long preoccupied art historians.[1] Whilst the activities of the various European East India Companies are at least partially documented, and there is a rich literature on seventeenth- and eighteenth-century collections of oriental objects, very little is known of the links between the arrival of the cargoes at European ports and the acquisition in Paris of objects for use and display.[2] This chapter considers the mercers' role within this series of transactions, and the ways in which they marketed and transformed the export goods for the Paris market.

Wholesale Importation from the Orient into Europe

Jacques Savary stated in 1675 that it was the mercers who were responsible for expanding French trade to the Indies.[3] Whilst this might have been true at the outset of this trade, the mercers who were retailing oriental goods in eighteenth-century Paris do not appear to have been major investors in the Companies. Whilst several mercers were shareholders in the French East India Company, the Compagnie des Indes, founded in 1664, this appears to have represented an investment strategy rather than a method of influencing access to the imports for the retail trade, and in relation to the capital sums of these companies the mercers' financial interest was negligible. Though European markets for oriental export porcelain, lacquer and textiles could be considered long distance trade, the series of intermediary companies and individuals limited the size of the capital outlay needed by the mercers to stock their Parisian shops. The major capital outlay was made by the shipping companies. On arrival at a European port, a whole consignment or parts of consignments were auctioned to wholesale merchants, who in their turn sold the goods on to retailers or other merchants.[4]

Oriental objects were known in France well before the eighteenth century, though they are frequently discussed in terms of individual collections and the acquisitions (gifts and purchases) of the court. By the second half of the seventeenth century a number of Parisian collectors, male and female, had assembled porcelain and lacquer of high value and quality.[5] The oft-reported visit in 1686 of the King of Siam and his entourage brought the orient to Versailles. This was the first of two Siamese trade missions to France to attempt to establish a base for the Compagnie des Indes in Bangkok, which acted as a staging post on the sea routes from east to west. With the Siamese came gifts to the French King of gold, tortoiseshell, fabrics, carpets, porcelain (over 1,500 items) and lacquer furniture.[6] These objects formed the basis of royal collections which were to be augmented during the following century, not least through purchases from mercers such as Thomas-Joachim Hebert and Lazare Duvaux of both old and new export porcelain.[7] And by the end of the eighteenth century, a hundred years after the visit of the King of Siam, the trade in highly valued antique (*ancienne*) Japanese porcelain was continued by mercers such as the Julliot family and Dominique Daguerre.

During the seventeenth century, the Dutch East India Company (VOC) was the principal source of oriental export porcelain. Holland had for some time been the source for the French merchants of ceramics, especially Delft-ware and Japanese porcelain[8] and in 1664, a third of the cargoes of the Dutch Company was estimated to have been destined for the French market.[9] Hans Huth cites an instance of French merchants buying lots from the cargoes of the VOC boats at the quayside of the docks at Amsterdam in about 1640.[10] The Dutch shared with the Chinese the monopoly on Japanese goods, and were said to have retained control of this market until the Compagnie des Indes was re-established in 1720,[11] although in 1709, the importation of all ceramic wares from Holland into France was prohibited.[12] Until this date, the import duty on ceramics had been fixed at 12 or 20 *livres* (the latter during times of war) per hundred pounds in weight of merchandise.[13]

That the Dutch continued to compete with the French in wholesale importation from the orient is exemplified by French records. For example, in 1708, a *marchand fayencier* named Braulard requested of the Conseil de Commerce in Paris permission to import from Holland six cases of *porcelaines d'Hollande et des Indes* for the Gobelet du Roi and for princely patrons.[14] Braulard also appears to have acquired goods on the Paris market – he appears as a debtor to Thomas-Joachim Hebert, mercer, in 1723.[15] As late as 1748, a merchant in Marseille proposed an import duty of 500 *livres* per quintal on imported porcelain, tea, cinnamon, cloves and nutmeg from Holland.[16] As in the case of printed cottons,[17] such prohibitions were neither popular amongst merchants and clients nor successful in promoting French commercial interests in imports and domestically produced goods.

French access to Oriental Imports

The extent to which the Parisian mercers could get luxury goods through the Compagnie des Indes is not entirely clear. Since the mercers' inventories do not link creditors' names with the objects in stock, it is not easy to determine the source of oriental export wares of different origins. In the case of the mercer Hebert a Dutch supplier is listed amongst his creditors. In 1724 Hebert owed 1231 florins 'pour reste de tous compte denvoy de marchandises' to Veuve Godefroy Dulong et Cie, merchants in Amsterdam.[18] The outstanding debt amounted to 2,600 *livres*. An announcement in the *Mercure de France* indicates that one other Parisian merchant, at least, also bought porcelain and lacquer imported by the Dutch company at this date. Gersaint advertised in December 1723 that he had just returned from Holland bringing back curiosities including *porcelaines singulieres*, small cabinets, boxes and other articles of *ancien lacque de la chine*.[19]

It is possible that in the case of Hebert and Duvaux, oriental lacquer and possibly porcelain bought from the Dutch cargoes was of higher quality than that available within the geographical boundaries of the French market place. Given that both mercers were supplying known collectors, at least part of their stock range would have consisted of the finest pieces. Finding lacquer of exceptionally high quality appears to have posed problems to the mercers, though it was certainly sought after in Paris. The Dutch stopped importing large pieces of Japanese lacquer in 1693 (though Chinese lacquer continued to be available to both French and Dutch companies). Gersaint alluded to this scarcity in the catalogue of the collection of Chevalier Antoine de la Roque in 1745, when he wrote of his expeditions to Holland

> . . . dans mon dernier voyage, malgré toutes les recherches que je pus faire pour m'en procurer, il me fut impossible de pouvoir en rapporter quelques Pieces satissfaisantes, & aujourd'hui le Lacq nouveau commence même à ne pas être commun.[20]

French importers become more ambitious in their trade with the East around the end of the seventeenth century. In 1681, a voyage on one of the royal ships had been proposed to bring back from the East a range of export goods not yet traded by the French 'dont la Compagnie ne faisait pas négoce, des gérofles, porcelaines et diamans'.[21] In 1700, the *Mercure de France* announced the return of the French boat L'Amphitre from the Indies to Port-Louis, with 181 cases of porcelain (advertised in part as 'modes et modèles et divers autres ouvrages de porcelaine très fine')[22] and almost as many cases of lacquer items, probably Chinese or Tonkin.[23] The consignment was sold by auction in Nantes. The ship made a subsequent trip, returning in 1703, but this second auction appears to have been less profitable.[24] These cargoes probably represented the first opportunity to buy oriental porcelain in bulk in France (see appendix 6). Little porcelain arrived after 1703 (except a cargo in 1706) until the 1720s, and Holland continued to supply the French market.[25]

Some mercers bought directly from the auctions at the French ports. Although trade at the ports was equally open to *négotiants* (plate 34), the aptly named mercer Orient bought wholesale volumes of cargo which arrived in St Malo on the Comte de Toulouse.[26] The auction took place on the 5th and 6th September 1720, and included cases of tea, lacquer screens, porcelain drinking wares and minerals. (The lacquer screens would have been Chinese.) He also bought four varieties of tea, screens worth 14,000 *livres*[27] and porcelain, predominantly cups and saucers[28] and also cases of dishes and pots for jam or sugar worth a total of 86,775 *livres*.

The sales of the Compagnie des Indes at Nantes in 1722 and 1723 were remarkable for the many thousands of items of porcelain, presumably Chinese, for sale at each. The total porcelain sales reached 683,032 *livres*, 470,679 of which resulted from the sale of cups and saucers of various sizes, forms and decoration.[29] Many must have been destined for Parisian shops, whose inventories from the early 1720's record a plethora of porcelain vases and other vessels for display of varied form, colour and pattern and an assortment of table wares. Cups and saucers were listed in their hundreds. According to Tournier, Parisian and Nantais merchants competed with each other at the auction. Tournier also lists twelve French merchants at these sales – from Lyon (1), Tours (2), Bordeaux (4), Rennes (1), Orleans (1), La Rochelle (1), Saint Malo (2), and two foreigners – Semith from Holland and Fourrat from Geneva.[30] This suggests that trading patterns within Europe were extremely flexible and that, dependant on the availability of information about forthcoming sales, merchants travelled considerably on the continent to acquire stock.

THE TRADE IN PORCELAIN IN PARIS

Within Paris, as in the case of other types of goods, oriental wares were circulated between merchants as well as sold directly to individual customers. Some mercers may have acted as wholesalers for oriental porcelain, though this is difficult to document comprehensively from the available evidence. The mercer Dubuisson certainly bought East India Company porcelain (*porcelaine des Indes*) in bulk from the firm of Jacquet and Tixier of the rue Bertin Poirée in Paris,[31] and sold it on in smaller volumes to a number of mercers, including Bailly[32] and also *fayenciers* including one Grouet in the rue de Richelieu.[33]

The retailing of these exotic goods was apparently an entirely different business from the wholesale dealing at auction. The sign painted for Edme François Gersaint's shop, A la Pagode, on the Pont Notre Dame in Paris in about 1720, shows a highly

Plate 34. La Boutique étant san chalan: adieu le negos, *French,* c. *1701. Bibliothèque Nationale de France, Paris.*

sophisticated environment within which a range of luxury objects including paintings, mirrors, clocks and lacquer were examined and sold (colour plate 9). Gersaint, who became a *marchand mercier* in 1720, is best known for his trade as a picture dealer.[34] However, this image shows his interest in new goods such as the large mirror on the left, with giltwood frame (*trumeaux*). The clock (left, on the table) represented the taste for Boulle marquetry and bronzes, and the toilet set depicted on the right was symbolic of exotic *chinoiseries*. Gersaint stocked fifteen such toilet sets in 1725, lacquered (*vernies*) in imitation of oriental lacquer, valued at 480 *livres*.[35]

By 1692, a kind of commercial almanac by Dupradel entitled the *Livre Commode des Adresses* gave a picture of the retailing of such wares. Du Pradel listed twenty dealers in Paris who specialized in objects of *Lachinage*.[36] Evidence of shops selling oriental goods before this date is limited. In 1644, John Evelyn observed of Paris that:

> among the Houses is a shop called Noah's Arke, where are to be sold all sorts of Curiositys, naturall & Artificial, for the furniture of Cabinets, Pictures and Collections, as of Purcelane, China . . . Shells, Ivory, Ebony: Birds, dryed *Fishes, Insects:*, &c of more Luxury than Use.[37]

Oriental imports are also known to have been sold in the seventeenth and eighteenth centuries at the Parisian fairs.[38] These were major, if passing, events, subject to their own trading regulations and attracting merchants from outside Paris into the city in large numbers.[39] By 1610, Portuguese merchants were selling such goods at the Foire St Germain[40] and Sauval noted in the 1660s that porcelain was on sale there. He said of the Foire St Laurent that

> on y vend, depuis quelques années, de la porcelaine et autres choses que les marchands vont acheter à grand frais aux extremités de la monde . . .[41]

The market at the Paris fairs for oriental porcelain must have been reasonably developed by 1678, when the Duchess of Cleveland sent her collection to be sold at the Foire St Laurent. The *Mercure Galant* announced

> Il s'en est vu cette année d'extraordinaires. Ce sont des porcelaines que Madame la Duchesse de Cleveland y a fait vendre . . . les plus rares ont étaient montées d'or ou de vermeil doré et garnies diversement de même matiere en plusieurs endroits.[42]

When Thomas-Joachim Hebert expanded his business between 1713 and 1724 the most striking development was the introduction into his stock of porcelain and lacquer wares. The business had been run by Guillaume Daustel in a shop Le Vase d'Or on the Quai de la Megisserie until his death in 1713 (see appendix 4). That year, Daustel's inventory lists neither porcelain or lacquer.[43] When the next inventory of the business was drawn up in 1724 the new products included a range of wares in both materials and the name of the shop had been changed to 'Au Roi de Siam'.[44]

Porcelain	No Items	Total Value	Average Value	As % of Total
porcelaine	1,686	7,993	5	23
ancienne	309	8,520	28	24
Chine	1,027	8,618	8	24
Japon	681	7,879	12	22
Chine/Japon	21	290	14	1
bleu et blanche	857	1,106	1	3
garnie (mounted)	19	910	48	3

Fig 14. Porcelain categories, 1724, T-J Hebert.

Chinese and Japanese porcelains were distinguished from each other in most inventories, as were old items from new. Although a number of objects in the inventories of the 1720s and 30s were described only as *porcelaine*, in all cases the *porcelaine ancienne*, both Japanese and Chinese, was distinguished from more recently made wares (*nouveau*), as was also the case for lacquer.[45] From the 1720s, the mercers' inventories generally included a combination of oriental porcelain distinguished by origin, age and decoration into the following categories – Chinese, Japanese and Persian, old and new, blue and white, monochrome and coloured. It was not until the 1770s that the mercers' inventories followed the practice of sale catalogues in classifying porcelain and lacquer by quality (first and second).[46] One type of European porcelain was similarly classified – by 1747, Meissen was divided into old and new. Sometimes porcelain (and lacquer) was referred to as *commune*.

Occasionally inventories and catalogues of porcelain collections used terms such as *fine*.[47] However, the quality of both porcelain and lacquer is more easily determined by the values given in the inventories. Within each, this tended to range from a few *livres* for porcelain plates, jars, cups, saucers and old lacquer coffers to over a thousand for furniture veneered with oriental lacquer and embellished with gilt bronze mounts. Some of the most valuable pieces of porcelain and lacquer were supplied as special commissions, such as the commode supplied by Darnault for 6,500 *livres* (see pp. 82–3), the value of which greatly exceeds the value of items in any mercers' stock. Most of the mercers' stock was of low to average value, and therefore probably not of exceptional quality. Hence the mercers can be seen to have been supplying not only a range of forms of vessels, ornaments and furniture, but also supplying a diverse market in terms of the connoisseurial and market value of their wares.

Of Hebert's stock as a whole, the porcelain (valued at 35,316 *livres*) represented 42% of the total stock value (83,335 *livres*). It was the single most valuable sector of the stock, the most numerous (4,600 pieces) and the sector with the widest range in value, from 1 to 223 *livres*. Of lowest value were the hundreds of cups and saucers which were in part the components of tea, coffee, chocolate and dining services. These included 456 large blue and white cups of Chinese porcelain, described as *commun* and valued at 182 *livres*. Cups, saucers, teapots and pots for preserves, sugar and milk, plates, dishes, etc. were stocked separately rather than in sets at this date. They were also sold separately by the Compagnie des Indes until the 1730s, when the first tea services were sold as sets.[48] Hebert also stocked a range of ready-assembled *cabarets*, imported as sets by the Compagnie des Indes from 1703.[49]

Hebert's Chinese porcelain included a number of vases and urns, some of which were inventoried in sets, creating *garnitures* of two, three, five or seven vessels (plate 35). A garniture of five pieces of

Plate 35. Garniture of five vases, Chinese, Kangxi, 1662–1722. J. Paul Getty Museum, Malibu, California.

Chinese celadon porcelain set in gilt bronze mounts was valued at 70 *livres* and sixteen pieces were listed together as *pour garnitures de cheminées*. A further twenty four pieces *de hauteur*, of varying heights and shape, of celadon, blue and yellow porcelain were specially for assembling garnitures according to demand. Other pieces for display, or curiosities, included a range of birds and animals and four celadon shells, one of which was broken (total value 200 *livres*).[50] Versions in celadon with bronze mounts dating from the mid-century survive (colour plate 10), and appear in the daybook of the mercer Duvaux.[51]

Most of Hebert's Japanese porcelain was described as coloured and of different *desseins* and probably therefore of the patterned Kakiemon or Imari style (plate 36). Some of the Chinese porcelain was described explicitly as being in the Japanese taste, of the type now termed 'Chinese Imari'. For example, the two *grands plats de porcelaine de la Chine gout du Japon a bords plats* (50 *livres*) would have been Chinese export porcelain decorated in the Imari palette of underglaze blue, iron-red and gold.[52] Sometimes this Chinese porcelain was described as *japonnée*.[53] In 1680, the Chinese stopped buying Japanese porcelain, and exported Chinese imitations of Imari porcelain. By 1720, this Chinese Imari was relatively standard (earlier wares were often of better quality and perhaps rarer).

It is particularly interesting to note that old Japanese porcelain formed a sizeable proportion of Hebert's stock and was, on average, more highly valued than any other category except mounted porcelain. Tablewares including cups and saucers, dishes, pots and also pot pourris and garnitures were classified as *porcelaine ancienne de Japon*. Some pieces, old and new, were mounted in silver and gilt bronze, and these were clearly more valuable than the unmounted version. Hebert sold porcelain mounted in silver, such as the four Japanese sugar bowls valued at 150 *livres*.

Plate 36. Garniture of three vases, Japanese, Arita, 1700–1722. J. Paul Getty Museum, Malibu, California.

Colour Plate 8. *Coloured drawing of a* sécretaire, *1780–85. Metropolitan Museum of Art, New York.*

Colour Plate 9. L'Enseigne de Gersaint, *1720–21, Antoine Watteau. Schloss Charlottenburg, Berlin, photo Jorg P. Anders, Berlin.*

Colour Plate 10. One of a pair of mounted shells, Japanese porcelain, late 17th century, the mounts c. 1750. J. Paul Getty Museum, Malibu, California.

Colour Plate 11. Urn, 1720–30, Chinese porcelain with French mounts. Victoria and Albert Museum, London.

Colour Plate 12. Lidded bowl, Japanese porcelain c. 1700, with French mounts, 1720. J. Paul Getty Museum, Malibu, California.

Colour Plate 13. Inkstand, early 18th-century Chinese porcelain, the mounts and lacquer c. 1750. J. Paul Getty Museum, Malibu, California.

Colour Plate 14. Nécessaire, *1749–56, rosewood box fitted with silver, glass and St Cloud porcelain. Victoria and Albert Museum, London.*

Plate 37. Pair of porcelain vases, Chinese, Kangxi 1662–1722, mounts French, 1745–9. J. Paul Getty Museum, Malibu, California.

Hebert's stock included more pieces mounted in bronze than silver.[54] Few large pieces were mounted with silver after the inventory of 1736 of Claude Antoine Julliot's stock.[55] Amongst Hebert's stock of porcelain mounted with gilt bronze fittings was a considerable amount of blue and white porcelain.[56] It included a fountain of Chinese porcelain with red and green colouring, of cylinder form mounted in gilt bronze valued at 120 *livres*. The colouring suggests that it was decorated in the Japanese style and would have been similar to a surviving fountain which was cut down at the neck before elaborate gilt bronze mounts were fitted (colour plate 11).[57] Many pieces in Hebert's inventory were described as broken or cut down, and those which retained high monetary values were almost certainly intended for mounting. For example, two square-sided bottles and fifteen large pieces, *urnes*, *rouleaux* and *cornets* were described as broken (perhaps in transit) and might have been intended for mounting. The two *urnes coupés* were almost certainly cut down in Paris before mounting, as in the case of the Chinese vases now in the J. Paul Getty Museum (plate 37). These were cut down by almost half from *rouleau* vases dating from 1700–1720 and set in gilt bronze mounts dated about 1750.[58] In 1768, Delahoguette's inventory included a similar piece, though mounted simply and valued only at 12 *livres* 'une moitié de bouteille de porcelaine bleu celeste monté sur une terasse avec feuillage de cuivre non doré'. He also had amongst his stock the top half of a *cornet* and a section of a *rouleau* vase, presumably for mounting.

Plate 38. Perfume burners, blanc de Chine *porcelain with silver-gilt mounts* c. *1700. Victoria and Albert Museum, London.*

Surviving pieces from the early eighteenth century are often made up of several different pieces (such as saucers, dishes and bowls) mounted together to form a single European vessel in metal mounts. For example, the body of each of a pair of perfume burners (*brûle parfums*) is formed from the lower part of a bulbous bottle with plum blossom sprigs in relief, which has been cut down and mounted in silver gilt (*vermeil*, plate 38). The covers were probably made from a lid of a Chinese tea-bowl, pierced with six vents, each framed with metal and the whole cover mounted with a silver-gilt border and knop. The porcelain and mounts are more or less contemporary, dating from about 1700. In another example, mounted in silver, three different pieces of Japanese porcelain have been used to assemble a covered bowl (colour plate 12 and plate 39). In the case of objects, usually lidded, which were comprised of several components of different pattern, the dominance of the French form and mounts of these finished objects presumably assisted the reading of the different pieces of porcelain as a single decorative scheme.

The inventories reflect this practice of assembling bodies and covers from different objects both in their wide range of individual vessels in stock which could be adapted for such purposes, and, in some cases by listing part-finished goods. For example Louis Bosseux had in stock 'deux pots a faire couverts de porcelaine de la chine garnis de cuivre doré d'or moulu' valued at 20 *livres*. Although the distinction was not often made in the inventories between mounts for use on furniture or porcelain, the gilt bronze 'gorge accompagnée de deux anses contournées et un fort pied' valued at 18 *livres* in Claude-François Julliot's inventory of 1777 was likely to have been destined for use either on a vase of porcelain, or of hard-stone – Julliot stocked an assortment of such items.[59]

The mounting of porcelain, at first with silver or silver-gilt but increasingly with gilt bronze, became a standard and lucrative practice for the mercers and examples are well documented.[60] The mercers trading in mounted porcelain appear to have had extremely close relations with the trades working with bronze, and were stocking a range of bronze andirons, wall lights and furniture with gilt bronze mounts. Although the inventories rarely give detailed enough descriptions to distinguish one bronze model from another, other evidence suggests that some mercers at least retained control of a particular design of bronze mount through commissioning and owning the mould itself (see chapter 3).

The value of mounted porcelains varied according to rarity and singularity of the piece, and the quality and design of its gilt bronze mount. Within a single inventory or product group, values tended to vary tremendously. For example Hennebert's inventory of 1770 included a rare garniture of five blue vases of *porcelaine de Perse* mounted in gilt bronze, valued at

Plate 39. Detail, components of lid of silver-mounted bowl. J. Paul Getty Museum, California.

500 *livres* and two small celadon urns, also mounted, of the same origin (30 *livres*).[61]

Alternative materials were used in some instances. For example, vases were occasionally mounted in giltwood, such as the three large urns embellished with giltwood ornements and valued at 200 *livres*, described in the 1768 inventory of Simon-Henri Delahoguette.[62] Delahoguette, mercer, stocked a number of paper maché vases, all painted to imitate alabaster. These were described as 'deux vases en carton peint en façon d'albastre garnie de pieds et couvercles de bronze doré dor moulu', and valued at 36 *livres*.[63] Another two vases of the same material were embellished on each side with giltwood mounts in the form of dragons, and placed on plinths of marble (d'Antin). They were valued at 24 *livres*. A third design was a gondola-shaped vase (*vase . . . en forme de nacelle*) valued at 30 *livres* which was mounted with handles of bronze, chased and gilt. Two vases made of paper maché (*carton*), and painted blue in imitation of Chinese porcelain, with fine gilt bronze mounts survive in the collection of the Musée Nissim de Camondo (plate 40). Whilst such imitations were not likely to deceive a connoisseur of porcelain or hardstones, they maintained their value as curiosities and were often, as in the blue paper maché vases, of high quality craftsmanship.

Oliver Impey states that Japanese porcelain was

Plate 40. Paper maché vases with gilt bronze mounts, French, c. 1740–55. Musée Nissim de Camondo, Paris.

exported in much lower volumes from the 1740s.[64] The fact that Japanese porcelain is listed after this date in the mercers' inventories might be explained in terms of a demand for Japanese porcelain which thrived on the limited number of goods available. Certainly its rarity attracted comment, and much old Japanese porcelain was circulated through the salerooms during the second half of the eighteenth century, much of it mounted. However, a number of mercers' inventories of this date also included new Japanese porcelain which suggests that it was still available in some quantity. Its scarcity was not the only factor in its high value. Chinese porcelain was less highly valued from the 1724 inventory of Hebert's porcelain. Those objects described specifically as Japanese were valued at an average of 12 *livres* each, whereas the Chinese objects were valued at an average of 8 *livres* each.

A number of mercers assembled porcelain from various origins and lacquer into ornaments (see chapter 3) and sets used for drinking tea and hot drinks, for travelling and for writing. Bosseux, for example, stocked lacquer trays for *cabarets* of various shapes – square octagonal, colours [tortoiseshell, red, black] and types of lacquer (European *peint en façon de la Chine* and *en gout de la Chine*). Cabarets assembled in Paris using oriental lacquer trays and European porcelain cups and saucers were stocked by Duvaux, Delahoguette and others.[65]

Like Gersaint, Bosseux stocked toilet sets. His

inventory includes sets in a number of colours – red, coffee-coloured (sometimes *caffé clair*), aventurine, black and a combination of *jaspée*, black and gold. The mercers combined lacquer and porcelain to make inkstands. For example, Bosseux had in stock two in 1726 which were already assembled. One was composed of a black lacquer tray with an inkwell, powder pot and sponge box of blue porcelain (*bleu celeste*) mounted with silver, valued at 120 *livres*. Another, valued at 100 *livres*, was assembled from three white cups mounted with silver, placed on a tray of black lacquer decorated, like the other *a relief facon du jappon*. This was a precursor of a surviving inkstand now in the J. Paul Getty Museum, with three white cups and three figures on a red lacquer tray, with branches for candles, leaves and other decorative mounts of gilt bronze (colour plate 13). The early eighteenth-century Chinese porcelain comprises the figure group and central cup from Dehua, and two outer cups from Jingdezhen. The lacquer and mounts are French and date to around 1750. This may well have been assembled by the same mercer responsible for the clock with *blanc de Chine* figures (see chapter 3, plate 28).

Many of the smaller items were used by the mercers to fit out boxes for smoking, drinking or travelling. These, like the garnitures, were wholly European in concept and function. Known as *nécessaires*, they were occasionally imported, but were more commonly made in Paris and were highly valued items. A late seventeenth-century travelling box fitted with nine flasks of Japanese porcelain appears to have been made in Japan for the Dutch East India Company,[66] though the French cargoes of the 1720's do not seem to include such items. The mercers used the imported porcelain vessels (and also European versions) to fit out boxes made in Parisian workshops. The mercer Louis Bossuet stocked in 1726 eleven boxes of rosewood (*palissandre*) and walnut (*noyer*), the most highly valued (300 *livres*) was fitted with drinking wares of silver, a mix of oriental porcelain and glass.[67] A comparable box veneered with rosewood, though of later date, is in the V&A (colour plate 14). Its accessories include porcelain from the French factory at St Cloud. A price list from the factory was found loose within the lining of the box. The silver items bear Paris hallmarks for the 1750s. Rougeux' other ten boxes comprised three rosewood boxes each with two tobacco jars of blue and white porcelain, one set of jars mounted in gilt bronze (*cuivre doré d'or moulu*), another mounted in silver (*garnie d'argent*) and each box also fitted with a silver spoon (one gilded). Smaller rosewood boxes contained one or two tobacco jars, of porcelain described as *japonnée* or Japanese *du Jap(p)on*. One box, lined with velvet, contained a single cup (goblet[68]) and saucer of white porcelain encrusted with gold. Two larger boxes, described as *tabagies* (smoking boxes) were fitted out with smoking accessories and porcelain tobacco jars with silver garnitures.[69]

EUROPEAN PORCELAIN

The mercers also stocked a range of European porcelain. The imitation of oriental porcelain and lacquer was driven by the marked success of the equivalent imports. These imported goods were clearly promoted in Paris by the mercers, to some degree in competition with both the factories and the sellers of ceramic wares (together members of the corporation of *maîtres* and *marchands faienciers*). The interests of the companies which imported oriental wares on the one hand, and of the French manufacturers on the other seem fairly clear – a case of commercial competition in which the manufacturers sought to achieve the quality and design of the imported goods. Mercantilist policies aiming to replace a range of imported luxury products with domestically produced goods were implemented in part through the apparatus of royal privilege. At first, privileges for the production of imitations of oriental porcelain, lacquer and fabric were accorded to the *manufactures royales* which were established from the 1660s,[70] and later to the workshops of Paris. Although many Europeans had been investigating the properties of lacquer and porcelain over a long period,[71] no successful lacquer and porcelain factories were set up in and around Paris until the early eighteenth century, other than the porcelain factory at St Cloud (1677?–1766). The Poterat family was given a royal privilege to manufacture porcelain in Rouen, a centre for the production of faience.[72] The porcelain factory at Chantilly was set up by the exiled Duc de Bourbon-Condé around 1725; another at Mennecy began production in the late 1730s.[73] The Meissen factory had been in operation since the 1710s, making imitations of Chinese and Japanese porcelain forms and decoration (plate 41).[74]

As the various European factories and workshops successfully built up production of wares which imitated the material qualities, forms and decoration of the oriental imports, and indeed developed new types of product, they looked towards the mercer's shops as retail outlets. Consequently, those mercers specializing in porcelain, lacquer and other oriental imports were juxtaposing in their shops the finest products of both east and west. The inevitable comparison between these oriental and European objects was at the very centre of late seventeenth- and eighteenth-century debates about the manufacturing of imitative wares, and also a considerable force in the development of a connoisseurship of such objects.

Plate 41. Vase and cover, 1727–30, Meissen. Victoria and Albert Museum, London.

The relationship between the oriental object and its European imitation is exemplified by the case of the Meissen imitations of the highly prized Japanese wares from Imari. This porcelain was known in Paris as *porcelaine de Saxe*. Rodolphe Lemaire, a French merchant (*négotiant*) is known to have negotiated with the officials at the Meissen factory for consignments of porcelain for the Parisian market. The surviving correspondence, published by Claus Boltz and summarized in English by John Mallett, suggests that during the late 1720s Lemaire was a driving force in the factory's efforts to imitate Kakiemon wares. Lemaire's involvement was twofold. He both sent white porcelain wares from Meissen to Holland to have them enamelled *dans le gout de l'Ensien Japon*, and he also offered the factory a market in Paris.[76] Meissen wares, he stated 'could surpass all the porcelain today being landed in Europe, and be similar to that of old Japan'.[77] As Hebert's inventory shows, the market for Japanese porcelain, especially Kakiemon wares, was fast developing by the 1720's. However, Japanese porcelain was never imported in such high volumes as Chinese porcelain and the market was therefore likely to accept porcelain in the Japanese style.

Lemaire has been credited with persuading the directors at Meissen to produce copies of Japanese (Kakiemon) wares which Lemaire guaranteed would be extremely successful on the French market. He would supply designs and models which would be appropriate for the Parisian shops. (It is interesting to note that Lazare Duvaux may have performed a similar role in Paris, though on a much smaller scale, using Meissen wares as a model for Sèvres,[78] and that towards the end of the eighteenth century Dominique Daguerre promised Wedgwood a market in Paris.[79]) Lemaire sought to persuade the factory to sell him porcelain without the Meissen factory mark of two crossed swords, which suggests that he was intending to sell the German porcelain in Paris as Chinese or Japanese.[80] He was prepared, however, to accept an oriental style mark, and in September 1729 agreed terms with the factory. A Meissen tureen of about 1730, now at Stanton Harcourt, is unmarked, and may be an example of the porcelain supplied by Lemaire with the intent to deceive Parisian buyers, merchants and clients. Lemaire was one of the factory's most important clients between 1729 and 1731. His privileged position with Meissen was terminated in 1731 – he was deported.

Given that Lemaire was importing Meissen into Paris at the end of the 1720s, it is interesting that no *porcelaine de Saxe* is described in the mercers' papers until the mid-century and it seems reasonable to speculate that the Saxon porcelain was indeed entering the market under the guise of Japanese imports.[81] Inventory descriptions are naturally of very little help in determining whether the objects described were of German or oriental manufacture. However, in some cases, objects are described only as *porcelaine*. When these objects are known to have been made both in Japan and Germany, speculation that the descriptions referred to Meissen versions might be justifiable. One such inventory survives from the 1730s. When Claude-Antoine Julliot's wife died in 1736, many of the products in stock were classified merely as *porcelaine*, including a number of types made at Meissen and in Japan for export.[82] Although Meissen was presumably by this date marking its wares, it is interesting that Julliot's inventory, whilst classifying some items as Japanese, did not specify the origin of others. Most of these unspecified pieces were animals (birds of prey, lions, tigers, cats) or vessels and difficult to attribute with any certainty. Surviving Japanese animals date from the late seventeenth to early eighteenth centuries and Meissen versions were in production by the 1730s.[83] Much of Julliot's stock at this date was Japanese, and all of the unspecified porcelain could have fallen into this category. No items listed were made exclusively at Meissen, and a number of European forms listed in the inventory could have been Japanese or Chinese export wares.[84]

Lemaire's enterprise presumed that his Parisian clientele, whether merchants or collectors, were largely ill-equipped to distinguish between Japanese and Meissen porcelain. It would appear that during the 1720s and 30s, very few individuals in Paris could confidently identify one kind of object from its imitator, and expertise in valuing these articles was also said to be of limited availability.[85] Ways of emulating the quality and decoration of oriental goods were the subject of much debate in Paris around this date. Dr Lister said of St Cloud porcelain 'J'avoue que je ne saurais distinguer ses produits des plus belles de la Chine . . . on avait égalé, sinon surpassé les chinois dans leur plus grande perfection'.[86] Such rhetoric was not surprisingly also to be found in the papers associated with the French factories established to imitate oriental porcelain, lacquer and fabrics (silks and printed cottons). In the mid-1720s the French were also seeking to imitate Kakiemon at the factory established around 1725 by the Duc de Bourbon at Chantilly. St Cloud, and to some extent Meissen, were especially known for imitations of *blanc de Chine*. Although the quality of Chantilly porcelain differs considerably from the Japanese, the products of the Meissen factory are still occasionally virtually indistinguishable from the Japanese originals.

Whether or not Julliot's shop, or indeed any other, stocked Meissen masquerading as oriental porcelain, the mercers' appear to have played a role in the development of the connoisseurship of porcelain. Their knowledge of their own stock, their relationships with known connoisseurs and collectors, and their involvement in the auction of extremely prestigious collections (including the authorship of catalogues) testifies to the expertise in porcelain held by at least a few mercers. They were thus closely linked with factories, merchants and collectors, all of whom were concerned with the differences between oriental and European objects in terms of their material characteristics and their value. We have to assume, therefore, that several mercers (but probably only a few) were highly skilled in matters of connoisseurship.[87] Clarke is of the opinion that at least one mercer was colluding actively in the deception of Parisian collectors. He states that the mercer Gersaint was responsible for removing the seals from the marked bases of Meissen pieces.[88] In 1747, he drew attention to the quality of the early Meissen imitations of Japanese porcelain. Certainly Gersaint was one of the first mercers to write catalogues of collections (de la Roque, 1745 and Fontspertius, 1747), and therefore to classify pieces for marketing purposes.

The Mercers and *Fayenciers*

The mercers' development of markets for porcelain imports of high quality and value was concentrated amongst those with sufficient capital to buy stock from the East India Companies and in bulk from other wholesalers, including Sèvres. These activities must be seen in the context of other parts of the ceramics trade. The mercers shared the right to sell ceramics with the *marchands fayenciers*. The latter were members of a corporation of makers and sellers of ceramic wares and glass, who were not permitted to trade in any wider a range of goods. When the corporations were dissolved, and then reconstituted in 1776 (see chapter 1), the nineteenth of the forty-four new *communautés* was the *Faienciers, Vitriers, Potiers de Terre*.[89] They were described as 'en concurrence avec le Mercier pour la vente des porcelaines' and 'en concurrence avec le Mercier pour la vente des poteries de terre'. It seems that a number of them sold ceramic and glass alongside beverages, and some stocked porcelain and up-market faience. For example, Dessus Le Montier, *marchand fayencier* at the sign of the Perroquet, rue de l'Arbre Sec, sold 'toutes sortes de vins de liqueur . . . toutes sortes de porcelaines, de belles fayence tant fines que communes, carasons de Seve et autres, verres fins, toutes sortes de vaisselle pour le chymie et verrerie . . .[90] Martin Lambert stocked faience from Rouen, Nevers, Flanders, Holland, and drinking glasses valued in total at 5,306 *livres*.[91] The 1720 inventory of the stock of the *fayencier* Guillaume de la Fond, rue Taranne, describes Dutch and French faience, cheap porcelain from Rouen and drinking glasses from Nevers.[92] Although Jean Baillet's inventory of 1732[93] shows an extensive network of suppliers within France and lists high quality faience and some porcelain, these wares were not described as imports and they were valued largely by the dozen, like glasswares.[94] The scale of these particular enterprises was considerably smaller than those of the mercers Hebert, Bosseux, the Julliot family, Duvaux and Delahoguette (see chapter 2), and the objects usually less valuable than those listed in the mercers' inventories.

Claude-Nicolas Cholet's enterprise in the rue St Honoré was more ambitious.[95] A *fayencier* from a large merchant family, he sold white fayence and 'fayence . . . nommé facon de porcelaine ou gros bleu' from Rouen, and white from St Cloud, Nevers and from the rue du faubourg St Antoine. He also stocked blue and white fayence from Rouen and of unspecified colour from Lisle. Glass wares were imported from Lorraine and Bohemia, and two items of English lead glass were listed.[96] In coloured porcelain he stocked pots, pots pourris in different sizes and a range of dessert and toilet wares, a service of twenty-two plates (250 *livres*). In blue porcelain were a service of twenty-six plates of different sizes (134 *livres*) and thirty-six dozen plates at ten *livres* the dozen. He also stocked candlesticks, cups and saucers, sugar pots and pomade jars from St Cloud. Several *garnitures* of silver were also listed, including two (13 *livres*) for mustard pots, which suggest that he, like the mercers, was co-ordinating the mounting of ceramic wares in metal mounts, though of silver rather than gilt bronze (typical of items destined to fit out *nécessaires*).

Another family of *marchands fayenciers* in this area traded from the rue du Roulle. Gilles Bazin, 'marchand mercier priviligié suivant la cour et marchand fayencier ordinaire de Sa Majesté', was listed in the sales registers at Vincennes and Sèvres from 9 April 1753.[97] He sold part of his business to Michel Joseph Lair in October 1756, at which point Lair also took over the rental of the shop at 1900 *livres* per annum.[98] Bazin was to continue in trade under his own name at Le Roy des Indes in the rue du Roulle. The last recorded purchase made by Bazin from Sèvres before selling the business was dated July 1757, but almost straightaway he was listed as buying 'pour Mrs Jacquesson et Brechant, which suggest that despite handing over the shop to Lair, he continued to act as an agent for Sèvres.[99] The registers document Lair's first purchase on 31 August 1757.[100]

Plate 42. Covered vase, 1749–50, Meissen, with French mounts. Cleveland Museum of Art, J.H. Wade Fund.

Michel Joseph Lair was born in 1732, the son of a Parisian mercer Louis Lair, who was described in 1756 as trading in Anjou as a *négotiant*. When Michel Joseph took on the shop in 1756 the goods were valued at 119,207 *livres*. Lair paid for the business with dowries and gifts from his parents and parents-in-law on the occasion of his marriage, also in October that year. He died at the age of twenty-six only two years after his marriage. By this date, Lair had expanded the stock considerably. He traded exclusively in glass, crystal, fayence and porcelain.[101] The ceramics comprised oriental porcelain (Chinese and Japanese) and European porcelain from Strasbourg, Frankenthal, Meissen, Sèvres, Vincennes, St Cloud, Sceaux, Villeroy and Chantilly. He was supplied by Hannong at Strasbourg and Helbig at Dresden. (Hannong had at least one other depot in Paris, with the widow Lachat.[102]) The Meissen wares included a range of tea and tablewares, and highly valued terrines. Several pot pourris were mounted with gilt bronze (plate 42). He also had in stock a garniture of five Meissen vases valued at 2000 *livres*. His papers include a record of insurance paid by Rouennais merchants for the transport of porcelain, crystal and flowers in a Dutch ship, which implies that Lair was exporting French porcelain. His orders included supplies for the *service du roi* at the Châteaux of La Muette, Bellevue, St Hubert, Choisy and Trianon, and for the services of the Dauphin and of the King's daughters *Mesdames*. Like the mercers, Lair sold mounted porcelain and ornaments assembled from porcelain and bronze of extremely high value, and his stock included porcelain flowers and Meissen figures which might have been intended for such use.

Madame Lair, Michel Joseph's widow, was twenty-two years old when he died. Their two sons were seventeen months and five weeks old. Madame Lair continued to run the business and was listed as one of the regular purchasers from Sèvres.[103] Her shop was described in an almanac of 1775, under *fayanciers* (a list of six, some described as retailers, some manufacturers, some advertising as both):

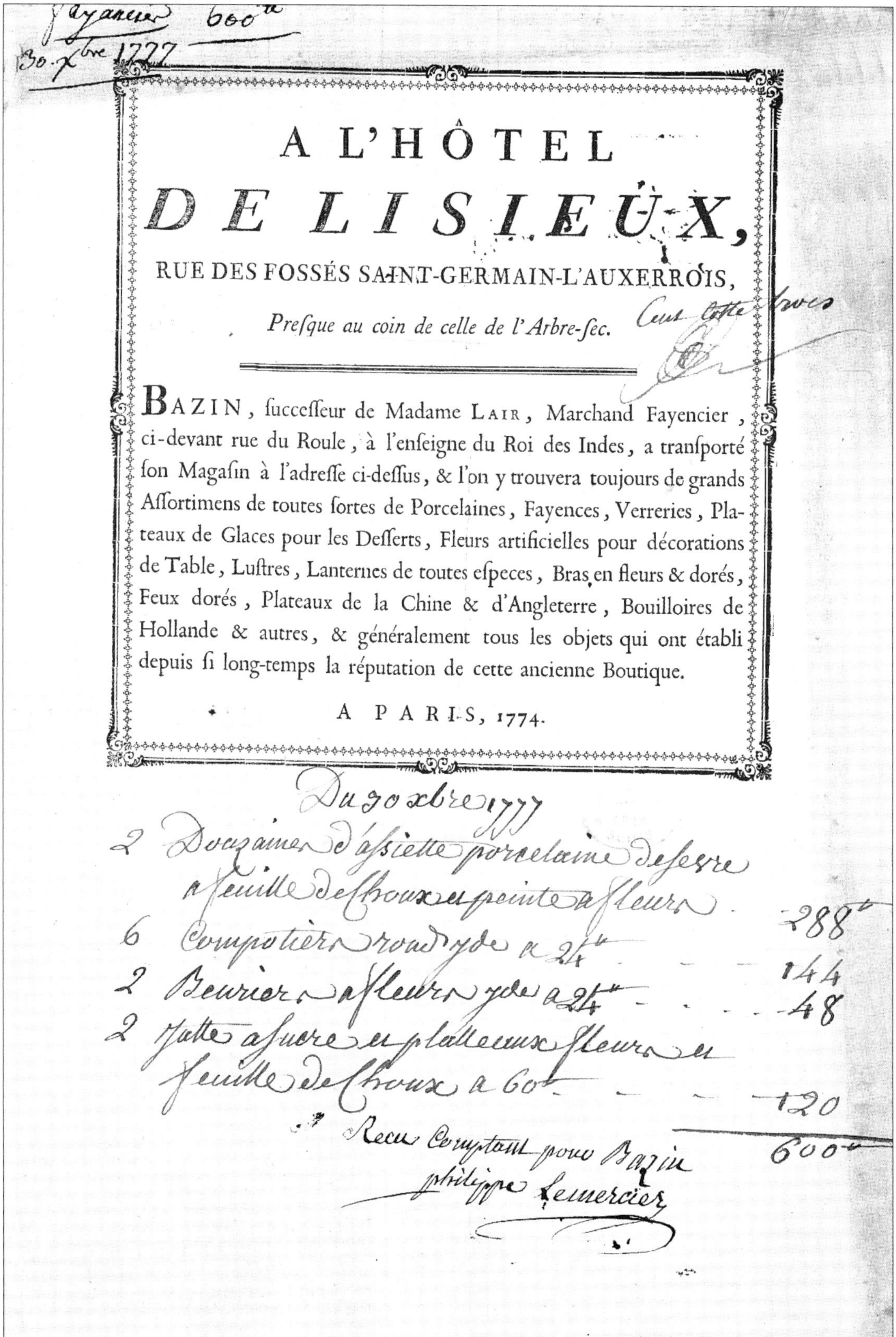

Fayancier 600[tt]
30. xbre 1777

A L'HÔTEL
DE LISIEUX,
RUE DES FOSSÉS SAINT-GERMAIN-L'AUXERROIS,
Presque au coin de celle de l'Arbre-sec.

BAZIN, successeur de Madame LAIR, Marchand Fayencier, ci-devant rue du Roule, à l'enseigne du Roi des Indes, a transporté son Magasin à l'adresse ci-dessus, & l'on y trouvera toujours de grands Assortimens de toutes sortes de Porcelaines, Fayences, Verreries, Plateaux de Glaces pour les Desserts, Fleurs artificielles pour décorations de Table, Lustres, Lanternes de toutes especes, Bras en fleurs & dorés, Feux dorés, Plateaux de la Chine & d'Angleterre, Bouilloires de Hollande & autres, & généralement tous les objets qui ont établi depuis si long-temps la réputation de cette ancienne Boutique.

A PARIS, 1774.

Du 30 xbre 1777

2	Douzaines d'assiette porcelaine de sevre a feuille de choux et peinte a fleurs	288
6	Compotiers rond ydes a 24	144
2	Beurriers a fleurs ydes a 24	48
2	Jattes a sucre et platteaux fleurs et feuille de choux a 60	120
		600

Reçu Comptant pour Bazin
philippe Lemercier

Plate 43. Trade card of Bazin, 1774. Archives de la Ville de Paris.

> Lair, Mme vve, au coin de la rue de l'Arbre Sec et les Fossés St Germain L'Auxerrois, à l'Hotel Lisieux, tient un des plus superbes magasins de porcelaines de Sevres, plateaux, lanternes en verres de Boheme, garnitures de cheminées et autres bijoux d'ornement.[104]

The almanac must have gone to print just before Madame Lair retired, for the trade card of the Hotel de Lisieux dated 1774 describes the proprietor of the same shop (l'Hotel Lisieux) as Bazin, successor of Madame Lair (plate 43).[105] It describes the products of the business and the long-standing reputation of the shop.[106] This trade card was used as an invoice dated 30 October 1777, for Sèvres tablewares.

Some twelve years after Bazin had taken over the business, he re-established a link with Gilles Bazin's early Sèvres purchases. In 1788, he commissioned a *vase pompadour* of similar form to a model originally launched in the early 1750's (plate 44).[107] Gilles Bazin is known to have bought such vases from the factory in 1753 and 1755, in December 1753 he bought a version in the fourth size, with a blue ground and birds very similar to one dated 1754 in the V&A collection (plate 45).

MARKETS FOR LACQUER

The mercers' business activities enabled them to develop the market for porcelain through importing and adapting objects, and they followed a similar approach in marketing lacquer goods. In the first instances, they sold such export wares without embellishment, but increasingly moved towards adapting and re-forming the lacquer to better suit European use and taste. By the early eighteenth

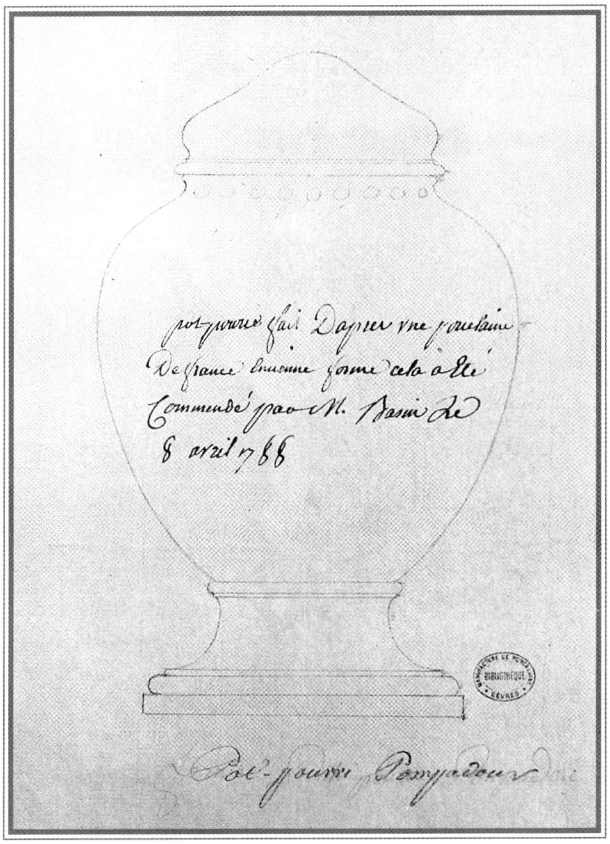

Plate 44. Drawing of a Vase Pompadour.

Manufacture Nationale de Sèvres.

Plate 45. Vase Pompadour, *Sèvres, date letter for 1754.*

Victoria and Albert Museum, London.

Plate 46. Cabinet on stand, late 17th-century, Japanese lacquer with French giltwood stand. Bibliothèque de l'Arsenal, Paris.

Plate 47. Trade card of Gersaint, 1740, François Boucher. Bibliothèque Nationale de France, Paris.

Plate 48. Commode, Japanese lacquer, late 17th-century, French giltwood stand, c. 1715. Nymphenburg, Pagondenburg.

century, the French appear to have been engaged in the practice of detaching lacquer panels from cabinets, chests and screens and re-using it to veneer and decorate modern furniture forms such as commodes, and new types of small boxes. Hebert's inventory shows the mercers' role in this process – the stock included both panels of lacquer (his raw material) and finished pieces newly veneered with the panels.

Hebert stocked fourteen pieces of Chinese lacquer furniture in 1724, including screens and cabinets.[108] His lacquer furniture was, on average, twice as valuable as his stock of furniture veneered with woods. The 'cabinet d'ancien la Chine a deux battans, plusieurs tiroirs et son pied de bois sculpté' was particularly highly valued at 700 *livres*.[109] Claude Antoine Julliot's inventory of 1736 included Japanese cabinets on stands, unaltered and placed on modern stands of giltwood or blackened wood. 'Un grand cabinet dancien japon monté sur son pied de bois doré' was valued at 437 *livres* 10 *sols* (plate 46). A similar cabinet of medium size (*moyen*) was valued at 125 *livres*, and a smaller version, also Japanese, at 150 *livres*.[110]

This form of cabinet, made exclusively for the European market, became almost iconic in Europe in that it was used to represent the idea of lacquer imports. An oriental lacquer cabinet on stand dominates the assortment of oriental goods represented in Gersaint's trade card (1740), designed by François Boucher (plate 47). The central place of lacquer in European display is also indicated by the representation of both red lacquer shelving and a lacquer cabinet of the now familiar type in a still life of the early eighteenth century (colour plate 15). The array of porcelain and terracotta wares parallels the profile of stock in the shop of a mercer, and indeed, this painting may represent a shop sign, or have hung inside a shop specializing in oriental curiosities.[111]

A cabinet on stand is a particularly interesting record of the development of the commode form and of the transformation of the oriental cabinet in France (plate 48). The doors have been removed leaving a carcase with ten drawers (plate 49). It retains its original mounts, which have been pierced to form escutcheons. In addition, it is embellished with gilt corner mounts and a low giltwood stand made in Paris.[112] The cabinet retains in its low platform the vestiges of the high giltwood stand typical of the late seventeenth-century presentation of these cabinets in France. This early eighteenth-century adaptation shows that the object was conceived partly as an oriental object, a cabinet, conventionally raised from the ground on a stand, and partly as a commode with Parisian corner mounts, drawer handles and with pronounced feet on its base, all of which parallel French designs for commodes of about 1710–15.[113]

Thus the mercers made substantial alterations to the standard export wares. Although the cabinets on stands continued to appear in inventories until the 1770's, they may have been used increasingly as raw material for veneering newly made carcases with the much-prized lacquer from the East.[114] Some may have been bought by mercers from clients as a source for lacquer panels for furniture veneers. For example, in 1782 the Darnaults bought at auction a Japanese lacquer cabinet from the collection of the Duc d'Aumont in 1782, from which five panels of very high quality were sent to the cabinet-maker

Plate 49. Detail, cabinet on stand, late 17th-century, Japanese lacquer with French giltwood stand. Bibliothèque de l'Arsenal, Paris.

Martin Carlin. He manufactured a commode with very fine gilt bronze mounts, which was supplied by the Darnaults after Carlin's death to Madame Adelaide for the exceptional sum of 6,500 *livres* (plate 50).[115] In the 1770s Roubo explained the process of removing such panels and re-using them on shaped carcases (see appendix 9 for full text).

Hebert's inventory describes two commodes which had been re-veneered in this way 'une commode de bois verny placquee la Chine, trois tiroirs fermant a clef', and another smaller version. The description of another furniture item in the inventory, a 'petite commode de trois pieds quatre pouces de long, avec dix tiroirs de verny de la Chine' valued at 120 *livres*, is more ambiguous. The term *commode* had been in use for fifteen years or so by this date, to designate French chests of drawers, usually with up to four drawers. Hebert's arrangement of ten drawers in commode form at this date is unusual.[116] A number of French examples of this type of commode survive, though from later in the century, (plate 51). This shows a French commode made in about 1750, veneered with small lacquer panels which were originally drawer fronts of Japanese cabinets.[117] On a commode by Joseph of about 1770, the ten oriental panels are combined to veneer only eight drawers, indicating that only the lacquer veneers were used, rather than the entire drawer or carcase.[118] However, in the example of another French commode, a set of ten drawers from a Japanese cabinet was fitted into a French carcase of 1787–90. The drawer sides, bottoms and fronts are all of oriental materials and construction.[119] It is probable that the 'quatre corps de tiroirs provenant de cabinet' valued at 300 *livres* in Lazare Duvaux' inventory of 1758 were destined to be used in just this way.[120]

The experts who drew up the inventories employed a number of terms to describe lacquer, and the distinction between oriental and French lacquer is not always easily discernible. When applied to new furniture forms such as commodes and corner cupboards, the term *verny la Chine* may well indicate a finish of European lacquer in the Chinese style, rather than a veneer of Chinese lacquer. Claude-Antoine Julliot's inventory of 1736 lists a number of types of furniture which might fall into this category, such as the 'deux encoignures de moyenne de la

Plate 50. Commode, French, 1785, stamped by Martin Carlin. Musée du Louvre, Paris (photo Réunion des Musées Nationaux).

Plate 51. Commode, 1740–50, stamped by BVRB II. Private Collection.

Chine fond noir avec leurs dessus de portour et chosson de bronze doré', valued at 150 *livres*.[121] Julliot also stocked small corner cabinets described specifically as decorated with Parisian lacquer ('six petittes encoignures fermantes verny de paris et figures', 90 *livres*). Two corner cupboards *verny a fleurs et pagode* were probably also wholly French. Some descriptions in the same inventory, in stating that the lacquer was *ancien*, indicate that old (or re-used) Chinese lacquer was used. For example, the 'commode verny ancien de la Chine garny de bronze doré avec son dessous de marbre de ver de mer' valued at 437 *livres* 10 *sols* and another 'commode de verny ancien de la Chine garny de bronze doré dor moulu avec son dessous de marbre noir incrusté de pierres de rapport' was valued at 750 *livres*. An

Plate 52. Medal cabinet, late 17th-century, attr. André-Charles Boulle. Bibliothèque Nationale de France, Paris.

unusual item was the coffer described as 'un grand bahut de verny d'italie sur son pied doré' (50 *livres*).

Perhaps the most spectacular items in terms of value and novelty would have been the bureau and filing shelves and the pair of armoires veneered with a combination of wood from the Cayenne Islands[122] and Chinese lacquer panels.[123] These are reminiscent of the two medal cabinets of Joseph Pellerin (1684–1782) made around 1730.[124] They are early examples of furniture of European form (*armoires*) with veneers of fine Chinese lacquer. One is veneered with borders of boulle marquetry (red turtleshell and brass) framing rectangular panels of Chinese Coromandel lacquer (plate 52). Its interior is partly decorated with Japanese lacquer. The other also bears panels of Coromandel lacquer, (plate 53), bordered by French lacquer in imitation. Both are decorated with gilt bronze mounts. They were probably made between 1725–30, and remained in Pellerin's ownership until they were transferred to the royal collection in 1782 for 2,000 *livres*, following the medal collection which had been given by Pellerin in 1762. A later example of a desk and filing cabinet similar in their use of exotic woods and high quality Chinese lacquer panels is the furniture, formerly at the Hôtel de Chatelet, now at the Château de Compiègne.[125]

The stocking of pieces of lacquer for re-use was common amongst the mercers specializing to any extent in modern pieces, largely cabinet furniture and small boxes, veneered with oriental lacquer.[126] Often

Plate 53. Medal cabinet, c. 1730. Bibliothèque Nationale de France, Paris.

Plate 54. Commode, c. 1750, stamped by Jacques-Philippe Carel. Musée du Louvre, Paris.

the lacquer in stock had been removed from its original chassis and was waiting to be reused, either in large pieces as panels for commodes, desks, tables and cabinets or for boxes (the inventories list drawers full of smaller pieces of lacquer for this purpose).

In almost all known cases, panels of oriental lacquer often of high value, were reused in Paris as furniture veneers rather than for display as a painting. (One possible exception to this pattern, however, is worth noting. In 1949, Lazare Duvaux supplied to M. de Villaumont 'un morceau de lacque garni en bronze doré d'or moulu' for the relatively high price of 960 *livres*.[127]) For use as furniture veneers, panels of Coromandel lacquer were valuable commodities and even currency amongst the trades. In the 1760s, the mercer Dubuisson had an agreement with the cabinet-maker Guignard that the latter would be paid for his work (180 *livres*) with two panels of Coromandel lacquer.[128] Along with three small screens of old Chinese lacquer were *deux planches de verny la Chine*. In Hebert's case, twelve leaves of screens of Coromandel lacquer decorated with flowers and birds were valued at 350 *livres*, and described as *douze feuilles* rather than *un paravent* which suggests that they had been dismantled and were stocked as individual leaves.[129] They were in part in poor condition, but several would have served as veneers for furniture. The doors of a commode stamped by Jacques-Philippe Carel are veneered with a single large piece of Coromandel lacquer (plate 54). In

1755 Delahoguette had *40 morceaux de Coromandel, endommagés* valued at 40 *livres* and other pieces of lacquer suitable for use as table tops (probably for tea tables) and *cabarets*.[130]

Julliot (1736) had in stock ten leaves from screens of Chinese lacquer valued at 500 *livres*. For veneers for smaller boxes, Julliot stocked fifteen small old pieces of Chinese lacquer. Hebert stocked '100 pieces de lacq rouge qui sont petittes boestes et dessous de boestes' (230 *livres*). A basket of pieces of lacquer and debris was valued at only 20 *livres*, but the high values accorded to the 83 *cabarets* with broken sides (160 *livres*) and the 170 others of 'verny de la Chine commun' in good and poor condition (worth 680 *livres*) suggest that the lacquer was valuable and reusable more or less despite its condition and age.

The mercers supplied these pieces of lacquer to the cabinet-makers and makers of small boxes (often goldsmiths) to be made up. This process may be followed in the daybook of Pierre Migeon. The *ébéniste*, himself involved extensively in sub-contracting, supplied work and goods to the mercer Thomas-Joachim Hebert.[131] Hebert had a current account with Migeon, and he made settlements of about half the outstanding sum every year or so.[132] Migeon first supplied him in November, 1731, with a *sécretaire* of rosewood and a small cupboard (100 *livres*) and in April 1732 with his first lacquer piece, a *sécretaire* veneered with lacquer and kingwood (*amaranthe*), for 120 *livres*. The daybook entry states clearly 'Ces luy quy ma fourny le vernit'. In August and December he supplied two more *sécretaires*, of lacquer, for 110 and 130 *livres* each, respectively. On 24 March 1733 is listed a *sécretaire vernis*, which presumably refers to a Parisian lacquer. Migeon continued to supply Hebert, along with other clients, with other lacquer pieces.[133] Other clients provided other types of materials for veneers; for example, on 18 July 1732, a Mr. Pettier de Fort bought a commode *en arbalete* (bow-fronted) of cayenne wood which the client had supplied. The carcase was of oak and 'il se tire un burot desous le dessus' which perhaps meant that it was an early example of a *bureau à pente*.[134]

The lacquer supplied by the mercers was glued onto or inset into furniture forms which more or less accommodated the panels of lacquer.[135] The edges had to be integrated into the surface decoration, and were usually framed with gilt bronze mounts. Migeon's daybook describes the process. Under an entry for a delivery to M. Guiton (perhaps a merchant) for a *sécretaire* of three feet 'il me fourny le vernis tout les join sont garnis de moulure en or moulu vendu 207 *livres*'.[136]

The type of work described here is represented by the mid-eighteenth-century commode from the workshop of BVRB II (see colour plate 5, chapter 3). Three seventeenth-century Japanese lacquer panels, originally from a chest (*bahut*) were used to veneer the commode.[137] The largest panel represents a landscape, and has been veneered across two drawers (*sans traverse*, that is, without framing each drawer with a border and thereby breaking the continuity of the design of the panels). The panels have been glued to the sides and front of this bombé commode and framed with a particularly delicate gilt bronze border, with integral handles on the lower edge. The upper drawer opens by using the key as a lever to pull the drawer forward. On the V&A commode, black French lacquer has been used to cover the carcase on the outside of the gilt bronze borders which form the corner mounts.

Plate 55. Box, unstamped, c. 1720. Victoria and Albert Museum, London.

Underneath the varnish can be seen the shape of the strips of wood veneer which have been glued diagonally to the carcase and which provided a smooth surface for the application of the varnish. The wood veneer also served the purpose of building up from the carcase wood (oak) to match the level of the Japanese lacquer panels. The lacquer panels are about 1.5 mm thick. An examination of the surface indicates that two different materials appear on the lacquer panels. French lacquer has been used to repair and varnish areas of the Japanese lacquer, which by the mid-eighteenth century, had not only travelled half way around the world, but was also about a hundred years old. Oliver Impey has shown through the examination of French furniture veneered with oriental lacquer that the surface was often repainted with Parisian *vernis* to repair or embellish the surface.[138] He has examined several pieces of French furniture veneered with Japanese lacquer and found that, in addition to this practice of varnishing over plain areas of old lacquer, the Parisians embellished plain areas which to French eyes invited additional ornament. Hence small motifs such as birds, insects and buildings were added in coloured varnish by *vernisseurs* in Paris as in the case of another commode in the V&A, attributed to BVRB II.[139]

Varnishes, coloured and clear, were used within the luxury trades for a range of decorative effects, on metal (tôle and alloys used for furniture mounts and wall branches), wood (furniture, *cabarets*) and porcelain.[140] In Paris, commercial almanacs list various specialists in lacquers and varnishes, sometimes for finishing bronzes. Roubo describes a lacquer 'connus sous le nom de Vernis d'Angleterre' for lacquering metals, especially metal mounts for furniture, to produce 'une belle couleur brillante approchant celle de l'or'. He gives the recipe in case the reader cannot find the lacquer at the merchants, some of whom he said would keep the recipe secret.[141] This English lacquer may have been the

> Veritable vernis anglois du Sr Torogood, rue de Tournon, qui imite parfaitement la plus belle dorure sur métaux et le plus beau noir de la Chine.[142]

Huth cites a M. Destorges who in 1762 is known to have been making painted tin panels for use in furniture.[143] In 1768, a workshop, La Petite Pologne, was established which made lacquered metal wares (*tôle vernie*) reputedly of inferior quality. The enterprise was evidently fraught with difficulties.[144]

The *vernisseurs* working with black and coloured varnishes which imitated oriental lacquers remain, with a few notable exceptions, largely obscure. A lacquer workshop was founded at the Manufacture Royal des Meubles de la Couronne at the Gobelins in Paris in 1673.[145] A Manufacture Royale de Vernis de la Chine was established in 1767, which was said by the Académie des Sciences to have produced a lacquer 'hard brilliant, tough and of a brilliant black'.[146] The Manufacture Royale set up by the Martin family to produce a varnish (*vernis*) which imitated Chinese lacquer was given its privilege to do so in 1733 and proved rather more successful than establishments such as La Petite Pologne.[147] In 1760, the Martins' work was considered by experts in Vienna to be on a par with at least one other Parisian workshop, that of Tremblin, who had just left the Gobelins workshops for Vienna.[148]

The mercers' inventories rarely give detailed information on the workshops who supplied furniture and boxes lacquered with these *vernis*. Neither did *vernisseurs* mark their work in any way. This frustrates many attempts to attribute work in European lacquer to specific workshops or individuals.[149] The *ouvrages de la Chine* produced in the Gobelins workshops and the output of the Martin family workshops therefore remains largely unidentifiable.[150] Hans Huth points to the temptation of assuming that the best quality lacquer work in Paris around the mid-century might be the product of the Martin family and more recently Anna Czarnocka demonstrates this approach with a string of attributions.[151] However, these are far from convincing, given that *vernis Martin* was evidently not very different from other solutions used in eighteenth-century Paris to imitate lacquer.[152] In

1773, Watin stated that ten different recipes for lacquer were being used in Paris,[153] and Huth cites Watin's assertion that by the 1740s at least, the real *vernis Martin* was being widely imitated (despite the royal privilege) resulting in a fall in value of the Martins' wares.[154] At about this date, the Académie de St Luc (to which a number of decorative painters working with lacquer belonged) were attempting to protect their stake in the market for *chinoiseries* from competition by the *tablettiers*.[155]

If twentieth-century connoisseurs attribute all too easily the best quality French lacquerwares to the Martin workshop, eighteenth-century practice is no more reliable. Writers, in praising the qualities of *vernis Martin*,[156] raised it not only to metaphorical status, but also transformed it into a generic term. In 1749, a ruling by the Parlement of Paris referred to works 'vulgairement appellez ouvrages et vernis de Martin'.[157]

The Martin name appears infrequently in the mercers' inventories used for this study. In 1755, Delahoguette's inventory included *une boite a cadrille de lac d'or, Les boetes de Martin garnies de bronze*, 60 *livres*.[158] Claude-François Julliot's lacquer goods included a *plateau rouge de Martin*.[159] An otherwise unknown mercer named Carreyvilliers, in the rue St Honoré, advertised himself as 'mercier, confiseur pour toutes sortes de bijouteries en sucre, boites a bonbons doublées de Bergamotte, et vernies de feu M. Martin. Fait des envois dans les provinces'.[160]

Although it is tempting to attribute to the best-known workshop in Paris the decoration of a commode, corner cupboards and writing table supplied by the mercer Thomas-Joachim Hebert to Madame de Mailly in 1742 (colour plate 16), there is no technical or documentary reason to do so – Hebert's inventories lists no *vernisseurs* as creditors. The fact that this was the first delivery of a piece of furniture lacquered with *vernis* in Paris to the French royal palaces might suggest that Hebert would indeed have chosen the family of whose name was associated, in literary terms at least, with the *chinoiserie* decoration of carriages, panelling and snuff boxes and who were themselves suppliers of decorative lacquerwork for various royal apartments. Certainly Watin stated that the Martin workshops were renowned for their white lacquerwork.[161]

The furniture was to be placed at the Château de Choisy in a room hung with blue and white moiré silk.[162] As John Whitehead has noted, the suite of furniture was supplied with blue and white wall branches.[163] Such blue and white lacquerwork appears to have become fashionable, and several other pieces of furniture, each supplied by a different mercer, survive.[164] A commode of simple form, decorated with a similar pattern of blue and white or cream (but with later mounts), bears the trade label of a merchant named Mesnard, who traded at the Duc de Bourgogne, in the centre of the Pont Notre Dame (colour plate 17). Ten years after the delivery to Madame de Mailly, Lazare Duvaux was supplying blue and white lacquer furniture to another female client. In March 1753 he delivered to the Duchesse de Mazarin for 30 *livres* 'une petite armoire de bois verni en blanc et bleu, à porte au milieu . . .'.[165] He is known to have used the Martin workshops for lacquering, cleaning and restoration work. For example, Duvaux' daybook records that he sent lacquer to the Martin family for repair and re-lacquering. In some cases, the work represented an almost complete re-surfacing of the carcase. For example, in September 1752 he charged the Marquise de Pompadour 175 *livres* for the following work:

> Le racommodage de deux commodes de lacq; rétabli les corps et tiroirs, regratté l'ancien vernis en aventurine refait en noir à neuf par Martin, rétabli le lacq, & ajouté des reliefs pour cacher les defauts , resaucé les bronzes et rétabli à neuf . . .[166]

The same entry describes the rejuvenation of 'deux figures vernies portant des cannes de sucre, fait reblanchir lesdites cannes d'argent & fleurs' for only

24 *livres*. One pair of such figures survives (colour plate 18). Duvaux used an un-named *vernisseur* to clean the commodes and corner cupboards owned by the Marquise de Pompadour at Bellevue. Duvaux had organized this visit in order to disassemble the mounted porcelains and clean and regild a number of the gilt bronze mounts, repair furniture and wash rock crystal chandeliers and the porcelain flowers at the Château de Bellevue in winter 1753.[167] The supervision of these tasks was entrusted to a skilled journeyman 'pour aider les ouvriers'.

The mercers' inventories give some further information on suppliers. The mercer Claude Rougeux declared during the taking of an inventory of his shop that he had sent to a *vernisseur* two small cupboards of pine carcase, 2½ ft wide and nearly 4 ft high.[168] He stated also that he had them made by a cabinet-maker named Sadon, in the rue Ste Margueritte, to whom he also owed money. Guignard supplied Dubuisson with two lacquered stands to match *cabarets vernis des Indes*.[169] Dubuisson's Parisian lacquerwork appears to have been done also by Bernard, *vernisseur*, who lacquered trays and part of a table.

In both porcelain and lacquer markets, the mercers' initial role as retailers of imported goods expanded to encompass both a range of activities and services, and new goods manufactured in Europe as a response to the consumption of oriental wares. Although some of the mercers' goods, oriental and European, old and new, were sold unaltered, the mercers' interventions were in many cases significant, namely the transformation, adaptation and embellishment of the oriental goods. By the early 1720s, and probably earlier, all of these practices are evident, and their implications for the Parisian market place during the eighteenth century were manifold. These interventions thus changed the function of objects, their form and their meaning.

Porcelain from the royal European factories of Meissen and Sèvres was treated in a parallel fashion – Meissen was adopted by connoisseurs and classified into new and old, and along with Sèvres, set in gilt bronze mounts. The mercers' control extended to the circulation of rare pieces within an internal market, and the re-arranging of porcelain and lacquer within the Parisian framework of fashion and taste. Altering ginger jars into pot-pourris, cutting down tall vessels and combining a number of oriental objects into a French form were all highly manipulative actions, giving the mercers control not only over the way that the market perceived oriental materials and design, but at a corporate level, over their market to the exclusion of other trades. No *fayenciers* (without using privilege) appear to have stocked oriental objects, unaltered or set in gilt bronze mounts, and none appear to have been buying at Sèvres. The *bronziers*, though employed by the mercers in many ways, were little in control of this market, and the cabinet-makers were dependant on the mercers not only for Sèvres plaques (see chapter 3) but also for oriental lacquer which would serve as veneers for furniture and boxes.

If markets were formed in part through demand, the mercers could be argued to have shaped that demand in this specialist market place through their control over the design, price and classification of oriental imports. Their interests were, however, also closely linked to those of wholesale suppliers and manufacturers, some of whom were supplying Paris with large volumes of export wares. Through changing their form and setting, the mercers were able to produce from these basic object types a range of highly differentiated goods. The mercers sat, it seems, between suppliers of goods and local finishing trades, and this position enabled them to produce considerable trading profits. Their strategy within the market place, of looking towards both suppliers and consumers but essentially pursuing their own business interests, perhaps raises the question of the usefulness of the 'demand or supply' question within this sector of the Parisian economy. This question is further explored using the case of markets for patterned silks in the next chapter.

NOTES

1. Schleuleer 1974, Clunas 1987, Levenson 1991, Howard and Ayers 1978, Honour 1961, Beurdeley 1962 and Picard, Kerneis and Buneau 1966.
2. For the history of the French Company see especially Dermigny 1990. On collecting and consumption, see Ayers, Impey and Mallet 1990, Impey 1977 and 1985, Thornton 1978 and 1986, and Watson and Whitehead 1991.
3. Jacques Savary, 1675.
4. When the mercer Orient purchased imported porcelain in bulk at the auction in St Malo in 1720 he spent 86,775 *livres* (BN FM 8259, 22 January 1721). The document does not make clear the means of payment, i.e. whether or not extensive credit was extended to such buyers. I would like to thank Katie Scott for this reference. This sum represented just over twice the value of the porcelain stock of the Parisian mercer, Thomas-Joachim Hebert, as recorded in an inventory of his shop. (The porcelain was worth some 35,000 *livres* (AN MC LIII, 224, 22 May 1724).
5. The accessibility of collections to tourists and *curieux* is recorded formally in guides to Paris, including *Les Noms des Curieux de Paris*, Paris, 1673, reprinted 1866. This mentions porcelain in several collections: M. de Creil, rue de Montmorency, M. Dovin, pres l'Hostel de Bourgogne, M. Niceronand. M. le Nautre, at the Tuileries had 'tableaux modernes, bronzes, estampes et vernis de la Chine fort rares'. The *Almanac Parisian, en faveur des étrangers et des personnes curieuses*, Paris, 1762, listed private and royal collections worth viewing, including the Garde Meuble du Roi in the former Hotel de Conti, Quai Conti.
6. Described by the Abbé de Choisy who was involved, prior to the visit, with the selection of gifts.
7. Some sixty-four porcelain items entered the collection of the Grand Dauphin, see Watson and Whitehead 1991, 1.
8. Tournier, 1953 17–20.
9. Belevitch-Stankevitch 1910, 146.
10. 'Mener moi au Portugais . . .', P. Scarron, *c.* 1640 cited in Huth 1971, 86.
11. The various French companies trading in the Orient were amalgamated into a single company, see Dermigny 1964.
12. Belevitch-Stankevitch 1910, 165.
13. Belevitch-Stankevitch 1910, 165. In 1720, the import duty on porcelain and *faience* from a factory in Lille (owned by the brothers Doré) was fixed at 50 *sols* the quintel plus 4 *sols* the pound (weight), (*Projet d'Arrêt* . . ., AN, F[12] 67, fo 171, 25 July 1720). This tarrif was also fixed for the products of other Lille factories, those of Jacques Fèvrier and Gaspard Cochon (*Projet d'Arrêt* . . ., AN, F[12] 70, fo 195, 19 November 1722).
14. *Placet du Dr Braulard* . . ., AN F[12] 54, 31 August 1708.
15. Sr Braulard, *md fayencier*, 30 *livres*.
16. AN F[12]95, fo 35, 17 January 1748. The proposal was rejected.
17. Chassagne 1980 and Chassagne and Chapman 1981.
18. AN MC, LIII, 226, 22 May 1724, Desgodets.
19. *Mercure de France*, December 1723.
20. Watson 1963, 104.
21. Tournier 1953, 19.
22. '167 baises ou caisses de porcelaines contenant urnes, jattes, bassins, aiguières, soucoupes, bassins à barbe, grands et petits plats, assiettes, pots à l'eau et à thé, bouteilles, gobelets, tasses, verrres, sucriers, salières, garnitures de cheminée, modes et modèles et divers autres ouvrages de porcelaine très fine.' (*Mercure Galant*, September 1700, cited in Tournier 1953, 20.)
23. 'Dix-sept caisses, de chacune quatre autres caisses de trois cassettes de vernis, et une écritoire à ramages d'or en relief . . . neuf caisses de diverses tables . . . quatorze caisses de cabarets et bassins à barbe . . . vingt-et-une caisses, de chacune un cabinet de verny fin, figures et ramages d'or . . . quatre-vingt-deux caisses, contenant quarante-cinq cabarets, seize bureaux, six coffres d'ouvrages du Japon . . .' (*Mercure Galant*, September 1700, cited in Bibliothèque Nationale 1989, 16).
24. Tournier 1953.
25. Tournier claims that the archives of the French Companies show that the early shipments (to 1722) consisted almost exclusively of fabrics, lacquer and saltpetre (Tournier 1953, 26–7).
26. *Valeur, qualité et quantité des marchandises saisies et inventoriées dans une salle des Grands Augustins, et au bureau des Epiciers*.
27. Five cases containing sixty leaves, four containing ninety-six and two containing fifty-four, making a total of thirty-five screens valued at 400 *livres* apiece.
28. *Gobelets* and *soucoupes*.
29. Tournier 1953, 27–35.
30. Tournier 1953, 34.
31. They are listed amongst his creditors in bankruptcy papers, AVP D[4]B[6] *carton* 39 *dossier* 2158, 30 October 1770, and in the daybook, AVP D[5]B[6] 2464, 13 January, 200 goblets and saucers, blue and white, 220 *livres*. This represented a wholesale quantity in relation to his sales of porcelain as single items or small groups.
32. AVP D[5]B[6] *régistre* 3499, *Brouillon*, 1 May 1764 Dubuisson. On 1 July 1766, Dubuisson sold to Bailly two services of Chinese porcelain for 1000 *livres*. AVP D[5]B[6] *régistre* 690, 7 January 1769, two fruit dishes from the Compagnie des Indes ('compotiers bleu des Indes a figures'), for 4 *livres* 10 *sols*.
33. D[5]B[6] *régistre* 1967, Dubuisson.
34. Neumann 1984 and see page 172.
35. Now best known for his activities as a picture dealer, Gersaint's clients included the King, Parisian collectors and merchants from Douay, St Omer, Ypres, Metz, Mons, Arras, Perigeux and

Valenciennes and Lille. His creditors do not appear to have included Dutch suppliers.

36. Du Pradel, 1692. In the 1691 edition by the same Lyonnais author (*Les adresses de la ville de Paris avec le trésor des almanacs, livre commode en tous lieux . . .*, Paris, 1691, seven shops were listed for Paris, one of which was a wholesaler (Belevitch-Stankevitch 1910, 151–2). Neither edition can be relied upon to give an exhaustive list – commercial almanacs commonly depended on individuals to supply information about their trade to the editor, so that most almanacs give conservative estimates of makers and merchants specializing in any given trade.
37. John Evelyn *Diaries*, 3 February 1644, cited in Wainwright, 1989, p. 46.
38. For more on the fairs in Paris see Isherwood 1986.
39. The *marchands forains* were permitted to trade in all sorts of goods at the fairs subject to the declaration of their goods. Their permits to trade were limited to the period of the fair plus a few days' grace at either end.
40. H. Huth 1971, p. 20.
41. H. Sauval 1724, vol. 1, 664, cited in Belevitch-Stankevitch 1910, 147.
42. Cited in Watson 1986, 13.
43. AN MC XXXIX, 271, 26 September 1713, Daustel. The stock comprised largely mirrors, tables, desks and commodes veneered with tortoiseshell or exotic woods, marble-topped tables, and clocks.
44. AN MC LIII, 243, 22 May 1724, Desgodets.
45. The translation of terms used in an inventory of 381 pieces of Chinese porcelain belonging to the Grand Dauphin in 1689 serves as a basis for identifying certain forms and decoration (Watson and Whitehead 1991). The collection comprised urns, bottles, vases and goblets, largely of blue and white Chinese porcelain.
46. It is no coincidence that the inventory which the stock is most precisely classified was that of Claude-François Julliot (1777, drawn up on the death of his wife). Not only was the stock to be sold by auction (hence a catalogue printed), but Julliot was himself engaged in organizing auctions and writing sale catalogues.
47. AN MC XCII, 469, 29 February 1732, Louis Armand de Bourbon, Prince de Conty.
48. Tournier 1953, 44.
49. Tournier 1953, 44.
50. Hebert's celadon wares included the shells and garniture described above and a teapot and dish mounted in silver, a large dish, twenty-six small cups (with no handles), two saucers, four salad dishes and a rock (*rocher*).
51. Watson 1986, 82.
52. Ayers, Impey and Mallet 1990, 233–38. A version of such a dish (Ashmolean Collection, Oxford 1962:83, armorial dish, Chinese, Jingddezhen, 1710–20) is illustrated, plate 259.
53. For example, in the case of Herbert (1724) and Bosseux (1726).
54. For the practice of setting porcelain in gilt bronze mounts, see Watson, Wilson and Derham 1982, and Watson 1986.
55. For example, 'deux sceaux de la Chine garnies d'argent' in Delahoguette's inventory of 1755 were valued at only 10 *livres*.
56. Blue and white mounted porcelain was stocked by Hebert (1724), Julliot (1736 and 1760 inventories), Delahoguette (1768) and Hennebert (1770).
57. He also stocked a smaller version of Japanese porcelain mounted in silver.
58. Watson, Wilson and Derham 1982, cat. no. 11. The Musée Carnavalet has two Japanese *rouleau* vases cut down and mounted in the same manner.
59. His hardstone vases with gilt bronze mounts were divided into the following categories, in order more or less of value: *vases de porphire* (maximum value for a pair of vases 3000 *livres*), *marbre verd antique, marbre breche porphire verd, grand roze, marbre verd d'Egypte* (including two items in the form of the Medici vases), *marbre jaune antique* (including a single Medici vase), *albatre orientale, albatre d'Italie, marbre de Sicile, marbre lumaquelle, marbre breche violette, marbre affriquain, marbre d'Ecosse, agathe orientale, jaspe universale* (a single vase, 91 *livres*). Most were mounted. Unmounted vases were stocked in both *marbre petit antique noir et blanc* and *marbre blanc*. Julliot also stocked some rock crystal items for which the bronze mounts might have been used, though these were more often in the form of objects for lighting than vessels. (A cut crystal vase of the 1770's in the J. Paul Getty Museum [no. 92. DK.1] is set in gilt bronze mounts.)
60. Watson, Wilson and Derhan 1982, Watson 1966 and 1986.
61. AN MC XLII, 521, 24 October 1770, Hennebert.
62. AN MC CXVI, 439, 23 December 1768, Delahoguette.
63. AN MC CXVI, 439, 23 December 1768.
64. Impey 1990.
65. Inventories of collectors and the mercers' clients include many such items, for example, AN MC XCII, 510, 28 June 1741, Madame Caroline Princesse de Hesse Reinfels, the porcelain valued by Hebert included a 'cabaret verni de la Chine garni de quatre tasses quatre soucoupes boite à sucre de porcelaine de Saxe dorée' (35 *livres*).
66. The lock-plate is of Dutch East Indies silver and the silver-mounted flasks are decorated with plants and scrolls and on the base with the monogram VOC for the Dutch East India Company (1993, pl. 44, and Ayers, Impey and Mallet 1990, pl. 53).
67. 'Une boeste bois de palissandre complet d'un necessaire composé d'une caffetiere une boete a thé un fusil un rechaud et son pied, un entrenoir une pince, quatre cuilleres letout d'argent, une theyere, une boete a sucre de porcelaine du jappon garnie d'argent quatre goblets quatre soucouppes de porcelaine japponnée, et deux flacons de cristal fondu garnis d'argent et un petit plateau de cabaret verny rouge de paris prisé trois cent *livres*', MC AN, CXV, 447, 6 June 1726.

68. A cup with no handles.
69. Une tabagie vernie facon d'ecaille doublée de satin bleu dans laquelle sont deux goblets, un bougeoir, un eteignoir deux bouts de tuyaux de pipes, deux palettes et un fusil letout d'argent, deux flacons de cristal fondu, deux pots a tabac de porcelaine japonnée garnies d'argent avec un couteau a manche de corne prisée cent quarante livres.

    Une tabagie a bois de noyer doublée de maroquin remplie de deux goblets, un bougeoir, un eteignoir, deux bouts de pipe, deux palettes un entonnoir et un fusil letout d'argent deux pots a tabac de porcelaine de St Cloud deux flacons de cristal fondu garni d'argent avec un couteau prisé cent dix livres.
70. The Savonnerie, The Gobelins, the Manufacture des Glaces at St Gobain, Aubusson.
71. For a brief history of these attempts, see Huth 1971.
72. De Plinval de Guillebon, 1992.
73. Alcouffe (ed) 1993, Le Duc 1993.
74. For comparison between Meissen and Japanese forms and decoration see for example Ayers, Impey and Mallet 1990.
75. Bold 1980, 3–101, and summarized in Walcha 1981, 7ff and Ayers, Impey and Mallett 1990, pp. 45–7.
76. Document dated August 11 1731, in part reproduced in French by Boltz, 1980, 58, and in German translation (57 and 69).
77. Mallett 1990, 45, citing Bolt, 1980 letter dated 17 December 1728.
78. Duvaux supplied the Duchesse de Mirepoix with 'une tasse de Vincennes faite sur un modèle de Saxe' (Courajod 1874, 161–2, no 1442, 12 June 1753).
79. Daguerre described the potential of the English market for Sèvres to the minister responsible for the factory, the Comte d'Angivilliers, 'M. Daguerre m'a temoigné dans l'entretien que j'ai eu avec lui le plus grand Zele à former un depot à Londres qu'il m'a assuré de faire un debit avantageux pendant les 4 premiers mois de l'année' (de Bellaigue 1995).
80. Mallett 1990, 45, citing Boltz, p.4 letter dated 17 December 1728. A Kakiemon-style basket probably from the du Paquier factory in Vienna, marked with 'four garbled Chinese characters' in blue on its base, illustrated in Impey etc, plate 309, is another example of a ceramic form produced by a European factory bearing pseudo-oriental marks in order to deceive.
81. In the daybook and 1758 inventory of Lazare Duvaux, the 1755 inventory of Delahoguette and the 1759 inventory of Lair.
82. AN MC XXXIX, 353, 7 December 1736, Fevrier.
83. Ayers, Impey and Mallett 1990, 175–189.
84. Julliot's fountains were clearly described as 'de la Compagnie des Indes' and other objects may also have been made in the East for the European market, following specifications made by the French company: the single branches (*bougeoirs*), four pairs of candlesticks decorated with silver mounts (*flambeaux*), four pairs of table chandeliers each with two branches (*girandoles*) and four pairs of wall-mounted lights (*bras*) with two branches. 'Several chandeliers' were imported by the French company in 1722 and 1723 (Tournier 1953, 34). Certainly Japanese versions of these forms are listed in other inventories – for example, Louis Bosseux' stock of Japanese porcelain included single branches and candlesticks described, like Julliot's, as mounted with silver.

    Although the Vincennes factory made clock cases of porcelain (see for example, J. Paul Getty Museum 81.DB.81, for a highly coloured soft paste porcelain case for a wall clock with gilt bronze and enamelled metal and a movement by Charles Voisin [Wilson 1981]), Julliot's 'pendule a cartel de porcelaine lapis monté en bronze doré d'or moulu mouvement fait a Paris par Le Noir horloger'(valued at 150 *livres*) was probably too early in date to be attributed to a French manufacturer. (Several clocks with oriental porcelain cases or figures with movements by Etienne Lenoir (1717–after 1778) survive. See Ayers Impey and Mallet 1990, 168 (ill. 147) for a Japanese elephant standing on an ormolu base and supporting monkeys which hold up the case of a round clock (Residenzmuseum, Munich K.V. D288). Another similar clock is at Burghley House (no. 160) and another model exists of a clock with a seated Kakiemon elephant (Residenz Museum). See plate 29 for a Meissen elephant supporting round clock with movement by Gudin.)
85. 'Le peu de connoissance que l'on a eu à Paris de la valeur de ces especes de machandises (sic), a causé une prevention si extraordinaire, que les seul gens d'honneur, d'équitté et de patience, pourrant en revenir par les preuves suivantes' (BN FM 8259).
86. Cited in Belovitch-Stankovitch 1910, 168.
87. For example, Hebert and Julliot were linked with the Duc de Bourbon-Condé', who owned an immense collection of porcelain and set up factories to imitate Japanese porcelain, lacquer and textiles from the orient, and could be expected to have been able to classify porcelain by its place and date of production. His porcelain collection comprised pieces from Japan and China, and the products of Chantilly, Meissen and St Cloud (Le Duc 1993, Nelson 1994 and Impey 1994). Julliot was called in as expert adviser for the inventory of porcelains in the Duc de Bourbon-Condé's collection in 1732 and Hebert advised during the taking of a later inventory in 1741 (AN MC XCII, 504, 17 February 1740). He also appeared at the taking of the inventory in another capacity – he stated the Duc had consigned a number of pieces of porcelain and lacquer goods to his care (AN MC XCII, 504, Condé, estimation Chantilly). Claude-Antoine Julliot and Thomas-Joachim Hebert were clearly particularly well-qualified to judge these matters.
88. Jackson-Stops 1985, 457. Citing Boltz, Clarke describes two tureens supplied by Meissen to Lemaire in 1730, and three more in 1731.
89. From 1776, this *communauté* charged annual fees of 500 *livres*

(pre-1776 they were 2,400), *Dictionnaire Portatif du Commerce*, Paris, 1777, 8° Z Le Senne 4221.

90. *Almanac des marchands, negotians et commercans de la Franc et du Reste de l'Europe*, Paris, 1770, 8° Z L Senne 3995.

91. AN MC XXIX, 368, 14 January 1723 Lambert.

92. The *porcelaines de Nevers* were valued at 4 *livres* 10 *sols* the dozen. The forty-four dozen *broderie de Rouen* items, were almost certainly blue and white porcelain valued at 9 *livres* the dozen. The *tres fines* from Rouen were the highest valued items at 16 *livres* the dozen. He also had one tea pot in stock, of *terre rouge facon de la Chine* and fifteen coffee cups.

De la Fond counted one *fayencier* amongst his debtors and also the maitres d'hotel of Monseigneurs Salleplage and de la Vrillière, and he owed money to a *marchand fayencier* in Rouen named Hugue, a Parisian merchant Robert, and for transport to Maronnet (*voiturier*) of Nevers.

93. AN MC XLII, 362, 29 avril 1732, Baillet. The business owed

Sr Tour manufacturier de St Cloud	100
Mde Bertin manufacturiere a Rouen	
Sr Mazors manufacturier a Nevers	1000 (billet)
	1500 (compte non arreté)
Serrurier manufacturier a Paris	150
Descarriere manufacturier a Paris Jourdan	2100 (billets)
manufacturier de cristal a Orleans	300 (billets)
Prignet md a Charlonnes	787
Soulons md de verres	489
Reverand md de porcelaine	100
Delafond md fayencier	108 (billet)
(tant du deffunt que son fils)	
Renault md a Charlon	240 (billet)
Mautemps md epicier a Paris	800 (billets)
Leclerc md fayencier	100
Alexandre md de terre d'angleterre	146 (billet)

94. Stock of Jean Baillet, *marchand fayencier*, rue Saint Honoré, 29 April 1732:
Fayence tres fine de Rouen
Broderie
Terre a bouillis de Rouen blanc et broderie
Jaspé de Rouen
Blanc de Rouen
Fayence d'hollande
Fayence de Lille
Terre de Flandre
Email fin
Fayence de Nevers blanc
Terre a Boulilere de Nevers bleue
Autre blanche
Fayence bleue de Nevers
Terre d'Angleterre
Porcelaine
Cristal
Verrerie d'Allemagne
Verrerie de France

95. AN MC XXIV, 5 avril 1741, Cholet. He had eighty-eight clients, half of whom owed him in total 2,537 *livres* in recoverable debts, and the other half owed 872 *livres* which were unlikely to be recoverable (*dettes douteuses*). The business owed considerable sums, including several which can be identified for goods supplied by manufacturers and merchants. To one Sulmont, *facturier* from Rouen he owed, in four promissory notes, 411 *livres*, presumably for the regular transportation of goods.

96. *Deux paires de bras double cristal d'angleterre* (30 *livres*) and the six paires *simples* (54 *livres*). This almost certainly refers to the English terms 'single' or 'double flint' lead glass. The dishes, pots, goblets, cups and saucers of *terre d'angleterre* were presumably English earthenware.

97. He bought goods, priced at 900 *livres*, 54 AQ1.

98. AN MC CXV, 698, 12 October 1756 Bazin, and AN MC CXV, 711, Bazin 7 December 1757.

99. 19 August 1757, 147 *livres*' worth of table wares, MNS 54 AQ1. Jacquesson may well be a French version of the English name Jackson.

100. My thanks to Rosalind Savill and Robert Darnley for giving me access to the microfilmed registers in the library of the Wallace Collection, London.

101. AN MC LX, 1481, 17 January 1759, Lair.

102. *Almanac Général des Marchands. . .*, 1770. Madame la veuve Lachat had a shop in the rue de Grenelle St. Honoré. Hannong's Strasbourg depot was run by the merchant Jollait.

103. The tradition of widows continuing a ceramics enterprise was evidently not new to the eighteenth century. Boileau, in *Le Livre des metiers*, Paris, 1268, stated that widows were able to take on the businesses of their deceased husbands, unlike the widows of glass-makers (*cristalliers*) and stone-cutters (*tailleurs de pierres dures ou précieuses*) who were prohibited from taking on the business because the work was considered too hard for women. In Rouen, fifteen women, mostly widows, were running businesses which produced faience.

104. *Ier Trimestre des tablettes royales de renommée, d'adresse perpetuelle et d'indication des négocians, artistes célèbres et fabriquants des six corps, art set metiers de la ville de Paris et autres villes du Royaume etc*, Paris, 1775.

Other *fayenciers* listed in this almanac were Billot, Delacour, Leulier, Locré and Sourreux. (Under *Correspondence*, the almanac lists 'Martin, chargé de la coréspondance de la manufacture de fayence de Niderwiller, pres Narebourg, generalité de Metz'.) Leulier's shop is described as 'un des plus fameux magasins de fayence et . . . tres renommé pour la bonne bierre'. Soureux was described as a manufacturer in the rue de la Roquette. He ran a 'fabrique considerable de plats, assiettes et autres vases de fayence japonnée, façon de porcelaine, dont il fait des envois considerable en province et chez l'etranger'. Locret was presumably the same individual as the *entrepreneur* of the Manufacture des Porcelaines, rue Fontaine au Roi, fauxbourg du Temple described as follows in 1786. 'Quoique les ouvrages qu'on y fait n'aient ni l'eclat, ni le luxe de ceux qui sortent des autres manufactures, ils sont néanmoins très recherchés, Almanac General des Marchands, negotians et amateurs de la France de l'Europe et autres Parties du Monde', Paris, 1786. BN Imprimées, V 21445, p. 508.

105. One of her four shop boys was François Charles Bazin, possibly a son or grandson of Gilles.
106. ADVP, 6AZ 291/20.
107. Bazin bought vases in the first and fourth sizes of this model, priced 216–360 *livres* (Savill 1988).
108. LIII, 226, 22 May 1724.
109. Another 'cabinet de la Chine avec dix tiroirs' was listed, valued at 400 *livres*.
110. A low cabinet veneered with Japanese lacquer (*bas d'armoire*), with its *serre-papier* of black wood with metal inlay ('un serre papier de bois noir a filets') was also listed.
111. Delahoguette's shop contained in 1768 a three-dimensional display of porcelain on shelves 'deux gradins contenants 72 pieces de porcelaine blanche' which may have functioned more as shop furnishings than stock. No other such example was found in the inventories.
112. De Reyniès 1987.
113. Thornton, 1986, plate 81, and for an early commode with three drawers decorated with European lacquer see de Reyniès, plate 1786.
114. Hebert's stock included a *bahut d'ancien la Chine de trois pieds sur son petit pied de bois sculpté* valued at 120 *livres*. This was almost certainly a standard Chinese export product (a round-topped chest), and, like screens and cabinets, was one of the sources of the lacquer panels which were veneered onto modern carcases, of commodes and sécretaires.
115. Only 5,500 of which was paid. See Alcouffe 1993, Lemonnier 1984.
116. It is unlikely that this commode was made in China. Export lacquer furniture tended to follow European convention (see the bureau with the Rabutin-Sevigné coat of arms, Far East, *c.* 1680, Huth 1971, plate 220 or the later Chinese export chest of drawers, Sotheby's New York, November 20, 1993, lot 208). Ten drawer cabinets with two doors were made in Europe in imitation of the oriental form, decorated with European lacquer finishes.
117. The carcase was newly made, and the sides decorated with french lacquer.
118. Kjelburg 1989, 511 (Commode veneered with Japanese lacquer stamped by Jean-François Leleu. See also Pradère 1989 for a commode with ten drawers of Japanese lacquer stamped by Joseph). Another of this type exists, though apparently with alterations, in a British Collection (Gorethorpe House, National Trust).
119. See Leben 1995 [3], 201 for a commode stamped by Bernard Molitor, of such construction.
120. The inventory also lists twenty-five more drawers of this type (described as *tiroirs* rather as *corps de tiroirs* which implies that the set was kept together), eighteen pieces of lacquer of different sizes, AN MC, XCIV,290, 29 November 1758, Duvaux.
121. MC AN XXXIX, 353, Julliot.
122. Listed by Roubo 1772, as a yellow and/or red veined (*jaune, rouge, veiné*) wood from the West Indies.
123. 'Un grand bureau de cinq pieds et demy de bois de cayenne a panneaux la Chine garny de bronze doré dor moulu avec son ser papier aussy garny de bronze doré dor moulu prisé a mille cinq cent livres'.

'Deux armoires a deux battans de trois pieds dix pouces sur cinq pieds de haut de bois de caienne a panneaux de verny la Chine prisées a trois cent soixante quinze livres'.

124. Pellerin held the positions of *Sécretaire du Conseil de marine, Commissaire of Brest*, and later of Rochefort, and from 1723 Ministre de la Marine until his retirement in 1745 (See Bibliothèque Nationale 1989).
125. Illustrated by Huth 1971, colour plate XIII.
126. Impey and Whitehead 1995.
127. Courajod 1874, 10, no. 101, 29 January 1749.
128. AVP D^5B^6 *régistre* 2464, Dubuisson.
129. The next item was described as 'un autre paravent de meme verny de six feuilles (300 *livres*)'.
130. D^4B^6 *carton* 14, *dossier* 677. In 1754, Madame de Pompadour supplied the Chinese lacquer top of a quadrille table transformed into two writing tables (Courajod 1874, 189, no. 1683, 15 January 1754).
131. *Livre Journal de Pierre Migeon, 1730–1736*. Other merchants supplied by Migeon include Mr. Juin of Anjou, who appears several times from October 1734. On 28 September 1735 his bill of 249 *livres* was reduced to 230. Bazar, marchant is listed on 13 October 1735.
132. December 1732, Hebert paid 192 *livres* against his outstanding debt of 360. On 27 Feb 1733 he paid another 96 *livres*.
133. The daybook lists the following:

15 Nov 1731	*sécretaire, palissandre*	100
22 Feb 1732	*sécretaire*	120
13 Aug 1732	*sécretaire de la Chine*	110
6 Oct 1732	*commode a la regence sans le marbre*	60
24 Dec 1732	*sécretaire de la Chine*	130
14 Feb 1733	*sécretaire de la Chine et d'amaranthe*	120

134. This may possibly have been a travelling, or combination, piece which had a set of drawers or document compartments in a section under the top, which could be released, such as examples by Oeben of the *tables à la bourgogne*. However, these all seem to date from the second half of the eighteenth century.

135. This practice varied, and sometimes oriental lacquer transferred to a flat surface was not glued onto the carcase. For example, a Weisweiler commode in the collection of the Kansas Museum of Art has panels which are secured in place without glue by bronze borders to each panel. (I am grateful to Oliver Impey for this information.) The veneers applied to the curved carcase on the BVRB (II) commode in the V&A (1094–1882, see colour plate 5) are held in place by glue.
136. On 4 May, a M. de Beauplant provided the lacquer for two corner-cupboards, also decorated in gilt bronze and with a marble slab (d'Antin).
137. Impey and Whitehead 1990.
138. Impey 1995.
139. V&A 1107–1882.
140. Two *manufactures de tôle vernie* were set up in the 1760's, see Jacquemart 1861, 311–313, and Volvesperges 1995.
141. Roubo, 1772, 1031–3.
142. 80 Z Le Senne 11630, *Almanac* 1775.
143. Huth 1971, p. 123.
144. Huth 1971, p. 123, and Volvesperges 1995.
145. See Huth 1971, Sonenscher 1989.
146. Jacquemart 1861, 311–313.
147. Sonenscher, 1989.
148. See Huth 1971, 89, and Sonenscher 1989, 223.
149. Gisela Haase has been able to document the work of Martin Schnell in Dresden, (Haase 1995).
150. With the exception of documented forms of pill box and the Martins' work at Versailles (Huth 1971 and Czarnacka 1994).
151. Huth 1971 and Czarnacka 1994.
152. This opinion, of Monsieur Payen of the Conservatoire des Arts et Métiers, is cited in Sonenscher, 1989.
153. See Sonenscher 1989.
154. Especially snuffboxes, see Huth 1971, 97.
155. Sonenscher 1989, 36.
156. Voltaire spoke of a coach 'bonne et brillante' with vernis martin lacquer panels and 'cabinets ou Martin a surpassé les arts de la Chine', from *Nanine*, act III, scene 5, cited in Sonenscher 1989, 211.
157. AN E1286e (10 April 1753, referring to a dispute in 1749), cited in Sonenscher 1989, p. 226.
158. AVP D^4B^6 *carton* 14, *dossier* 677.
159. For some reason at the end of a list of *nouveaux lacques du Japon*, AN MC IX, 666 November 1777, Julliot.
160. Roze de Chantoiseau 1768, BN V 25838.
161. Huth 1971, 93 and note 21.
162. Verlet 1990, 6–8, Alcouffe 1993, 144–149.
163. Lazare Duvaux had repainted for the Abbé de Malherbe a pair of small blue and white candlesticks (Courajod 1874, 2, no. 15, 11 October 1748).
164. A small *sécretaire en pente* stamped Dubois, in the Musée des Arts Décoratifs, is another example of the use of a blue pigment, but the combination of gold and blue, with gilt bronze mounts, makes this piece rather distinctive from the blue and white group. Huth illustrates a blue and white lacquered commode, with unexceptional bronze mounts formerly with A. and R. Ball, New York (Huth 1971, pl. 243).
165. Courajod 1874, 154, no. 1378, 25 March 1753.
166. Courajod 1874 135, no. 1213, 9 September 1752.
167. Courajod 1874 178–9, no. 1582, 27 November 1753.
168. The name is difficult to decipher. AN MC XXIV,704, 8 avril 1746.
169. AVP D^5B^6 *régistre* 2464, Dubuisson, 12 *livres*.

5 Design and innovation: markets for patterned silks

Disons un mot du riche pais des Bourdonnais. C'est-là que le luxe vous conduit dans des Pérons en magasins, ou les lingots d'or et d'argent se mesurent à l'aune . . .[1]

An understanding of the relationships between design and innovation, and between innovation and fashion is of fundamental importance in determining the mercers' role in dictating or influencing the look of their wares, and it is these overlapping areas which form the subject of this chapter. In the case of Lyonnais silks, it has been possible to discover something of the interrelationship and interdependence of the two cities Lyon and Paris – the first a city whose economy was based on a highly specialized form of production, the second the international centre of a *commerce de luxe* whose luxury economy was largely based on a network of specialist retailers. At the top end of the market, for expensive woven silks (patterned fabrics of coloured silk and often gold and silver threads), the market in Paris was highly sensitive. Both the Parisian merchants and Lyonnais suppliers were acutely aware of this, and indeed the segmentation of the market was described by the latter group in 1731.[2] At this date the Lyonnais petitioned the King for support during a period of recession and a large part of the document was taken up by an analysis of the market.

Both the Lyonnais and the Parisians recognized that the newest, and by implication the most expensive, designs should first be sold to the court, and that adaptations and older designs would be accepted by distinct consumer groups within Paris, the provinces, foreign cities and courts, and the colonies. The newness of the pattern was but one element in its market value, however. Quality and price were other factors, and in the case of price, the mercers were in a position to set a price which was acceptable to the appropriate market. As long as the the mercers judged their market correctly, and negotiated a good price with their suppliers, they could sell new fabrics woven to both new and older designs.[3] Even old fabrics, clothes and furnishings also retained their value within the second-hand trade, particularly at the high quality (luxury) end of the market.

The history of textiles has not so far been able to document or explain the nature of the market for silks, and has, instead, fallen back on the assumption that the continued bouyancy of the market for silks depended on major changes in design, in terms of pattern, colour and weave, across the product range. The interpretation put forward in this chapter suggests, rather, that whilst this was true for certain commissions, the Parisian demand for novelty and fashion could be satisfied to a large extent by minor changes to existing designs.

In line with assumptions about innovation and luxury markets, the literature on patterned silks woven in Lyon in the course of the eighteenth century lays much emphasis on the theme of novelty and constant change in design. The tendency to attribute the success of the industry to a very few designers, principally Jean Revel and Philippe Lasalle, encourages a view of an industry whose success depended on a high degree of product innovation led by these named designers.[4]

Since Peter Thornton's work (published in 1965) only the special exhibitions and studies of the staff at the Mobilier National in Paris have attempted to put the silks themselves into their social and economic context.[5] The Royal Commissions (*Commandes Royales*) which they document, however, represent only a fraction of the actual production of Lyonnais looms and might be considered atypical both of commissions from clients and of the relationships between the Lyonnais and their markets.[6] Jean Peyrot has gone some way towards unravelling the way in which commercial manufacturing houses worked, though his interests lay not in the design of the silks but rather in the mechanics of the business of production.[7] Evidence of the relationship between Lyon and Paris suggests that neither the business nor the fabrics can be understood purely through an examination of production, but form part of a more complex discourse between mercers, manufacturers and designers. To reveal this discourse requires a reassessment of both the role of novelty (*nouveauté*) in the sale of silks and also the role of the mercers as finishers (*enjoliveurs*) of part-finished goods.

Newness, *nouveauté*, or difference from some other design or object was undeniably a strong force within luxury markets. However, novelty appears to be a concept created within the market place, within a web of cultural references to time and style. The evidence for gauging the differences between things, and the timescales of change within the context of eighteenth-century fashions is limited and problematic. There exists a large literature which is concerned with the discourse on fashion, but as in the parallel case of the luxury debate, these writings do not necessarily document the entire range of practices of designers, producers and consumers of fashionable articles. Along with the literature on the history of silks, much writing on the subject of fashion encourages a view of constant change and innovation.[8]

PARIS–LYON

The research outlined in this case study has resulted from work undertaken collaboratively with Dr. Lesley Miller, whose research on the silk designers of eighteenth-century Lyon shows their preoccupation with how best to respond to the demand from Paris.[9] This chapter draws heavily on Dr. Miller's references from the Lyon archives.[10]

Of the documentary sources in the Paris and Lyon archives, inventories and a series of commercial correspondence detail the relationships between the Lyonnais merchants and their retail outlets in Paris, the mercers. The correspondence of several commercial houses which went bankrupt in Lyon in the second half of the eighteenth century reveal that Parisian correspondents outnumbered those from any other national centre.[11] For example, the majority of commercial correspondents in the papers of the manufacturing houses of Carret, Fayet, Fiard and Seilhade were based in Paris. The firm of Fayet, active between the 1730s and 1758 had forty-two correspondents in Paris and no more than a dozen elsewhere. Paris was just ahead of Geneva in Seilhade's letters with thirty correspondents as compared with twenty-four, and in the papers of Carret, Paris compared favourably with Bordeaux but poorly with Amsterdam (43, 36 and 67).

The Lyonnais listed in the Parisian inventories seem, predictably enough, to have been the wealthy merchant manufacturers, *marchands fabricants*. Those listed in the Parisian mercer Jean-François Barbier's bankrupcy accounts of 1762, for example, numbered eighty, about forty of whom can be identified in the Lyon tax records (appendix 9).[12] Most of these were paying relatively high rates of tax, over 100 and up to 288 *livres*, and their businesses were initially founded on a capital investment of between 40 and 150 thousand *livres*.[13]

In contrast to the Lyonnais, the wealthiest of the Parisian mercers established their businesses on higher capital sums, as discussed in chapter 2. Of

Abbeville	Orleans
Alençon	Paris
Amiens	Picardy
Avignon	Rennes
Cambray	Rouen
Elboeuf	St. Denis
Fontainebleau	St Etienne
Lyon	Sedan
Marseilles	Tours
Meaux	Troyes
Nîmes	Versailles
Jouy	Villefranche

Fig 15. Manufacturing areas in France supplying mercers.

those documented as trading with the Lyonnais, several were in partnerships with combined capital of more than half a million *livres*, as in the case of a marriage and partnership between two well established silk dealing families in 1738.[14] In Paris, a considerable number of silk mercers were grouped in the rue St Honoré and the surrounding streets, especially the rue des Bourdonnais. When Joubert recommended that Lyonnais designers stay in the heart of the silk dealing district, he suggested that they stay in the rues Bétizi, de la Limace and Cloître Sainte Opportune. This area housed not only the mercers' shops but also the Halle à la Toille and the Halle aux Draps through which the trade in cotton and woollen (and woollen-mix) textiles was controlled.[15]

An impression of the dependancy of the Lyonnais on Paris can be gained from the inventories in terms of the number of suppliers and the value of the stock in Paris. The Paris shops carried stock ranging in value from under 100,000 *livres* to more than a million. The stock of Jean-François Barbier, supplier to the King and over 200 high ranking clients, was valued in 1762 at over a million *livres*.[16] Admittedly, this sum was unusually high, and was valued during a period of slow turnover. Other examples of stock valued at over half a million *livres* include Jean-Baptiste Buffault's silks, valued in 1772 at 567,778 *livres*.[17]

Most mercers combined the products of the Lyonnais looms with other French silks and often imported fabrics. For example, the trade card for Buffault's shop advertises silks from Lyon, Tours, Nîmes, the Levant, Marseille, Avignon, Milan, Italy, Antwerp, Holland, Genoa and Switzerland.[18] Inventories for the Parisian mercers show that they were importing textiles from at least twenty manufacturing areas in France (fig. 15). The most frequently listed areas in the inventories were Paris, followed by Lyon, Tours and Rouen. Those mercers dealing in luxury patterned silks from Lyon constituted the second of Savary de Bruslons' twenty catagories of mercers, those who specialized in silks, woven gold and silver threads (*étoffes de soie, d'or et d'argent*). Amongst Barbier's Lyonnais suppliers was Galy Galien and Company of Lyon, one of whose designs, dated 1762, may represent the style of patterned silk stocked by Barbier at this date (colour plate 19). The most expensive silks listed in the mercers' inventories were valued at a hundred *livres* or more per ell *aune*, and were all woven with silver and/or gold threads (see appendix 9). They were stocked in only very small quantities (often 2 ells, enough for a waistcoat) in

Plate 56. Trade card of Berthollon.
Archives de la Ville de Paris.

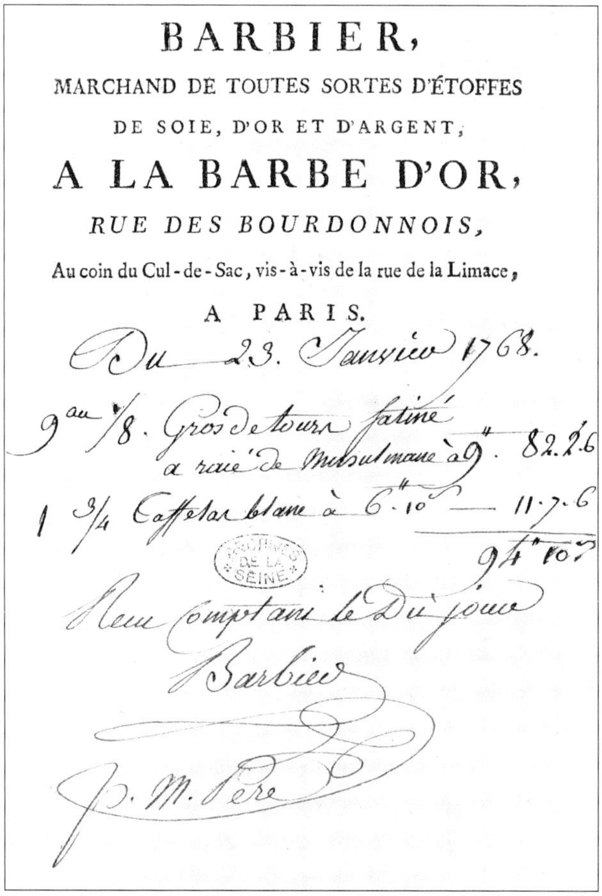

BARBIER,
MARCHAND DE TOUTES SORTES D'ÉTOFFES
DE SOIE, D'OR ET D'ARGENT,
A LA BARBE D'OR,
RUE DES BOURDONNOIS,
Au coin du Cul-de-Sac, vis-à-vis de la rue de la Limace,
A PARIS.

Du 23. Janvier 1768.
9 au 1/8. Gros de tours satiné a raie de Musulmane à 9ᵗ. 82.2.6
1 3/4 Taffetas blanc à 6.10 — 11.7.6
94ᵗ 10
Reçu comptant le dit jour
Barbier
p. M. Père

Plate 57. Trade card of Barbier with bill dated 23 January 1778.
Archives de la Ville de Paris.

comparison with the longer lengths of silks and fabrics valued at under 50 *livres* per ell. Velvets and cheaper silks, often of two colours, striped or with simple patterns but also including many plain colours, were stocked in much longer lengths (colour plate 20).

Miller gives the 1751 retail price in Lyon for silks woven with gold and silver threads as between 13 and 400 *livres* per ell.[19] Few examples of priced silks survive. Rare samples of such silks supplied by Parisian merchants for the Garde Robe of the King of Portugal in 1736 included silks woven and brocaded with gold and silver threads, priced at 140–150 *livres* the ell, and elaborately worked velvets at 35 *livres* (colour plate 21).

Although most mercers traded in silks from a number of areas, several shops in Paris were advertised as depots with specific links to Lyonnais suppliers.[20] Berthollon of Lyon advertised a Paris shop, Au Grand Cerf, selling not only Lyon silks but also velvets from Genoa and other Italian fabrics (plate 56).[21] A general depot for Lyon silks was established at the sign of La Bienfaisance, whose trade card stressed the advantage of buying at fixed prices direct from the manufacturers.[22] Thon, Joly et Compagnie of Lyon, at the Corbeille Galante, rue St. Honoré alongside the Hôtel d'Aligre also advertised their silks at manufacturers' prices, according to a surviving trade card dated 1777.[23] For those wishing to deal direct with the manufacturers and merchants in Lyon, the names of agents in Lyon were advertised in Paris

Barbier	À La Barbe d'Or, rue des Bourdonnais
Bourjol	Au Lyon d'Or, rue St Denis
Doucet	À la Croix d'Or, rue St Honoré
Duchesne	Aux 3 Moines, rue St Denis
Leveque	rue St Denis
Lenormand	Au Grand Turc, rue St Honoré
Leroux et Delasalle	rue St Honoré
Martin	Au Couronne d'Or, rue des Bourdonnais
Nau	À l'Image de Notre Dame, rue de la Lingerie
Grugelin	rue St Denis

Fig 16. Silk dealers from the Etat des Marchands, *1785.*[30]

Colour Plate 15. Still life, c. 1725. Musée des Arts Décoratifs, Paris.

Colour Plate 16. Commode, 1742, stamped by Mathieu Criard. Musée du Louvre, Paris, photo Réunion des Musées Nationaux.

Colour Plate 17. Commode, c. 1750, unstamped. Photo Christie's Images.

Colour Plate 18. Pair of painted bronze figures with silver canes, 1745–50. J. Paul Getty Museum, Malibu, California.

Colour Plate 19. Design for a silk, dated 10 February 1762, Galy Galien & Cie, Lyon. Victoria and Albert Museum, London.

Colour Plate 20. Merchant's order book of woven silks, French c. 1760–64. Victoria and Albert Museum, London.

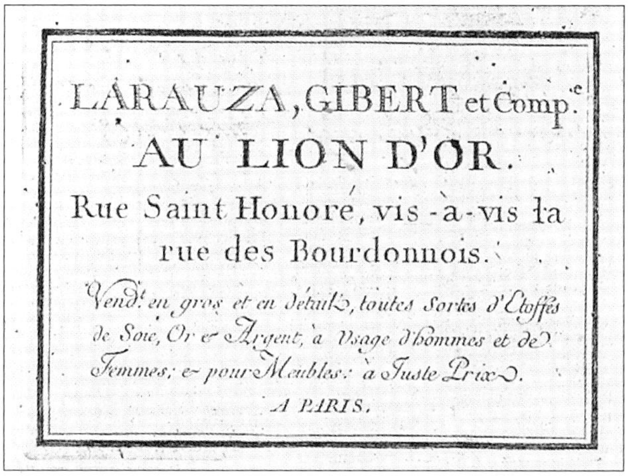

Plate 58. Trade card; Larauza. Archives de la Ville de Paris.

Plate 59. Trade card of Bourjot. Archives de la Ville de Paris.

Plate 60. Trade card of Lenormand. Archives Nationales, Paris.

Plate 61. Trade card of Leroux and de la Salle. Archives de la Ville de Paris.

almanacs.[24] New products were also advertised. For example, an almanac of 1775 advertised a new fabric sold by Watrin in Paris,[25] and another of 1788 announced the 'nouvelle machine de l'invention du Sr Rivey de Lyon, à l'effet d'executer des tricots soie et laine a fleurs nuees. On trouvera de ces étoffes chez MM Bertrand, Delpech et Cie, rue St Honoré, au Duc de Valois'.[26] Occasionally, a designer advertised in the almanacs. For example, Adventurier, 64, rue de Grenelle St Honoré, styled himself 'dessinateur des manufactures de velours de lyon, pour étoffes de soie etc'.[27]

Jean-François Barbier was one of the sixteen silk dealers ('les fameux Magasins d'étoffe de soie') whom Joubert recommended by name to the Lyonnais designers in 1765 (plate 57).[28] The others were Bourjol, Laurozat, Nau, Despeignes, de Courcy, David, le Roux, Doré, Mercier, Buffault, Martin, Doucet, le Boucher, Gregelu and le Sourd. These names are echoed in a list printed in an almanac of 1785 (figure 16) and surviving inventories and trade cards testify to these mercers' stocks of silks woven with gold and silver threads (plates 58–61).[29]

The mercers sold to a range of clients, private and commercial. They advertised silks for men and women, for furnishing and upholstery of both furniture and coaches, for mourning and religious use, operas, theatre and the *spectacles du roi*. The mercers' commercial clients included the upholsterers (*tapissiers*), tailors (*tailleurs*) and the milliners (*marchand(es) de modes*).

The correspondence of Jean-François Barbier with his clients, first published by Mary Schoeser, serves to illustrate the ways in which the purchasers of silks expressed their demands.[31] Often selections were made from samples (*echantillons*) suppplied by Barbier (colour plate 22). Many were to be delivered direct to the tailor or milliner. An order letter of 1783 requested '16 aulnes d'etoffe pareille à cet échantillon mais absolument pareille tant par le travail que par la nuance . . .'.[32] Other clients used the samples as a basis for ordering a fabric which differed slightly from the sample, such as an order for a taffeta like the sample, but if possible with 'le violet . . . un plus foncé'.[33] Some customers left the choice of pattern to Barbier – the Comtesse Demouleau wrote in her order for a dress which would be wearable in three seasons 'je men raporte a votre honneté pour luy dire les etoffes et les couleurs qui son plus à la maude. Je vous soite [souhaite] le bonjour et a Md Tetare'.[34] One client asked him to recommend a fabric 'avec un dessein courant ou il y ait beaucoup de fleurs de toutes sortes de couleurs surtout en couleurs de rose . . .' and in another letter he was asked to send samples of autumn fabrics and to indicate *les plus à la mode*.[35]

Although some silks were sent to the court direct from Lyon, others were supplied via Paris. For example, during the 1760's, Nau supplied the Garde Meuble du Roi with *taffetas chinés*, and later with worked velvets and satins.[36] Nau was amongst the principal suppliers of Lyonnais silks to the Garde Meuble during the eighteenth century.[37] Buffault, Lenormand and Leroux-Lasalle also appeared, though less frequently, in the Journal du Garde Meuble.

The family networks of these prominent silk dealers were extensive. For example, the Nau family was extremely active in a number of geographical regions and branches of commerce, with a history of manufacturing in Lyon during the seventeenth century, and by the eighteenth century trading in Lyon and Paris. A trade card advertised Nau, Germain et Compagnie at L'Image Notre Dame in the rue de la Lingerie, at the corner of the rue St Honoré. They were selling Lyonnais silks with gold and silver thread for men and women's clothing and damasks from Genoa for upholstering furniture.[38] As well as the part of the family which dealt in silk markets from shops in Paris, branches of the Nau family in Paris were also *marchands bonnetiers* and *drapiers*.[39] A portrait attributed to François de Troy, now in a private collection, is said to represent the family at the turn of the eighteenth century (colour plate 23).[40]

The family of Jacques Bourjot, *marchand d'étoffes de soie*, was equally well-connected. The Bourjots were related by marriage to the important dynasty of merchant drapers and textile manufacturers, the Quatremère family of Sedan and Paris.[41] Bourjot, a regular correspondent and indeed visitor to Lyon, died in 1788, in the rue d'Anjou.[42] Just before his death, he liquidated his partnership with Pierre Porte, remaining a sleeping partner (*en commandité*).[43] Barbier and Buffault also married strategically and linked their families with other merchant dynasties. (Barbier was related by marriage to the silk-dealing families Cuvillier and Tetard.) By the time they died, Barbier and Buffault had long retired from business to enjoy the fruits of their commercial success, leaving the shops in the hands of their successors. Buffault remained a sleeping partner after his business, Au Grand Turc, was taken over in 1772 by Lenormand et Compagnie, who continued to trade at this address until at least 1851.[44]

The interest on the part of the Lyonnais in supporting bankrupt businesses in Paris bears further witness to their commercial dependency on the mercers. For example, a slump in Barbier's sales led him to declare bankrupcy in 1762 due to severe cashflow problems. His debts and assets each totalled over 4 million *livres*. The potential turnover of this single enterprise was considerable, and both the King and the Lyonnais considered his role between maker and market so crucial that a syndicate was set up to oversee the continuation of the business. The Lyonnais agreed to continue to supply him with stock for the shop, sending over 1,300,000 *livres*' worth of silks to him between January 1762 and May 1763. By the latter date, a general air of optimism about improvements in commerce and the recovery of debts enters the records. Plans were made for supplying him with stock for the coming autumn and winter.

In another instance, the Lyonnais were involved in prosecuting a Parisian mercer who had continued to buy stock from them on extended credit whilst concealing from them the fact that he had sold the merchandise. Lorieux' creditors included forty-two suppliers from Paris, thirty-eight from Lyon, nine from Tours, four each from Nîmes and Avignon and two from England (London and Manchester).[45] In addition to his aristocratic clients were listed Le Boucher and Lenormand. His assets in 1788 amounted to a third of a million *livres* but were dramatically outweighed by his debts of 1,100,100 *livres*.[46] Eventually he was exposed by Jean-Baptiste Perrin, *négotiant* from Lyon (lodged at the house of Perrin and Gamel in Paris, rue des Deux Ecus) and Gervaise Pigalle (rue des Bourdonnais, Paris), and as a result of a prosecution he was imprisoned at the Châtelet. The syndicate, led by Perrin and Gamel, Pigalle and Lucy (Denis Lucy, *négotiant* from the rue du Four St Honoré, who also acted on behalf of Pierre Davoton and Cie and Jean Jacon and Cie of Lyon) reported that Lorieux had been trading without keeping books since 1781. His assets were seized and creditors resigned themselves to the probability of recovering only 10 per cent or so of their debts.[47]

Precarious credit arrangements and market confidence were features of these markets. Barbier's business was governed by the syndicate for almost ten years before it picked up, and soon after the final business report Barbier retired from business and left it in the care of his former partner and son-in-law, Tetard. He died in 1787.[48] In other bankrupcy case filed in June 1759, the business partners Jacques-Denis David and Henry-Paul Eve (both mercers) recovered their debts rather faster than Barbier. They had made considerable losses in their trade with the French colonies during the Seven Years War and had lost consignments whilst en route by ship to or from the islands. They were given four years by their syndicate to recover debts and pay their creditors, and in June 1762 they reported that they had achieved this in only eighteen months.[49] However, the continuing success of their business depended in part on their repute and on credit from their suppliers. They requested of the Paris Parlement that a notice be posted all over Paris, including at either side of the doors of the offices of the Compagnie des Indes and the corporation of *marchands merciers*. Though not trading in silks, the evidence of their difficulties throws some light on the dependence of mercers in all branches of commerce on good relationships with their creditors, particularly when engaged in capital-intensive commerce and trade with distant markets.[50] In Barbiers' case, his close relationship between the Lyonnais and his suppliers in Tours, and the mutual interest served by their continued supply of his shop gave him a strong foundation for balancing his books and continuing in business.

MARKET SENSITIVITY

Commercial links between Lyon and Paris were close, but a number of practical constraints affected the market directly. These included communications, events dictating certain codes of behaviour and dress in Paris, the availability of information and the speed of production. Apparently efficient postal and passenger services operated between Paris and Lyon in the second half of the eighteenth century. According to Cobban, the journey from Paris to Lyon by coach took ten days in the seventeenth century and five by the late eighteenth.[51] The runs of regular commercial correspondence reveal the impatience of intermediaries in the capital if they did not receive letters by return of post (in other words within approximately six days). They complained not only of written communication, but also of lack of speed in expediting packages of silks which seem to have been transported by post and barge.[52] Although the journey to Paris was expensive at 100 *livres* one way, the Lyonnais manufacturers felt the need to write it into their partnership contracts.[53] Evidence about the jaunts of one designer suggests that these stays could be quite long. In 1723, he spent three full months between the end of August and the beginning of November in the capital.[54]

Events in Paris, such as periods of mourning, war, the absence of the court from Paris and the weather conditions are all highlighted in the correspondence with Lyon as negative effects on the market. Conversely, prestigious weddings and royal or public festivities and spectacles stimulated the consumption of luxury silks. For example, the Lyonnais welcomed with relief the accession to the throne of Louis XV: 'La cour d'un jeune Roy seroit brillante et remplie de fêtes'.[55]

The influence of the court within the market was viewed by the Lyonnais as central to the fortunes of the industry. The top end of the market for these patterned silks was seen as dependent on the refined judgement of members of the court, and in particular on the consumer ability to distinguish new from old designs:

> Cette consommation [at court] n'est que pour le plus beau le plus parfait et le plus nouveau . . .[56]

The approval of a new pattern by the court greatly enhanced consumption within Paris and abroad. Whether supplied direct from Lyon or by Parisian mercers such as Nau,[57] the Lyonnais recognized that the court represented the highest cultural authority in these matters of taste. The court, stated the Lyonnais,

> à toujours été l'objet principal de ce commerce c'est elle qui par ces decisions sur le gout et sur les modes autorisé des nouveautés qui sans son autorité n'auroient aucune faveur. C'est elle qui par son gout et son magificence sert de modele à toutes les cours etrangeres qui dans l'emulation qu'elles ont de l'imiter se laissent avec empressement entrainer a son exemple . . .[58]

Markets within which consumers were motivated to imitate the French court included foreign courts, Parisian consumers and the provinces:

> La Cour est imitée par Paris qui à son tour est imitée par les provinces, ainsy la Cour donné a l'un et a lautre un exemple qui regle leur gout et leur depense, et cette imitation de la Cour qui sied parfaitement bien aux gens de condition de Paris a passé jusqu'a la plus petite bourg-eoisie qui porte scrupuleusement les deuils de la Cour, comme si cette bourgeoisie avoit l'honneur d'etre alliée destestes couronnéees et des princes a la memoire desquels la Cour paye atribut.[59]

As well as representing a market in its own right, the court was thus useful in marketing terms. Other commentators observed the effect of the purchasing habits of court personalities on city fashions. Casanova de Seingald described in his mémoires a visit to Paris in 1753. Seeing a crowd in a shop in the rue St. Honoré, he asked his companion for an explanation. 'Ne riez pas', replied Patu (a lawyer) 'c'est le magazin de la Civette. Toutes les bonnes gens attendent leur tour pour faire remplir leurs tabatières'.[60] Casanova assumed that this was because snuff was only sold at that shop. Patu denied this:

> Nullement, on en vend en mille endroit. Mais, depuis trois mois, personne n'en vent plus que celui qui se vend ici, il faut être un croquant pour ne pas avoir dans sa tabatière du tabac de la Civette.

Patu explained that it was no better than other snuff, and when Casanova asked him why, then, it was so fashionable, he answered that the Duchess of Chartes had started the trend, though with relatively little effort:

> Deux ou trois fois, en descendant de ses appartements du Palais-Royal elle a fait arreter sa voiture devant cette boutique, y a fait rempli sa tabatière et a dit bien haut à la marchande que son tabac était le meilleur de Paris . . .

Casanova reflected that the duchess must have had no idea of the effect she was having on the shop's fortune, reputed to amount in sales of snuff to 100 *écus* a day. This was not the case, explained Patu. The motivation behind the duchess' visits was to support the young shopkeeper, who had just married.

In another instance, Granchez directly exploited the marketing potential of royal patronage by marketing copies of models supplied to the d'Artois family (the Comte d'Artois was the brother of Louis XVI). In January 1777, just before the d'Artois were buying and comm-issioning on a large scale for the construction and furnishing of the Bagatelle, Granchez advertised candelebra after models supplied to the Comtesse d'Artois.[61] The announcement in the Mercure de France read:

> Petits flambeaux, forme d'Athénienne en albâtre et bronze doré au matte. Les premiers ont été présentés et vendus à Madame la Comtesse d'Artois. Boucles, argent et or, supérieurement ciselées, imitant les diamans, modèle de M. le Comte d'Artois.[62]

These instances recall McKendrick's description of Wedgwood's use of royal patrons to promote his creamware range.[63] As these examples suggest, the Lyonnais were not the only group to see that by successfully placing new designs at court, consumption elsewhere would be encouraged. Neither did they miss the potential to market successful designs elsewhere, and to find more distant markets for the sale of patterns which would have been deemed unfashionable at the top end of the market in Paris. In order to empty the Parisian shops of silks which were not selling well in the period leading up to 1731, the Lyonnais proposed that they be sold in South American markets. Despite difficulties in competing in such foreign markets, the Lyonnais were prepared to cut their losses, seeing that this might be the only means of shifting large quantities of old stock and thus encouraging the mercers to start placing new orders.[64]

The Life of a Design

The question of the diminution in value of patterned fabrics over time is complex. The high premium placed on the most fashionable wares was often quickly reduced to a lesser profit margin, and the mercers were often concerned to point this out. Evidence from Lyonnais sources supports the case that stock did not always retain its value over time. Both design theft cases and ensuing copyright legislation bear witness to the life of a fashion pattern, in terms of aesthetic and monetary value, indicating that the value of a particular fabric diminished by approximately 25 per cent the season after it first came onto the market. There is no indication however that this fall from top fashion meant that sales were impossible.[65] In fact, merchants in Paris deliberately packed up stock ready for sale the following year. Their manufacturing counterparts in Lyon still felt justified in complaining about the theft of designs when they had been weaving them into fabric for two to three years and they objected when national copyright legislation imposed a six year life on designs for dress fabrics and fifteen years on furnishings in 1787.[66] One of their objections was that a design might, in fact, have a lifespan of fifteen to twenty years – and clearly they sometimes received new orders for 'old' designs.[67] In fact, choice of fabric was consistently seen in terms of price, quality and pattern.[68] If the price or quality were not right, the pattern would not suit the mercers or their clients.

The devaluation of stock which was old, or at least not a new season's pattern is occasionally defined in the inventories of stock of fabrics and accessories. In particular, stock held up unexpectedly at customs barriers on its way into Paris was susceptible to depreciation. For example, a case of muslin ordered by the milliner Jean-Joseph Beaulard from Dame Baille of Lyon was held up in customs for two years and was therefore valued at half its normal price.[69]

That the practice described by the 1731 document of sending less satisfactory or less fashionable goods to the provinces and colonies was also followed later in the century is borne out by evidence in Beaulard's inventory. Duval et Compagnie held some of his old stock, which was to be sent to Marseilles in an attempt to find a market, and *anciennes marchandises* were handed over to two ships' captains in Le Havre in order to sell them in America. They were all goods which could not be sold in Paris and were valued for the inventory at half their Paris market price.[70] Very infrequently were goods totally written off. Beaulard's inventory contains only one example – he declared that the Jewish merchants would not take at any price ribbons which had been in stock for five years.

Beaulard was compelled to write off satin ribbons described as out-of-date and of *mauvaises couleurs*. They were reduced in value for the purposes of his bankruptcy inventory by 40 per cent. He purchased a ribbon factory in 1787, perhaps to better control the quality and design of ribbons for both his Paris market and his shop in the rue Mikolsky in Moscow.[71] He supplied the latter outlet with fabrics and ribbons from Paris, Nîmes, Lyon, St Etienne, London and Neufchâtel. Beaulard's suppliers included Falsom of Lyon, to whom he owed 8,178 *livres* and Barbier and Tetard, who supplied him with almost 40,000 *livres*' worth of goods. The management of the Moscow branch with his partner Martin was fraught with difficulties linked to the design and pricing of ready-made clothes and accessories. Goods 'mal choisies et mal ordonnées' such as hats which were priced too high for the market, gloves and metal wares were all written off in 1789 as bad debts, to the tune of 10,000 *livres*. Perhaps to avoid this problem, in 1790 Beaulard sent an *ouvriere en modes* to Russia for four years. He paid her exceptionally high wages, presumably in the hope that the partnership might gain control over the Moscow market and reduce losses on the most fashionable lines.[72]

It is likely that merchants selling clothing and fashionable accessories made from silks and trimmings were particularly susceptible to the diminution in value of their stock. For example, the milliner Madame Julien's sales of fashionable goods were disappointing, and in 1790, on the point of bankruptcy, she stated that she had had to take apart some of the out-of-date fashions to sell the goods at a loss ('faire défaire la plus grande partie des marchandises . . . pour pouvoir s'en procurer la vente).[73]

Usually, however, old fabrics and clothes retained a second-hand value and could eventually be sold at knock down prices or for the value of their component threads at the end of their fashionable life. For example, the widow Parmentier, Au Soleil d'Or, made, sold and bought all sorts of fashionable dress, both old and new but emphatically 'des plus à la mode'. She specifically stated on her trade card of 1734 that she bought wardrobes which came from the court. Described on her trade card as *marchand d'habits*, she would have been a member of the corporation of *marchands fripiers* specializing in the second-hand trade in clothing (plate 62). She rented

Plate 62. Habit de Fripier, c. *1680, Nicolas de l'Armessin. Bibliothèque Nationale de France, Paris.*

out goods for mourning and marriage, and bought all kinds of furniture upholstered in velvet, damask and fabric of all types. She also bought old braid of gold and silver, presumably for re-cycling or for its melt-down value.[74]

Court furnishings also retained their value – a fabric first supplied to Versailles in 1731 was re-used in 1753, 1785, and finally melted down in 1793.[75] Other examples demonstrate the surprising length of time over which a fabric might retain its value. For example, the *marchands fripiers* are known to have sold in the 1730s the hangings from the bed made for the château of Vaux-le-Vicomte sometime after 1660. Two swatches are conserved in volume 1 of the *Echantillons Richelieu* in the Bibliothèque Nationale (colour plate 24).[76] The description of the hangings and lining is followed by the explanation that the *fripiers* cut up the fabric and sold it in 1735.

Design Theft and Copying

The practices of plagiarism, design theft and reproductions bear witness to the marketability of variations on fashionable designs, and of a long period of currency and even supremacy of certain models in both silk design and other luxury markets. Adaptions and reproductions were put into production with reasonably little effort in comparison with a brand new design, and by no means at a loss of profit. For example, the Boulle workshops at the Louvre stored a repertoire of designs, templates and models for bronze mounts, ready to be reused or adapted as appropriate. An inventory of stock destroyed or damaged in a fire of 1720 at the workshops listed an extraordinary range of drawings, paintings and designs, as well as templates for marquetry and models for casting bronze mounts.[77] This repository was used by Boulle as a design archive. Other inventories of the workshop (in 1715 and 1732) include descriptions of part-made reproductions of successful models such as the Trianon commodes, a reproduction of which was ordered by the mercer Thomas-Joachim Hebert in 1723.[78] As in the case of silks, the lifetime of a successful furniture design might be surprisingly long.

The prevention of plagiarism was a concern for many trades. In the 1730s the cabinet-maker Cressent stated that the reason that furniture makers kept their own models for mounts and contravened corporate regulations by having bronze mounts gilded in their own workshops was that 'they fear that their models will be stolen'.[79] It was not until the 1760s that a more formal document was drawn up by the *bronziers* requiring that designs and models for mounts be registered with the office of the corporation, in order to control and prevent 'the theft and plagiary which are made daily of their models'.[80]

A further parallel with the preoccupations of the silk merchants of Lyon in the 1760s may be drawn here. In this particular decade their deliberations on the problems of the theft of designs centred around the dispatch of sample books to Paris, the provinces and abroad, and culminated in legislation of 1765 and 1766 banning such activities.[81] Evidently the practice of sending such books to potential clients had been formalized in the 1740s. Unfortunately, however, the dissemination of information in this way led to corrupt practices. Once *commissionaires* and potential clients had the samples in their hands, they were able to commission the same design from another source. Not only would the motif be within their grasp, but so too would be the art of combining dyed yarns in the appropriate way and also the basic weave structure which could be analysed warp-and-weft thread by warp-and-weft thread. According to one rather inflated estimate, about nine tenths of what the Lyonnais produced as samples was copied in Hamburg, Naples, London, Germany, Holland and Flanders. Only one tenth was actually ordered from Lyon and made up there. Even Paris came in for some criticism for trying to pirate such information, hence the follow-up legislation in 1766.[82]

That the Parisians were guilty of malpractice had surfaced at the same time as the first drive for legislation in 1760–1. The *marchand mercier* Nau had received samples from the Lyonnais firm Thevillon & Vingtain, and had shown them to the Queen who was seeking a *chiné* silk for furnishing her appartments at Versailles. The Queen had not been altogether happy with any of the samples although one had seemed almost to her taste. Nau then approached Jean-Baptiste Saint Michel who came from the competing firm of St Michel, Dany et Cie. and asked him to alter the design. This he did to the satisfaction of the Queen and to the disgust of Thevillon et Vingtain. Unfortunately for St Michel, his fabric was recognized on the loom and he was prosecuted.[83]

DESIGN PRACTICE IN LYON – A RESPONSE TO THE PARIS MARKET

When in 1731 the Lyonnais spoke of the sensitivity within the top end of the market to new designs, they were recognizing the commercial disadvantages to their industry of such refined consumer behaviour:

> la delicatesse des personnes qui composent la cour est si grande, l'attention si exacte et leur connaissance si parfaite que par quelque deuil ou par quelque autre evenement, aura en la malheur de n'avoir pas été vendu dans la saison pour laquelle elle aura été faite n'aura point de bonheur d'etre vendues dans les saisons suivantes pour peu qu'elle puisse etre soupçonnée de n'être pas absolument nouvelle . . .[84]

By implication, it would seem, the Lyonnais recognized that the market for patterned silks could not be based entirely on supplying brand new designs to such a critical consumer group. In practice they appear to have found alternative ways of responding to a wider market which thrived on novelty, by introducing changes and adaptations to existing designs rather than constantly designing new patterns.

Within the silk industry of Lyon, design theft cases record a very clear picture of the way in which designers acquired ideas, and the simplicity of some changes in design – in other words, how easy it was to update designs. On the one hand, they testify to the existence of seasonal change within this branch of the trade, and perhaps overemphasize the speed with which the particular design might descend from fashionability into common currency. On the other, they underline the fact that most 'new' design constituted only minor changes in the motif or background of a brocaded silk. This applied to both the tiny patterns for men's suiting (*droguet*), and the more expansive patterns for women's dress and for domestic furnishings.[85] In this context the role of the design studio within a firm (*fabrique*), and that of the archive of designs (*fond des dessins*) were seen as complementary.[86]

The design studio in Lyon worked in two ways. Firstly, it turned out new designs and secondly it altered – or 'corrected' – (*corriger*) old designs in the archive. The addition of a new motif or change of colour combinations or background effect transformed an old design into a new design. Like motifs and patterns in silks, designs for bronzes were adopted to create new and improved models, and legislation for design registration accomodated this practice. The bronze workers' corporation had some difficulty in controlling design copyright in the face of alterations to existing, registered designs:

> Que celui qui aura deposé le dessin au Bureau vouloit faire quelque changement, soit qu'il le fit plus grand ou plus petit, il sera obligé de faire un autre dessein de la même grandeur et forme dudit modéle . . .[87]

However, unlike the case of the bronze workers' system of registering designs with the corporation, the Lyonnais firms retained individual control of their designs. The company archive was made up of all the designs produced or changed during the years of the firm's existence. It was regarded as one of the firm's assets which allowed constant and legitimate manoeuvering to suit both mercers' and consumers' taste. At the end of the century some 400 merchants had considerable archives, reputedly worth between 30,000 and 40,000 *livres*.[88] To give a concrete example of the problem of creativity versus servile copying is essential. In the dispute between Ribier & Bertrand and Assada & Reynard in the 1740s, the defendants pointed out that the whole system of designing relied on the practice of taking inspiration from existing designs and adaptating ideas. They stated – as did others in the same position – of the Lyonnais designers:

> It is only by copying different designs from manufactured fabrics in Paris that their taste is formed and they compose other designs which are then executed by their merchants, seizing from those which have already appeared what they like most and correcting the mistakes . . . the Grande Fabrique supports this practice.[89]

This documentary evidence relates very well to surviving silks as inspection of a sample book of 1763 in the collection of the Victoria and Albert Museum reveals.[90] In this sample book, the fabric swatches from thirty-one Lyonnais manufacturers show that the same basic pattern or design could feature several times with minor alterations (see colour plates 25 and 26). The alterations consist of changes in the size of the motif – a flower of 22 inches in height may be reduced to 1 inch. In the weave and pattern of the background, a stripe may be added or subtracted (colour plate 27) or in the addition of a brocaded motif a new leaf may be added to or subtracted from a basic floral motif.

Verbal descriptions of this process of alteration also survive in merchants' correspondence between Paris and Lyon, and are quite precise. Usually the writer, a mercer or *commissionaire*, instructed the manufacturer in ways of changing his samples to suit his taste. For example, when Bentabole wanted changes in a sample of striped satin, he suggested:

> cut the grey stripe in the way that we have marked it [on the sample] by a feathered line and leave the straw coloured stripe as it is, but to render the stripes equal, diminish the size of the straw stripe to what we've cut back on the grey stripe.[91]

Silk producers thus exploited existing designs as a response to the demand in Paris for *nouveauté*. This case study has emphasized that distribution was a crucial link in the chain of relationships and activities that affected the final look of the product. In the case of the market for patterned silks, a strong reactive thread in the creation of eighteenth-century fashion can be determined. Design of these fashionable products, which have often been described in fine art terms, was neither as original nor as revolutionary as historians have inferred.

The mercers' role in this is reasonably clear. They acted as intermediaries who communicated the information about Parisian demand and the rhythm of the market which was to affect the look of the finished silks, and make them desirable to a market which thrived on novelty. They were not, on the whole, acting as designers.[92] The mercers depended on both suppliers and clients for profit, and both these groups depended on the mercers for access to information about fashion. Serving their own business interests, they were able to make vast profits through dealing in high-premium goods, and also through finding markets both near and distant for distributing goods which the more sensitive end of the Parisian market would not accept.

NOTES

1. Rivière du Frény, *Amusements sérieux et comiques des boutiques de la rue des Bourdonnais*, Paris 1731, cited in Havard 1894, 531.
2. *Mémoire général* 1731.
3. The papers of the Parisian Police (AN Y series) include a number of disputes between wholesale and retail merchants over the price of textiles.
4. This literature follows on from de l'Hiberiderie's small manual on silk design of 1765, receiving a boost in the early twentieth century (Leroudier, 1908). Stylistic change is charted by Thornton, 1965. The recently renovated Musée Historique des Tissus in Lyon picks out some of the more sophisticated silks which incorporate gold and silver threads and sets them alongside the signed works of Revel and Lasalle, the paintings of Jean Pillement and several models of looms of the period. This is not surprising given the problems of survival and attribution of such fragile items, but it is sobering to note that out of over 600 designers known to have worked in Lyon in the eighteenth century, only a handful can actually be associated with specific fabrics and designs (Miller 1988).
5. Thornton 1960, and Musée Historique des Tissus Lyon 1989.
6. Musée Historique des Tissus, Lyon 1989.
7. Peyrot, 1973.
8. For critical studies of fashion see for example Brewer and Porter 1993 and Styles 1996.
9. Miller, 1988 and 1996.
10. All references to documents held in Lyon were given by Dr. Miller. Earlier versions of this paper include Miller and Sargentson, 1993, and see also Miller 'Paris–Lyon–Paris: dialogue in the design and distribution of brocaded silks in the eighteenth century', in Fox and Turner 1996.
11. ADR, Série B (*commerçants*). See Léon 1976 for more details.
12. AML CC178 *Rolle de capitation* (*grande Fabrique*), 1758–9.
13. ADR Série B Formations de Sociétés.
14. AN MC LXXXIII, 363, 4 August 1738, Boscheron-Bauvin and 29 September 1738 Bauvin Aubertin. I would like to thank M. Jollain for this reference.
15. Both of these served as customs points for cloth imported into Paris.
16. AN MC LXXV, 672, 26–28 February 1762, Barbier.
17. According to the partnership established on 30 August 1772.
18. AVP 6AZ 440.
19. Miller 1996. Worked velvets ranged from 16 to 70 *livres* and plain velvets from 17 to 26 *livres*. Below 30 *livres* were silks brocaded with silk (4–30 *livres*), plain silks (2–14 *livres*) and plain and mixed silk (with wool or linen) at under 10 *livres*.
20. This was also true for the Paris depots of other manufacturing centres. For example, the mercer Papion was described as the depot for the Manufacture Royal at Tours (*Almanac General*, 1778, Z Le Senne 4178).
21. The manufacture of Camille Pernon advertised its Paris depot with Grognard, at the Maison Lignereux, rue du Helder. A surviving trade card in empire style dates from the early nineteenth century, and describes fabrics of silk and gold thread for clothing, furnishing and church ornaments.
22. Lyon, Musée Historique des Tissus, no. 81496/8217. A La Bienfaisance Depot de Lyon. Magasin d'Etoffes de Soye, or et Argent, en tous Genres. Rue St Honoré, près celle des Bourdonnais Cet Etablissement a pour principal objet de mériter la confiance du Public par des Prix fixes par le choix et le gout des Etoffes expediées directement des Manufactures. Prix de fabrique et prix fixe.
23. AVP 6AZ 440 '. . . tiennent toutes sortes d'étoffes en soie, or et argent pour Dames, pour Hommes et pour Meubles. Aux prix de fabrique et comptant'. The bill for coral-coloured satin sold to the Marquise de Janson was dated 11 December 1777.
24. Levent, 1778, Z Le Senne 4178, which listed under Lyon 'fabriquants et negotiants, MM Agnel Huet et Cie', and then as *commissionnaires-changeurs*, Andre Scodelly et Cie. In the section titled *Idée generale de la France et de son Commerce* were listed the Deputés des Villes et des colonies pour le commerce, including for Lyon in 1767, Pernon, Chausee d'Antin.
25. *Tablettes Royales*, Z Lesenne 8418 (1).
26. Z Le Senne 11630.
27. *Essai sur l'almanac général* . . . 1769, V25838.
28. De l'Hiberderie 1765, 86.
29. Inventories and other papers were found for a number of these dealers, including Barbier (AN MC LXXV, 672, 26–28 February 1762, Barbier, AN MC VII, 414, 13 November 1774, Barbier-Tetard, AN MC VII, 447, 16 August 1780, Bardin-Barbier, AN MC VIII, 462, 29 January 1784, Pingot, AN MC VII, 483, 23 November 1787, Barbier, AN MC VII, 486, 12 June 1788, Bardin, AN Y13579, 22 November 1787, Barbier, AVP DC[6] 282, 12 February 1788, Barbier, AVP 6AZ 1521 12 July 1788, Barbier-Tetard). Bourjol or Bourjot (AN M2.417 Placard de décès Bourjot, AN MC XXXIV, 758, 29 April 1788, Bourjot-Sorte and 14 July 1788, Bourjot, AN XXIV, 980, 14 October 1790, Bourjot, Y13980 28 April 1788, Bourjot). Buffault (AN MC CXVIII, 801, 1 September 1755, Fayan-Buffault, AN MC CXVII, 802, 27 October 1755, Buffault-Peeters, AN MC LIII, 394, 7 January 1765, Thibert, AN MC LIII, 488, 30 August 1772, Buffault-Lenormand, AN MC LII, 492, 24 October 1772 Buffault-Fayan, AN MC LIII, 535, 30 November 1777, Peeters). Lenormand et Compagnie took over the premises of Buffault, at the Grand Turc.
30. Levent, Etat des Marchands, V58825 *Etat des Marchands*, Levent, 1785.

31. Schoeser 1979 and 1981.
32. Comtesse Delage de Volude, 25 September 1783 (V&A 86.QQ.11).
33. St Fort, 25 September 1785 (V&A 86.QQ.11).
34. 28 October 1785.
35. An order to Testard dated 17 February 1784.
36. Musée Historique des Tissus, Lyon 1989, 32 and 49.
37. For example, during the first six months of 1787, Nau, Germain et Compagnie supplied furnishing fabrics for the Châteaux of Versailles, Compiègne, St. Cloud and Rambouillet to the Garde Meuble de la Couronne for which 53,652 *livres* were paid against a bill of 53,752 *livres* (AN O[1]3641, Ier semestre 1787).
38. AVP 6AZ 440. A Nau was trading individually at this address in 1779 (*Almanac* . . . 617 8⁰ V58825).
39. The *bonnetiers* included a Nau, *doyen des marchands bonnetiers*, who was interred in 1715 at St. Germain l'Auxerrois (AN *Placard de décès* 364), and Nau de la Grange, *doyen* of the corporation, who was interred at the same church on 15 December 1743 (AN *Placard de décès* 366). Marc and Marc Antoine were *drapiers*, the latter formerly *garde du corps de la draperie, ancien juge consul*.
40. I would like to thank Alexis Kugel for providing this photograph of the painting, which was shown at the Biennale in Paris in November 1994.

    The group in the centre foreground showing a crouching figure with game and hunting dogs is more accomplished than the surrounding figures and heads of the family members. This suggests that the painting could even be attributed to Jean-Bapiste Oudry, François Desportes, or indeed the figure on the far right of the painting, or conceivably be a collaborative effort. This figure was holding a *porte-crayon* and was apparently wearing the order of St. Michel. I would like to thank David Maskill for these observations, which form part of his Ph.d. research on eighteenth-century French portraiture (Courtauld Institute of Art).
41. AN MC XXIV, 980, Bourjot, wife of Nicolas-Etienne Quatremere, AN MC XXII, 60, 21 September 1789, Berrieux.
42. AN Y13980 28 April 1788, Bourjot.
43. AN MC XXXIV, 758, Bourjot.
44. A trade card Au Grand Turc, 248 rue St Honoré, opposite the rue de l'Echelle, advertises Lenormand as 'breveté de Sa Majesté l'Imperatrice Reine'. It bears the imperial coat of arms and is anotated overleaf with a receipt on behalf of the Princess Josephine for 354 *francs* 82 *centimes*, dated 10 January 1851 (AVP 6AZ 440).
45. AN MC VII, 486, 5 July 1788, Lorieux. The syndicate reported that Lorieux had been trading without keeping books since 1781. Despite severe and untenable cashflow problems he had con-tinued to order silks from his suppliers. Eventually he was exposed by Perrin (from Paris, rue des Bourdonnais) and Pigalle (from Lyon), and as a result of a prosecution he was imprisoned at the Châtelet. His assets were seized, and creditors resigned themselves to the probablity of recovering only 10 per cent or so of their debts.
46. The goods in stock represented only 25,000 *livres*, his country house 120,000 and sums owed to him on credit 100,000.
47. AN MC VII, 486, 5 July 1788, Lorieux.
48. And was entered on 23 November 1787 (AN *Placard après décès* 2.417).
49. *Lettres de rehabilitation sur contrat d'atermoyement (sic) pour les Sieurs David et Eve*, Paris, 23 June 1762, BN F23627(47).
50. As highlighted by Savary in *Le Parfait Négotiant* 1675.
51. Cobban 1957, 46.
52. Eighteenth-century *Almanacs Royaux* specify that the journey took five to six days according to the season, and that mail took approximately three days. This is borne out by correspondence between manufacturers and their Parisian counterparts throughout the eighteenth century (ADR Série B, Fonds de Vitry et Gayet, *liasse* 1 and Fonds Fiard, *liasse* 1).
53. De l'Hiberderie (1765) mentions this aspect of partnership aggreements and surviving contracts bear out his claim. See for example ADR 3E3866 Dalier (Lyon): 11 October 1753 *Société* Pernon, Pernon, Aubert.
54. ADR Série B, *Fonds de Vitry et Gayet*, *liasse* 1.
55. *Mémoire général*, 18.
56. *Mémoire général*, 30.
57. AN O[1] 3641 *Journal du garde Meuble du Roi*.
58. *Mémoire général* 1731, 29. The text continues 'que dans les temps ou la cour de France n'a été dans le gout de la parure et de la dépense ou s'est toujours apercu de la diminuation de celle des cours etrangeres'.
59. *Mémoire général* 1731, 31.
60. *Mémoires* of Casanova de Seingald, cited in Henard 1908–9, 429.
61. On the furnishing of the Bagatelle see
62. *Mercure de France*, January 1777, 198–201.
63. McKendrick 1982.
64. Following the Missisippi crisis, the patterned silk industry (*étoffes de soyes or et argent*, that is, luxury production) was experiencing difficulty in South American markets in competition with English and Dutch fabrics. Taxes and customs inhibited success in other markets (in Sardinia, and in Venice they were banned completely) but the illegal imports of the French East India Company were considered the most significant threat to the French silk industry:

    La Compagnie de Indes inonda, et inonde encore actuellement la cour, Paris et les provinces d'etoffes prohibées que malgré les ventes qu'elle paroit en faire à Nantes pour les pays etrangers elle fait par une collusion condamnable reverses en France apres les avoir seulement pour la . . . fait sorter du port de Nantes (*Mémoire général* 1731, 17).
65. BML, *Imprimé* 354461 *Mémoire sur l'envoi d'echantillons de la fabrique de Lyon*, 1760, ff. 92–3. Correspondence between merchants and their representatives in Paris reveals that goods

were kept for the following season when they were sold. See for example ADR Série B, *Fonds Fiard*, *liasse* 1, *Correspondence Achard/Fiard*, 2 September 1758 and 9 July 1773.

66. BML *Imprimée* 113949, *Arrêt*, 14 July 1787.
67. BML *Fonds Coste* ms 1005, f.2v.
68. See for example correspondence between Bourjol père and Carret 1772–4 in ADR, *Série B, Fonds Carret*, *liasse* 1.
69. AN MC XCIII, 17 September 1787, Beaulard. I would like to thank Michael Sonenscher for this reference.
70. They included *gazes gauffrées, chapeaux de paille, viellies plumes*.
71. AN MC LXVI, 685, 2 June 1788, Blette-Beaulard.
72. Madame Joly was paid 1300 *livres* during the first year, and for each subsequent year was to receive an additional 100 *livres*. Her travel costs to Moscow (1200 *livres*) were also paid by Beaulard (AN MC XCIII,187, 13 August 1790, Beaulard).
73. AVP D^4B^6 *carton* 109 *dossier* 7772, Julien.
74. AVP 6AZ 291/4.
75. Miller, 1996.
76. I am extremely grateful to Madame Bonnardel for allowing me to study the original volumes. The samples were assembled into seven annotated bound volumes by Richelieu before the mid-eighteenth century. Entries on the manufacturing areas of France and Europe comprise fabric samples with prices, dimensions, and prices per unit. Some entries give a history of the region's textile production, estimates of its output and comments on the markets for which the textiles were destined. These volumes are unique in the number and scope of samples – silks, woollen textiles, cottons, ribbons, lace and other materials from French manufacturers and foreign goods. Another sample book for the purposes of comparing the products of competing woollen manufacturers in Europe was compiled by the Italian merchant Moccassi, and presented to Count Bogino in about 1760. It is conserved in the Bibliothèque Forney, and contains swatches, descriptions, prices and dimensions (*Exposizione delle Manuffatture di Francia, Inghilterra ed. Olanda*. BF FN 677.064).
77. Samoyault, 1979, Wilson 1974.
78. See Sargentson, 1992.
79. Cited in Pradère 1989, 130.
80. Reproduced by Eriksen, 1974, 271–6.
81. BML *Imprimés* 113923 and 113925 *Arrêt* . . . qui homologue la deliberation de la cmmunauté des maître marchands et maître-ouvriers facbriquans en étoffes d'or, d'argent et de soie de la ville de Lyon du 15 mars 1765 concernant la prohibition de l'envi des échantillons des mêmes étoffes hors laditte ville, 14 mai 1765. Also *Arrêt* . . . qui permet aux syndics-jurés et maîtres-gardes de la communauté des fabriquans en étoffes d'or d'argent et de soie de la ville de Lyon d'établir un commis au bureau de la régis de Paris, à l'effet de visites et perquisitions des échantillons de leur fabrique, qui pourroient y êtres envoyés en contravention; et de faire des recherches chez tous les dessinateurs et fabriquans, commis et autres de la ville de Lyon, logés à Paris et chez tous particuliers soupçonnés de recevoir lesdits échantillons et d'en favoriser l'exportation, etc., 6 mars 1766.
82. BML *Imprimés* 113925 *Arrêt* . . . f.4.
83. AML HH139 Saint-Michel, Dany et Compagnie contre Thevillon et Vingtain, 5 documents 1761–2.
84. *Mémoire général* 1731.
85. This is born out by the range of cases which deal with different fabrics. Ten or so are to be found in AML. HH139. They range in date from 1673 to the 1770s.
86. BML *Fonds Coste* ms 1005, f.2.
87. Eriksen 1974, 273.
88. BML *Fonds Coste* ms 1005, f.4.
89. AML HH139 *Mémoire pour les sieurs Ribier et Bertrand contre les sieurs Assada et Reynard c.* 1740, f.2v.
90. T373–1972, see Rothstein 1990.
91. ADR Série B *Fonds Fayet liasse 1*, 17 January 1749 letter Rohault/Fayet..
92. Lesley Miller argues that the Parisian mercer Bourjol was far less influential than he claimed in supplying the Lyonnais industry with new and successful designs (*esquisses*) in the 1740s (Miller 1996, 13).

6 Parisian shops and the 'magasins anglais'

Le 28 Mai, Madame de Beckendorf vint me prendre de bonne heure, et nous sortîmes toute la matinée chez les marchands. Nous restames plusieurs heures au Petit Dunkerque. C'était l'enseigne d'un bijoutier demeurant à la descente du Pont Neuf. Rien n'est jolie et brillant comme cette boutique, remplie de bijoux et de colfichets en or, dont on paye la façon, dix fois ce que vaut la matière.[1]

'La mérite personel du Marchand ne fut plus un titre suffisant pour se concilier les suffrages du public. Il le fallut séduire par les apparences'.[2]

Commercial and design relationships between manufacturers and retailers give some sense of the pattern of demand and response within the specialist market of patterned silks. This chapter turns to the question of the marketing strategies employed by the mercers which, along with their role in the design process, allowed them to market highly fashionable goods at the top end of the market. In particular, it focuses on the presentation of imported goods and French imitations in the *magasins anglais*, exemplified by Madame Blakey and Charles-Raymond Granchez. When Madame d'Oberkirch spent several hours at Granchez' shop on 28 May 1784, she was entering one of the most remarkably designed shops in Paris. Decorated with mirror glass and fittings of mahogany and giltwood, the attention paid to its interior design recalls that of Fouquet's shop, dating from around 1900, now in the Musée Carnavalet. Like Gersaint's premises on the Pont Notre Dame (colour plate 9), both Fouquet's and Granchez' shops are examples of shop interiors within which commodities such as furniture, porcelain and trinkets were on display. The design of the shop, from the exterior to the innermost rooms, was intended to create a memorable context within which the highly designed luxury objects on sale could be viewed and purchased. This chapter explores the idea that the identities of these Parisian shops were created and presented by their proprietors as part of their marketing strategies, and looks particularly at several examples of English-style shops, the *magasins anglais*, between the 1760s and 1780s.

Anglo-French Trade

The origins of the symbolism of the *magazins anglais* lie in the history of Anglo-French trade. Commercial competition between Britain and France had long stimulated comment and debate. Much of this revolved around competition in markets for textiles, from woollen cloths to the luxury silks discussed in the previous chapter. For instance, whilst the French were collecting samples of European silk and woollen production from the 1730s and comparing their price and quality (colour plate 21),[3] in 1734 the British were collecting French woollen samples and details of pricing for examination by Parliament.[4]

French imports into Britain, especially to London, have been the subject of several studies. These have documented the taste within the English metropolis for French silks, furniture, silver and porcelain. English tourists such as Walpole and Cole were keen shoppers, and ambassadors including the Duke of Bedford and Coventry made important purchases in Paris which eventually found their way back to Britain.[5] Much (though by no means all) of this purchasing activity took place after the Seven Years War (1756–1763). The traffic, however, was two-way, and after 1763 French travellers were once again crossing the channel to England. Nicole de Blomac describes, for example, visits by Frenchmen to Epsom, Newmarket and York, and their discovery of 'le racehorse' and the benefits of membership of the Jockey Club, founded in 1751.[6] The French fashion for imitating the English style of horse riding encouraged the acquisition by the French of imported horse flesh, saddlery and accessories for équipage.[7] In the female domain the association of tea-drinking with English fashions (*thé à l'angloise*) largely replaced its association with the orient in the late eighteenth century.[8] Literary and political circles also followed English customs and studied the thinking of their English counterparts. Grieder discusses the expression of anglomania in literary texts from the 1740s.[9] During the second half of the eighteenth century this was manifest in various other forms such as the French interest in English gardens and the opening in 1774 of *le Wauxhall,* a Parisian version of London's Vauxhall pleasure gardens. The Marquis de Marigny's purchases of English furniture and the Comte d'Artois' lifestyle at the Bagatelle are but two examples of an interest in English furnishings and customs.[10] Gordon and Déchery have described in detail the relationship between Marigny and Reinach, who acted for him in acquiring English goods.[11] With the exception of the purchases of English goods by Marigny in the 1760s, and the decoration at the Bagatelle by the Comte d'Artois in the 1780s, the taste for English luxury goods in Paris has been little studied.[12]

Trade between France and England, however, involved far more than the occasional aristocratic engagement with British culture. The author of Beawes explained that most of the British exports to France were sent via the free port of Dunkirk. His list of the exports for 1751 from London to France is reproduced in appendix 10. Luxury objects imported into France from Britain were listed in 1784 by François Lacombe (fig. 17), who remarked that the importation of English textiles and metal goods took place 'à profusion à la honte du Ministere de Versailles, presque toutes par contrabande & fraude'.[13]

Draps fins, bleus & rouges & autres couleurs.
Bas de laine, tricots, flanelles, etamines, doublures & shalons.
Gazes a fleurs, soie moirée, soie crue, petits satins, & rubans.
Bazins picqués, couvertures de cotton, velours de cotton bleu & autres.
Acier et quincaillerie, boutons de chasse, crayons, verres blanc, cristaux, lunettes et instruments, la potée, étain, limes, aiguilles, épingles, lignes & hamecons, chappes, grilles et foyers.
Fayence et terre blanche, carosses, resorts & roues. Estampes, cartes & livres.
Cuirs et sellerie & bottes fortes.
Cabarets à thé & tables de mahogony.
Chevaux, boeuf salé, suifs etc.

Fig 17. English imports into France, after Lacombe 1784.

As in the case of oriental imports, the French attempted to imitate and compete with the imported goods. Linda Colley explained the case of the imitation of French high style in Britain as a strategy of competition; 'by catering for the public's taste for the French fashions, they reduced the demand for French imports and thus advanced England's own fine art and decorative industries'.[14] Imports into France stimulated similar attempts, often supported by royal privilege, whose endeavours were described and advertised in the Parisian press. Hence the 1789–90 edition of the *Tableau Général du commerce* devoted considerable attention to the promotion of Parisian manufacturies which imitated English goods, especially metal wares.[15]

Though luxury markets in Paris were experiencing extreme difficulties, Gournay, author of the *Tableau Général*, celebrated French achievements and promoted commercial optimism. Gournay, highlighted significant success in markets for French luxury bronzes and porcelain and in the metal industries. For example, a *manufacture royal de placqué et doublé d'or et argent* employing 100–200, set up in 1777, was offered a royal privilege to manufacture 'dans le genre anglais, tous les objets placqués concernant l'équipages'. It also made snuff boxes, buckles and souvenirs and had ostensibly achieved notable success by the mid-80s. However, Gournay was forced to recognize a certain lack of ability in this factory to compete strongly enough with English goods, and interpreted this as a failure in marketing. He observed that the entrepreneurs, two goldsmiths named Tugot and Darmy, had paid insufficient attention to advertizing, which was necessary in order to counter the public perception that English metal goods were better.

Manufacturers of steel fancy goods were in competition with English goods, in terms of both quality and price.[16] Another factory, owned by Dauffé, sought to produce goods (including snuff boxes, buckles, corkscrews and furniture mounts) at a price considerably lower than English imports. He was awarded an annual pension for his successes, directed at bringing to a close 'l'importation en France des bijoux et autres ouvrages d'acier d'Angleterre'.[17] Arthur Young, however, presented a very different picture in 1789, when he argued that English steel, textiles and stoneware seriously rivalled French production.[18] Goods clearly travelled in both directions and whilst the British aped the styles of the French aristocracy and court, the French saw in Britain, with its constitutional monarchy, a tradition of enlightenment thinking and a corresponding taste for simpler forms and distinctive style.[19] The consumption of English goods in Paris thus took place within this rhetoric of commercial competition and was fuelled, in markets for luxury goods, by the anglomanie within both high and popular culture (exemplified by Marigny and Le Wauxhall) in Paris.

MADAME BLAKEY'S *MAGASIN ANGLAIS*

Although English goods had been sold in Paris by the mercers for many years, the mercers appear to have presented their shops as *magasins anglais* only from the 1760s, following the end of the Seven Years' War. Madame Blakey, née Margueritte Elizabeth Aumerle, ran such a shop in the rue des Prouvaires between 1766 and 1776.[20] In 1762, she married Guillaume (William) Blakey, named in the marriage contract as *auteur des bandages elastiques*. These were hernia bandages which he sold all over Europe. He was the son of the English spring-maker, William Blakey, who was involved with a network of Anglo-French clockmakers and the early eighteenth-century French imperative to stimulate the French clockmaking industry.[21] When Guillaume abandoned his business interests in Paris, his wife continued to trade as *quincaillière priviligiée du roi suivant la cour*, and to act as her husband's agent in Paris, until selling out to Jean René Jousset de Lizy, *marchand drapier mercier*, Quai de la Mégisserie.[22] The sale of the business took place in 1776, the year of the dissolution and reconstitution of the Parisian corporations, hence his combined profession of mercer-draper (see chapter 2). The sale was agreed at 46,579 *livres*, 10,000 representing the *pot de vin* and the rest of the sum the value of the stock.

Four years earlier Madame Blakey had declared bankruptcy, following a particularly difficult year.[23] She was in deficit to the tune of over 200,000 *livres* – her obligations amounted to about 380,000 and her assets to only 170,000. She reported that having just returned from England, she was unable to balance the books, despite her attempts to defer payments and extend her credit.[24] In particular she cited the problem of a consignment of goods sent to England, valued at 72,000 *livres*, half of which was held up at customs, and the other half of which had been sold at a loss of 50 per cent. An illness on the way to England had forced her to entrust goods worth 35,000 *livres* to agents, who were unable to prevent them from being seized at customs. This occurred despite her written requests to suppliers not to write in English on the packaging, because of the risk of the goods being held up at Dunkirk.[25] She maintained that any delay of goods so marked would be the responsibility of the British exporters.

Her list of necessary business expenses between the establishment of her business and her filing for bankruptcy in 1772 totalled 172,600 *livres* and covered the following items:

Construction of the shop	10,000
Rent of the shop @ 2,000 p.a.	14,000
Travelling expenses @ 2,500 p.a.	17,500
Household expenses @ 3,000 p.a.	21,000
Transport and customs	34,000
Interest and exchange rates, losses,	
Thefts, Paris & England	72,000
Postal costs	1,500
Capitation and other costs	1,600
TOTAL	172,000

Fig 18. Business expenses Madame Blakey 1765–1772.

She valued her stock in Paris at over 50,000, and in other places at 8,000 *livres*. Two privileges were listed amongst her assets, that of *mercerie* valued at 7,600 *livres* and that of *bonneterie* at 3,000. Although some debtors were Parisian, she was owed large sums for goods sent to the French provinces and the colonies.[26] A cutler in the Cap Français ordered French metal goods from her, which she obtained from Garnier, *coutelier*, at the Place Mont Michel.[27] A number of provincial clockmakers, who presumably bought tools from her, were listed amongst her debtors, including a Vanrobais at Courtray, Chartier at Bordeaux and Baron at Caen. She also supplied a number of Parisian clockmakers including Merlier, at the Porte St Martin, Dubois in the rue St Jacques and a Sr. Bekaers. To British suppliers she owed well over a hundred thousand *livres*.[28] She also owed money to individuals in Flanders, Caen, Geneva, Lyon, Versailles, Bayeux, Calais, and Seville.

Her interest in the importation of British merchandise is further documented in her support of a fellow merchant, Nicolas Augustin Bournisien d'Epineville, who established a *magasin anglais*, also on the Quai de la Megisserie.[29] She helped him both by putting up capital (50,000 *livres* in return for 2,500 income per annum in perpetuity) and by advice in setting up and running the business defined as follows: 'que la De Blakey a beaucoup contribué à la formation de ce magasin, par ses peines & soins qu'elle s'est donné et qu'elle se donne journellement'. He both housed her and gave her his power of attorney to buy and sell goods, and to arrange credit as befitted the interests of the business.

In 1776 the stock included a wide range of decorated tinwares (*taule peinte*). These included seventy-four trays valued at 440 *livres* and twenty-two pots, many for coffee and tea caddies, cabarets, candlesticks, inkstands, vases, salts, goblets, flower baskets.[30] A number of tables were composed of painted tôle trays on stands, some of which were described with *pieds tournants* (plates 63 and 64). Only two tables, one square, one round, were described as two-tiered. This range of tables was in part imitating the finer and more valuable tables which were mounted with porcelain plaques and trays and sold by Poirier and Daguerre (see plates 20 and 21). Two such tables with tôle stands were valued together at 272 *livres*. One table top was painted with a seascape, the other with fruits, and both were described as *très bien peints*. Since they were distinguished by the number of cups (*tasses*), they can be assumed to have been tea tables.

Tablewares of various metals were listed. Silver-

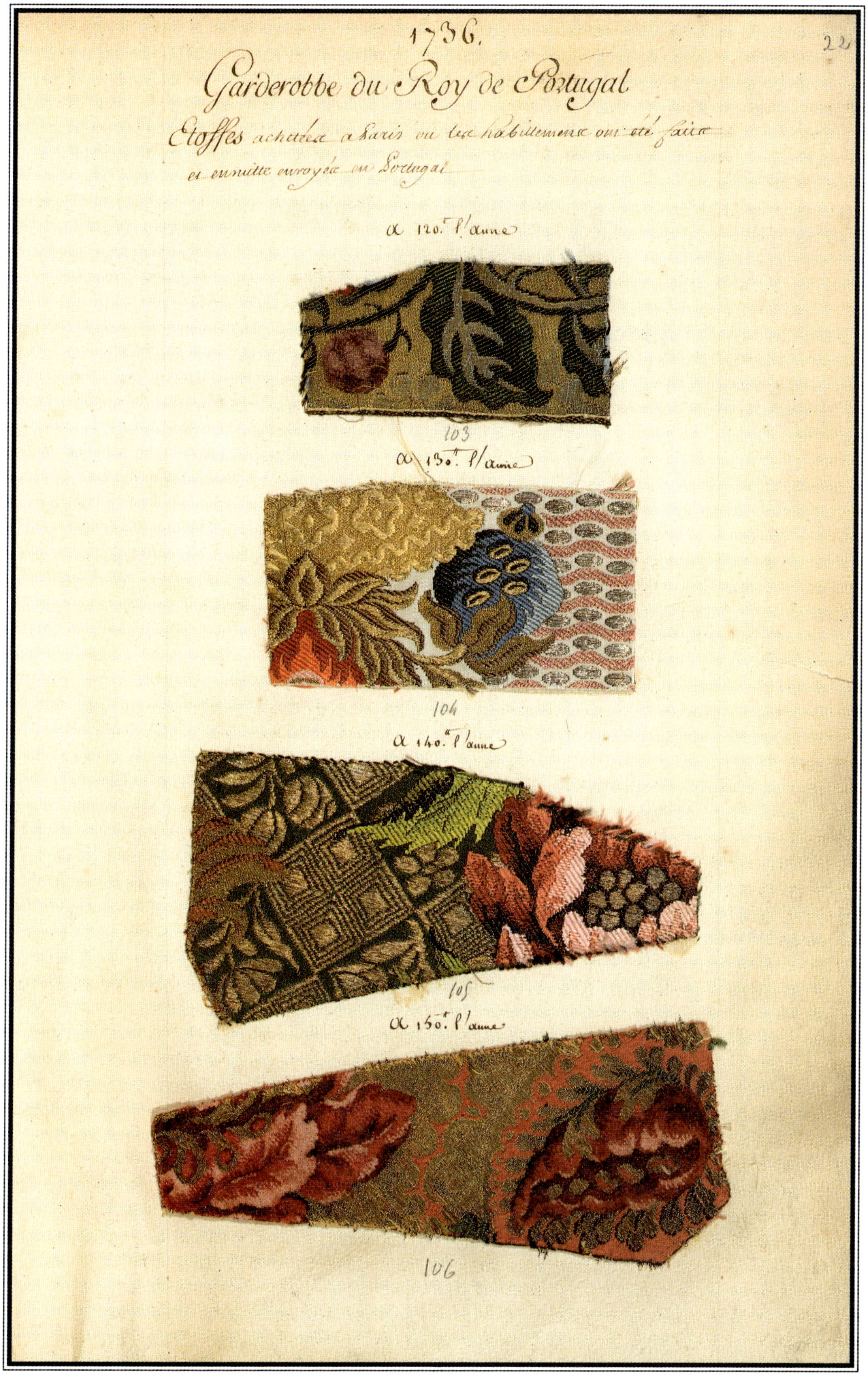

Colour Plate 21. Brocaded silks and velvet, Lyon, c. 1736. Bibliothèque Nationale de France, Paris.

19

M.d de Maupeou ~~Prie~~ Mr barbier de donner au porteur treize aunes de l'étoffe dont elle luy envoie l'échantillon moiré; il voudrat bien les porter sur son Mémoire. a Atheiges le 31 aoust 1789 Cmtesse de Maupeou

Mr George

19

Colour Plate 22. Order letter for silks, Comtesse de Maupeou to Jean-François Barbier. Victoria and Albert Museum, London.

Colour Plate 23. Portrait, possibly of the Nau family, 1700–15, attr. François de Troy. Private collection, photo courtesy Kugel & Co, Paris.

Colour Plate 24. Hangings from the bed of Nicolas Fouquet, c. 1660. Bibliothèque Nationale de France, Paris.

Colour Plate 25. Merchant's order book of woven silks, French c. 1760–64. Victoria and Albert Museum, London.

Colour Plate 26. Merchant's order book of woven silks, French c. 1760–64. Victoria and Albert Museum, London.

Colour Plate 27. Merchant's order book of woven silks, French c. 1760–64. Victoria and Albert Museum, London.

Colour Plate 28. Guéridon *with flip-top, stamped Joseph Canabas. Photo Christie's Images.*

Colour Plate 29. Commode, *c. 1770–75, stamped by Dubois, Jacques or René. Waddesdon Manor, National Trust.*

Colour Plate 30. Etui, *c. 1770, English, the knife blades marked by Thomas Gray. Photo Christie's Images.*

Colour Plate 31. Interior panelling from the Café Militaire, 1762, Claude-Nicolas Ledoux. Musée Carnavalet, Paris.

Plate 63. Guéridon, 1770–80. Photo Christie's Images.

Plate 64. Detail, plaque, painted rôle, 1770–80. Photo Christie's Images.

plated goods included coffee pots, compartments for inkstands and pans.[31] These appear to have been supplied by Huntsman and Asline of Sheffield, who complained forcefully about Blakey's unwillingness to settle even part of her account.[32] The same company supplied samples, and a range of metal goods including tools for various trades, scissors, and knives, some of which were described as *couteaux de poche à la française*. They supplied Madame Blakey with silver-gilt salts, porcelain *nécessaires* and many enamelled boxes. References to transport costs indicate that they sent some of these consignments via Liverpool. Others travelled via Charles Granges in London to Dunkirk, where they were handled by the agent Des Graviers. Blakey's English ceramic wares in 1776 included one stoneware teapot (brown), and several white teapots and cups decorated with flowers.[33] These may have been purchased in Paris – Madame Blakey was a client of the mercer Dubuisson (a specialist in porcelain, see chapter 4) and bought from him English-style salts *salières d'angleterre*, possibly of porcelain, and English tea caddies of various sizes. Tin wares (coffee pots and kettles) and a range of plain and cut glass items were listed, some clear, some blue.[34] An assortment of candlesticks in the form of broken fluted columns with garlands were variously decorated in silver and gold (the columns were either gilded or silvered and the garlands or fluting picked out in the other colour). They were relatively highly valued at between 48 and 72 *livres* the pair.[35]

Small enamelled wares included snuff boxes and salts (listed in two sizes) and 474 enamelled labels for wine bottles valued at 237 *livres*.[36] The stock included a range of tools and small metal wares for sculptors or carvers and joiners, upholsterers and clockmakers.[37] A range of metal buckles and buttons of various descriptions, jewellery, spectacle frames and belt buckles were made of steel (*acier*).[38] Some items were described specifically as made of cut steel, such as the shoe buckles of *acier taillées en diamant*,[39] and four pairs of buckles were described as silvered steel.[40] The steel goods were variously described as polished (*poli*), burnished (*brûlé*), and sometimes of especially fine quality, (*fin*). Other pieces of jewellery were set with precious stones and marquisite. A few buckles and chains were supplied by Wm Brott in 1768, but more significant orders were made to Oppenheim of Birmingham in November of the same year. They supplied buckles, buttons, boxes and *étuis*, some of silver and others of *pinchebecq* (pinchbeck, an alloy of copper and zinc with a gold appearance). They also supplied steel candlesticks at 24 and 28 *livres* the pair.[41] Another Birmingham supplier, Glover and Chamot, sent two crates of steel and lacquer goods in 1768, priced at a total of 11,438 *livres*. William Hanscombe of London supplied fine saddlery in May 1769 and Richard Snow, also of London, sent six saddles with stirrups, and blankets or covers for horses in the same year.[42] Madame Blakey also bought saddles, martingales, girths and other items from Goddard, Williams and Co, saddlers to her majesty, of Great Queen St, Lincoln's Inn Fields and at Southwark.[43] Other imported items included gloves and stockings, watch glasses, canes, innumerable small boxes of varying finish and children's toys.[44] A range of boxes was covered with imitation tortoiseshell, paper maché and shagreen (plate 65).

Some of her imported goods are clearly recognizable from their descriptions as English forms which were soon to be imitated in Paris. In the case of mahogany tables, it would appear that Madame Blakey acted solely as importer. The 1776 list of stock describes English dining tables in mahogany, for four to twelve covers (*couverts*), the largest square, the others round.[45] Grangés of London supplied her in 1769 with tea tables and dining tables.[46] An unusual item of furniture in the 1776 list of stock was the *lit anglais de forme de secretaire* valued at 40 *livres*, which was apparently not a form known in Paris at this date.

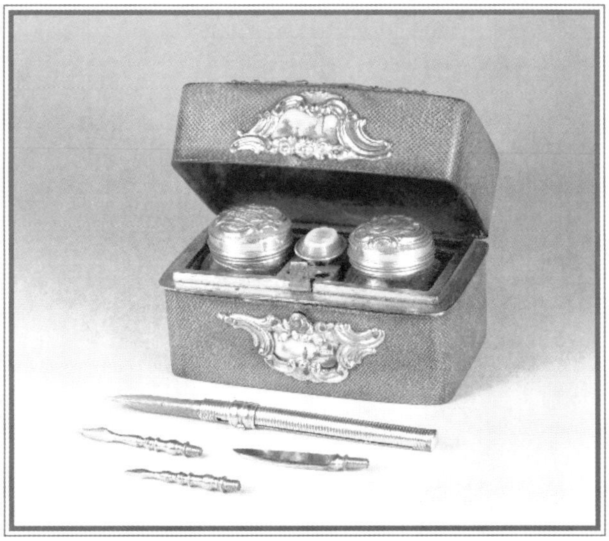

Plate 65. Box, South Staffordshire, c. *1760. Victoria and Albert Museum, London.*

By the 1760s, English tea tables were being copied in Paris and sold by other mercers. In his description of *guéridons* and tables, Roubo explains

> On fait encore d'autres Tables ou Guéridons nommées *à l'Angloise*, apparémment parce qu'elles ont été inventées en Angleterre.[47]

Even earlier, the mercer Dubuisson was selling mahogany tables supplied to him by Canabas, who is now best known for his range of furniture in solid mahogany and often following English forms, (colour plate 28).[48] One round and one square mahogany table with marble tops and several screens, including one described specifically as *à la grec*, were supplied by Canabas in October 1765.[49] Canabas supplied Dubuisson on a running account from 1766 onwards, mainly with round mahogany tables. These included two *tables tournantes*, one smaller than the other, delivered on 29 January 1767, priced 40 and 36 *livres* respectively.[50] Canabas took lacquered goods (4 *cabarets*) in part-payment.[51] He packed and sent a two-tiered mahogany table (*à deux-étages*), the top of a tray of lacquered English tin – *tolle d'angleterre verni* valued at 160 *livres*, along with forty-eight blue and white cups and saucers, to the Marquis de Narbonne Pelet.[52] Two trays of the same material were sent on the following day to the Ambassador of the Low Countries.[53]

Dubuisson's English goods also included six-and-a-half rolls of green and white English wallpaper, but these items formed only part of his stock, which comprised Chinese wallpapers, many other oriental imports, especially porcelain and lacquer goods, and French furniture and bronzes and porcelain and faience from many parts of Europe (see chapter 4). Amongst Dubuisson's customers was Madame Blakey, who bought from him goods such as glass and metal wares, tea and tea-drinking apparatus and English ceramics (see above). A list of his clients included several English names such as a Madame Henry, the Comte Waldener and a M. Opkins, all of whom purchased tea.

CHARLES RAYMOND GRANCHEZ

Amongst Dubuisson's suppliers of English goods was a M. Granché, rue St Honoré, near the Oratoire, from whom he purchased *quatre paires de salieres d'angleterre dorées* in June 1767.[54] A Charles-Raymond Granchez moved from Dunkirk to Paris to open a *magasin anglais* on the Quai de Conti in the same year. However, a building with shop space called Le Port de Dunkerque in the rue St Honoré existed as early as 1748.[55] Whether or not this was Granchez' first address in Paris, or perhaps his father's, is not clear.[56] Charles-Raymond Granchez was born in Versailles and his wife Margueritte Leveque in Paris. They were married in Paris on 13 September 1761.[57] Granchez brought from his business at Dunkirk 20,000 *livres*, and her dowry was 12,000. Granchez traded in Dunkirk at the sign of the Perle d'Orient in the rue du Commandement, and stated in an advertisement of 1768 that after the opening of the shop in Paris he would continue the Dunkirk trade in *bijouterie et quincaillerie anglaise*.[58] The Perle d'Orient was still in existence in 1787.[59] Granchez' first child, Marie Therese Charlotte, was born in 1762. When she was twenty-two she married a lawyer, L-A Leprevot.[60] In 1767 Granchez became a member of the Parisian corporation of *marchands merciers*.[61] In May 1774 he was appointed *bijoutier du Roi*, and by the following year, *bijoutier de la Reine*.[62] Margueritte Leveque died in 1784. When, three years later, Granchez declared himself insolvent, his son, Charles François, was described as a minor.[63]

Granchez' wife inherited over 50,000 *livres* from her parents' estate in 1766, which may have provided the means for Granchez to expand his business in the following year. He announced the opening of his new *magasin anglais* in Paris in December 1767, on the Quai de Conti.[64] The original shop sign, a representation of the port of Dunkerque, was painted in 1767 by Joseph Vernet.[65] (Louis XV had commissioned from Vernet in 1753 a series of the ports of France which, due to the financial impact of the Seven Years' War, was never completed.[66]) Like Gersaint's sign, which entered the collection of ?? within several weeks of its completion, Granchez' sign was apparently bought by the Duc de Villeroy some fifteen years after its execution by Vernet in 1782.[67] The premises were at 3, Quai de Conti, at the corner of the rue Dauphine and across the river from the goldsmiths' shops around the place Dauphine and the Quai des Orfèvres.

The building survived until the demolition of the block in 1914 to allow for the widening of the rue Dauphine. A modern building now stands on its site.[68] A photograph shows a shop front consisting of four arched windows, decorated with a Greek key pattern and fully glazed (plate 68). The sign illus-trated in the photograph, which is conserved in the collections of the Musée Carnavalet, is made of worked steel and represents a ship surrounded by a border of grapes, vine leaves and heads of Bacchus (plate 69). The Petit Dunkerque appears to have subsequently moved to the rue de Richelieu, at the corner of the rue de Menard (plates 66 and 67),[69] and to have remained there until at least 1813.[70] At some point after Granchez left the premises at Quai de Conti, they were taken over by a *marchand de vins*.[71]

Plate 66. Eugène Atget, 3, Quai de Conti, 1900. J. Paul Getty Museum, Malibu, California.

The association between Granchez and Dunkirk was important commercially and in terms of the image of the Parisian shop Au Petit Dunkerque. The port of Dunkirk was a key trading post for the movement of goods between Britain and France. As a result of the 'Battle of the Dunkirk Dunes' (1658), between the allied French and British armies and the Spanish, it was ceded to the British. Lord Clarendon acted for Charles II in selling it to the French a few years later in 1662. The identity of both Granchez' business at Dunkirk and the Parisian shop was strongly associated with the port. Both trade cards were designed with a framed image of the port (plates 70 and 71) and the Paris shop sign between 1767 and 1782 was a high-quality painting representing the port.[72] All of these images of ships associated with the shop directly recall the armorials of the corporation of *marchands merciers* (see plate 1) and the emblems of the city of Paris (discussed in chapter 1), linking the symbolism of Anglo-French trade via the port of Dunkirk with that of the city of Paris, the Six Corps of merchants and overseas trade.

Even some of the goods on sale at the Petit Dunkerque were decorated using the same iconography. A commode attributed to René Dubois, bearing the inscription 'Au Petit Dunkerque' was painted with a port scene after Joseph Vernet (colour plate 29).[73] Other goods marked with the name of the Petit Dunkerque survive. A number of gold boxes bearing this inscription on their flanges were sold by Granchez (plate 72).[74] He launched a new snuff box every year, sometimes commemorating a specific event. Mercier said of this ritual 'chaque année on baptise ces petits bijoux d'un nom particulier et bizarre'.[75] For example, boxes named *la consolation dans le chagrin* were covered with black shagreen and were decorated on their lids with portraits of Louis XVI and Marie Antoinette. They were advertised after the death of Louis XV in 1774.[76]

Such novelties attracted considerable attention. Mercier described the crowds which flocked to the Petit Dunkerque during the first few days of the New Year, no doubt to see the latest box.[77] The value of these kinds of goods was expressed in terms of pleasure derived from their novelty, and their rarity.

Plate 67. Sign Au Petit Dunkerque, *c. 1782, steel. Musée Carnavalet, Paris.*

Plate 68. Trade card, Au Petit Dunkerque. Private Collection.

Plate 69. *Trade card, Au Petit Dunkerque. British Museum, Banks Collection.*

Plate 70. *Trade card,* Á La Perle d'Orient. *Waddesdon Manor, National Trust.*

If Mercier was making a comment on the regrettable lack of 'real' value of objects when he said 'l'on juge des objets, non sur leur bonté réelle mais sur les rareté', Madame du Châtelet was more willing to engage in the pleasures and satisfaction to be gained from the consumption of fashionable goods:

> Je ne ris plus que personne aux marionettes, et avoue q'une boîte, une porcelaine, un meuble nouveau sont pour moi une vrai jouissance.[78]

Plate 71. *Trade card,* Au Petit Dunkerque. *Waddesdon Manor, National Trust.*

Some of Granchez' novelty goods were made, or partly made, in England. For example, the *étui* decorated with the arms of the Choiseul family contains a knife whose twin blades were hall-marked for Thomas Gray of London (colour plate 30).[79] Gray was listed amongst Granchez' creditors in 1787, owed 3,181 *livres*, and the Duchesse de Choiseul was amongst his debtors.[80] When Granchez declared bankruptcy in 1787, Gray went to Paris but was represented formally in the business by the mercer Dominique Daguerre, who was by this date living and trading in London in partnership with Martin-Eloi Lignereux who remained in Paris.[81] It is interesting to note that Madame Blakey was selling similar goods in 1776. Ten of her *étuis*, finished in black shagreen with English clasps, were each fitted with six English razors, a sharpening stone, a pair of scissors and a flask (plate 75).[82]

No doubt the small scale of some of the objects in stock motivated Granchez to employ some form of security at the shop. Often, said Madame Oberkirch of the Petit Dunkerque in 1782, the number of visitors to the shop was controlled by a guard.[83] The interior of the Petit Dunkerque was described in great detail in the inventory taken after Granchez' wife's death in 1784, not least because the fittings were so valuable (3,000 *livres*).[84] The ceiling was composed of 250 pieces of mirror glass (each 8 inches high and 6 wide) and the back wall of the shop was similarly decorated, with 54 pieces of mirror glass (14 by 18 inches each). Three columns of mahogany (one larger than the others) were partly gilt and decorated with curved pieces of mirror glass. Two corner display cabinets, and a variety of other cabinets in the shop were also of parcel gilt mahogany and curved mirror glass. Drawers were built into two large counters which were themselves described as in the form of galleries, and made of mahogany and glass. A small mirrored counter with balusters was mobile (*roulant*). Four lanterns, three of which were in the form of griffins, provided lighting, and twelve globes of silvered glass (*boules en verre étainés*) were also listed. Heating was provided by a stove.

The shop design was based on a glittering combination of mirror glass, mahogany and giltwood, and the objects and surroundings alike would have been reflected in the mirrors at the back and on the ceiling of the shop. The use of mirror glass recalls a fashion in the contemporary interior design of cafés, described as the *magie des glaces* in the example of the interior of the Café Militaire in the rue St Honoré (colour plate 31). A café in the rue Montmartre was also fitted out with alternate mirrors and painted panels. This was imitated by Roy, owner of the Café de la Régence. Roy had very explicit ideas about the establishment. He opened his doors only to people whose appearance pleased him, and was not prepared to admit soldiers or servants, nor anyone who might disrupt the 'tranquillité de la société'. Above all, he wanted, his café to have the air of a salon, not a shop.

Granchez' mirrored interior provoked comment in various quarters.. The Baronne d'Oberkirch described the shop as *étincelant*, and Mercier said that 'rien n'est plus brilliant à l'oeil que cette boutique: rien n'est plus triste à la réflexion . . .' (for the full transcript of Mercier's decription of the Petit Dunkerque see appendix 12).[85] The author of the *Correspondance Secrète de Métra* was presumably describing the Petit Dunkerque when he spoke thus of an academy of fashion in Paris:

> J'indiquerai . . . l'emplacement pour ce vaste magasin, que j'entends être plafonné, boisé et planchéré de glaces.[86]

Granchez' interior inspired a fellow merchant from Dunkirk, Jean Lafaye, who opened a Paris shop selling perfumes and accessories. An almanac of 1778 descibes it thus:

> Lafaye, rue Platriere, aux Armes de Soubise. Parfumeur, tient un des plus superbes magasins & des lieux assortis en Poudre, Pommade, Parfums & Bonbons de premiere qualité. Ce magasin est dans un genre aussi galamment decoré que celui du Petit Dunkerque, & mérite d'être vu par les Etrangers.[87]

A poem dedicated to the Petit Dunkerque, celebrating a visit from the Dauphine, was published in the *Mercure de France* in October 1773. To be sung to the tune of the 'fanfare de St. Cloud' it went as follows:

> Marchand du Petit Dunkerque
> Tu primes sur tes voisins:
> L'heureux vainqueure de Stinkerque
> Eut envié tes destins.
> La fortune te rend maître
> De mille effets précieux,
> Et puis elle vient te mettre
> En commerce avec les Dieux.
>
> Pour charmer notre DAUPHINE,
> Chez toi l'on voit réunis
> Et d'Angleterre & de la Chine
> Les bijoux les mieux finis:
> Mais la jour que cette Belle
> Vint en choisir de sa main,
> Non, rien de si rare qu'Elle
> N'étoit dans ton Magasin.

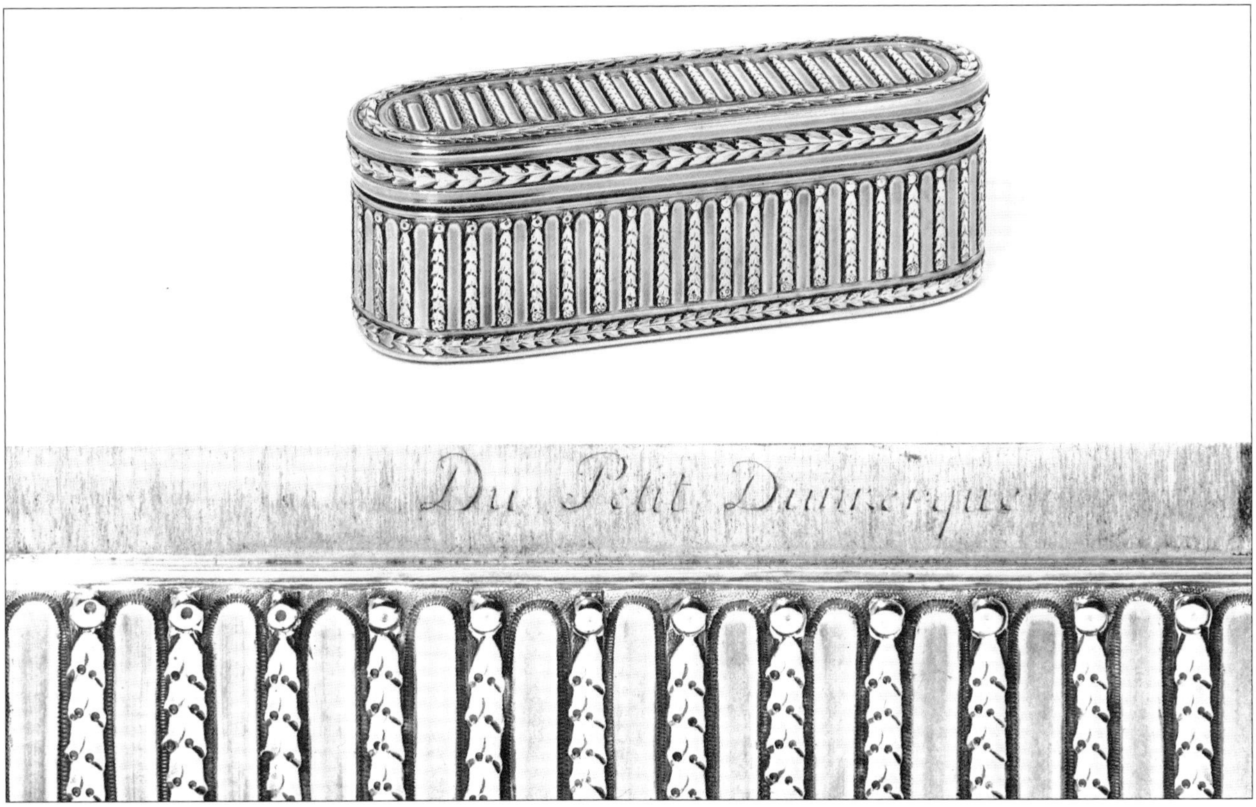

Plate 72. Gold box, 1775–81, and detail of inscription. Victoria and Albert Museum, London.

De cette époque brillante
Tu peux rien t'enorguellir,
Et d'un voix triomphante
Chanter ainsi ton plaisir:
"Pour un mortel ordinaire
"Quels momens délicieux! . . .
"Hélas! Sans quitter la Terre
"Je me suis vu dans les Cieux![88]

This royal visit and its consequent impact on public awareness and consumer behaviour recalls the visit of the Duchesse de Chartes to *La Civette* (see pages 104–5). Granchez was quick to exploit such patronage. After 1775, he had printed a new set of bill headings with his title *Bijoutier de la Reine*.[89] He publicized his business through a series of announcements from 1767 to 1778 in the *L'Avant Coureur*, and from 1774 in the *Mercure de France*.[90] In his advertisements in the *Mercure de France* during the 1770s, he announced the availabilty of a number of items which had been supplied to prestgious clients. In 1777 he was marketing small candlesticks *à l'athénienne* which he had first presented to the Comtesse d'Artois, and buckles 'du modèle de M. le Comte d'Artois' (who owed him 1,173 and 1,902 *livres* respectively in 1784).[91] Also in 1777, he described a small clock named *de lit à tirage*, of gilt bronze, the gilding both burnished and matt of which *le premier modèle a été fait pour la Reine*.[92] In the same advertisement he offered watch chains each decorated with a round bell (*grelot*) of gold and nine new trinkets (*brelogues*), the first of which was made for Madame (the sister of the King), who owed Granchez 2,326 *livres* in 1784.[93]

Small boxes decorated with portraits provided a means of creating objets which had both market appeal and linked Granchez' shop with illustrious personalities, some of whom were clients. In 1776, he advertised a range of snuff boxes each with a gold medallion portrait in relief of the Comte d'Artois after an engraving by Trebouchet, at various prices. In 1775 he advertised new boxes with portraits of the Queen, priced from 30 *livres*. The same portrait in miniature was available on snuff boxes, as was the portrait of her brother, the Archduke of Austria. In 1774, gold rings *à l'antique* with enamelled portraits in relief under glass were on sale. They represented the King and Queen, Henry IV, the Emperor and Empress, all after engravings by Wurtz, were declared 'chef-d'oeuvre de resemblance' and priced at 36 *livres* each.

The advertisements emphasized the novelty of products (*nouveaux modèles*) available at the Petit Dunkerque. In the *Mercure de France* Granchez announced the availability of a new range of buttons in pinchbeck, steel silver and enamelled silver. A collection of objects was made of English paste imitating rock crystal (*crystal factice*) – chandeliers, candlesticks, garnitures for chimney pieces and vases, many of which were mounted in Paris in gilt bronze. New forms made in painted tôle with some silver content[94] included small candlesticks, toast baskets, teapots and fountains for making tea and salts and inkstands of ebony decorated with tôle plaques with cut crystal compartments.[95] In 1771, Granchez announced in *L'Avant Coureur* that he was now employing two artisans who had formerly worked at the ill-fated Petite Pologne (a *manufacture de tôle vernie*, see page 88).[96] However, in 1777, the objects of the tôle and silver alloy were described as imports (*de l'Etranger*). Other novelties included innumerable small boxes and buckles, silver tablewares, punch bowls, spurs with rowels on springs which facilitated walking, and mechanical toys. Despite the promotion of annual, and indeed seasonal, changes in the design of boxes (Mercier described the difference between lightweight summer boxes and heavier boxes for winter use), the design of boxes associated with the Petit Dunkerque sometimes had a rather longer life. Snowman has noted that a circular box dated 1783–4 by Louis Lecarrière, with the inscription 'Du Petit Dunkerque' on the flange, is remarkably similar in design to another made by Le Bastier twelve years earlier.[97] Its pink ground with leopard skin spots of black enamel recalls Granchez' advertisement of a circular box in 1777, *bonbonnières en or et émail tigrées*.[98]

Plate 73. Etui for razors, English 1750–60. Victoria and Albert Museum, London.

Some of the items advertised were clearly of exceptional quality and several were described as unique. Candlesticks and vases of the highest quality work, of marble and bronze were priced at 1,000 to 2,000 *livres*. An ornament for a chimney piece in the form of a Chinese pagoda 'travaillée en philigrame d'une délicatesse comme il n'est pas encore paru en Europe' was priced at 2,400 *livres*. Chandeliers of paste cost 900 to 1,100 *livres*.

When Granchez first advertised the *magasin anglais* in Paris at the end of 1767, he announced the sale of *bijouterie anglaise* imported from England. For example, Granchez' patronage of Gray indicates that price was not the only factor in commissioning English goods. In September 1771 he advertised a collection, 'un choix très complet' of English wares supplied by Wedgwood and Bentley. However, in 1777, although some imports were listed, the emphasis in Granchez' announcements seems to have shifted away from English imports and towards the promotion of French products. In 1777, he advertised plate-warmers of a model 'copié de l'anglais', which he said held many more plates than other types. Of the quality and design of the small articles of hard paste porcelain from the factory at Clignancourt (first advertised in 1775), he said that they represented the proof of 'la possibilité d'établir en France des ouvrages en tout genre à l'imitation de l'Angleterre, & sur les desseins plus variés'. As well as buying gold boxes from the Parisian goldsmiths, in 1787 Grancher owed 1,281 *livres* to Dauffer, *marchand orfèvre*, who may well have been the same individual who ran the factory imitating English steel products (see page 115).

Granchez' patronage of Parisian suppliers can be quantified in part by looking at the list of his creditors in 1784 (in the inventory drawn up after the death of his wife).[99] Amongst the fifty-nine creditors, only four English names appeared – Thomas Gray of London, Baumgartner and Hoffsletter of London, Glover and Frey of Birmingham, Holy and Wilkinson of Sheffield. Other than one Genevan merchant, who was owed 2,300 *livres*,[100] all the other creditors were Parisian, mainly goldsmiths, suppliers of bronzes and inlay-workers. However, these English suppliers were owed 37,448 *livres* in total – over a third of Granchez' debts in 1784.[101] When Reinach was shopping in London for Marigny's metal goods, he testified to the differences in quality between different suppliers in England. He said that although Birmingham wares were a third cheaper than London prices, they were much lighter plated than those to be found in London. Of Birmingham wares he said 'C'est la ou Mr. Gronché et autres tire leurs marchandise. Examiné l'ouvrage de votre epée' [supplied by Thomas Gray] 'et comparez avec celui des épée de ces Mrs vous trouverez la difference'.[102]

As some of the advertisements showed, many of Granchez' products were costly. However, the Petit Dunkerque was perceived as competitive. Mercier remarked that Granchez sold at fixed prices, and that claims made by merchants to the contrary were merely motivated by jealousy.[103] Granchez was not the only shopkeeper to advertise fixed prices, however. Although trade cards most often use the term 'à juste prix', the mercer Delfrenaye, who had a shop in the Palais de Justice, advertised as early as 1737 at 'prix fixe'.[104]

The financial realities behind the 'fine outside' of Granchez' shop were more or less invisible, except to his creditors. The finances of the business were both extensive and at times precarious, particularly from the mid-1780s. He had for some time been managing an extensive network of credit, consistently buying goods on credit from individuals in Paris, London, Birmingham and Sheffield. In 1784, he owed almost 100,000 *livres* to fifty-nine suppliers and planned further payments of 304,988 *livres* over a period of fourteen months.[105] Cashflow was a constant problem in the years preceding his bankruptcy. In May 1785, his assets of 476,540 *livres* had outweighed his debts by a mere 6,000 *livres*, and subsequently he succeeded in paying off his debts. As de Bellaigue has shown, he managed to avoid declaring bankruptcy twice that year.[106] However, in September 1787, his margins were only slightly more healthy,[107] his creditors lacked confidence and formed a syndicate to control the settlement of outstanding sums and ongoing orders.[108]

Despite periods of commercial uncertainty, Granchez' shop attained a symbolic status by the 1780s, and a series of associations with Le Petit Dunkerque continued to be made through the nineteenth and the early twentieth centuries in publications as diverse as Balzac's *Cousin Bette* and

Larousse.[109] In the eighteenth century, the highly fashionable designs of at least some of his goods and certainly the dazzling environment of the shop, went some way to placing him on what Mercier described as his throne. Granchez painstakingly controlled the cycle of his fashions, frequently advertising them as *nouveau* and launching and naming new products annually. Through these means, he created a sense of difference, novelty and an élite quality at the Petit Dunkerque. The fashionable status of Granchez' goods was reinforced by a programme of advertising, and the shop's fortunes were aided by public royal and aristocratic patronage, carefully publicised by Granchez himself, by Mercier and by Granchez' customers. The goods advertised themselves; 'Ne faut-il dire en étalant une boite: c'est du Petit Dunkerque'.[110] Through all these means, Granchez created a sense of difference, novelty and an élite quality at the Petit Dunkerque.

It is difficult to discuss the strategies and fortunes of an individual merchant, particularly one who was in many ways extraordinarily successful, without falling into the trap of assuming that he was the only mercer to employ marketing strategies such as those outlined above. It is by no means the intention in this chapter to present Granchez as the Parisian version of Josiah Wedgwood, whose singular status within the literature on eighteenth-century English marketing was established in the 1960s.[111] A glance at Gersaint's shop sign of *c.* 1720 and his trade card of 1740 shows that sophisticated commercial environments were already envisaged in Paris much earlier (colour plate 9 and plate 47). As a postscript and balance to Granchez' creation of the Petit Dunkerque, the final part of this chapter will look at the ways in which other merchants and shopkeepers worked in similar ways, employing designers and artists of varying calibre and cost.

Marketing and the Design of Shops

The presentation of luxury shops was achieved through a number of means, from exterior symbols such as trade cards, shop signs and shop fronts to interior decoration, display and behaviour. The imagery of the trade cards for the Petit Dunkerque and A La Pagode, produced by printing from engraved plates were unusually elaborate. Many of the trade cards circulating in eighteenth-century Paris were very simple, especially amongst the furniture trade (plates 11 and 15).[112] Claude Carelu's order for 1000, for example, cost him only 30 *livres*.[113] However, at the top end of the market, specialist designers and engravers supplied images such as Gersaint's card of 1740, designed by François Boucher before he became *peintre du roi*.[114] A number of merchants ordered trade cards, often with neo-classical frames, from the engraver Choffard, and these are now conserved as much for their quality as engravings as for their interest as commercial ephemera (plates 74 and 75). Larger format cards (more or less the modern A4 size) were used as bills, and one shop inventory refers to items of jewellery being wrapped in *etiquettes*.[115]

If the trade card bore an image of the shop as well as text, that image was often used for the shops sign (*l'enseigne* or *le tableau*). The *enseignes* were made of various materials, and were sometimes three-dimensional.[116] The *tableaux* ranged from those of Gersaint and Granchez to much cheaper versions. For example, in the rue St Honoré shop of Michel Hugot in 1726 were 'Deux morceaux de draps vert et deux ronds debois rouge peinte nom de Jesus servant detalage une enseigne de tolle avec ses potences de fer' valued at 30 *livres*.[117] In Menard's hardware shop on the Quai de la Mégisserie, amongst the items valued for an inventory in 1778 were 'les marchandises servant d'etalage tant en dehors que dedans . . '. These included the sign and a decorated *plafond*, which might have been the ceiling. Gersaint described his sign as a *plafond*, an overdoor painting on the exterior of the shop. 'L'enseigne et le plafond avec le chiffre' were together valued at 330 *livres*.[118] At Madame Pucelle's linen shop in the rue St Honoré, both the sign and ceiling of overdoor were painted with images of Ste Anne. The inventory described 'une enseigne qui a

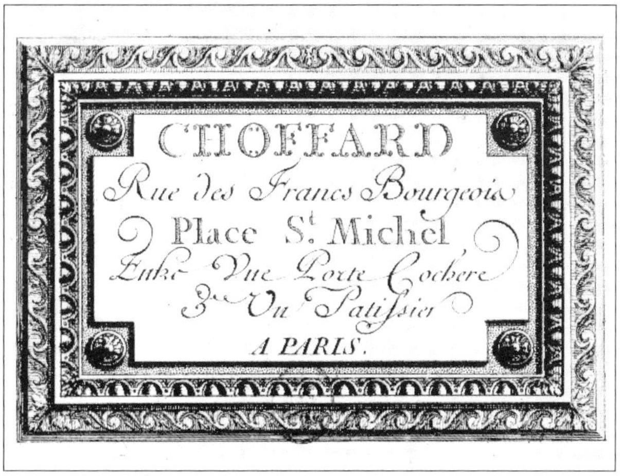

Plate 74. Trade card, c. 1770, Pierre-Philippe Choffard. Bibliothèque Nationale de France, Paris.

Plate 75. Trade card, Remy. Bibliothèque Nationale de France, Paris.

pour titre Ste Agnès et le plafond qui represente la même Sainte' were valued together at 20 *livres*.[119] According to a document of 1761 produced by the Six Corps of Paris as a response to a proposal to alter the disposition of signs, many merchants spent up to 400 *livres* on their signs. This statement was made in an attempt to preserve the signs, which were, from 1761, no longer permitted to overhang the street.[120] Before 1761, hanging signs had been suspended from brackets of wrought iron (plates 76 and 77). They allegedly blocked views, obscured light and were in danger of falling onto passers-by. This was part of a long-running dispute, which had resulted in similar legislation in 1666.[121] Despite appeals by the Six Corps, who argued that overhanging signs were 'plus avantageuses au Négoce', that the expense involved in making alterations was excessive and that 'l'enseigne d'un marchand décide souvent le valeur de sa boutique', at the end of December 1761 the police ordered that all signs should be fixed to the wall. In August 1792, all merchants in Paris were ordered to 'supprimer tous emblêmes qui rappeleroient au peuple le temps d'esclavage sous lequel il agemi depuis longtemps'.[122]

The sign, whether it meant the physical shop sign or the name of the shop, was the primary means of identifying a shop. It was strongly associated with an individual and his or her trade, and sometimes explicitly formed part of the value of a business. When Bentabole terminated his partnership with the Rohault brothers (see p. 127), he reserved the right, should he decide to remain in business on his own account, to use the sign La Toison d'Or.[123]

The appropriateness of the symbolism of the shop sign and the pretensions of proprietors were a matter of occasional discussion, as shown by the following conversation about the optician Sick:

> mon père m'avait demandé d'excellentes lunettes; j'allait les lui acheter chez Sick, l'opticien du Palais Royal. Celui-là aussi prenait un air d'importance à mourir de rire; il était, disait son enseigne, *fournisseur de l'Académie*.
>
> – Ah, disait Beaumarchais, si le pauvre Sick mettait sur sa boutique: *fournisseur des Quinze-Vingts*, (a hospital for the blind), cela nous donnera bien plus de confiance.[124]

Certain elements of the temporary display set up outside a shop were described as the *étalage*. These consisted of *tapis* to which were pinned small items, such as prints, buckles, ribbons etc. For example,

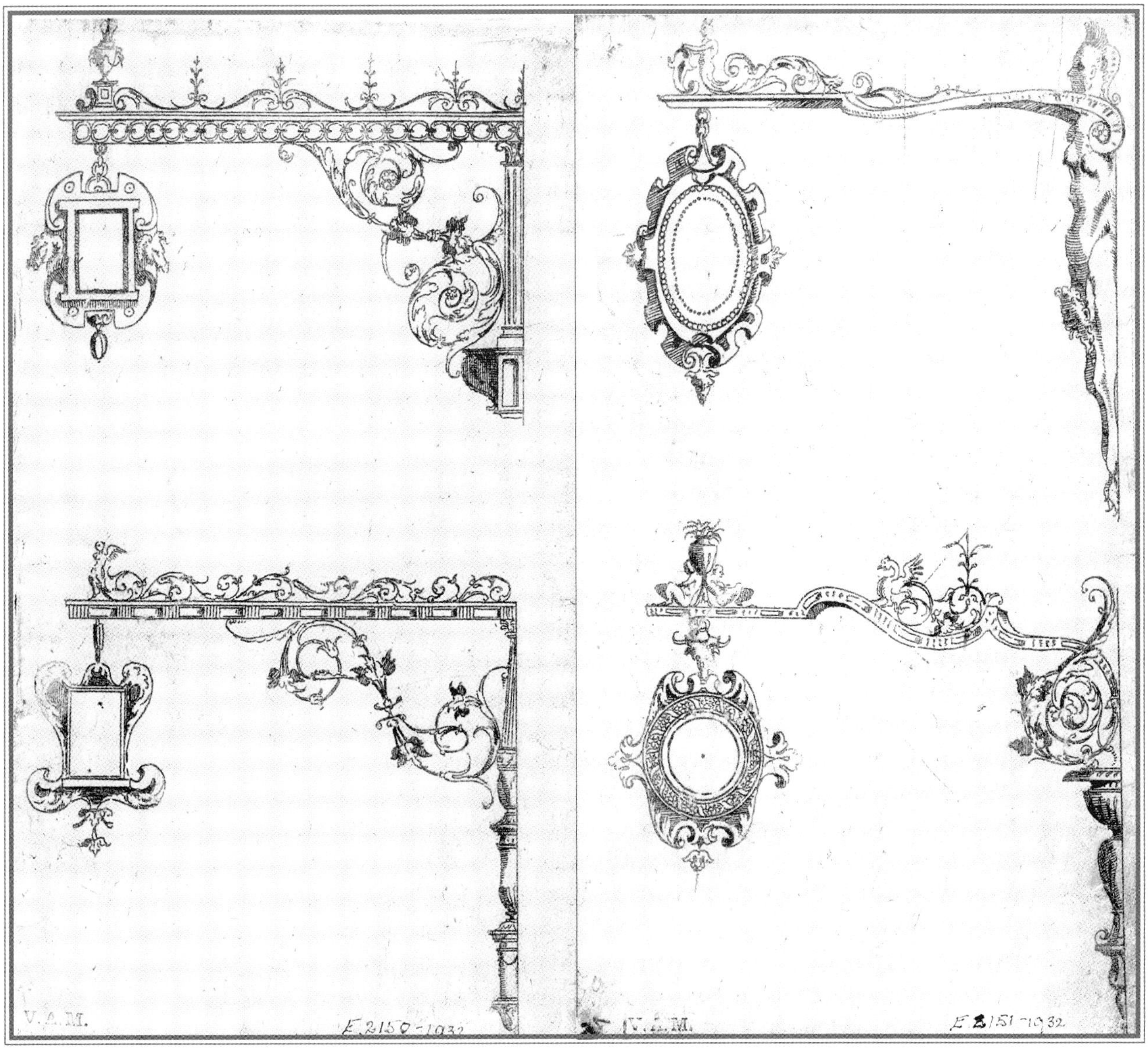

Plate 76. Designs for brackets and shop signs, Jacques Androuet du Cerceau. Victoria and Albert Museum, London.

'2 tapis de drap vert garnys d'Echantillons de rubans et de taffetas, et quatre battons garnys de bottes de paille couverts de papier blanc et noir, letout servant d'etalage' hung outside the shop of Guillaume Joseph Sornier in 1738, and were valued at 12 *livres*.[125] Three rods decorated with *étalages* and three *tapis d'étalage* were inventoried along with a glazed display case (*un montre vitrée d'étalage*), drawers and counters, a lantern, mirrors and various forms of seating in the shop of the perfumer Jean de Louy, rue St Honoré, in 1751.[126]

A dispute over shop display in Rouen uncovers something of the hostility towards the holders of privileges.[127] In August 1739, a *fayencier* named Delafosse told the guards of his corporation that, having received the title *priviligié suivant la cour* three months earlier, he had displayed outside his shop an appropriate sign and hanging. He complained that, immediately the signs were in place, the guards of the corporation arrived and compelled him to close the shop, tore down the signs and confiscated 30,000 *livres*' worth of goods. He pointed out that his

Plate 77. Design for a bracket, Louis Fordrin, 1723. Victoria and Albert Museum, London.

Plate 78. Shop, eighteenth century, rue des Prouvaires.

privilege gave him the right to use a special display, though his assertion that he was obliged to use them was probably not . . . 'son tableau et le tapis que les privilèges sont obligés de faire mettre au devant de leur boutique'. The corporation in Rouen argued that artisans were protected only in Paris, perhaps because they associated the privilege more closely with the practices of the Parisian corporations than with the King. After all, although the privilege itself gave considerable commercial advantages, the title was by this date merely symbolic of a much older system within which the King and court moved away from Paris, and were dependant on the merchants and artisans appointed to supply them as part of *la suite*. The legislation relating to the *marchands suivant la cour* is now somewhat obscure, but the Rouen document explains that formerly, when the King and court were outside Paris, the corporation of shoemakers (*cordonniers*) attempted to force them to close their shops, and thereby to prevent them trading in Paris under privileged protection when, by right, they should have been *suivant la cour*. Henri IV ordered that any individual in any part of France who held the privilege of artisan or merchant *suivant la cour* should be permitted to open shops wherever the court should be. Delafosse won his case.

Surviving evidence of the design of shop fronts, show them to have been decorated with fashionable motifs and, by the mid-century, glazed (plates 78 and 79). Honoré Guibert, sculptor and wood carver (*c.* 1720–1791) worked in Paris from about 1760. Eriksen has described his known work for private patrons as largely for commercial premises.[128] He made a shop front in the rue Saint Denis in about 1761, with a doorway in 'une architecture grecque', and a shop sign for the rue Saint Honoré in 1764 – a forty-foot high obelisk decorated with hieroglyphs. Guibert might be a candidate for the design of Granchez' shop. He was recommended to the *Batiments du Roi* by Joseph Vernet, for whom Guibert supplied frames for the paintings of the ports of France.[129]

It would appear that the glazing of shop windows was not customary much before the mid-century. In 1728, a French visitor to London said of the shop-windows he saw:

> What we do not, on the whole, have in France is glass like this, generally very fine and very clear. The shops are surrounded with it and usually the merchandise is arranged behind it, which keeps the dust off, whilst still displaying the goods to passers-by, presenting a fine sight from every direction.[130]

Plate 79. Shop front, Paris, c. 1750. Metropolitan Museum of Art, New York.

Crowds were often attracted to the shop window by a particular event or display. The Baronne d'Oberkirch described the shop of Daguerre in the rue Saint-Honoré:

> On ne pouvait approcher de son magasin, tant il y avait de monde; la foule se pressait devant un buffet de salle à manger d'un travail admirable. Il devrait etre porté en Angleterre chez le Duc de Northumberland.[131]

By 1745, at least, the finery of Parisian shops was notable. Daniel Defoe devoted a chapter in *The Complete London Tradesman* to the subject of the appropriate layout and decoration of shops, in which he proposed moderation and decency. He was appalled by the excesses of the French mode of painting and adorning a shop with gilding and carving in order to make a great show. Apparently this was becoming a vogue in England, and in true anti-Gallican polemic, he said:

> I take this to be a French humour, or a spice of it, turned English. And indeed we are famous for this, that when we do mimic the French, we generally do it to our hurt, and overdo the French themselves.
>
> The French are eminent for making a fine outside, when perhaps they want necessaries; and indeed a gay shop and a mean stock, is something like one of those people, with his laced ruffles without a shirt.[132]

The shop interior was very different from the environment of the workshop (plate 80). Luxury shops in the rue St Honoré, consisted of a *boutique* and *magasins* (plate 81). At the sign of the Grand Turc, Jean-Baptiste Buffault also dedicated a room to

Plate 80. Le Menuisier en meubles, L'Encyclopaedie, *1769. Victoria and Albert Museum, London.*

Plate 81. Le tapissier, L'Encyclopaedie, *1771. Victoria and Albert Museum, London.*

book-keeping.[133] The rooms directly behind the shop fronts seem to have been fairly narrow, and often other rooms in the building were used as commercial space. A contract for a five-floor building in the rue St Honoré shows a shop (*boutique*) at ground level and other rooms above.[134] These could be rented out as commercial or living accommodation. Inventories testify to this flexibilty, often describing a room filled with goods on an upper floor as a *chambre servant de magasin*. Gersaint's sign may represent the idea of the *boutique*, with a number of showrooms behind accessible through the open door at the centre back of the painting. In the 1760s, William Cole described Poirier's shop, Au Couronne d'Or in the rue St Honoré, as 'a Magazin of several lower Appartments'.[135] The inventories show that goods were often distributed over both ground and first floors. Matthew Boulton said that 'unprivate shops are only customary in London for at Paris all their finest shops are upstairs'.[136]

Like the names of the shops, several interiors were decorated to allude to royal patronage. Portaits of royal clients were hung in the shop of Rose Bertin, and described by one of her clients in May 1783:

> Je devais les bontés de mademoiselle Bertin au souvenir de madame la comtesse du Nord dont elle avait conservà la pratique. Elle avait son portrait dans son salon à coté de celui de la reine et de toutes les têtes couronnées qui l'honoraient de leur protection . . .[137]

Madame Eloffe, milliner to Marie Antoinette, also had a portrait of the Queen in her shop.[138] In the shop of the milliner Madame de St Quentin, *Au Magnifique* in the rue St Honoré, the customers and women working in the shop were presided over by a statue of Minerva, goddess of stitching (plate 82). Madamoiselle de St Quentin was famous for her *poupées de la rue St Honoré*, dolls dressed in the latest Paris fashions and circulated in foreign markets. Mercier described this as a 'mannequin précieux . . . enfin le prototype inspirateur'.[139]

Luxury shops formed part of the itinerary of Parisians and visitors alike. When in 1814, an almanac recorded the custom of promenading around the Parisian shops, the author was not recording a new phenonenon:

> Quand le mauvais temps interdit la promenade, la manière la plus ordinaire de gagner l'heure du dîner est de rendre des visites et de parcourir les magasins des joailliers, des lingères et des plus célèbres marchands de meubles, de modes ou de raretés.[140]

When Cole and Walpole went to Paris in 1765, they visited several mercers. Cole describes such a day:

> "After taking an airing about the Place Louis 15, we went to the shop of Madame Dulac, where the Earl of Fife with Mr Sheffield, son of Sir Charles Sheffield, were making Purchases . . . From this dangerous shop we went to another not a whit less so, Mr Poirier's, where the China and Toys and fine cabinets were rather richer and in greater abundance; being a magazine of several lower appartments full of them.[141]

In May 1782 Madame d'Oberkirch spent several hours in Granchez' shop, and she left having purchased a *joujou à la mode*.[142] She described an afternoon's leisure in the following terms:

> Après avoir diné avec les Beckendorf je fis des visites d'après-midi, et j'allai avec Madame de Skzrawonski aux *Variétés amusantes*, ou nous nous amusames beaucoup à *Jerome pointu*. La salle était plein de gens de la cour, qui riaient à gorge déployée. En sortant de la comédie, nous retournames dans les boutiques, en particulier chez les ébenistes et les quincailliers. Nous y vimes les plus belles choses du monde. J'étais rentrée chez moi à neuf heures.

Within the shop, conversations took place about the quality, price and availability of goods.[143] Although

Plate 82. Au Magnifique, *1777, Gabriel de St Aubin. E. Dacier* Gabriel de St Aubin, peintre, dessinateur et graveur *(1724–1780) 2 vols, Paris 1921–31.*

relationships between mercers and clients are less easy to document than many other aspects of Parisian commerce, several diaries record something of the quality of these relationships and suggest that the personality of the proprietor was often an important element in the process of purchasing. In 1765 Cole described his seduction by Madame Dulac and her wares, in

> that extravagant and expensive shop; where the Mistress was as tempting as the Things she sold, and where a younger man than myself would run the risk of losing that which is of more value than Money, except he was much upon his guard: so that it is no wonder that such a shop was thronged with customers, or that the Mistress of it might boldly set what price she thought proper upon her commodities: for both her person, tho' drawing towards forty, as well as I could judge, voice and manner, were so engaging, that it was almost next to impossible to refuse her what she asked for them, or to go away without purchasing something both to remember where you bought it, as well as the manufacture itself.[144]

His companion Walpole also remembered clearly the proprietor of this shop, and that of Poirier which they visited the same day. He wrote to Madame du Deffand in 1771 'I know the faces of every snuff-box and every teacup as well as those of Madame du Lac and Monsieur Poirier', thought it must be said that this observation may have been as much a comment on slow turnover and a disappointing lack of new stock as the attraction of the merchants.[145]

The seductiveness of female proprietors and shop assistants was notorious, and sexuality or sexual availability was sometimes a very clear part of a commercial transaction, particularly amongst those trades such as linens and sewing which principaly employed women (plate 83). Female consumers were similarly cast as seducers – of Granchez' shop, Mercier claimed that:

> Elle étincelle de tous ces bijoux frivoles que l'opulence paye, que la frivolité, que l'on donne aux femmes honnêtes qui n'acceptent de l'argent mais bien colfichets en or, parce qu'ils ont un air de décence.

The wives of less grand artisans and small-scale merchants were deemed by Mercier 'l'âme d'une boutique' and many female proprietors conducted their business with impressive condescension.[146] Of Madamemoiselle de Bertin's response to a visit from the Baronne d'Oberkirch, who was in search of a bonnet, the latter said:

> Elle m'en montra, ce jour-là, *elle-meme*, ce qui n'àtait pas une petit faveur, au moins une trentaine, tous différents . . .[147]

Personnal attention from a shopkeeper of particular repute was clearly a bonus. In order to be well-served by a proprietor, clients were sometimes obliged to put up with somewhat erratic behaviour from their suppliers. Madame Oberkirch explained her relationships with the milliners Bertin and Beaulard as follows:

> Après le concert de M. d'Albaret, j'allais chez Baulard, le marchand de modes et de colfichets. Alexandrine et lui étaient autrefois les deux célèbres, mais mademoiselle Bertin les a détrônés. Elle est venu de son quai de Gèvres, ou elle est restée si longtemps obscure, triompher de ses rivaux et les mettre tous au second rang. Baulard avait cependant la vogue pour les mantes; il les garnissait avec un gout exquis. Il me retint une heure en démonstrations et en cris contre mademoiselle Bertin, qui prenait des airs de duchesse, et qui n'était pas meme une bourgeoise. Je finis par m'arracher de ses confiances, que du reste il offrait à chaque nouvelle arrivant, et j'allai à la Comédie Italienne . . .[148]

A later visit was made to Beaulard to order a formal outfit for Oberkirch's presentation to the Queen.

> J'avais acheté l'étoffe et fait faire l'habit chez Baulard, mademoiselle Bertin m'ayant trop fait

Plate 83. Marchande lingère dans sa boutique, *1688. Bibliothèque Nationale de France, Paris.*

> attendre. L'étoffe était d'un brocart d'or, à fleurs naturelles, admirablement beau; j'en reçus mille compliments. Il n'y entrait pas moins de vingt-trois aulnes; c'était d'un poids énorme.[149]

On 4 June, she returned to buy a coat from Baulard and remarked that 'Il fut plus discret cette fois'.

Her diary makes clear both her dependence on and her personal opinion of both Baulard and Bertin. Of the latter's bankruptcy in 1787, she reported:

> Cet empire des modes subit un grand cataclysme. Mademoiselle Bertin, si fière, si haute, si insolente même, qui *travaillait* avec Sa Majesté, mademoiselle Bertin étalant sur ses mémoires en grandes lettres *Marchande de modes de la reine*; mademoiselle Bertin vient de faire banqueroute. Il est vrai que sa banqueroute n'est point plébéienne, c'est une banqueroute de grande dame, deux millions! c'est quelque chose pour une marchande de chiffons.[150]

The polite behaviour represented in diaries and in paintings such as Gersaint's sign and the dialogues between merchant and client contrasted with the apparently frequent occurences of brawls and thefts, documented in the records of the *commisssaires de police*. For example, a merchant upholsterer Jean-Michel de Lerpine alleged that he had experienced an assault in December 1756 by a *traiteur* named Desmoulins, which was motivated by de Lerpine's refusual to pay his bill of 133 *livres* 8 *sous*.[151] The shop's apprentice upholsterer, Gautrot, was in the shop with de Lerpine's wife at the time (the shop was full of people, he said) who described Desmoulins' entry with a bayonet at the end of a gun. Another upholsterer, Charles Antoine Languigneux, aged thirty-nine, experienced a theft, though was fortunate enough to avoid any violent confrontation. Indeed, he did not even observe that a piece of Gobelins tapestry two and a half ells high by 4 wide, worth 600 *livres*, was missing for some time.[152]

Some of these police reports are useful not only in revealing another side of commercial life, but also because the precision with which each witness's testimony was recorded often included descriptions of shops and the way in which goods were displayed. For instance, small items were notoriously easy to steal. A goldsmith in the rue St Honoré reported that a pair of women's buckles had been stolen from the glass surface of a display case.[153] In another case, René Laflaiche was on his way back to his shop in the Palais Royal at about 6pm. His wife told him that a thief had been taken to the *corps de garde*. Whilst she was replying to someone who was bargaining with her over some buckles, she had seen the thief examining several pairs of buckles attached to some chains which were hanging on a hook outside the shop – a typical *étalage* of the late eighteenth-century arcades of small shops at the Palais Royal. The thief took the buckles in his hand, then at a moment when he thought she was not watching, tore off a pair which he threw to the ground when he heard shouts of 'thief'. The buckles and the piece of chain were taken to the guard. Laflaiche declared that the buckles were his and identified them by means of their description and a tag attached to them with the number 2756 in his writing.[154]

Despite these intrusions, the environment of luxury shops in Paris seems to have been controlled in a number of ways – in terms of comfort, security, sophistication and style. The design of exterior and interior elements of a shop contributed to the distinction of one business from another, and, in the most successful examples, helped to create an impact which entered into printed and conversational discourse. Although Granchez is an exceptional example, both because of the range and success of his marketing strategies and the amount of surviving eveidence which provides a basis for documenting his career, many of the devices employed by him were used by other merchants seeking to occupy the high throne of fashion and to seduce the public.

NOTES

1. *Oberkirch* Paris 1970, 172.
2. *Memoire à consulter at consultation pour . . . les mds de . . Paris*, 1761.
3. The *Echantillons Richelieu*, see chapter 5.
4. 'A Gentleman . . . had nicely examined into the Cost of every Sort and we as exactly compared them with our own, and found them to be considerably under the Price of the same here; and what added to their Value, they were generally more substantial than ours, though for less Money: the Collector of these samples has been dead for some years, and I fear the good Use that might have been made of them died with him, which is the more to be regretted . . . (Beawes, 6th edition 1773, 514).
5. The list of shops patronized by the English Embassy during the 1760s and 70s has survived, and was published recently Pradère 1993.
6. On English racehorses in Paris and the tradition of riding in the English manner see de Blomac 1994.
7. On *anglomania* in France from the 1740s to 1780s see Grieder 1985.
8. See, for example, the painting entitled *Thé à l'angloise*, Musée du Louvre.
9. See Grieder for a list of novels and stories 1740–89 (Grieder 1985, 151–162).
10. See Eriksen 1962 and 1972, Gordon and Déchery 1980 and L'Objet d'Art, 1988.
11. Gordon and Déchery 1980.
12. Gordon and Déchery 1980.
13. Lacombe 1784, 173–4. I would like to thank John Styles for providing this reference.
14. Snodin (ed.) 1984, 16. The Anti-Gallican Society, founded in London in 1745, produced a print 'The Imports of Great Britain from France' which commented specifically on French luxury imports (reproduced C24 in Snodin (ed.) 1984, 49). For further discussion of the Rococo in Britain see also Hind (ed.) 1986. The plethora of studies on the consumption of French fashions in Britain include de Bellaigue 1967, 1968, 1977 and 1995, John 1995, Gilbert and Murdoch 1993, Snodin and Cornforth 1992, Watson 1967 [1].
15. Gournay 1789–90, 562.
16. On luxury steel production in Paris see Leben 1995 [1].
17. Gournay 1789–90, 564.
18. Young 1789.
19. Marigny stated his preferance for simplicity when ordering English furniture (Gordon and Déchery 1980).
20. Her daybook (AVP D^5B^6 2813 *Blakey*) covers the period between November 1766 and March 1769.
21. Turner, 1993.
22. AN MC LXXVIII, 817, 29 December 1776 *Blakey à Jousset de Lizy*.
23. AVP D^4B^6 *carton* 44 *dossier* 2490, 10 March 1772 *Blakey*.
24. Some of her creditors drew on the London bankers John and Jacob Baumgartner. Her credit normally extended to six months, and in one case to twelve.
25. AN Y13701 *Factures diverses de Londres 1769*.
26. Brest, Bordeaux, Bourgogne, Lorient, the port of Paix, Lisle Bourbon (26,262 *livres*), and Perou. Goods worth 4800 *livres* sent to the Cap Francais in 1766 were still not paid for in 1772. Over 3000 *livres* was owed by Delary in St Mare, Isle St Dominique, for bandages and clocks sent via La Rochelle. Tardivy, also in St Domininque, owed 25,000 *livres* outstanding from a transaction which involved an exchange of goods between Mme Blakey and the colonies. She had been paid only 11,000 *livres* to date.
27. The merchandise was to be shipped via Nantes. (AN Y13701 *Factures diverses de Londres 1769*).
28. Granges of London owed 10,000, Huntsman and Asline owed nearly 80,000 *livres*, and Gorterat about half that sum.

29. AN MC LXXVIII, 786, 24 November 1773, *Blakey & S. Bournisian*.
30. Barbers' bowls were of 'cuirs peints a fleurs' and trays for bottles were of painted wood.
31. The smallest *casserolle* was valued at 30 *livres* apiece, medium at 36 and large at 48. Bills in English translate these as 'plated stew pans'. Other silver plated goods were *sceaux* and *verrieres*.
32. Who appeared as regular suppliers in the 1760s (AN Y13701 *Factures diverses de Londres 1769* and AN Y13702 *Régistre de factures de marchandise tirées de'Angleterre commence le 27 mai 1766*. I would like to thank Christian Baulez for suggesting that I look at these papers).
33. 11 cups and 2 saucers were valued at 6 *livres* 10 *sous*.
34. 7 vases 'non garnies' (total 21 *livres*) and 1 garniture of three with mounts (300 *livres*).
35. A typical example was the pair 'de flambeaux a colonne brizée cannelure dorée guirlande argenté' 48 *livres*.
36. Labels of this description were supplied in 1769 by James Monbray of London (AN Y13702).
37. Including carving tools ('80 outils de sculpteur') screwdrivers, compasses, components of clock movements and clockmakers' tools (15 *outils d'horloger d'acier*), hammers, pinions, gilded nails for wooden panelling (*boiseries*) and gilt bronze door handles for glazed doors.
38. Spectacles were supplied in November 1768 by Dolland, near St Paul, London (AN Y13702 *Régistre de factures de marchandise tirées de'Angleterre commence le 27 mai 1766*).
39. 27 pairs were valued at 252 *livres*.
40. 'Acier couvert d'argent'. (AN Y13702).
41. AN Y13702.
42. Blakey bought from Hanscombe many whips, including '4 beaux fouets de Cabriolet de 5 pieds et demie garnis d'argent avec touches de soye', 16 *livres* 16 *sois* each and 'six grands fouets d'academie à la Rochefouchuld garnis d'argent et giselé proprement for the total price of 64 *livres* 16 *sous* (AN Y13702 *Régistre de factures de marchandise tirées de'Angleterre commence le 27 mai 1766*). A letter to her from Hanscombe states that her whips were ready (i.e. made to order), and that they would be sent with six months' credit. British suppliers provided cloth for riding habits. For example, Jacques Charles Grangé supplied cloth for redingotes, along with superfine cloth and watchglasses (AN Y13702).
43. AN Y13701 *Factures diverses de Londres 1769*.
44. *Tabatieres* and *bonbonnieres* were listed of both tortoiseshell and 'carton' in pink, grey and other colours . In the latter material were listed a particular form of box called 'platitudes'.
45. For Marigny's correspondence with Reinach on the merits of English mahogany dining tables see Gordon and Déchery 1980, 94.
46. The largest and most expensive item was the mahogany table in three sections priced at 176 *livres* 8 *sous*. Two dining tables and a tea table were priced together at 108 *livres* (AN Y13702 *Régistre de factures de marchandise tirées de'Angleterre commence le 27 mai 1766*).
47. Roubo 1772, 973.
48. AVP D5B6 *régistre* 1967. Kjellberg gives a brief biography and quotes from the inventory taken after the death of Canebas' wife in 1769: 'sécretaires, commodes, guéridons, bureaux, tables à coulisse et à patins, tables de nuit à cylindre, consoles, toilettes d'homme et de femmme, chiffonières, fauteuils de bureau et autres objets, pour la plupart en acajou massif, ornés de cuivre et dans le meilleur goñt' (Kjellberg 1989, 146).
49. Also '2 ecrans a table moyens garniture argenté et pied garnie et le bougeoir' (132 *livres*) and 2 small screens *a panneaux*, delivered on 6 November 1765. (Joseph Canabas became *maître* in 1766, see Kjellberg and de Bellaigue 1974).
50. Other types of mahogany table included 'une table à deux étages a rebords découpés laditte en bois d'acajou monté sur 4 pieds de biche, 60 livres and a pied en bois d'acajou sculpté à cremailliere et tournante sous un plateau de tole d'angleterre vernis 29 *livres*' (AVP D5B6 régistre 1697 Dubuisson). On 11 Febraury 1769, he supplied two each of the following; *pied a bascule*, *pied tournante*, *pied a deux etages*, for 36, 26 and 32 *livres* respectively (AVP D5B6 690 *Brouillon 1767*). The term *bascule* refers to a table designed with a mechanism which allows the table top to be fixed vertically when not in use.
51. AVP D5B6 2464 Dubuisson.
52. AVP D5B6 2464 Dubuisson, 10 October 1767.
53. M. Peeter.
54. D5B6 régistre 2464 Dubuisson. The salts cost 36 *livres*.
55. AN MC CXVIII, 454, 18 December 1748 Bentabole-Rohault.
56. Verlet gives Granchez' father's name as Jean-Baptiste who died 8 August 1749 (Verlet 1989, 444). The names of Charles and Jacques Charles Grangés of London in the late 1760s in Madame Blakey's correspondance are intriguing – however no documents have yet come to light suggesting a family relationship with the Parisian Granchez. The names have been gallicised, and in fact the true English name may well have been Granger. I would like to thank Patrick Leperlier for giving me access to his notes on Granchez.
57. The marriage took place on 13 September 1761. Her parents were Pierre Leveque, *perfumer*, and Marie Therese Lefevre.
58. *L'Avant Coureur* 1768. Lemattre described in 1913 a *brocanteur* in Dunkirk who was so impressed by Granchez' success in Paris that he attempted to set up a similar enterprise in the rue St Julien in Dunkirk some time before 1808 (Lemattre 1913).
59. The papers of the notaries of Dunkirk were largely destroyed, and no record of Granchez' early business practice appear to have survived.
60. The marriage took place on 12 June 1784. He was an *avocat en Parlement*, living in the rue Guenegaud, Paris.
61. AN Y9331 9 April 1767, cited by de Bellaigue 1974, 861.

62. De Bellaigue 1974, 861.
63. In 1787, following the registration of Granchez' bankruptcy, a contract was drawn up to protect his future inheritance from his mother (AN MC IX, 817, 17 September, Granchez and 2 October 1787, Granchez.
64. *L'Avant Coureur*, December 1767.
65. Vidal and Duru 1911, 218.
66. See Manuevre and Reith 1994.
67. Vidal and Duru 1911, 218. In an inventory of 1784, the Duchesse de Villeroy was listed as owing Granchez 938 *livres*.
68. *Le Monde Illustré* 28 March 1914. I would like to thank M. Porhel for sending me information on Lemattre's history of the Paris shop.
69. De Bellaigue 1974, 861.
70. Bill dated 1813,(AN 301 AD 209). I would like to thank Patrick Leperlier for this reference.
71. At the end of the nineteenth century, Lemattre described the eighteenth-century shop and assumed the Carnavalet sign to have been the original. He said 'Le vogue du Petit Dunkerque, battue en brèche par la concurrance, diminua d'importance au déclin du siècle dernièr . . . L'immeuble . . . est aujourd'hui occupé par des marchands de vins et des bureaux de tabacs' (Lemattre 1898). He failed to secure the sign for the museum at Dunkirk, and it subsequently entered the collection of the Musée Carnavalet in Paris.
72. Clarendon's London house was said to have been named the 'Petit Dunkerque' (*Archives Historiques et Littéraires* 1852, 119–20).
73. In Dubois' inventory was a list of painted furniture (de Bellaigue 1974).
74. Five examples are conserved in the Musée du Louvre (Grandjean 1981, cat 45, 128, 145, 147, 255. 145, a snuff box and 147, a sweet box, are both marked by Charles Le Bastier).
75. Mercier 1787, 82.
76. Advertised in the *Mercure de France*, 1774, see Snowman 1966.
77. Le Mercier 1787, 82.
78. Henard 1908–9, 433.
79. A Thomas Gray, jeweller, was trading at this date from 42, Sackville St, London (*The London Goldsmith 1200–1800* 1935, 163). Gray appears to have acted as an agent of sorts, in that he found suppliers of English goods for Reinach, who was during the 1770s making orders in England on behalf of the Marquis de Marigny (see Gordon and Déchery 1980). I would like to thank Tessa Murdoch for sending me details of this piece, and Richard Edgecumbe for providing information on Thomas Gray.
80. AVP D^4B^6 *carton* 91, *dossier* 6280, 15 September 1787.
81. AN MC IX, 814, 22 October 1787, Granchez.
82. AN MC LXXVIII, 817, 29 December 1776 *Blakey-Jousset de Lizy*.
83. Oberkirch reprinted 1970, 172.
84. AN MC XI, 888, wife of Charles-Raymond Granchez. Most inventories gave valuations for shop fittings under 1,000 *livres* and often considerably less than this. Another shop with a highly valued interior was that of Jean-Baptiste Buffault, Au Grand Turc, rue St Honoré (see chapters 2 and 5).
85. Oberkirch reprinted 1970, 172, Mercier 1787, 81.
86. Vol IV, 135, cited by Havard, 531.
87. 8^0 Z Le Senne 11630. Jean Lafaye was born in Grasse, Provence in 1728. His marriage contract with Marie Therese Noel from Reims, in which he was described as *marchand parfumeur* from Lille, was drawn up at Dunkerque on 24 May 1752. One of the witnesses was Noel Joseph Julien *geographe du roi*. Lafaye and his wife had 6 children born between 1758 and 1769. I would like to thank M. Porhel of the Archives de la Ville de Dunkerque for supplying this biographical information.
88. *Mercure de France*, October 1773, 48–9. I am grateful to Ulrich Leben for sending me this reference.
89. Two such bill headings survive in the household papers of the Chevalier de Fitz-James (T186) and the Duc de Tremoille (T1051), dated 1775 and 1777 respectively.
90. *L'Avant Coureur*: December 1767, January 1768, January 1770, April 1770, May 1770, December 1770, April 1771, September 1771, October 1771, July 1772, November 1772. I am indebted to Patrick Leperlier for these references. Granchez' advertisements in the *Mercure de France* were dated: September 1774, April 1775, January 1776, July 1776, January 1777.
91. AN MC IX 795, 4 October 1784 Leveque.
92. *Mercure de France*, January 1777.
93. AN MC IX, 795, 4 October, 1784, Leveque.
94. Tôle amalgamé en argent' (*Mercure de France*, April 1775).
95. An inkstand with twelve such plaques, with the inscription 'Du Petit Dunkerque', was sold in 1912 (Hotel Drouot, 7 June 1912, lot 231). A plant holder with two pots also of painted tôle were sold a few years later ((Hotel Drouot, 30–31 May 1919, lot 48). I would like to thank Patrick Leperlier for these references.
96. *L'Avant Coureur*, October 1771.
97. Snowman 1990, 233, plate 478.
98. *Mercure de France*, January 1777.
99. AN MC IX 794, 4 October 1784, Leveque.
100. Pierre Henri Mallet was listed, for the firm of Mallet and Bourdillon, Geneva.
101. Baumgartner and Hoffsletter 26,128 *livres*, Glover and Frey 7,113, Gray 3,181, Holy and Wilkinson 1,026.
102. For example, in 1778 'Vous trouvez les serrures chers . . . Tout et diablement cher ici quand on veut avoir quelque chose de bien fait'. (Gordon and Déchery 1980, 105).
103. See appendix 11.
104. See Delafrenaye's trade card dated 1737 (British Museum).

105.

October 1784	26,957
November	20,836
December	29,567
January 1785	47,745
February	29,696
March	27,465
April	27,478
May	22,452
June	24,944
July	20,406
August	10,982
September	8,700
October	5,875
November	1,685
TOTAL	304,988

AN MC IX 813, *inventaire après décès Margueritte Leveque*.

106. AVP DC[6] 29 fos 89v° and 176v° (de Bellaigue 1974, 861).

107. Assets of 392,598 against debts of 374,898 (AN MC IX 813, *Leveque*).

108. He had over two hundred clients in 1787 (including Vernet, who owed him 117 *livres*) and was committed until 1790 to make payments to suppliers every three months. He owed money to 100 suppliers, about a third of whom were present for the assessment of his financial state. The formal bankruptcy papers are dated 15 September 1787 (AVP D4B6, 91, 6280).

109. The *Larousse du XXe siècle* stated that 'L'usage de ce nom [le Petit Dunkerque] persista bien après la fermeture de ce magasin, et il est plusieurs fois fait allusions dans les romans de H. de Balzac, à des colfichets du 'petit Dunkerque'. Lemattre cited such a passage from Balzac – 'Sur le manteau de velours de la cheminée s'élevait la pendule alors à la mode. On voyait un peit dunkerque assez bien garni, des jardinières en porcelaine chinoise luxueusement montées' (H. Balzac, *Cousin Bette*, 1846, in Lemattre 1898). According to Lemattre, painted tôle wares were generally called 'Petit Dunkerques'. He cited Ernest d'Hervilly's memories of furniture highly valued by his grandparents as follows. 'Un Petit Dunkerque est un meuble de salon de la taille d'une chiffoniere , en acajou, en bois de St Lucie ou en marqueterie, couvert d'un joli marbre, gris, blanc ou bleu, avec galérie à jour de cuivre ciselé . . . Très suvent un dossier également proportionnée, avexc un miroir fixe,sélevait garni de tablettes . . . On en voit au Musée des Arts Décoraifs . . . et au Louvre parmi les meubles amenés de Saint-Cloud; à Trianon également et enfin dans les estampes d'intérieur des jolies petits maîtres du XVIIIe siècle' (Lemattre 1898).

110. Mercier 1787, 82.

111. See in particular McKendrick, Brewer and Plumb 1982. For later critiques on this, see especially Brewer and Porter 1995.

112. A later trade card with an image *Au Bonheur* (Musée Carnavalet).

113. AVP D[5]B[6] *régistre* 2464.

114. Many of the highly designed cards were made for merchants who had strong links with the engraving trades, such as the painters and goldsmiths (see for example, Antione Dieu's trade card of 1698 and Formey's card of *c.* 1740).

115. AN MC XXXVIII, 609 Gaillard.

116. Mercier descibes some of these in an oft-cited passage in *Le Tableau de Paris* 1787. The collection of ironwork of the Musée le Secq de Tournelles in Rouen includes many signs, often painted on metal or of forged metal, as well as brackets and other architectural ironwork. See also Paris, Musée des Arts et Traditions Populaires 1977.

117. AN MC II, 425, 1 August 1726.

118. AN MC XC, 476, 20 Jan 1778, *inventaire après décès* Marie Francoise Richard, wife of Antoine Marie Menard, *marchand mercier quincaillier*.

119. AN MC CXVII, 800, 25 May 1755, Pucelle.

120. *Ordonnance du bureau des finances de la généralité de Paris, concernant les Enseignes dans toutes l'étendue de la ville et faubourgs de Paris*. Paris, 25 Mai 1761. *Reflexions des six corps* . . . , Paris 1761, *Memoire à consulter at consultation pour . . . mds de* . . Paris, 1761, *Ordonnance de Police*, 17 Dec 1761. The merchants' appeal was turned down, by *Arrest de la Cour de Parlement*, 7 Dec 1761. *Vidal et Duru, p. 253*.

121. According to the *Reflexions des six corps* . . . , shop signs in 1666 were limited to a height above the pavement of 13½ feet with a maximum overhang of 3 feet. The dimensions of the sign were to be 18 inches × 2 feet high maximum.

122. *Arrêt de commune*, August 1792, cited in Vidal and Duru 1911.

123. AN MC CXVIII, 454, 18 December 1748 Bentabole-Rohault.

124. Oberkirch 1970 , 312. (A guide to Paris describes the hospital 'L'Hopital des Quinze Vingts, bâti par Eudes de Montreuil, et fondé par S. Louis vers l'an 1260 pour trois cents aveugles, dont on publie que les premiers qui l'ont occupé, eurent les yeux crevés par les Infidéles dans la guerre de la Terre Sainte. Mais l'opinion commune est que l'Histoire ne faisant point mention de ce fait, il est plus raisonable de croire que ça été pour retenir des aveugles mendians, comme cela est à present. Cet hopital se divise en aveugles, & en voyans pour conduire les aveugles . . .' *Curiositez de Paris* 1733 vol. 1, 280).

125. AN MC LIII, 286, 24 January 1738, Sailly.

126. AN Y11314, 24 December 1751, de Louy.

127. AN V[3] 192 fo 191 r°.

128. Eriksen 1974, 189. Guibert's work is illustrated in plates 66–7, 345–8.

129. Eriksen 1974, 189.

130. *Voyage en Angleterre*, 1728, f° 29, cited in F. Braudel, 1982.

131. Oberkirch 1970, 306.

132. The passage continued 'I cannot but think a well-furnished shop, with a decent outside, is much better to a tradesman, than a fine shop and few goods. I am sure it will be much more to his

satisfaction when he casts up his year's account; for his fine shop will weigh but sorrily in his account of profit and loss; it is all a dead article, it is sunk out of his first money before he makes a shilling profit; and may be some years a recovering, as trade may go with him. Some people tell us indeed, that putting a good face upon things goes as far as the real merit of the things themselves; and that a fine, painted, gilded shop, among the rest, has a great influence upon the people, draws customers and brings trade. And they run a great length in this way of talk; which is only satirizing on the blindness and folly of mankind; and showing how the world are to be taken in, and deluded, and imposed upon, by outside and tinsel. But I do not grant that the world in general is thus to be deluded; perhaps in some cases it may be so, where the women, and they must be the weaker of the sex, too, are chiefly concerned; or where the fops and fools of the age resort . . . (Defoe, 210–211).

133. AN MC LIII, 488, 30 August 1772, Buffault-Lenormand.

134. For living arrangements within buildings in Paris see especially Roche (1981) and Pardailhé Galabrun (1988).

135. Cole 1931, 245.

136. Cited in Henard 1908–9, 430.

137. Oberkirch 1970, 311–12.

138. Eloffe, vol 2.

139. Mercier, 1787, 291.

140. *Almanac de modes et annuaire des modes réunis*, 2ème année, Paris, 1815, BHVP Rés 700613, 20.

141. Cole 1765, 244–5. My thanks to Clive Wainwright for suggesting that I look at Cole's diary. Cole describes the purchases at these two shops as follows. From Dulac 'Mr Walpole, among other Things, bought three most beautiful Vases for a Chimney, of Blew enamel, set in gilt Copper, as a present for Mr. Chute of the Vine in Hampshire: they cost nineteen guineas, and were the most elegant Ornaments for the place they were designed, the middle one being larger than the two others'. At Poirier's 'Mr Walpole, amongst other things, bought an elegant tripod of gilt Copper, in an antique fashion of about 4 Inches high to burn Incense, or Pastilles à bruler, on: it cost 3 guineas. I bought a single coffee cup and Saucer of the enamelled Chantilly manufactured china, for which I gave 12 livres, or half a guinea'.

142. Her companion, Maria Feodorovna, travelling incognito in Paris as the Comtesse du Nord, purchased many items to be shipped back from Russia. (Her purchases in Paris also included a number of items from Daguerre, amongst which was the 'bureau plat' illutrated in colour plate 6).

143. For a discussion on conversation in the work of Antoine Watteau see Vidal 1992, especially 'L'Enseigne de Gersaint and the Conversational Structure of the Artistic Sign' (173–202). Unfortunately Vidal does not discuss the examination of the toilet set except in terms of the celebration of narcissism.

144. Sèvres porcelain, said Cole, "is of an admirable beauty and texture . . . Indeed it ought to be superabundantly eminent and excellent, as the Price is excessive. I was with Mr. Walpole one Day at a great shop in Paris, Mr. Poirier's, where it was sold, and saw him give 10 louis or guineas for a single coffee cup, saucer, and a little square sort of Soucoupe, or under-saucer, to set them on; they were indeed the highest finished Things of the Kind which can be conceived: perfect jewels that deserve to be set in gold frames to be admired and looked at, but never to be used for fear of breaking them: at the same time, at another shop of the same sort, in the rue Saint Honoré, at one Madame Dulac's, he bought a chocolate cup and saucer for his nephew, the Bishop of Exeter, which cost between three and four guineas, and was a great beauty of a less gaudy cast. I was tempted to purchase two or three things of the lowest price I could meet with, a specimen of this beautiful manufacture: accordingly I bought half a dozen cups with saucers, for coffee, which cost 9 livres each Cup and Saucer, the whole 54 livres, (or above 2 guineas considerably), for the Set, with a neat sugar dish and Cover at 12 livres: being the lowest priced things I could meet with in that that extravagant and expensive shop Cole (1765, 233–4).

145. p. 233 fn. 1, letter to Mme Du Deffand, July 31, 1771.

146. Mercier 1787, 173.

147. Oberkirch reprinted 1970, 311–12.

148. Oberkirch reprinted 1970, 317.

149. Oberkirch reprinted 1970, 324.

150. The text continued 'Les petites-maitresses sonr aux abois; à qui s'adresser désormais? qui tournera un pouf? qui arrondira un toquet? qui posera des plumes? qui inventera un nouveau juste? On assure que mademoiselle Bertin cédera à toutes les larmes et continuera son commerce. On dit aussi qu'elle a été ingrate pour la reine, et que sans cela Sa Majesté ne l'eut point abandonné dans son malheur, bien qu'elle fut occupé de tristes choses et d'intérêts plus graves'. (Oberkirch reprinted 1970, 478).

Rose Bertin's business is discussed in detail by Langlade 1911, and in summary by Garland 1968. The façade of her shop, rue de la Loi, no. 26 was illustrated in *Collection des Maisons de Commerce de Paris les Mieux Décorées*, Musée Carnavalet, Paris. It was called the Grand Mogul, after prevailing taste for Turkish things (Langade 1911).

151. AN Y11314, 4 December 1756.

152. AN Y15000 5 Novembre 1779. Languigneux' shop was in the rue de la Harpe, paroisse St Benoit. The tapestry was described as a 'Piece de tapisserie de Gobelins fraiche comme neuve representant des enfants jardinieres a petittes bordures doublée en plain de grosse toile grise de la valeur de 600 livres environ'.

153. AN Y11370, 12 July 1768, Maillard.

154. Y12644, 10 sept 1789, 'vol d'une paire de boucles d'argent fait à la boutique du Sr. Laflaiche md bijoutier au Palais Royal suivant procès verbal 29 aout 1798'. Other witnesses

elaborated – the *lieutenant* Roussel described the buckles as 'boucles d'argent de forme ovale ciselée à poites de diamans avec chapes et ardillons de fer.' Louis Seguneau, *bourgeois de Paris*, 66, rue de Clery, was looking at some buckles when the theft took place. François Fenart, another mercer, at no. 30, Palais Royal, who was thirty-four years old, followed the rush over to the guard, and declared that he recognized Leroux as the man who had stolen three pairs of silver buckles from him on two separate occasions in May 1789. Leroux had been arrested a few days later for stealing silver buckles from Venant, *md bijoutier* at the Palais Royal. He said that Jean Baptiste Leroux was a *garçon tappissier*.

CONCLUSION

The case study of an individual such as Granchez provides much in the way of detailed information about the strategies of an individual mercer who sought to compete at the most fashionable end of the market. However, broader questions about the mercers' role in eighteenth-century French commercial developments, and their significance within the history of design remain to be evaluated. Colbert's grand plan to turn France into a great manufacturing and trading nation clearly depended, in part at least, on the commercial activities of the mercers, and his support of the Six Corps of merchants and his special relationship with the mercers is indicative of their significance in his mercantilist scheme. Evidence of the mercers' intersection with so many of the trades in Paris and provincial France, the large European trading companies importing from the Orient, other specialist European merchants and factories and with the colonies, shows that there were very few branches of commerce within which they did not play some role.

Statistics on the macro-economics of the French luxury trades are virtually non-existent. At the individual and neighbourhood levels, however, it is possible to investigate the role of these trades in some detail. In the area surrounding the rue St Honoré, the mercers appear to have been central to the development of a *quartier de luxe* which, by the end of the eighteenth century, was a market place internationally renowned for its shops, goods and fashionable street culture. Their strategies were based on stocking a wide range of goods in terms of design, quality and price and on pricing these goods aggressively both at the novelty end of the market and at the end of their fashionable life in second-hand markets.

The structure of the eighteenth-century luxury market place was well understood by the mercers. They knew that the most novel designs and expensive patterns of silks were best marketed first at Versailles, and that the Court's authentication of these patterns was as close as they would get to a guarantee that they would be able to market them successfully in other quarters. A hierarchy of markets based on a diminishing sensitivity to novelty in design placed Paris after Versailles, followed by the provinces, foreign courts, cities and the colonies. This pattern of marketing was by no means exclusive to the silk industry – Granchez exploited court approval of his designs and Mademoiselle Bertin was notorious for palming off out-of-date fashions (in Parisian terms) onto provincial clients.

These markets were closely related to the profiles of stock held by mercers specializing in a number of different branches of commerce, as the inventories demonstrate. Each inventory included a range of goods, in terms of design, value and quality. A premium could be charged for goods which combined new design, expensive raw materials and high quality workmanship. Special commissions of furniture and bronzes supplied to the court and aristocracy were far more costly than the items held in stock in the mercers' shops. The demand for novelty was met by a number of design strategies which included new designs created in their entirety (often on paper), adaptations of existing designs and alterations made to existing objects. Although many of the mercers' goods were ready-made (particularly those which were imported), the form, decoration and function of many of these goods were transformed by the mercers' practive of *enjolivement*. The combination of elements of different materials, origins and dates, such as the porcelain, lacquer and bronze confections described in chapter 4, exemplifies another approach to design employed by the mercers. This practice of assembling new forms of ornament from objects kept in stock seems to have represented a new kind of design process unique to these merchants. Their role was therefore often very different from the kind of design process which produced drawings and prints, and which forms the subject of the historiography of design in early modern Europe.

These design strategies allowed the mercers to manipulate the concept of *nouveauté* in collusion with their suppliers, in order to satisfy demand with relatively minor design changes. Up-market objects often differed only slightly and the desire for a certain level of difference, or distinction could apparently be satisfied by the introduction of relatively minor changes into a range of forms. Thus designs for patterned silks were considered by the Lyonnais to have a life of fifteen to twenty years, a series of *bonheurs-du-jour* with Sèvres porcelain plaques were made over a period of fifteen years or so with only minor variations and even Granchez' gold boxes were not always of such novel design as he might wish his clients to believe. Even direct copies were not denigrated in the way that they now are. A lively second-hand market encompassed goods of extremely high value such as old Boulle and Japanese lacquer furniture and porcelain classified by origin, date and pattern. The high cost of materials and workmanship were two factors in the maintenance of high values within the market place for second-hand luxury goods. However, old styles and used objects could also be sold down at competitive prices at the end of the fashion cycle, and fierce disputes between the corporations of mercers, upholsterers and second-hand dealers over the rights to trade in old goods bear witness to the lucrative nature of this market.

In all of these markets, the mercers operated at the nexus of the supply-demand cycle. This very phrase immediately conjures up a history of debates about production and consumption. However the question 'supply or demand?' which has long been linked to historical enquiry into the nature of nineteenth- and twentieth-century economies seems in some ways unhelpful for discussions of the luxury trades. This is in part because luxury markets are perhaps more likely than any other to be 'demand-led', in the sense that they usually comprise consumers who are especially sensitive to changes in novelty, fashion and taste, and who demand highly differentiated goods. A further complication in using the supply-demand equation in relation to the eighteenth-century French luxury trades is that it is rather difficult to define the point at which supply meets demand, and therefore to characterize the relationship between the two. Were the mercers suppliers or were they, in a sense, demanding consumers in their own right – themselves representing a market to many workshops and factories? What of their place within a string of intermediaries, and their role as finishers (*enjoliveurs*) of part-finished goods? The mercers specializing in luxuries were in many ways much closer to their consumers than to their suppliers. This relationship is represented symbolically in Gersaint's shop sign, in which the three clients examining the toilet set are positioned on both sides of the sales counter.

What is perhaps more interesting in the case of the mercers is the question of their position *between* consumers and clients, and their negotiations with each group over the look, price and quality of goods in pursuit of their own business interests. To best serve their own aims, they exploited information about fashion and taste in order to acquire from suppliers goods which were highly likely to be desirable to their clientele (often adapted or finished to the mercers' or clients' precise specification), whilst simultaneously creating a sophisticated context around these commodities in their shops which would encourage their customers to believe in the credibility of the mercer and the fashionability of the objects on sale. Purchasing luxuries was, in many ways, an act of faith, and the mercers were uniquely positioned to manipulate demand and create confidence.

The mercers' activities thus raise important questions about the life cycle of objects and the way they were valued, the trading options of merchants who operated within narrow margins of credit and cashflow, and relationships between different corporate groups who were jostling for position and advantage within the eighteenth-century French *commerce de luxe*. Whilst the practices of the mercers do not necessarily signal a revolution in consumerism at this period, their influence within the market place surely indicates that developments in eighteenth-century French commercial life, such as the accumulation and exploitation of capital, market manipulation and sophisticated interventions in the design process, were very much part of the eighteenth-century luxury economy.

List of Appendices

1 Article XII of mercers' corporate statutes.
Article XII, *Ordonnance de Louis XIII servant de statuts aux Marchands Merciers, Grossiers, Joailliers de cette ville de Paris*, January 1613 (AVP IAZ 51, pièce 19).

2 Disputes between mercers and other corporations, 1600–1800.

3 Stock profiles of a selection of mercers in Savary's thirteenth category.

4 Thomas-Joachim Hebert, 1713–1774.
From AN MC LIII, 226, 22 May 1724, Desgodets, AN MC XXIII, 654, 26 August 1763, Legras and AN MC LIII, 502, 15 January 1774, Hebert.

5 Lazare Duvaux, monthly turnover 1750.
After L. Courajod *Livre Journal de Lazare Duvaux, marchand-bijoutier ordinaire du Roi 1748–1758,* Paris 1874.

6 Cargoes of French Companies, 1700–1730.
From figures published by Tournier, 1953.

7 The use of oriental lacquer as a veneer, 1772.
J-A. Roubo, *L'Art du Menuisier Ebéniste*, Paris, 1772.

8 Lyonnais suppliers of silks to Jean-François Barbier, Paris.
From AN MC LXXV, 672, 26–28 February 1762 Barbier and *Rolle de Capitation*, 1758–9 (information supplied by Lesley Miller [from Miller 1988]).

9 Values for silks in Parisian inventories, 1753.
Antione Porlier, Rue St Honoré, AVP D^4B^6 *carton* 12 *dossier* 560.

10 British exports to France from London, 1751.
W. Beawes, *Lex Mercatoria Redivava* or, *the Merchant's Directory*, Dublin, 1773, 517–20.

11 Le Petit-Dunkerque, L. S. Mercier, *Le Tableau de Paris*, Amsterdam, 1787.

Appendix 1

Article XII of Mercers' Corporate Statutes

Article XII, Ordonnance de Louis XIII servant de statuts aux Marchands Merciers, Grossiers, Joailliers de cette ville de Paris, January 1613 (AVP IAZ 51, pièce 19).

Pourront lesdits Marchands Merciers acheter, vendre & débiter, troquer & échanger, tant dans la Ville, Prevôté & Vicomté de Paris, Villes circonvoisines d'icelles, & en tous autres lieux du Royaume, même dans les Pays étrangers, en gros ou en détail, toutes sortes de marchandises:

D'or, d'argent, soyes, ostades, serges de Florence, razes & estamets de Milan, serges de Seigneur, de Leyde, de Moüy, de Chartres, d'Orleans, d'Ascot et de toutes autres sortes, Pays & façons.

Camelots, burails, moncahiards, étamines, futaines, doublures, frises, revêches, boucassins, treillis & bougrans.

Draps de Borde, d'Espagne, Angleterre & autres Pays étrangers.

Toiles de toutes sortes, ouvrées & non ouvrées, tant Françoises qu'étrangeres, grosses, moyennes & fines; chemises, mouchoirs, collets, & toutes autres sorte de lingerie.

Chanvres, lin, fil de toutes sortes teints & non teints, cordes, cordages, ficelles, sangles, panneaux & filets tant de chasse que de pêche.

Castors à faire chapeaux, laines filées & non filées, teintes & non teintes, bonnets, chapeaux, bas de chauffe tant de soye, laine, que fil ou autre étoffe, camisolle, cotons filez & non filez.

Maroquins, cuirs de Levant, chamois, bufles, buffetins, chevrotins, velins, peaux de moutons parées, cuirs de megie, & generalement toutes sortes de cuirs.

Fourures, pelleteries, gands, mitaines & tous ouvrages faits des susdites étoffes.

Tapisseries, coutils, courtepointes, couvertures, castelognes & autres.

Franges, passemens, dentelles, lassis, points coupez, rubans, cordons, boutons d'or, d'argent, de soye, fil, crin, & de toutes autres étoffes, & de tous pays & façons, même l'or & l'argent tant fin que faux, filé sur soye ou sur fil.

Ensemble argent de Chipre, soyes cruës & non écrues, teintes & non teintes.

Pareillement toute sorte de joüaillerie, d'or, d'argent, pierres precieuses, perles, joyaux d'or, & d'argent & d'autres metaux, corails, grenats, agathes, calcidoines, cristal, ambre, amatistes & toutes autres sortes de pierres taillées & non taillées & toute sorte de paternostrerie.

Droguerie, épicerie, bresil, pastel, cochenille, graine d'écarlate, garance & toutes especes de teintures.

Fer, acier, cuivre, airain, leton, ouvrez & non ouvrez, neufs ou vieux, même fil de leton & médailles.

Epées, dagues & poignards, lames, gardes & garnitures d'iceux, & éperons, étriers, mords de chevaux, fers et clous.

Ciseaux, lancettes, canivets, razoirs, couteaux, épingles & aiguilles.

Ceintures, porte-épée, peignes, éponges & aiguillettes.

Serrures, cadenats, fermetures d'huis, portes, fenestres, coffres & cabinets.

Dinanderie, quinquaillerie, coûtellerie, & de toutes autres sortes de marchandises de cuivre, fer, fonte, acier, & toutes autres oeuvres de forge & fonte.

Miroirs, images, tableaux, tant en bosse qu'autrement, peintures, heures, pseautiers, catechismes & autres livres de prieres.

Plumes, gaînes, étuis, boêtes, écritoires, & generalement toutes autres sortes & especes de marchandises.

Appendix 2

Disputes between Mercers and Other Corporations, 1600–1800

Date	Corporation	Source
1612	Ribbon-makers	Chardon 1752
1638	Locksmiths	Chardon 1752
1662	Engravers	Chardon 1752
1662	Coachmakers and wheelwrights	Chardon 1752
1667	*Marchands priviligiés*	Chardon 1752
1669	Furniture-makers (*menuisiers*)	Chardon 1752
1672	Lead-workers	Chardon 1752
1676	Nailsmiths	Chardon 1752
1679	Locksmiths	Chardon 1752
1682	Furrier	Chardon 1752
1682	Spice merchants	Chardon 1752
1691	Paper-makers and pasters	Chardon 1752
1691	Carders	Chardon 1752
1692	Fan-makers and glove-makers	Chardon 1752
1692	Upholsterers	AN AD XI/22
1696	Sword-cutlers	Chardon 1752
1697	Stocking-makers	Chardon 1752
1697	Upholsterers	Chardon 1752
1697	Dyers	Chardon 1752
1697	Second-hand dealers (clothing)	Chardon 1752
1699	Furriers	Chardon 1752
1699	Paper-makers and pasters	Chardon 1752
1699	Pedlars (*artisans colporteurs*)	Chardon 1752
1700	Inlay-workers	Chardon 1752
1706	Hatters	Chardon 1752
1707	Furniture-makers (*menuisiers*)	Chardon 1752
1711	Weavers	Chardon 1752
1715	Mirror-makers	Chardon 1752
1716	Inlay-workers	Chardon 1752
1718	Button-makers	Chardon 1752
1719	Inlay-workers	AN AD XI/22
1721	Spice merchants	BHVP 323217

DATE	CORPORATION	SOURCE
1723	Upholsterers	AN AD XI/22
1724	Furniture-makers	AN AD XI/22
1725	Pin-makers	Chardon 1752
1725	Curriers	Chardon 1752
1736	Furriers	Chardon 1752
1736	Fan-makers	Chardon 1752
1736	Candlemakers from Blois	BN Mss Joly de Fleury 2018 fo 104
1737	Mirror-makers	AN AD XI/22
1738	Dyers	Chardon 1752
1745	Lead-workers	Chardon 1752
1747	Dyers	Chardon 1752
1747	*Marchands forains* (merchants visiting fairs)	Chardon 1752
1749	Furniture-makers (*menuisiers*)	Chardon 1752
1751	Workers in cloth of gold and silver thread	Chardon 1752
1751	Engravers	Chardon 1752
1752	Upholsterers	AN AD XI/22
1766	Tailors	BHVP 132243
1766	Glovemakers	BHVP 132242
1767	Ribbon-makers	BHVP 132245
1767	Wig-makers	BHVP 132244
1768	Curriers	BHVP 132248
1768	*Marchands forains* (merchants visiting fairs)	BHVP 132247
1769	Goldsmiths	BHVP 134181
1769	Secondhand dealers (in paintings)	BN Z le Senne 104
1772	Ribbon-makers (against mercers and drapers)	BN Est Mss Joly de Fleury 1426 fo 261
1772	Ribbon-makers	BHVP 132245
1774	Drapers	BHVP 132252
1774	Inlay-workers	BHVP 132232 and 132253
1775	Goldsmiths	BHVP 132254
1775	Inlay-workers	BHVP 132251
n.d	(but before 1776) Drapers	BHVP in 8⁰ 4088
1777	Upholsterers and mirror-makers	AN ADXI/22
1781	Inlay-workers-musical instrument makers-fan-makers	BHVP 132256

APPENDIX 3

STOCK PROFILES OF A SELECTION OF MERCERS IN SAVARY'S THIRTEENTH CATEGORY

THOMAS-JOACHIM HEBERT, 1724

STOCK BY VALUE RANGES

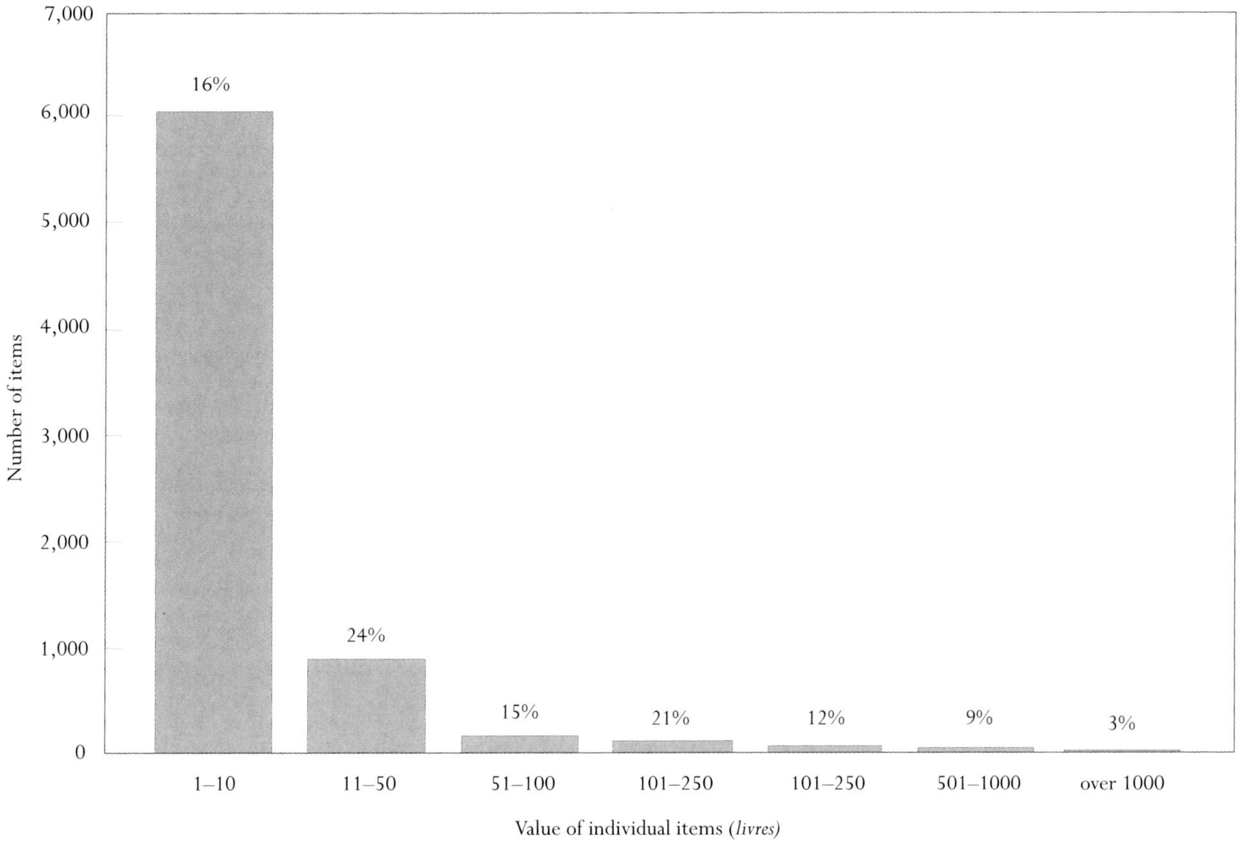

Figures above bars represent stock as % of total stock value

CLAUDE ANTOINE JULLIOT, 1736
STOCK BY VALUE RANGES

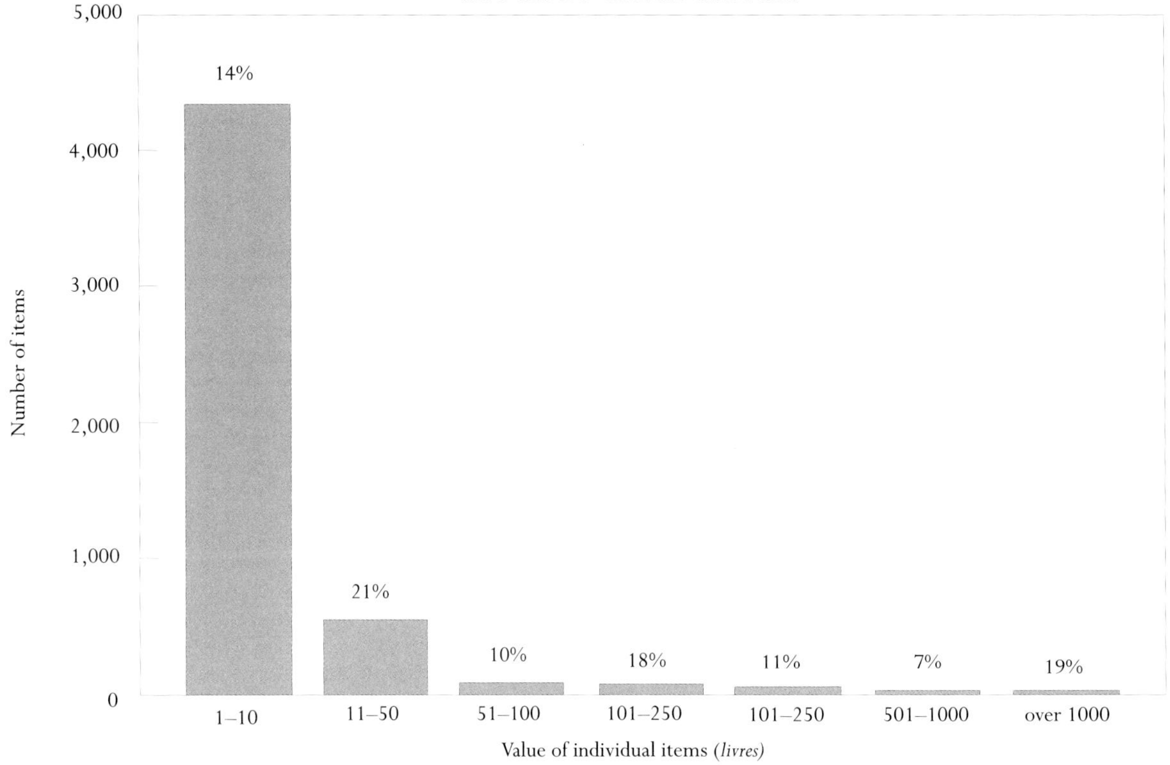

CLAUDE ANTOINE JULLIOT, 1760
STOCK BY VALUE RANGES

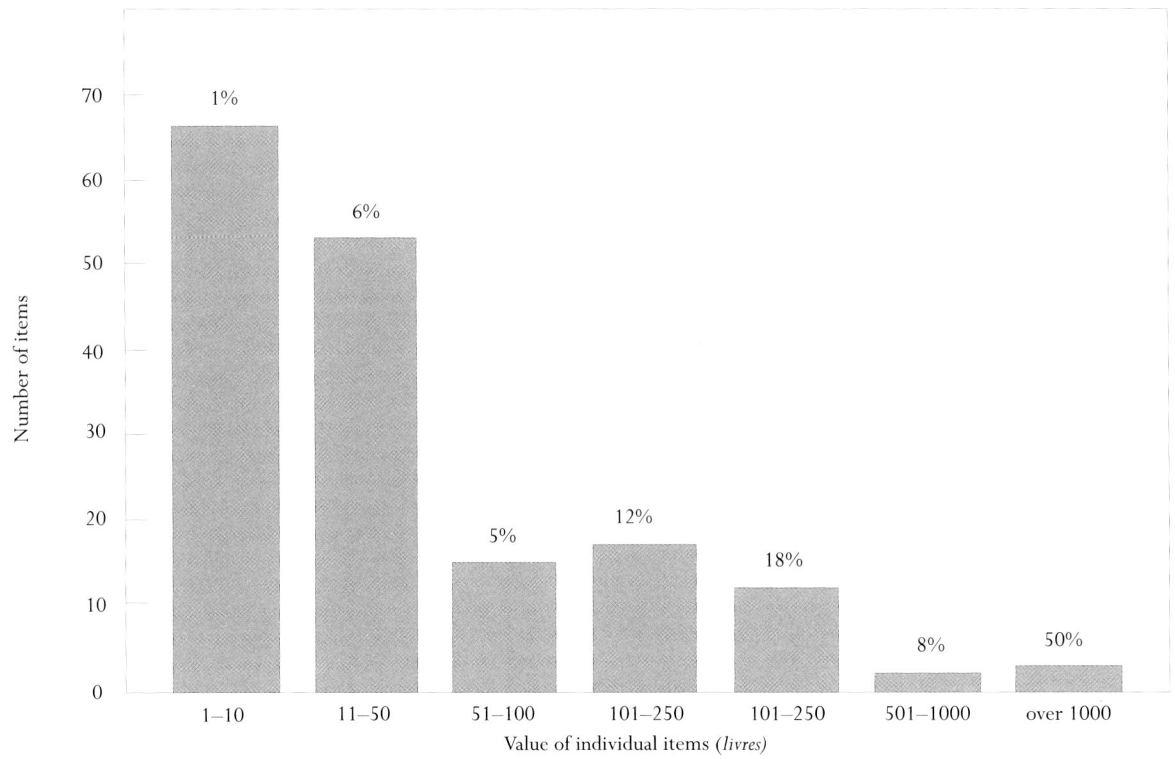

SIMON HENRI DELAHOGUETTE, 1768
STOCK BY VALUE RANGES

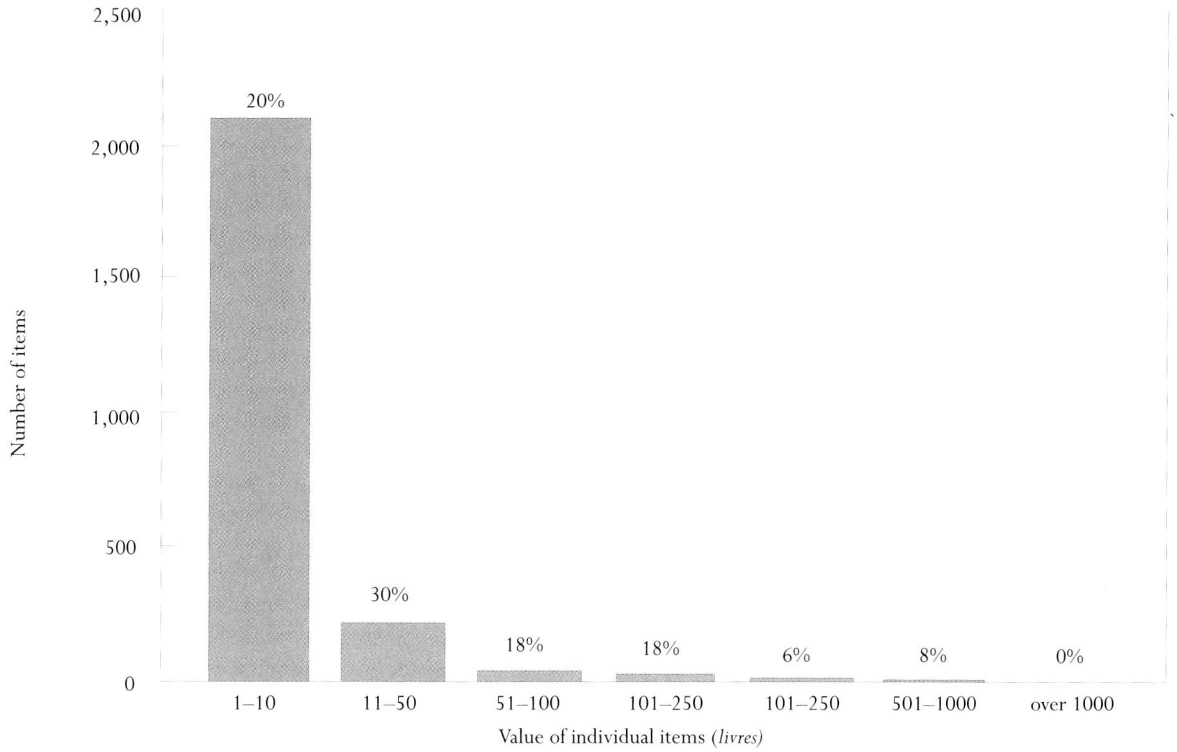

MARTIN HENNEBERT, 1770
STOCK BY VALUE RANGES

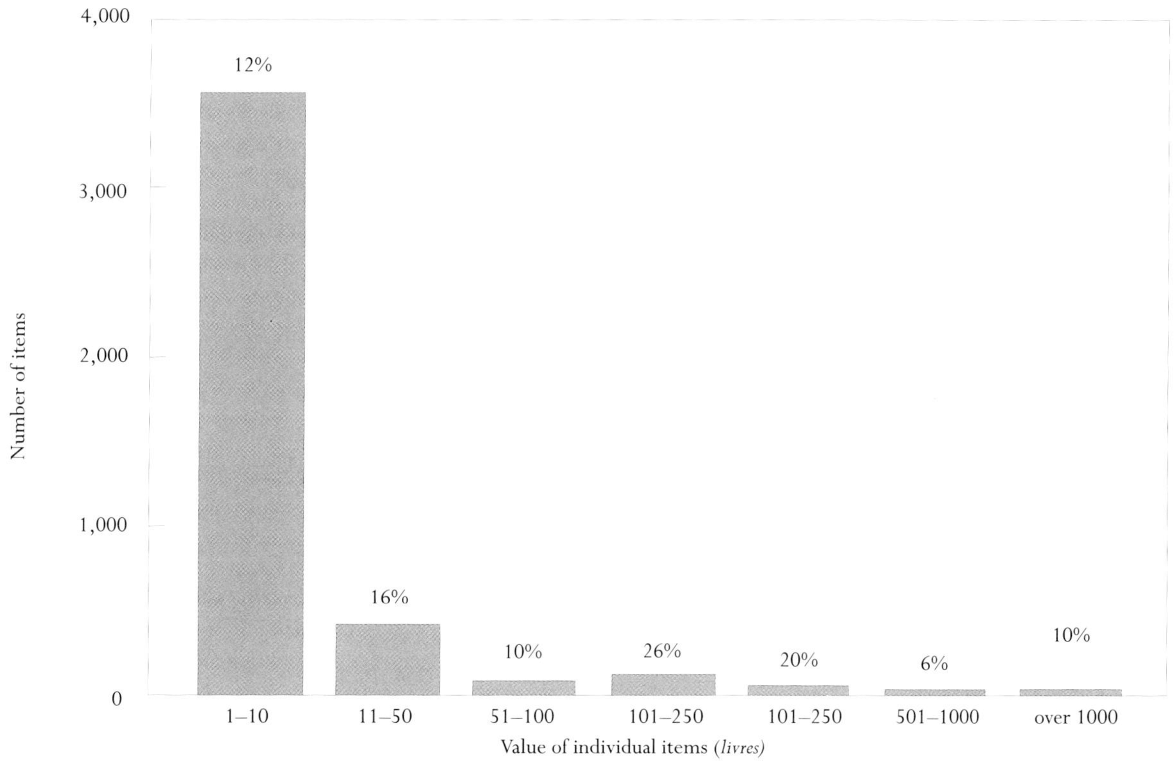

APPENDIX 4

THOMAS-JOACHIM HEBERT 1713–1774

From AN MC LIII, 226, 22 May 1724, Desgodets, AN MC XXIII, 654, 26 August 1763, Legras and AN MC LIII, 502, 15 January 1774, Hebert.

1714 Married Louise Desgodets. Her dowry 16,523 *livres* 3 *deniers*. Her first husband N.G. Daustel, a *marchand bijoutier*, d.1713, Quai de la Megisserie, *La Vase d'Or*. Stock on death worth 27,495 *livres* 10 *sols*. She had carried on business, then handed it over to Hebert on marriage.

1719 Inherited house at Maule worth 1000 *livres*.

1724 First wife died.
Hebert described as *marchand joaillier bourgeois,* address Quai de la Megisserie, *Au Roy de Siam*. Stock worth 82,915 *livres* 10 *sols*, 457 items, average worth 181 *livres* 10 *sols*; furniture, porcelain, mirrors, clocks, bronzes, boxes, etc. Clientele include over half *ducs, duchesses, comtes(ses), marquis(es), chevaliers, mareschals, abbés, ambassadeurs, financiers*.

1730 Married Marie Jeanne Legras. Her dowry 30,000 *livres*.

Hebert's assets:	121,526 *livres* 12 *sols* 1 *denier*	(goods and cash) +
	124,940 *livres* 10 *sols*	(owed to his business)
TOTAL	246,467 *livres* 2 *sols* 1 *denier*	

1763 Second wife, Marie Jeanne Legras, died. He described as *ecuyer, conseiller secretaire du roy, maison couronne de France et de ses finances*.

1774 Hebert died.

DATE	INVESTMENT	INCOME P.A.	CAPITAL	RATE	TYPE
1724	*Rente*	180 *livres*			*rente viagere*
1731	House	6,000	64,000		
1737	House	1,300	36,000		
1737	*Rente*	1,310	26,200	20 *deniers*	*Duras*
1738	*Rente*	943 *livres* 15 *sols*	18,867		*Richelieu*
1740	House	6,000	21,000		
1740	*Rente*	400	8,000	20 *deniers*	*Villars*
1744	*Rente*	600	12,000	20 *deniers*	*de la Valliere*
1744	*Rente*	200	4,000		*duc de Boufflers*
1744	*Rente*	40	800	20 *deniers*	*Baron de Quintin*
1745	House	3,700	29,000		
1745	*Rente*	88			
1746	*Rente*	300	6,000		*de la Valliere*
1746	*Rente*		22,000	20 *deniers*	*Prince de Soubise*
1748	*Rente*	425 *livres* 19 *sols* 9 *deniers*	8,519 *livres* 16 *sols*	20 *deniers*	*Princesse de Bourbon*

DATE	INVESTMENT	INCOME P.A.	CAPITAL	RATE	TYPE
1749	*Rente*	200	4,000		*duc de Vallars*
1750	*Rente*	325	6,500		*duc de Bouillon*
1752	*Rente*	40	2,000	50 *deniers*	*Ladvocat*
1752	Office		110,000		from *Ladvocat*
1756	*Rente*	2,000	40,000		government
1756	*Rente*	600	12,000		*Dargenson*
1756	*Rente*	1,500	30,000		*de Machault*
1759	*Rente*	250	5,000		government
1761	*Rente*	100	2,000		government
1761	*Rente*	14			*rente viagere*
1770	Shares	1,680	35,000		East India Company
TOTAL		28,196 *livres* 14 *sols*	242,886 *livres* 16 *sols*		

APPENDIX 5

LAZARE DUVAUX, MONTHLY TURNOVER 1750

After L. Courajod Livre Journal de Lazare Duvaux, marchand-bijoutier ordinaire du Roi 1748–1758, Paris 1874.

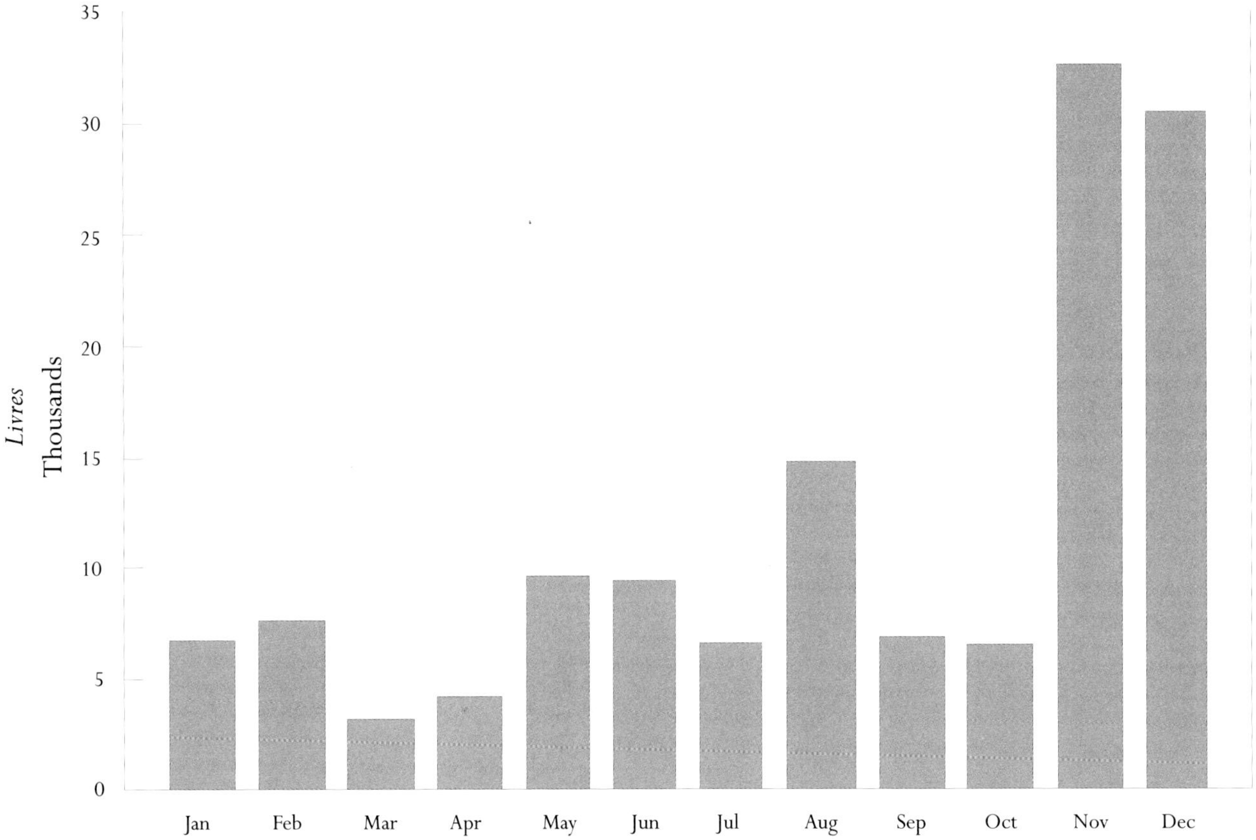

Total sales for 1750: 137,721 livres

APPENDIX 6

CARGOES OF FRENCH COMPANIES, 1700–1730

From figures published by Tournier, 1953.

DATE	PORT(S)	CARGO
1700	Nantes	181 cases* porcelain
1703	Nantes	porcelain
1706	Brest,	
	Port-Louis	some porcelain
1715	Nantes	4 cases porcelain
1716		173 pieces porcelain
		30 plates, porcelain
		6 cups, 4 cornets
1721		367 pieces porcelain,
		Chinese and Japanese
1722		333,060 pieces porcelain
1723		349,972 pieces porcelain
1725	Nantes	141,338 pieces porcelain
		5 cases porcelain
1727		4,057 cabarets vernis
		33,863 pieces porcelain
1729		71 cases porcelain
1730		121 cases porcelain
		1 case of samples
		7 cases of 400 cabarets vernis

* One case is estimated by Tournier to contain more or less one thousand pieces of porcelain.

APPENDIX 7

THE USE OF ORIENTAL LACQUER AS A VENEER, 1772

J-A. Roubo, L'Art du Menuisier Ebéniste, Paris, 1772, 1020–21

La laque qu'on emploie ordinairement en Ebénisterie, se prend dans des feuilles soit de cabinet ou de paravent venu de la Chine ou du Japon, qui, pour la plupart, sont vernies & peintes des deux côtés , & qu'on refend au milieu de leur épaisseur pour les diminuer ensuite au rabot & les mettre en état d'être plaquées sur des fonds de Menuiserie ordinaire. Il faut prendre beaucoup de précautions, tant pour refendre ces feuilles, que pour les diminuer, de crainte de faire fendre ou éclatter la vernis; c'est pourquoi, lorsqu'on les refend, il faut les mettre dans la presse entre des coussins ou de couvertures de laine. Il faut avoir la même précaution lesqu'on les rabote par derriere, c'est-à-dire, qu'il faut mettre sur l'établi une couverture ployée en double, pour que les inégalités qui sont à la surface du vernis à l'endroit des fleurs ou autres ornements, entrent dans l'épaisseur de cette couverture.

En diminuant l'épaisseur des bois qui portent la laque ou vernis de la Chine, il faut prendre garde de leur laisser assez de consistance pour qui'il ne se rompent pas; c'est pourqoi il faut leur laisser au moins une ligne d'épaisseur; après quoi on les plaque sur l'ouvrage à l'ordinaire, en prenant toutefois la précaution de les faire chauffer, ainsi que les bâtis qui doivent les recevoir, & d'étendre sur la laque des couvertures, par-dessus lesquelles on met des coussins ou des calles de bois avec des goberges ou des presses à coller, selon qu'on le juge nécessaire; mais il ne faut jamais se servir de valets pour faire ces collages, de crainte qu'en frappant dessus pour les serrer, on n'étonne le vernis, & qu'on ne le fasse fendre.

Autant qu'il est possible, on entoure les joints des ouvrages de laque de rapport avec des ornements ou des cadres de cuivre, parce que quelques précautions qu'on prenne en coupant les feuilles de laque, il est bien difficile de n'y pas faire quelques éclats, qui font paroître la place des joints, ce qui fait un très-mauvais effet; de plus, quand on pourroit parvenir à couper la laque avec toute la propreté possible, les arêtes des ouvertures qui ne seroient pas ainsi garnies, ne tarderoient pas à être gâtées, ce qui feroit toujours mal.

On imite en France les vernis de la Chine (du moins autant bien qu'il a été possible jusqu'à présent) ce qui fait de l'ouvrage plus solide que celui où on plaque ceux de la Chine. Dans ce dernier cas, c'est-à-dire, quand on vernit les meubles, il faut avoir grand soin que leurs bâtis soient construits de bon bois très-sec, & avec toute la solidité possible, comme je l'ai enseigné dans le cours de cet Ouvrage.

Appendix 8

Lyonnais Suppliers of Silks to Jean-François Barbier

From AN MC LXXV, 672, 26–28 February 1762 Barbier and Rolle de Capitation, *1758–9 (information supplied by Lesley Miller [from Miller 1988]).*

Occurence in *Barbier* papers, Paris	Occurence in *Rolle de Capitation*, Lyon *marchands* who paid more than 20 *livres*
* François Claviere, ancien echevin et négotiant (for Claviere père et fils) logé chez Sinard négotiant, cul-de-sac des Bourdonnais	Veuve Claviere et fils, rue Puy Gaillot
* Jean Jacob, négotiant logé chez Despiegnes garde de la mercerie, rue St Denis	Jean Jacob et Cie, rue Lafond
* Antoine Lucy (for Lucy, Colliot et Cie) logé chez Foisenfant, limonadier rue St Honoré, au coin de celle des Bourdonnais	Lucy, Colliot et Cie rue St Marcel
* Leonard Gay, négotiant (for L. Gay et Ribouté) logé chez Campagniac marchand chapellier, rue St Honoré	Gay et Riboutte, rue Puy Gaillot (?Ribaudy, rue Neuve)
* Pierre Emery (for Emery, Mary et Cie) logé chez Foisenfant, limonadier rue St Honoré, au coin de celle des Bourdonnais	
* Monlong, Lagneau et Seve	Monlong, Lagneau et Seve Place des Terreaux
Thomas Deschamps et Cie	Thomas Deschamps Place des Terreaux
Morel oncle et neveu et Beau	Morel, rue Puy Gaillot

OCCURENCE IN *BARBIER* PAPERS, PARIS	OCCURENCE IN *ROLLE DE CAPITATION*, LYON *MARCHANDS* WHO PAID MORE THAN 20 *livres*
Claviere et Rambeau	Claviere et Rambaud, rue Ste Catherine
* Geneve	Geneves frères, Place des Carmes
Pierre Pavy et Cie	
Levasseur et Cie	Frères Billet et Levasseur, Place des Terreaux
Bonnet et Durand frères	Durand, rue Thomassin
* Marrechalle et Richard	Marichal et Richard, Quay de Retz
Galy Gallien et Cie	Galy et Cie, place des Terreaux
Durand Grandmaison et Cie	
Duperret Jabié et Cie	Duperrel, Jubier et Cie, rue Puits Gaillot
Baujon frères	Beaujon, rue Ste Catherine
Justin Courtois et Cie	
Pilat frères	
Peynard Vial et Cie	Vial et Cie, rue Puy Gaillot
La Salle et Cie	Lasalle, Boucher et Charrier, Quay de Retz
Gardelle Chrisan et Cie	
Lemoine et Savy	Lemoine et Savy rue Puy Gaillot (Savy l'ainé et Cie, rue des Puits Gaillot)
Cesar Fonneral et Cie père et fils	
Chardivy	

Occurence in *Barbier* papers, Paris	Occurence in *Rolle de Capitation*, Lyon *marchands* who paid more than 20 *livres*
Roque et Galon	
* Dutilleul et Cie	
* Arcis et Dupré	Arcir et Dupré, rue Pizay
Thevenet et * Giraudin	Thevenet et Giraudin, rue Buisson
Henry Brosse et Cie	Henry Brosse, Petite rue Merciere
Foray frères	Frères Foray, rue Desirée
Jaillon et Bouvard	
Gontelle Falsan et Cie	
Savy et Cie	
Etienne Jacques	? Jacquette, Place de la Croix Pacquet
Constant l'ainé	
Clerc et Cie	
Eymard et Tete fils	Teste père et fils rue Puy Gaillot
Louis Rebout	Reboul, rue Puy Gaillot
Constant et Cie	
Seve et Cie	
Romier et Meunier fils	
Gerard et Cie	
Bouvet et Cie	
Poulle Genetelly et Cie	? Poully, Montée de la Glaciere

Occurence in *Barbier* papers, Paris	Occurence in *Rolle de Capitation*, Lyon *marchands* who paid more than 20 *livres*
Petit et Cie	
Richard et Marquis	
Marquis Balley et Cie	
Etienne Reu et Cie	
Bilet frères et Cie	Giraud et Bilet, rue Bat d'Argent
Veuve de René Imbert et fils	Veuve Imbert et Guilloux, rue Ste Catherine Imbert, Petite rue Merciere
Labarre, Vial et Bridan	Frères Labarre, rue Ste Marie
Bisserdan frères	
Jean Baptiste Beaucousin et Cie	Beaucousin, Quay de Retz
Brossard et Cie	
The following *négotiants* were represented by the syndicate:	
Guignard Courvoisier et Rodier	
Nayron et Cie	
Faure frères et Cie	
Villenot et Cie	? Villennes et Vuty, rue Bressée
Bellache et Cie	
François de Varenne et Cie	
Goudon et Breton	Goudon et Bretton, rue Puy Gaillot
Ribier et Doyal	Ribier et Doyat, Quai de Retz
Marc Doyal	
Jean François Raiboudy	

OCCURENCE IN *BARBIER* PAPERS, PARIS	OCCURENCE IN *ROLLE DE CAPITATION*, LYON *MARCHANDS* WHO PAID MORE THAN 20 *livres*
Reverony frères	Reverony frères et Cie
The *négotiant* Leonard Millanois was represented individually by Leonard Gay.	Milanois et Cie rue Puy Gaillot
The following *négotiants* were represented by Charles Claude Briasson, *ancien échevin, logé chez Briasson, libraire, rue St Jacques*	
Frederic Greffe et Cie	
Jean Claude Durand (for Jean Claude Durand et fils) logé chez Fontrobert, rue des Mauvaises Paroles	
Jean Antoine Servant fils logé chez Briasson libraire	
* Seignoret et Cie	? Signoret fils, Montée de la Glaciere (? Sonnerat fils et Cie, rue Genty)
Rigod et Cie	Rigod et Cie, rue Ste Catherine
Gaspard Fontaine (for Gaspard Fontaine et Chorel)	Fontaine fils et Chorel, rue Puy Gaillot
[Baujon frères et Cie were also listed as represented by François Careaud, rue Cocqueron, Paris]	
Roque et Galon were represented by Claude Roque, *agent de change*, rue du Mail, Paris	
Antoine Ignace la Feaume	
Nicolas May was represented by Jean Pierre Razuret, *négotiant* rue St Honoré, Paris	(Razuret, rue Ste Catherine)

* members of syndicate (of twelve creditors from Lyon, twelve from Tours and one from Paris)

Appendix 9

Values for Silks in Parision Inventories 1753

Antoine Porlier, Rue St Honoré, AVP D^4B^6 *carton* 12 *dossier* 560

Fabric Type	Inventory Value	Total Length of Fabric in Stock
silks brocaded with gold and silver	64–110 *livres*	103.75 *aunes*
velvets	14–27 *livres*	142.25 *aunes*
brocaded silks	4 *livres* 12 *sous*–17 *livres* 10 *sous*	884.25 *aunes*
coloured silks (usually two colours, patterned with stripes/checks, flowers etc)	4–18 *livres*	9,628 *aunes*
plain silks	3 *livres* 19 *sous*–11 *livres* 10 *sous*	3,351.25 *aunes*
waistcoats	23–60 *livres*	40 waistcoats

APPENDIX 10

BRITISH EXPORTS TO FRANCE FROM LONDON, 1751

W. Beawes, Lex Mercatoria Redivava or, the Merchant's Directory, Dublin, 1773, 517–20

EXPORTS TO FRANCE, FROM THE PORT OF LONDON ONLY, IN THE YEAR 1751			EXPORTED		
Allum	3,161	C.	2,212	14	0
Apoth.	6	C.	24	0	0
Bays	400		1,800	0	0
Barley	410	Qr.	307	10	0
Beans	1,765	Qr.	1,853	5	0
Beer	21	Hhds.	63	0	0
Bellows	24	Doz.	24	0	0
Books	11 1/2	C.	11	10	0
Brass, wrought	550	C.	4,400	0	0
Butter	530	Firk.	530	0	0
Clock-work	3	C.	9	0	0
Cloths, long	556		5,560	0	0
short	81		648	0	0
Copper	50	C.	275	0	0
Coals	42	Cha.	52	10	0
Cheese	32	C.	40	0	0
Cordage	130	Tons	3,250	0	0
Cottons and Plains	290	Goads	26	2	0
Copperas	8,680	C.	2,821	0	0
Coach and Harness	1		70	0	0
Harness	1		6	0	0
Chaise	1		30	0	0
Earthen Ware	17,800	Ps.	74	3	4
Frize	250	Yds.	37	10	0
Fustians	20	Pcs.	20	0	0
Fustick	1,813	C.	498	11	6
Flannel	1,730	Yds.	86	10	0
Garters	438	Gro.	438	0	0
Grindstones	2	Chal.	1	6	0
Glass	7,200	Ps.	240	0	0
Gunpowder	800	lb.	24	2	2
Glue	330	C.	412	10	0
Habdash.	29	C.	290	0	0

Hose	314	Doz.	376	16	0
Hats	10	Doz.	25	0	0
Iron	25	Tons	375	0	0
Cast	74	Tons	894	0	0
Wrought	6,134	lb.	109	10	8
Kersies	263		460	5	0
Leather wrought	60		4	10	0
Lead	1,832	C.	1,103	17	11
Lanthorn Leaves	15,940		1,115	16	0
Litharge of Lead	57	C.	69	16	6
Linen	24	C.Ells	200	0	0
Oats	200	Qrs.	125	0	0
Oil	452	Gal.	55	12	1
Pewter	57 ½	C.	373	15	0
Pipes	100	Gro.	7	10	0
Plate, wrought	74	Oz.	25	18	0
Red Herrings	140	Bar.	105	0	0
Rye	5,200	Qr.	3,640	0	0
Serges	80	Qr.	160	0	0
Stuffs	2,146		4,292	0	0
Snuff	600	lb.	60	0	0
Stone Ware	200	Ps.	1	13	4
Shot	605	C.	423	10	0
Shoes	280	Doz.	140	0	0
Shumack	67	C.	36	17	0
Silk, mixt	602	lb.	451	10	0
wrought	3,668	lb.	7,336	0	0
Tin	606	C.	2,272	10	0
Train oil	2	T.	46	0	0
Skins, Goat	85	Doz.	106	5	0
Wheat	57,380	Qrs.	83,201	0	0
Wheat Meal	15,082	Qrs.	32,804	7	0
Wood, Brazeletto	150	C.	65	12	6
Lignum Vitae	8	T.	64	0	0
Logwood	4,738	C.	2,724	7	0
Nicaragua	170	C.	178	10	0
Redwood	1,510	C.	2,642	10	0
	DRUGS				
Gum Seneca	38	C.	361	0	0
Oil Vitriol	566	lb.	42	9	0
Unrated goods			5,354	0	0
	TOTAL OF EXPORTS		177,966	11	4

EXPORTED BY CERTIFICATE TO FRANCE, FROM THE PORT OF LONDON ONLY, IN THE YEAR 1751.

Almonds	8	C	42	16	0
Books	81	lb	0	14	5
Calicoes	6,870		14,083	10	0
Cambricks	697		1,394	0	0
Cassia Lignea	351	lb	29	5	0
Canvas	27	C Ells	157	10	0
Cocoa Nuts	402	C	1,457	5	0
Coffee	153	C	1,250	15	6
Elephants Teeth	23 1/2	C	211	10	0
Ginger	7	C	29	6	3
Hemp	758	C	748	0	0
Handkerchiefs	436		19	18	8
Ditto	1	Ps.	1	1	0
Indigo	937	lb	240	2	1
Iron	2	Ton	32	0	0
Lawns	14		28	0	0
Linen	19,100	Ells	1,591	13	4
Foreign	332	Pcs.	996	0	0
Diaper	210	Yds.	14	0	0
Mother of Pearl Shell	10	C	55	0	0
Nuts	10	Bar.	3	6	8
Oil	23,523	Gal.	2,800	7	2
Pepper	219,699	lb	10,069	10	9
Pimento	56,459	lb	2,822	19	0
Prints	323		21	3	0
Raisins	10	C	12	10	0
Rice	5,647	C	5,435	4	9
Sago	7	C	77	0	0
Shellack	905	lb	307	1	1
Silk, wrought	46	lb	57	10	0
Skins, Cat	80	lb	2	0	0
Kid	200	lb	6	0	0
Snuff	120	lb	12	0	0
Tobacco	3,270,688	lb	40,883	12	0
Tortoise Shell	921	lb	368	8	0
Wine	5	T.	175	0	0
Wools, Sheep's	26,988	lb	2,698	16	0
Lambs	250		18	15	0
Vigonia	3,912		1,369	4	0
Blue long Cloths	56		168	0	0

DRUGS

Cortex Peruv.	1,200	lb	360	0	0
Ipecacuanha	327	lb	100	2	10
Manna	218	lb	42	13	10
Quicksilver	740	lb	132	11	8

EAST-INDIA GOODS

Bandanoes	375		393	15	0
Carradarries	35		19	18	0
Cherconnaes	6		8	2	0
Chints	62		62	0	0
Chucklae	1		1	16	6
Coopees	70		56	17	6
Damasks	17		85	0	0
Dimity	1		2	0	0
Ginghams	28		18	4	0
Gorgoroons	3		12	15	0
Guinea stuffs	217		32	11	0
Jilmils	2		2	13	0
Lampassy	1		5	10	0
Nillaes	30		24	15	0
Palempores	41		143	10	0
Paduasoys	5		27	10	0
Paper Fans	600		105	0	0
Pieces China	400		20	6	0
Pelongs	99		111	7	6
Photaes	60		49	10	0
Romals	4,170		1,824	7	6
Salempores	39		72	3	0
Sattins	7		31	10	0
Silks, wrought	42	lb	52	10	0
Seersuckers	110		192	10	0
Sooseys	110		176	0	0
Taffetys	294		374	17	0
		TOTAL OF EXPORTS BY CERTIFICATE	94,233	5	6

Appendix 11

L.S. Mercier, Le Tableau de Paris, Amsterdam, 1787

CHAPITRE DLV
Le Petit-Dunkerque

C'est la boutique d'un marchand bijoutier, à la descente du Pont-Neuf. Elle étincele de tous les bijoux frivoles que l'opulence paie, que la fatuité convoite, que l'on donne aux femmes honnêtes qui n'acceptent point de l'argent, mais bien des colifichets en or, parce qu'ils ont un air de décence.

Rien n'est plus brillant à l'oeil que cette boutique: rien n'est plus triste à la réflexion; on ne sait si l'on doit sourire ou gémir de ce luxe puérile. On admire les graces qu'on a su donner à des riens. Ces superfluités sont les joujoux des grands enfans, & c'est dans ce lieu sur-tout qu'un philosophe pourroit dire: que de choses dont je n'ai pas besoin!

De nombreux tiroirs sont remplis de mille bagatelles, où le génie de la frivolité a épuisé ses formes et ses contours. Le prix de la façon vaut dix fois le prix de la matiere. L'or a pris toutes les couleurs; le crystal, l'émail, l'acier, font les miroirs taillés à facettes, & les enfantillages de l'industrie délicate sont là sur leur trône. Un homme descend de voiture, entre dans la boutique du bijoutier, & achete des breloques à un tel prix que la moitié auroit suffi pour faire subsister pendant une semaine entiere plusieurs familles nécessiteuses.

Nos petits seigneurs prennent ces petits bijoux à crédit, les distribuent d'un air de nonchalance; & ces dépenses de fantaisie excedent les dépenses nécessaires. Il est triste de voir des sommes considérable offertes à un luxe aussi petit. Dans les premiers jours de l'année, la boutique est remplie d'acheteurs; on y met une garde. Ne faut-il pas pouvoir dire, en étalant une boîte: c'est du Petit-Dunkerque? Chaque année on baptise ces petits bijoux d'un nom particulier & bizarre.

Mais après avoir gémi en philosophe, il faut rendre justice au goût du maître. Il anime, il dirige les articles; il imagine ce qui doit plaire. En donnant la vogue à plusieurs colifichets, il a fait travailler dans la capitale ce qu'on étoit obligé de faire venir à grands frais de l'étranger. La bijouterie a fait plus de progrès, depuis qui'il a mis sous les yeux du public des modeles élégans & variés, qu'elle n'en avoit fait depuis longtems.

D'ailleurs chez lui le prix des bijoux est fixe & invariable; & si la rivalité fait dire aux autres marchands, qu'on paie le double au Petit-Dunkerque, c'est la jalousie qui parle. La grace & le fini des bijoux ne les rendent pas là plus chers qu'ailleurs.

Voltaire, lors de son dernier séjour à Paris, se plaisoit beaucoup dans le riche magasin de cette maison curieuse. Il sourioit à toutes ces créations du luxe; il appercevoit, je crois, une certaine analogie entre ces bijoux brillans & son style.

Comme le luxe change continuellement d'objets, & que les modes varient avec rapidité, les ouvriers du luxe éprouvent des vicissitudes ruineuses: & leur sort est toujours incertain, tandis que celui de l'agriculture ne l'est pas. Tel colifichet perd de sa faveur, & voilà des hommes qui tombent inopinément dans le besoin.

Un autre jour s'accrédite un nouveau genre: des ouvriers qui mouroient de faim se trouvent dans une abondance imprévue, & suffisent à peine aux demandes des amateurs. Mais ces artisans, soumis aux idées de fantaisiem n'ont que des moments de vogue; ils ne savent à quel objet s'attacher, pour assurer leur subsustence. Quand le caprice vient à changer, plusieurs ne sont plus en état d'embrasser une profession nouvelle. La pénurie kes desseche, & l'état perd des citoyens dont les bras & la tête sont devenus absolument oisifs.

Si l'on dit que les ouvriers favorisés jouissent à leur tour de la souffrance des autres, & dédommagent l'état de la perte des malheureux, il faudroit pouvoir ajouter que cette abondance sera durable. Mais non; ils tombent invinciblement dans l'abyme de la misere, ces futilités changeantes exigeante une adresse particuliere. Prisée la veille, nulle le lendemain, cette industrie n'est point applicable à des objets utiles; elle est trop ou trop peu payée, selon le cours de ces joujoux bizarres. Aussi l'artisan qui connoit lui-même l'instabilité de sa profession, n'ose jamais statuer sur rien, & la population ordinairement ne gagne pas avec lui.

Chaque siècle a son moule qui passe de mode Tout s'y jette; on le change: les deux siecles n'ont presque plus la même physionomie.

Qui découvrira les chaînons imperceptibles, mais existans, par lesquels nos manieres tiennent les unes aux autres? Quand les femmes portoient de grands paniers, on forgeoit chez les orfevres des assiettes d'une grandeur extraordinaire. Les bijoux du Petit-Dunkerque semblent d'accord aujourd'hui avec nos petits appartements, nos jolis meubles, notre habilement & notre coëffure. Il est donc en tout des rapports secrets, qui ont leur origine & leur liaison.

List of Illustrations with Notes

Colour Plates

1. The Resurrection of Christ, 1674, Charles Lebrun (1619–90), 1676, Height 4.8 m, width 2.65 m.
Musée des Beaux-Arts de Lyon, A 203.
Montgolfier 1960, Mairie de Paris 1988.

Painted for the *confrérie* of the corporation of *marchands merciers* for the church of St. Sépulchre, rue St. Denis. The altar was described thus a hundred years later 'Le grand autel a quelque chose de majestueux; il est orné de sculptures et de belles Figures en bois, tant en haut qu'en bas; et au milieu est un Tableau de Résurrection par Le Brun; Colbert le Protecteur du Commerce, y est répréesenté tenant un bout de linceul' (*Voyage Pittoresque* Paris 1770, 36).

2. Commode, French, *c.* 1750, (attrib. Joseph Baumhauer d. 1772, *ébéniste priviligié du roy* in 1749). Oak set with panels of Japanese lacquer and painted with aventurine and black *vernis Martin*; gilt bronze mounts; *campan mélangé vert* marble top. One trade label of the mercer François-Charles Darnault pasted on top of carcase and another pasted underneath.
Height 88.3 cm, width 1.46 m, depth 62.6 cm.
J. Paul Getty Museum, Malibu, California 55.DA.2.
Augarde 1987, Bremer-David 1993, Kjellberg 1989, Pradère 1989.

Another commode of this model is stamped by Joseph, but without trade labels (Victoria and Albert Museum, London 1105–1882). The areas surrounding the Japanese lacquer panels are painted with black *vernis martin* in place of the *aventurine* used on the Getty piece.

3. *Sécretaire à dos d'âne*, stamped RVLC (Roger van der Cruse or Lacroix, 1728–1799, master 1755). Oak veneered with rosewood, satinwood and boxwood, some woods stained; gilt bronze mounts; *breche d'alep* marble top. Inscription in ink on underside of one of interior drawers: '*Poirier 3 pieces argentées*'.
Height 83 cm, width 64 cm, depth 37 cm.
Bernheimer & Co, London.

As de Bellaigue has suggested, such examples of furniture inscribed with Poirier's name, alongside instructions for assembly or finishing, were thus marked because Poirier co-ordinated their manufacture, sending out either drawers for the fitting of writing materials, or tables for mounting with Sèvres porcelain plaques (de Bellaigue 1974).

4. Coloured drawing of a commode decorated with bronze, partly gilt and partly patinated green, inset with plaques of *pietre dure*. Pen and watercolour. Inscription at bottom: *Ce dessin a été fait pour . . . /en datte du 7 Septembre 1784/Sous la direction de P.F. Julliot fils*.
Musée des Arts Décoratifs, Paris, Inv. 25180.

Arts Council 1960, Lemonnier 1983, Leben 1995.

At the end of the first line of the inscription, the surface of the paper is distressed, which suggests that a name might have been erased at a later date.

5. Commode, French, *c.* 1750, stamped twice on top of carcase beneath marble BVRB for Bernard II van Risamburgh (after 1696–*c.* 1766, master by 1730) and six times JME for the *juré des menuisiers ébénistes*. Oak and pine set with panels of Japanese lacquer, around which the carcase veneered with fruitwood and painted with black *vernis Martin*; gilt bronze mounts; *griotte d'Italie* marble top.
Height 83.3 cm, width 115.2 cm, depth 53.3 cm.
Victoria and Albert Museum, London 1094–1882.
Bremer-David 1993, Whitehead and Impey 1995, Pradère 1989.

In the collection of the *Musée de Dijon* is a commode stamped by BVRB of identical form and with the same mounts veneered with red lacquer. Other versions of similar design include commodes in the J. Paul Getty Museum, Malibu, the Metropolitan Museum of Art, New York (Wrightsman Collection), and in a private collection, New York. Some of the mounts also appear on the lacquer commode supplied by Thomas-Joachim Hebert for the Queen Marie Leszczynska at Fontainebleau in 1737 – the first documented royal purchase of furniture veneered with lacquer.

6. *Bureau plat*, French, 1778–1784, stamped M. Carlin (*c.* 1730–1785, master 1766), the stamp partly effaced and JME under front right rail; mounted with fourteen soft paste Sèvres plaques, marked variously with the date letters AA for 1778 and paper labels inked with the prices 30 *livres* (plaques on front and back rail) and 96 *livres* (shaped end drawer plaques); gilt bronze mounts; eight of the plaques gilded by Jean-Baptiste Emmanuel Vandé *père*; trade label of Dominique Daguerre underneath left-rear rail; three Russian inventory numbers painted on carcase; paper label inked with Duveen inventory number 29615.
Height 77.5 cm, width 1.31 m, depth 62 cm.
J. Paul Getty Museum, Malibu, California 83.DA.385.

Christie's London December 1 1983 lot 54, Kjellberg 1989, Pradère 1989, Wilson, Sassoon and Bremer-David 1983. See also Bremer David 1993 for full bibliography, especially for provenance.

Daguerre's purchases from the Sèvres factory in 1778 include an entry for two plaques at 96 *livres* each, and several entries which might refer to the other plaques. This *bureau plat* was owned by the Grand Duchess Maria-Feodorovna of Russia, who placed it in her bedroom at Pavlovsk near St. Petersburg. She is known to have made significant purchases from Daguerre, Au Couronne d'Or, rue St. Honoré on May 25 1784. See Sotheby Monaco June 24 1976 and Watson 1966–70 (vol. 1, 105) for two *sécretaires* with Sèvres porcelain plaques also assumed to have been sold by Daguerre to Feodorovna at the same date.

7. *Bureau plat*, French, *c.* 1780, stamped M. Carlin (*c.* 1730–1785, master 1766) and JME three times, on front right, back left and end right rails. Mounted with panels of Japanese lacquer; gilt bronze mounts.
Height 74.3 cm, width 1.30 m, depth 61.6 cm.
Victoria & Albert Museum, London 1049–1882.

This model differs from that illustrated in colour plate 6 in the design of the legs (the *chandelles* are different) and the gilt bronze mounts (the end drawer mounts with swags and tassels do not appear on the model set with Sèvres plaques, though they are used on the tables illustrated in plates 18 and 19).

8. Coloured drawing of a *sécretaire* mounted with porcelain plaques, pen, black ink and grey and coloured wash, inscribed at the top *C'est encore imparfaitement que le dessin rend leffet de la bauté de la secretaire qui est orné de 4 bas reliefs en porcelaine de franc biscuit sur un fond petit bleu et bronze doré au mat* and at the centre *secretaire/ 30 pouces de large & 46/pouces de haut* at left *N° 3*.
Metropolitan Museum of Art, New York MMA 59.611.10
Dauterman and Parker 1960, Dauterman, Parker and Standen 1964, Huisman and Jallut 1971, Baarsen 1986, Myers 1991, Lemonnier 1983.

The *sécretaire* is mounted with Sèvres plaques made in imitation of Wedgwood plaques. A number of furniture forms were decorated with blue and white plaques and medallions of this type, notably *sécretaires* by the *ébénistes* Martin Carlin, Adam Weisweiler and Bernard Molitor (see Lemonnier 1982, Leben 1992 and 1995). The Weisweiler pieces are likely to have been made for Dominique Daguerre, who may also have sold Molitor's mounted furniture. A surviving *sécretaire* in the Metropolitan Museum of Art, attributed to Weisweiler, is similar to this drawing. It is mounted with a single large plaque on the fall-front, flanked on each side by small Wedgwood medallions.

9. *L'Enseigne de Gersaint*, Antoine Watteau (1684–1721), 1720–21.
Height 3.06 m, width 1.66 m.
Schloss Charlottenburg, Berlin.
Adhemar 1964, Alfassa 1910, Laurel 1913, Morgan-Grasselli 1984, Neuman 1984, Posner 1984, Vidal 1992.

The sign was painted by Watteau for his friend and dealer Gersaint soon before the painter's death. After only two weeks in use as a shop sign, it was bought by the collector Gluck and later entered the collections of Frederick the Great. It was engraved by Aveline in 1732 (*L'Enseigne gravée d'aprè le Tableau en Plat-Fond peint par Watteau pour son amy Marchand/Sur le Pont Notre Dame... qui est a present/dans le cabinet de Mr de Jullienne*). It has long been held to be symbolic of Watteau's artistic testament. The giltwood mirror (right), the Boulle clock (left) and a *vernis Martin* toilet set (right) represented some of the most fashionable and high quality luxury goods on sale in Paris in 1720. The painting represents a secular act of worship (in front of the painting to the right of centre), the examination of goods (the toilet set on the right, which recalls the *vanitas* theme but also the interest at this date in the distinctions between oriental and European lacquer and porcelain) and sophisticated conversation (between well-dressed shopkeepers and clients over the commodities). Neuman convincingly interprets the contemporary significance of the image as a carefully constructed commentary of the art market and as an apology for luxury within the context of the *commerce de luxe* in the 1720s. The combination of traditional emblems, such as paintings within a painting, and the conventional apparatus of the *vanitas* (the mirrors and clock) with a modern iconography of luxury and consumption make this a complex image worthy of consideration from many viewpoints.

10. One of a pair of mounted pot pourri vases, the porcelain Japanese, Arita or early Hirado kilns, late seventeenth century, the mounts French, *c.* 1750. Hard paste porcelain, polychrome enamel decoration, gilt bronze mounts.
Height 15.2 cm, width 18.7 cm, depth 16.5 cm.
J. Paul Getty Museum, Malibu, California 77.DI.30.

Bremer-David 1993. These vases probably belonged to the well-known collector Pierre-Louis Randon de Boisset. They were sold from his collection on February 3 177 (lot 603) to the Duchesse de Mazarin for 660 *livres*. The same vases or a similar model subsequently appeared in a number of sale catalogues in Paris: of the mercer Claude François Julliot 20 November 1777 (lot 331), the collector Radix de Sainte-Foix, 22 April 1782 (lot 55, 120 *livres*), the dealer Jean-Baptiste-Pierre Lebrun, 11 April 1791 (lot 698, 120 *livres*). They were bought from the latter sale by Paillet, dealer and auctioneer.

11. Urn, the porcelain Chinese, Jingdezhen 1715–30, the mounts French, 1715–30. The porcelain of underglaze cobalt blue with overglaze iron red enamel and gilding, gilt bronze mounts.
Height 33.7 cm.
Victoria and Albert Museum, London 166–1879.
Clunas 1987, Ayers , Impey and Mallet 1990.

This is a particularly fine example of the Chinese imitations of Japanese Imari porcelain. A large jar and cover have been mounted in gilt bronze to form an urn for dispensing coffee or chocolate.

12. Lidded bowl, the porcelain Japanese, Imari *c.* 1700, the silver mounts French *c.* 1717–22.
Height 27.9 cm, width 34 cm, depth 27.5 cm.
J. Paul Getty Museum, Malibu, California 79.DI.123.a.–b.
Wilson 1980, Wilson, Watson and Derham 1986.

Three pieces of porcelain of different decoration have been fitted in silver mounts to form a covered bowl. A number of pieces of silver mounted porcelain dating from this period survive, though after about 1730, gilt bronze mounts were preferred, except in the case of glass and porcelain fittings for *nécessaires*, which were often of silver.

13. Inkstand, Chinese hard paste porcelain, early 18th-century, *vernis Martin* French *c.* 1750, gilt bronze mounts French *c.* 1750.
Height 20.3 cm, width 35.6 cm, depth 26.7 cm.
J. Paul Getty Museum, Malibu, California 76.DI.12.
Wilson, Watson and Derham 1982.

This ornate inkstand combines a group of three Chinese porcelain figures with writing vessels formed from three porcelain vessels in the form of libation cups, set on a lacquered tray and embellished with two candle sockets at the back. The group of *blanc de chine* figures, made in Dehua, China, resembles that used in a clock (plates 27 and 28).

14. *Nécessaire* (toilet case), box veneered with rosewood and lined with silk, fitted with silver (most pieces with Paris discharge marks of 1750–56), glass and St. Cloud porcelain, and with a piece of paper pasted into base of box marked 28 July 1749.
Height 17.8 cm width 28.4 cm.
Victoria and Albert Museum, London C575–V–1920.

Havard suggests that the term *nécessaire* came into use around 1715 (Havard, vol. 3, 966). He cites the *Dictionnaire Trevoux* of 1752, which describes such fitted boxes thus: 'Petite boîte divisée par compartiments, pour renfermer différentes choses nécessaires ou commodes en voyage comme aiguilles, soucoupes, tasses, cafetières, theières, chocolatières etc'.

15. Still life, French, *c.* 1725.
Musée des Arts Décoratifs, Paris INV 29896.
Height 1.06 m, width 1.39 m.

The painting is probably contemporary with Gersaint's shop sign (colour plate 9), and may also have been made as a commercial sign. Its condition indicates use in an interior, and it may have hung inside a shop. Alternatively, it may represent a modest private collection of oriental curiosities. It is in the manner of Desportes but does not approach the quality of his best work. The foreground of the painting is more skillfully executed than the objects on the shelves which suggests a degree of collaboration.

Porcelain was traditionally displayed on lacquer cabinets, and was often stored inside them whilst in transit from the East. Most of the objects types depicted here are identifiable, and date from the end of the seventeenth/early eighteenth century. The objects relate closely to the trade in oriental curiosities discussed in chapter 4. The lacquer cabinet and shelves (*étagère*) are used in other images – for the cabinet see plate 46 and 47, and the shelves appear to the far right of the composition in François Boucher's *Le Déjeuner* (Musée du Louvre). The porcelain standing directly on the cabinet includes a covered bowl with gilt bronze mounts *c.* 1700 (centre right) and a bowl with an inverted shallow dish acting as a lid (centre). On the shelves are early Persian ewers, monochrome garnitures, pagods and *blanc de chine* libation cups. Some artistic license has been used in the decoration of the porcelain and lacquer, which makes it difficult to determine whether oriental or European objects are represented. For example, the lacquer cabinet is decorated in a wholly European manner, and may represent a European japanned cabinet rather than an oriental object. The monkey may feature merely as a *chinoiserie* motif, along with the array of objects, but it may play a stronger role in alluding to the French practice of aping oriental forms and decoration.

16. Commode, French, 1742, stamped M. Criard (*c.* 1689–1776), oak veneered with fruitwood, painted with blue and white *vernis Martin* attr. Guillaume Martin; silvered bronze mounts; *bleu turquin* marble slab. Stamped once on top of carcase beneath marble at rear right, number N° 1290 painted in black on back, printed ticket with number 10177.
Height 85 cm, width 1.32 m, depth 63.5 cm.
Musée du Louvre, OA 112292.
Alcouffe 1993, Czarnocka 1994, Salverte 1927, Whitehead 1992, Verlet 1958, Musée du Louvre 1995, AN $O^1$3313, fol. 99 v°.

This appears to have been a prototype for a series of commodes with these distinctive bronzes made by Criard, with veneers of lacquer or wood, the bronzes marked with the crowned 'c' for 1745–9, including one delivered in 1748 by Hebert for the cabinet of the Dauphin at Versailles (Musée de Versailles). The commode was delivered by Thomas-Joachim Hebert for Madame la Comtesse de Mailly (1710–1751) for her bedroom at the Château de Choisy, and was subsequently moved to the Garde Meuble de la Couronne in Paris (1775), and to the Château de Versailles (1787), where it was used by the children of the King. The Château de Choisy was purchased by Louis XV in 1739 for his mistress. She is said to have spun the threads of the blue and white moiré silk which were then woven by Louis XV and hung in the bedroom in which the commode was placed in 1742. The room was painted in blue and white, and Hebert supplied a writing table, corner cupboard and shelves *en suite* with the commode, blue and white porcelain and fittings for lighting. The blue and white wall hangings, curtains, *portières* and upholstered furniture (bed, fifteen chairs and a screen with wood painted in blue and white) were supplied by the *tapissier* Sollier. Madame de Mailly fell from favour and never lived in this chinoiserie creation.

17. Commode, French, *c.* 1750, blue and white *vernis Martin*; later bronze mounts; yellow marble top.
Height 83 m, width 1.02 m, depth 50 cm.
Christies', London 13 June 1991, lot 50.

This commode bears the trade card of Mesnard *AU DUC DE BOURGOGNE, au Milieu du Pont Notre Dame, vend Glaces, Trumeaux, Miroirs, Commodes, Secretaires, Tables de marbre, Toilettes, Paravents, Ecrans, Feux, Bras, . . . Bureaux et toutes sorted d'ouvrages d'ebenisterie.*

18. Pair of painted bronze figures with silver canes, the bronzes stamped with crowned 'c's for 1745–49, the silver hallmarked for 1738–50; lacquer painting attr. Etienne-Simon and Guillaume Martin.
J. Paul Getty Museum, Malibu, California 88.DH.157.
Height 22.8 cm, diameter 15.2 cm.
Courajod 1874, Bremer-David 1993.

19. Design for a silk (point paper), Galy Galien & Cie, Lyon, dated 10 February 1762.
Victoria and Albert Museum, London T404–1972.
Rothstein 1990.

Galy Galien and Company of Lyon were listed in Jean-François Barbier's accounts in late February 1762 (see appendix 8). This point paper represents the stage in the design process at which the painted design has been transferred to scale onto ruled paper.

20. Merchant's order book of woven silks, French *c.* 1760–64.
Victoria and Albert Museum, London T373–1972, 4v°.
Rothstein 1990.

Each page of this volume is inscribed with a note of the type of silk and the initials of the supplier. The samples on this page are checked silks *angleterres* and plain silks *gros de florence*. The supplier's initials are V. M.

21. Garderobbe du Roi de Portugal, *c.* 1736.
Bibliothèque Nationale de France, Paris, Département des Estampes, Echantillons Richelieu, Lh45, vol. 1, 22 r°.

The inscription indicates that the fabric was purchased and made up into clothing in Paris in 1736. The top three samples are of brocaded silk, with gold and/or silver threads. The lower sample is of worked velvet. They are typical of the highest quality production from Lyon at this date.

22. Order letter for silk with sample of striped dress silk, Comtesse de Maupeou to Jean-François Barbier.
Victoria and Albert Museum, London 86.QQ.11(G).
Schoeser 1979 and 1981.

The letter reads 'Md de Maupeou prie Mr barbier de donner au porteur treize aunes de l'étoffe dont elle luy envoie l'echantillon choisie; il voudrat bien le porteur sur son memoire, a ableiges le 31 aoust 1789. CMesse de Maupeou'.

23. Portrait, possibly of Nau family 1700–15, attr. François de Troy (1645–1730).
Private collection, photo courtesy Kugel & Co, Paris.

The group in the centre foreground showing a crouching figure with game and hunting dogs is more accomplished than the surrounding figures and heads of the family members. This suggests that the painting could conceivably have been a collaborative effort, or that it might be attributed to other painters such as Jean-Bapiste Oudry or François Desportes. The figure on the far right of the painting, who holds a *porte-crayon* and apparently wears the order of St. Michel may represent the painter.

24. Etoffe du Lit du M. Fouquet, 1736.
Bibliothèque Nationale de France, Paris, Département des Estampes, Echantillons Richelieu, Lh45, vol. 1, fo 25 v°.

The bed was presumably made originally for Fouquet's château of Vaux-le-Vicomte, built by Louis le Vau between 1657–1661. The upper sample was taken from the hangings of the bed, and the lower sample from the lining.

25. Merchant's order book of woven silks, French *c.* 1760–64.
Victoria and Albert Museum, London T373–1972, 9r°.
Rothenstein 1990.

These samples are silks with floral motifs, with backgrounds of lines, checks and squares. Samples 173 and 175 share the same floral motif, in different colours and on different backgrounds. Sample 174 is a slight variation on the same motif, in the replacement of the small leaves at the top of 173 and 175 with berries. All are *florences brochez* supplied by J.C.B. and priced between 6 *livres* 15 *sols* and 7 *livres* 5 *sols* the ell.

26. Merchant's order book of woven silks, French *c.* 1760–64.
Victoria and Albert Museum, London T373–1972, 27v°.
These satins, supplied by R.C. and priced at 11 *livres* the ell, show variations in the stripes, floral motifs and background colours.

27. Merchant's order book of woven silks, French *c.* 1760–64.
Victoria and Albert Museum, London T373–1972, 27v°.
Rothenstein 1990.

These samples show the addition of stripes to silks brocaded with floral and geometric motifs.

28. Table, French, stamped by Joseph Canabas (1712–1797, master in 1766), mahogany.
Height 72.5 cm, diameter 110 cm.
Christie's Monte Carlo, 4 December 1988, lot 256.

This form of circular table with tip-up top mechanism and tripod base is typical of the Parisian imitations of English tea tables described by Roubo (1772, 973), which had been in use in England from about 1725. Other Parisian *ébénistes* who specialized in mahogany tables such as these include Bernard Molitor (see Leben 1992 and 1995) and to a lesser extent Adam Weisweiler (for example a table veneered with fine mahogany, stamped by Adam Weisweiler, in the Victoria and Albert Museum, London, W11–1919).

29. Commode, French, *c.* 1770–75, stamped twice on the back I. Dubois and JME, painted in ink on the back panel *au petit Dunkerque* (reproduced on page 119), the reverse of the four swag mounts incised M or W, the drapery moulding surrounding the marble top stamped ten times J. PIRET (Jules Piret, active 1856–1870). The stamp is that of the Dubois family used by the widow of Jacques Dubois (d.1763) assisted by René, or after 1772, by René Dubois (1737–1799, master 1755).
Height 87.2 cm, width 74.3 cm, depth 37.2 cm.
The National Trust, Waddesdon Manor, W1/26/2.
De Bellaigue 1974.

De Bellaigue has shown that Jacques Dubois appears to have specialized in painted furniture, listed in an inventory of 1772 as painted on a green ground. The pieces painted with scenes were highly valued (such as 2 *sécretaires* @ 1,200 *livres* and 2 corner cupboards painted green @ 400 *livres*). The inventory lists a Du Bois as a painter, suggesting that the decoration was undertaken within the family. Other green-painted furniture stamped Dubois survives in the Wallace Collection (F330, F178 and F287). These coastal scenes are painted in the manner of Joseph Vernet, whose series *Les Ports de France* was commissioned by Louis XV and later engraved. The scenes painted on the commode are in the manner of Vernet, but cannot be linked to any particular painted or engraved source. It is interesting that the decoration of some of Granchez' goods related closely to the image of his shop. His shop sign, a painted scene of the Port of Dunkerque, was commissioned from Joseph Vernet in about 1767.

The mounts on this piece occur on furniture by RVLC, Garnier and Montigny. Piret specialized in repair work and high-quality reproductions.

30. *Etui*, *c.* 1770, gold and enamel, containing gold-mounted steel scissors, a reeded gold pencil mount with diamond finial, a folding knife with mother-of-pearl handle banded in gold, the twin blades marked *Gray*, one gold-plated, and a gold bodkin.
Length 9.2 cm.
Christie's London, 25 November 1987, lot 42.

The coat of arms on the *étui* was one of those used by the Choiseul family. The Duchesse de Choiseul was amongst Granchez' clients in the 1787 (owing 709 *livres*) though was not listed in the 1784 inventory. Following an illustrious career as Minister of Foreign Affairs, the Duc de Choiseul fell from favour after supporting the Jesuits and was exiled to Chanteloupe until his recall to Paris by Louis XVI in 1774. He acted unofficially as intermediary between Wedgwood and France in the 1770s.

31. Interior panelling from the Café Militaire, 1762, oak carved and partly gilded, and mirror glass, by the architect Claude-Nicholas Ledoux (1736–1806).
Musée Carnavalet, Paris.
Kalnein 1995.

The fashionable Café was in the rue St Honoré, and its design demonstrates both the quality of carving and gilding used in commercial interiors, and the use of large areas of mirror glass. Ledoux' decorative scheme was based on military trophies and symbols such as pikes and helmets and the attributes of Mars and Minerva. His work at the Café Militaire is described by Kalnein as a 'spectacular Parisian début' which launched him as the 'fashionable architect of Parisian society' (Kalnein 1995, 192). His subsequent commissions included the Hôtel de Hallwill (1766–8), the Hôtel d'Uzès (1768–9) and later the pavillion at Louveciennes for Madame du Barry (1771). He is best known for his revolutionary work dating from the 1770s, exemplified by his plans for the ideal city, Saline des Chaux.

BLACK AND WHITE PLATES

1. Armorial of the corporation of *marchands mercers*, plaquette printed in 1674.
Bibliothèque Nationale de France, Paris, from Vidal and Duru 1911 (4° Z Le Senne 975 [1] 352).

The coat of arms at centre top was that of the *grande garde*, and the other six of the *gardes* of the corporation. The design of this armorial dates from 19 June 1629.

2. *Jeton* (medal or coin) struck for the mercers' corporation, 1704.
Bibliothèque Nationale de France, Paris, Cabinet des Médailles.
Lespinasse 1886–94.

These coins were distributed to the current and former *gardes* and *grandes gardes* of the corporation and were allocated to the guards at formal meetings and assemblies of the corporation. In 1662, each of the Six Corps was required to pay 66 *livres* to buy silver *jetons*, four for exceptional meetings, two for ordinary meetings – the same number of guards was mandatory for such assemblies. Other examples survive, dated 1588 (single ship, St Louis on back) and 1656 (three ships, St Louis on back).

3. *Der Kramer*, German, late 16th- or early 17th-century.
Bibliothèque Nationale de France, Paris, Département des Estampes Oa 60 (71).

This image of the itinerant merchant (*marchand ambulant* or *colporteur*) bearing his panier and crying his wares appeared in many parts of continental Europe at this date. For example, several German and French book, almanac and print sellers are depicted as hawkers, some with paniers (Taubert 1966, plates 51, 62, 71, 96). This form of merchandizing appears to have been practised by large numbers of travelling merchants who hawked their wares around the countryside, towns and cities of Europe (Fontaine 1993, and see also Choux 1980).

4. Le *Mercier*, French, late 17th or early 18th-century, engraved by Jean-Baptiste Bonnart 1654–1726.
Bibliothèque Nationale de France, Paris Département des Estampes. Oa 53 (51).

The panier and comb were symbolic of the mercer's trade (see the proverbs from the *Dictionnaire Trevoux* following title page). The comb was one of the official attributes of *mercerie*, though became redundant in practical terms as a symbol of their commerce, since it represented only a minor branch of their trade *menue mercerie* (see chapter 1 fig 6).

5. *Le marchand de frange dor et dargent*, French, late 17th-century pen and wash.
Bibliothèque Nationale de France, Paris, Département des Estampes.

The verse indicates that this merchant specialized in gold and silver threads used for trimming men's clothes, particularly military dress.

6. *Le marchand de rubans*, French *c.* 1700, pen, ink and wash on paper.
Bibliothèque Nationale de France, Paris, Département des Estampes.

The merchant appears to stock fabric and ribbons, which he sells to a female client, presumably for trimming clothing and possibly hats.

7. Façade of the headquarters of the corporation of merchant drapers, *c.* 1655–60, by Jacques Bruant.
Bibliothèque Nationale de France, Paris.
Blunt 1977.

The building no longer survives, except the façade, which was moved in the nineteenth century to the courtyard of the Musée Carnavalet, Paris. Bruant may also have been involved with Bullet in the building of a Paris house for the banker Everhard Jabach, which was later the address of the mercer Noel Gérard and other merchants (see Sonenscher 1993, Augarde, and Pradère 1989).

8. Frontispiece and title page *L'Office de Saint Louis, Roy de France et Confesseur A l'Usage de Messieurs les Marchands Merciers, Grossiers et Jouailliers de la Ville de Paris*, Paris 1749.
Victoria and Albert Museum, London 111.RC.K.36.

9. Trade card of Périer, *marchand quincaillier*, 1767, Gabriel de St Aubin (1724–1780). Etching and drypoint reworked with pen and brown ink. 127 mm x 183 mm (plate). Signed end of counter *GD/SA/1767*; on edge of curb, lower left *gravé par gabriel de s[t] aubin 1767*; inscription along top *A La Teste Noire Perier M' Quai De La Megisserie*.
Metropolitan Museum of Art, New York, Elisha Whitney Fund 1979.650.
Dacier 1914, Dacier 1931, Maillard 1898, Metropolitan Museum of Art 1980.

This is a working proof for the trade card, the final state of which has more cross-hatching than this and stronger lettering along the top. St Aubin added details to this state in pen and brown ink, which were incorporated into the final etching. A further preparatory stage is documented by an existing drawing which shows more merchandise (Dacier 1914 no 44a). In no known surviving version is the blank space created against the drapery folds filled with text, which was the convention for the layout of trade cards. The sign of the shop is represented at top left by the black turbanned head. The overall composition of the trade card is similar to another, by de Saint Aubin's younger brother Augustin, designed for Jacques François Quillau, bookseller (Maillard 1898, 24).

10. *Trumeau* with two *parcloses*, French, 1745–1753, gessoed and gilded oak; modern mirror glass; two trade cards of François-Charles Darnault, one pasted on the back of the central panel, the other on the back of the proper left *parclose*.
PHOTOGRAPHED DURING CONSERVATION TREATMENT
Height 3 m, overall width 1.98 m.
J. Paul Getty Museum, Malibu, California, awaiting accession number.

11. Trade card of Darnault, from *trumeau*, plate 10.
The trade card is dated 1751, and is from the shop A la Ville de Versailles in the rue du Grenier St. Lazare, which Daranult *père* left in 1753. The Darnault trade card more usually found pasted on furniture from this family gives the address from *Au Roy d'Espagne* in the rue de la Monnaie (such as that on the commode illustrated in colour plate 2). A later trade card for *Darnault frères* was recently published by Pradère (1993). See also plate 50.

12. Frontispiece of *Recoeil de Fleurs de Caprice inventé et dessiné par Jean Pillement*.
Victoria and Albert Museum, London.

Jean Pillement, painter to the King of Poland, produced a myriad of designs which were widely used by the decorative trades, especially for silks and also as motifs in European lacquer furniture and boxes. In July 1770, the *Mercure de France* advertized books of ornament prints suitable for woven silks, printed cottons, and flowers especially for Persian style fabrics, available from *Leviez, marchand d'estampes à Paris, rue Saint-André des Arts*.

13. Drawing of a screen, pencil on paper, 1760s.
AVP D^5B^6 *régistre* 2813 *Journal de vente* Madame Blakey.
Archives de la Ville de Paris.

14. Commode with *pietre dure* plaques *c.* 1785, attr. A. Weisweiler (1744–1820, master 1778) oak, pine and beech veneered with ebony and mahogany, pewter stringing, the plaques French and Italian, mid-seventeenth to late eighteenth-century, *portor d'Italie* marble tops.
Height 1.02 m, width 1.5 m, depth 54.5 cm.

J. Paul Getty Museum, Malibu, California 76.DA 9.1–2.
Bremer-David 1993, Freyburger 1981, Gonzalez-Palacios 1982 and 1991, Kjellberg 1989.

This commode has been traced to a sale of 1790 in Paris at which it sold for 3,100 *livres*. It is paired with a commode of identical form and dimensions and similar decoration, dating from about 1810. The pair may have been owned by William Beckford at Fonthill Abbey and subsequently they entered the Hamilton Palace Collection and were sold at the famous Hamilton Palace sale in 1882. (Susan, Duchess of Hamilton, wife of the 10th Duke, was related to Beckford.)

15. Trade card of Daguerre from *bureau plat* (colour plate 6).
J. Paul Getty Museum, Malibu, California 83.DA.385.

The trade card is of simple design, printed from a wood block.

16. Detail, Sèvres plaque 1778, from *bureau plat* (colour plate 6).
J. Paul Getty Museum, Malibu, California 83.DA.385.
Bremer-David 1993.

The two large curved plaques with *bleu celeste* borders are the only known surviving plaques of this form. They are each marked on the back with the price 96 *livres*. See colour plate 7 for comparable mounts used to frame lacquer panels.

17. Detail, panel of Japanese lacquer, from *bureau plat* (colour plate 7).
Victoria and Albert Museum, London 1049–1882.

The lacquer panels have been cut to fit the curved carcase and the shape of the framing mounts. When the swag mounts which hold the lacquer panels in place were removed, as shown here the *nashi-ji* lacquer borders underneath were found to be bright red, in contrast to the faded dull brown colour of the lacquer which has been exposed to light.

18. Coloured drawing of a table mounted with plaques of Sèvres biscuit porcelain, French, 1770–1785, pen, black ink and watercolour, in the style of Martin Cochin.
Metropolitan Museum of Art, New York, 59.611.5.
Myers 1991.

In its form and use of plaques, this drawing resembles the *bureau plat* illustrated in colour plate 6.

19. Detail, console table, French 1770–80, attr. Martin Carlin (*c.* 1730–1785, master 1766), veneered with ebony and set with panels of Japanese lacquer; gilt bronze mounts; *griotte* marble slab.
Height 94 cm, width 119 cm, depth 44 cm.
Sotheby's Monaco 18 June 1994.

This detail of the front of a console table shows the use of a gilt bronze swag mount to frame a piece of Japanese lacquer, identical to the mount used on the curved ends of the *bureau plat* mounted with porcelain illustrated in colour plate 6. The lacquer panel and mount are in this case applied to a flat surface. Curved lacquer panels with simpler mounts are applied to the curved ends of the table. A coloured drawing in the Metropolitan Museum of Art (59.611.1) shows a table of similar form with the same central mount.

20. Table, French *c.* 1773, stamped M. Carlin (*c.* 1730–1785, master 1766): oak veneered with tulipwood, holly and ebony, set with four soft paste Sèvres porcelain plaques; gilt bronze mounts. The circular porcelain plaque dated 1773, attributed to Jacques-François Micaud.
Height 73.3 cm, diameter 40 cm.
J. Paul Getty Museum, Malibu, California 70.DA.75.
Bremer-David 1993, Kjellberg 1989, Pradère 1989, Sassoon 1991.

21. Table, French, *c.* 1785, stamped M. Carlin (*c.* 1730–1785, master 1766) and J. Pafrat (d. 1794, master 1785). Tulipwood inlaid with sycamore, gilt bronze mounts, set with Sèvres porcelain plaque; label bears inscription 'Sèvres china table, the gift of Queen Marie Antoinette to Mrs Eden, afterwards Lady Auckland, in 1786. G. Eden, 1852.'
Height 76 cm, diameter 73 cm.
Victoria and Albert Museum, London 1058–1882.
Dawson 1980.

Eleanor Eden was the wife of William, who successfully negotiated the Treaty of Navigation and Commerce on behalf of the British in 1786. A service of Sèvres porcelain was given to Eden (Lord Auckland from 1793) and this table and another mounted with Sèvres plaques were given to his wife (Victoria and Albert Museum, London, 1057–1882).

22. *Bonheur du jour*, French *c.* 1765, stamped M Carlin (*c.* 1730–1785, master 1766). Tulipwood on oak, with seventeen Sèvres plaques, one dated 1765 and bearing the reversal of the mark usually used by the painter Antoine-Toussaint Cornailles.
Height 80.5 cm, width 68 cm, depth 41 cm.
Bowes Museum.
De Bellaigue 1974 and Medlam 1992.

This appears to have been the prototype for a series of *bonheurs du jour* with slight differences in the decoration of the plaques and wood veneers. De Bellaigue describes a further ten of these flat-panelled writing tables, all with plaques of apple-green ground, the plaques dating from 1766 to 1774. He compares minutely the differences between the woods of the small drawers and veneers of the underside of the writing flaps. After the acquisition of the Bowes example, Medlam suggested that it was the first to have been made, not only because of the early date of the 1765 plaque, but also because several of the plaques had been incorrectly fitted by Carlin, despite markings on the reverse of the plaques to indicate their orientation.

23. Vase with gilt bronze mounts *c.* 1785, the Sèvres hard-paste porcelain of *bleu nouveau* ground and of form vase *à monter Daguerre*, the mounts attributed to Pierre-Philippe Thomire (1751–1843), the plinth of *rouge griotte* marble.
Height 37.5 cm, width 34.3 cm, depth 26.1 cm.
J. Paul Getty Museum, Malibu, California 73.DI.77.1–2.
Ottomeyer and Proschel 1986, Savill 1988, Sassoon 1991.

This Sèvres form is assumed to have been produced from 1786, after a drawing inscribed *Vase de Monsieur Daguerre oval donné a faire Dapres un modele en bois Le Mois de 9bre 1786*. The shape is a simplified version of the vase and cover introduced from 1763 possibly after a design for a vase of similar shape was published by Joseph-Marie Vien in 1760. It is one of a group of shapes (including round vases) named *vases à monter Daguerre* – this shape was called *Daguerre ovale* or *cassolette à monter*.

24. Vase with gilt bronze mounts *c.* 1785, the Sèvres hard-paste porcelain of *bleu nouveau* ground and of form *vase à monter Daguerre*, the gilt bronze attributed to Pierre-Philippe Thomire (1751–1843), grey marble base.
Without mounts: height 14 cm without cover, width 31.4 cm.
With mounts: height 37.5–53 cm, width 38–39.7 cm (depending on cover).
Wallace Collection C342.
Savill 1988.

This example is the only known example of this form of vase with a gilt bronze cover (see plate 23 for a vase with porcelain cover). An outline drawing of a vase of almost identical shape to this and plate 23 is inscribed *Vase Casollette pour Etre Monté par M. Tomir fait d'un 10e plus grand que le model ce 20 Avril 1784*.

25. Combined candelabra and pot pourri vases, French *c.* 1765, apple-green Sèvres porcelain, gilt bronze mounts.
Height 42 cm.
Christie's, London 4 December 1975 lot 51.
Verlet 1987.

The cover of each vase is upturned to reveal the three-light candelabra. Other vases of this form, of blue ground, were produced at Sèvres. A related model was bought in 1765 from Dulac by Horace Walpole for his friend John Chute, and survives at The Vyne, Hampshire.

26. Clock, French, mid-18th century; gilt bronze with flowers of Vincennes porcelain and three figures of Meissen porcelain; the backplate of the clock movement engraved *Jolin A Orleans* (possibly Louis Jolin, d. 1781); the movement or dial a later replacement.
Height 54.5 cm, width 40.2 cm, depth 20.3 cm, diameter of dial 11.5 cm.
De Bellaigue 1974.

The figure of the shepherdess dates from *c.* 1748, and is attributed to J. J. Kaendler. The other two figures, which date from 1755–60 are thought by de Bellaigue to be later additions, since the gilt bronze base on which the right-hand figure stands juxtaposes awkwardly with the form of the bronze base. As he points out this could have been an eighteenth-century adaptation.

27. Clock, the dial signed NOEL BALTHAZAR A PARIS, the movement signed *Noel Balthazar a Paris* (master 1717), soft-paste porcelain flowers, French *c.* 1740–50 and a group of four figures of *blanc de Chine* porcelain, Chinese, Dehua, Fukien province, bronze mounts French *c.* 1740–50, restored.
Height 36 cm, width 20 cm, depth 15 cm.
Christie's, Monaco, 2 December 1994, lot 23.

The clock combines coloured European porcelain with Chinese export *blanc de chine* porcelain figure group (see plate 28), the porcelain base of which is framed and raised on a platform of gilt bronze which also supports the bronze tree trunk. The trunk bears the drum case for the clock and French porcelain flowers.

28. Group of figures of a Dutch family, Chinese *blanc de chine* porcelain, Dehua, Fukien province, *c.* 1700.
Victoria and Albert Museum, London C108–1963, Ionides Bequest.

Dutch merchants and traders trading with China presumably inspired the design of these figures.

29. Clock, mid-eighteenth-century, the porcelain German (Meissen), the movement and gilt bronze base French, the movement by Gudin.
Height 44.5 cm, width 33 cm, depth 21 cm, diameter of dial 12 cm.
The National Trust, Waddesdon Manor, W2/48/6*.
De Bellaigue 1974.

As de Bellaigue has noted, Lazare Duvaux sold Meissen figures to Gudin in 1753. The fact that Delahoguette had in stock a figure of an elephant supporting a clock case without its movement throws new light on the question of Gudin's role in supplying clocks for such ensembles, suggesting that in at least some instances, the production of such items was co-ordinated by the mercers. A drawing in the Houthakker collection for a clock mounted in a bronze frame is very similar to this clock, though differs in the depiction of a Meissen horse and Moor in place of the elephant. The drawing is marked with Gudin's name in the clock drum (Fuhring 1989, cat. no. 583).

30. Detail, bronze base of clock (see plate 29).
The National Trust, Waddesdon Manor, part of W2/48/6*.

An unused shelf within the base, and the protruding semi-scroll at the back are pierced, apparently to take screws which would secure whatever was originally intended to be placed on the base. The figure of the elephant, however, does not come into contact with these holes, which suggests that the base was intended for some other composition such as the horse and Moor described above. Perhaps it was a stock item adapted to fit available figures rather than a special design.

31. Model armchair (*fautueil*), French, probably 1763–1768, stamped Tilliard (stamp used by Jean-Baptiste Tilliard (1686–1766, master 1717),Jacques Jean Baptiste Tilliard (1723–1798, master in 1752), the webbing marked in black ink *fecit petrus urbare? Sieg 126?* (probably Jean Baptiste Petrus, *marchand tapissier*).
Height 54 cm, width 17 cm, depth 27.7 cm.
Christie's London, 16 June 1992.

The graining, upholstery and rear legs seem to be nineteenth-century work. The chair may well have been altered at this date for use as a child's chair – the worn patches on the seat and back are compatible with such use.

32. Coloured drawing of a mounted vase.
Gouache, with brown and grey ink. 235 mm x 378 mm. Inscribed at upper left, '*2 Pied. 3 pouces. 2 Lignes.*' and below *No. XIII. Une Piece. I pied 4 pouces/Les Ornements en Rameaux de fleurs et de joncs de ce Vase sont un peu en relief. Il est d'un verd un peu plus foncé que les Suivants/et tirant sur le gris. La monture est en bronze* and at bottom right in red ink '*20*'.
Metropolitan Museum of Art, New York 61.680.1(7).
Myers 1991, Watson 1981 and 1986.

The colouring and inscription indicates that the vase was of celadon porcelain with gilt bronze mounts. The design of the mounts dates to the 1750s. The drawing may date from this period, though is more likely to have been made in the 1770s or 80s, alongside others in the Esmerion bequest to the Metropolitan Museum of Art which are thought to have represented the stock of Poirier and Daguerre at this period. The ongoing taste for old porcelain in finely worked bronze mounts was exemplified by the pieces sold in the Gaignat sale catalogue dated 1768, complied by Simon-Philippe Poirier, one of which was drawn by Gabriel de St Aubin. (Amongst

Lazare Duvaux' sales of celadon porcelain set in specially designed mounts was the sale to Gaignat on 16 March 1754 of two covered celadon urns set in gilt bronze mounts designed by Duplessis, for the price of 2,920 *livres*.)

33. Vase, Chinese celadon porcelain, gilt bronze mounts French, *c.* 1750.
Height 76 cm.
Sotheby's, Lot 13 December 1974 no. 137.

Several other versions of this model survive, although some of these recorded at auction may be the same as other cited examples: Musée Carnavalet, Paris, (Collection Henriette Bouvier no. 89) and a second from the Bouvier Collection, possibly sold Christie's London 3 December 1981 lot 33, also Christie's London 29 September 1969 lot 96, Sotheby 21 June 1974 lot 31, Galerie Georges Petit Paris 10–14 May 1886 lot 279, possibly sold at Sotheby 13 December 1974 lot 137, Sotheby 11 June 1993 (later with Jean Lupu, Paris and advertised in *Burlington Magazine* May 1990). These vases vary in height between about 75 and 77 cm high.

34. *La Boutique étant san chalan: adieu le negos*, *c.* 1701, Paris.
Bibliothèque Nationale de France, Paris.

The *traffiquant* and the *négotiant* (holding tobacco leaves?) are here shown dealing in wholesale goods at a port. Neither were members of a corporation and thus traded freely in imports and exports (see Bergeron 1978). The verse beneath alludes to the long-term credit which formed part of the transaction.

35. Garniture of three lidded and two open vases, Chinese, Kangxi, 1662–1722, hard paste porcelain, underglaze blue decoration.
Height 31.8 cm, diameter 27.3 cm (lidded vases).
Height 28.3 cm, diameter 12.7 cm (open vases).
J. Paul Getty Museum, Malibu, California, 72.DE.1-.5.
Bremer-David 1993.

36. Garniture of three vases, Japanese, Arita, first half of the eighteenth century, hard paste porcelain, underglaze blue decoration; polychrome enamel; gilding.
Vase 1: Height 32.1 cm, diameter 17.8 cm.
Vase 2: Height 32.1 cm, diameter 18 cm.
Vase 3: Height 32.4 cm, diameter 17.8 cm.
J. Paul Getty Museum, Malibu, California, 87.DE.26.1-.3.
Bremer-David 1993.

37. Pair of vases, the hard paste porcelain Chinese, Kangxi (1662–1722), the gilt bronze mounts French, stamped with crowned 'c's for 1745–9.
Height 31.7 cm, width 35.5 cm, depth 26.7 cm.
J. Paul Getty Museum, Malibu, California, 79.DI.121.1-.2.
Bremer-David 1993, Wilson 1980, Wilson, Watson and Derham 1982, Watson 1981.

38. One of a pair of perfume burners, Chinese *blanc de Chine* porcelain, Dehua, Fukien province *c.* 1700, the silver-gilt mounts French, early 18th-century.
Height 19.1 cm, width 11.5 cm.

Victoria and Albert Museum, London 816&a–1882.
Victoria and Albert Museum 1924.

The design of the mounts recalls that of the covered vase of coloured porcelain in the foreground (to the left of the monkey) in the still life illustrated in colour plate 15. Note especially in the painting the tripod feet of gilt bronze or giltwood. Another vase of *blanc de chine* porcelain of about the same date with later mounts in neo-classical style is now in the J. Paul Getty Museum (78.DI.359, see Watson 1981, Bremer-David 1993).

39. Components of lid of bowl with silver mounts (colour plate 12), porcelain, Japanese, Imari *c.* 1700, silver mounts French 1720.
J. Paul Getty Museum, Malibu, California 79.DI.123.a-.b.

40. Pair of vases, French *c.* 1740–55, blue lacquered cardboard (*carton*) or paste, gilt bronze mounts.
Height 20 cm, width 10 cm.
Musée Nissim de Camondo, Paris, Inv 82.
Musée Nissim de Camondo, 1986.

The body of these vases imitates Chinese blue porcelain. The chased and gilt mounts are of extremely high quality design.

41. Vase and cover, Meissen, 1727–30, the porcelain painted in enamel and a pinkish lustre; marked with the monogram 'AR'.
Height 39.6 cm.
Victoria and Albert Museum, London C 48–1971.

42. Covered vase, the porcelain German (Meissen) 1749, the gilt bronze mounts French. *c.* 1750.
Height 31.1 cm.
Cleveland Museum of Art, Purchase from the J. H. Wade Fund, 44.230.

43. Trade card of Bazin dated 1774 with bill for Sèvres porcelain plates, jam pots, butter dishes and sugar bowls, total 600 *livres*.
Archives de la Ville de Paris 6AZ 291 fo20.

44. Drawing of a *vase pompadour* with inscription.
Manufacture Nationale de Sèvres, Archives, photograph J.P. Harmand/MNS.

45. *Vase Pompadour*, Sèvres porcelain, 4th size, turquoise blue ground with birds, date letter for 1754.
Height with lid (knob missing) 20.2 cm, height without lid 16.4 cm, diameter 12 cm.
Victoria and Albert Museum, London C421–1921.

46. Cabinet of the Duchesse de la Meilleraye, Japanese lacquer 1680–1700, giltwood stand French, *c.* 1690.
Bibliothèque de l'Arsenal, Paris (photo Bibliothèque Nationale de France, Paris).
Whitehead and Impey 1988.

47. Trade card of Gersaint, François Boucher 1740.
Bibliothèque Nationale de France, Paris.
Watson 1967 (2), Thornton 1986.

As Thornton noted, the composition of the trade card was reproduced in colour in the corner of a painting dated *c.* 1760 of the Countess Tessin, whose father-in-law had been Ambassador to France. The painting, in the National Museum, Stockholm, shows the Countess sitting at her French-style desk in a room hung with painted Chinese silk. The cabinet is coloured red and gold, the pagod is clothed in a striped blue outfit and the coral, fans, shells etc are also highly coloured.

48. Commode, Japanese lacquer cabinet with brass mounts, late 17th-century, the giltwood stand and bronze corner mounts French *c.* 1715.
Pagodenburg, Nymphenburg.
Huth 1971.

49. Detail, cabinet of the Duchesse de la Meilleraye, Japanese lacquer 1680–1700, the giltwood stand French, *c.* 1690 (plate 46).
Bibliothèque de l'Arsenal, Paris (photo Bibliothèque Nationale de France, Paris).

50. Commode, French 1785, stamped M. Carlin (*c.* 1730–1785, master 1766), oak veneered with ebony and satin-wood, the lacquer Japanese, black and aventurine *vernis Martin*, gilt bronze mounts and white marble top.
Height 96.7 cm, width 1.513 m, depth 53.5 cm.
Musée du Louvre OA 5498.
Verlet 1958, Samoyault 1971, Lemonnier 1984, Alcouffe 1993.

The Darnault brothers acquired a Japanese lacquer cabinet from the sale in 1782 of the collection of the Duc d'Aumont. They supplied Carlin with the five panels from that cabinet for this commode soon after, and when he died in 1785, it was listed in his inventory as only partly complete. It was finally delivered to the Château de Bellevue for Madame Victoire in April 1785, for the price of 6,500 *livres*. Alterations to the carcase suggest that a part-made carcase was adapted to take the lacquer panels. The columns were described in the description of the commode made on its delivery as 'colonnes chinoises sur les angles'. The commode has drawers veneered with matchbook veneers of satin-wood. In the nineteenth century the commode was used at the Tuileries and Fontainebleau; it was copied several times in the late nineteenth century.

51. Commode, 1740–50, stamped by Bernard II van Risamburgh, Japanese lacquer, gilt bronze mounts, marble slab.
Private Collection photo Edimedia.
De Reyniès 1987.

The Japanese lacquer panels have been let into larger black lacquer backgrounds, which are framed with gilt bronze mounts. This arrangement suggests that the drawer fronts from a Japanese lacquer cabinet were removed from their drawers and reused on larger drawers which were made specifically to fit the dimensions of this large commode.

52. Medal cabinet late 17th-century, attr. André-Charles Boulle, veneered with ebony, burr walnut, marquetry of brass on red-stained turtleshell, Chinese lacquer; gilt bronze mounts.

Height 2.28 m, width 1.33 m.
Bibliothèque Nationale de France, Paris, Cabinet des Médailles.
Bibiothèque Nationale, 1989.

The exterior is set with oriental lacquer panels, and the interior with European imitations. The Boulle marquetry borders frame four panels of a burnt orange ground, producing a highly coloured result. The design of the Boulle marquetry is based on identifiable designs conserved in the Musée des Arts Décoratifs, Paris. The inside of the doors are decorated with four carved and lacquered panels of burr walnut made in France, each representing a bird of prey, probably copied from Japanese lacquer panels.

53. Medal cabinet, veneered with Chinese Coromandel lacquer, early 18th-century, European lacquer, the mounts French, *c.* 1730.
Height 2.27 m, width 1.34 m.
Bibliothèque Nationale de France, Paris, Cabinet des Médailles.
Bibiothèque Nationale, 1989.

The Chinese Coromandel lacquer panels come from a large screen, as in the example of the commode illustrated in plate 54. The interiors of the cabinets are fitted out with shallow drawers for medals.

54. Commode French, *c.* 1750, stamped by Jacques-Philippe Carel (master 1723, archive 1724–50) oak veneered with Coromandel lacquer, *vernis Martin*, purplewood and fruitwood; gilt bronze; Sarrancolin marble top.
Height 93.3 cm, width 1.47 m, depth 69 cm.
Musée du Louvre, OA9488.

The commode was made *en suite* with two corner cupboards which were presumably veneered with panels from the same Coromandel lacquer screen. All three pieces were in the Château de Valençay in the nineteenth century.

55. Box, Paris, *c.* 1720, red *vernis Martin* with gilt ornaments; gilt metal locks and hinges.
Height 10 cm, width 22.75 cm, depth 29 cm.
Victoria and Albert Museum, London 8507–1863.
The box is decorated with arabesque designs in gold on a red ground, and in one of its interior compartments is fitted a smaller removeable box of similar decoration.

56. Trade card of Berthollon, with bill dated 3 August 1790, for 5 *aunes* of blue *florence*, total 15 *livres*.
Archives de la Ville de Paris 6AZ 291 fo41.

57. Trade card of Barbier, with bill dated 23 January 1778, for *gros de tours satiné* with Muselman stripes, and white taffeta, total 94 *livres* 10 *sous*.
Archives de la Ville de Paris AZ 291 fo13.

58. Trade card of Laroza with bill made out to Monsieur Vilery, dated 9 February 1764, for 15 *aunes* of satin, total 180 *livres*.
Archives de la Ville de Paris 6AZ 291 fo10.

59. Trade card of Bourjol.
Archives de la Ville de Paris AZ 291 fo9.

60. Trade card of Lenormand.
Archives Nationales, Paris. Conti papers.

61. Trade card of Leroux and de la Salle with bill made out to the Marquis de Despinchal, dated 16 October 1773, for yellow satin, grey satin and black velvet, total (with outstanding debt of 246 *livres*) of 412 *livres* 13 *sols* 4 *deniers*.
Archives de Paris AZ 291 fo17.

62. Habit de Fripier, French *c.* 1680, Nicolas de l'Armessin.
Bibliothèque Nationale de France, Paris, Département des Estampes Oa 60 (26).

The *fripiers* specialized either in second-hand clothing or second-hand furnishings, hence the two sides of this figure's costume.

63. *Guéridon*, French, 1770–80, marquetry of rosewood and amaranth; plaque of painted tôle gilt bronze mounts.
Height 76 cm, diameter 57 cm.
Christie's, Monaco 16 June 1990, lot 215.
Photo Christie's.

The table is an imitation of the round tables mounted with porcelain plaques such as those illustrated in plates 20 and 21. The gilt bronze mounts are unexceptional, unlike the distinctive swag mounts used on furniture stamped by Martin Carlin (see especially plate 21). The inlay of the darker amaranth on the legs imitates fluting, which is both carved and often decorated with gilt bronze *chandelles* on the Carlin tables and *bureaux plats*.

64. Detail, plaque of painted tole, 1770–80 (plate 63).
Diameter 57 cm.
Christie's, Monaco 16 June 1990 lot 215.
Photo Christie's.

The plaque is painted on a faux marble ground, itself on a pink background with highly coloured garlands and a village scene in the manner of Teniers. It imitates the circular plaques produced at Sèvres for mounting on furniture (see back jacket).

65. Box, South Staffordshire, 1760s, wood covered with shagreen, 3 plaques of painted enamel on copper, mounted in brass; fitted with glass inkpot and pounce pot with brass *repoussé* covers and an onyx seal mounted in brass; two steel erasing blades and 1 cutting blade for gold holder.
Height 4.75 cm, width 7.3 cm, depth 4.25 cm.
Victoria and Albert Museum, London C415–1914.

The box was probably made in Birmingham, Wednesbury or Bilston, the three main manufacturing centres in the South Staffordshire area known for their painted enamel wares.

66. Trade card, Au Petit Dunkerque.
Private collection.

The label is pasted to the lower half of a cardboard fan box which is decorated in a bright green in imitation of shagreen and has a pink interior.

67. Trade card, Au Petit Dunkerque.
British Museum, Banks Collection 133.86.

68. Eugène Atget, *3, Quai de Conti, 1900*.
Atget neg. no. inscribed in negative. Title and negative no. 4133 and *Ancien magasin de bijouterie/de Marie Antoinette/Au Petit Dunkerque* inscribed verso in pencil.
J. Paul Getty Museum, Malibu, California 90.XM.45.1.
Baldwin 1991.

Atget's repertoire of photographs of Paris include a number of eighteenth-century shop fronts. This photograph, with ghost figure of a waiter exiting, was taken fourteen years before the building was demolished, and shows it in use as a bar. The detail of the surrounds of the windows and of the sign are particularly clear.

69. Sign 'Au Petit Dunkerque' *c.* 1782, steel.
60 cm x 65 cm.
Musée Carnavalet, Paris.

The sign replaced the painted sign of the Port of Dunkerque by Joseph Vernet, and appears to have hung at the shop between *c.* 1782 and its demolition in 1914. It is attached to the façade of the shop in the manner described by the legislation of 1761 which banned overhanging shop signs (see chapter 6, page 130).

70. Trade card, A La Perle d'Orient.
The National Trust, Waddesdon Manor.

71. Trade card, Au Petit Dunkerque c. 1768 J. M. Moreau.
The National Trust, Waddesdon Manor.

72. Gold box, French, 1775–81, makers' mark of J-C Genu and Paris discharge marks for 1775–81 and 1775–6, and detail of inscription 'Du Petit Dunkerque' on flange.
Victoria and Albert Museum, London 168–1878.
Bury 1982.

73. *Etui* for razors, English 1750–60, wood covered with white shagreen and mounted in silver; five steel razors with handles of tortoiseshell mounted in silver, four blades marked Gordon, one marked Tyrer; leather stop.
Height 18.2 cm, width 7.7 cm.
Victoria and Albert Museum, London, M18–G–1965.

The case is lined with pink velvet, now faded, and trimmed with a silver gallon. It is divided into seven compartments. The top of the box is decorated with a plate which bears the initials of H.W. and a crest (a squirrel eating a nut on a crown).

74. Trade card of Choffard, *c.* 1770, Pierre-Philippe Choffard (1731–1809).
Bibliothèque Nationale de France, Paris, *Département des Estampes*, Ef 180 Rés. f4.
Roux 1940, Maillard 1898.

Choffard specialized in various types of *petites estampes* including copper plate designs for trade cards. This was his own advertisement.

75. Trade card of Remy *c.* 1770, Pierre-Philippe Choffard (1731–1809).
Bibliothèque Nationale de France, Paris *Département des Estampes* Ef 180 Rés. f4, 23.
Roux 1940.

The neoclassical frame was a typical device used by Choffard, for example on the trade card of Vallayer, *mercer Au Soleil d'Or*, rue du Roule (he was the father of the painter Anne Vallayer-Coster).

76. Designs for brackets and shop signs, Jacques Androuet du Cerceau.
Victoria and Albert Museum, London E2150–1932, E2150–1932.

These are rare survivals of French designs for architectural ironwork, and show that there was in Paris a tradition of decorating domestic and commercial spaces with elaborate brackets well before the eighteenth century. Such designs do not appear to have changed radically over time (see plate 78 and H.R. d'Allemagne 1924).

77. Design for a bracket, 1723, Louis Fordrin, from *Le Nouveau Livre de Serrurerie*.
Victoria and Albert Museum, London.

This page of designs for decorative metalwork is from the book of designs for churches, houses and royal and princely residences, gardens, staircases, sign brackets and balconies. Fordin announced himself on the frontispiece as *Serrurier ordinaire du Roy et de ses Monnoyes*. The book was produced under royal privilege (*avec privilège du roy*).

78. Shop, 18th-century, rue St Honoré, from *Revue Générale de l'Architecture et de Travaux Publics* 1866, vol. XXIV pl. 26.
Bibliothèque Nationale de France, Paris, Cabinet des Estampes.

Like the Wrightman shop front (plate 79), this shop front comprises glazed windows and distinctive carved woodwork.

79. Shop front, Paris, *c.* 1750 from 3, Quai Bourbon, Paris; carved oak, the sign a replacement (though in the manner of eighteenth-century signs and close to du Cerceau's designs, see plate 77).
Metropolitan Museum of Art, New York, 20.154.

Fully glazed shops both protected the merchandise from theft and dust, and made it possible to create interior comforts such as warmth within.

80. *Le menuisier en meubles*.
Diderot *L'Encyclopaedie*, vol. VII, 1769, plate I.
Victoria and Albert Museum, London.

This workshop was called an *atelier* by Diderot, a term not used in the inventories, and depicts a workshop which specialized in upholstered goods. Diderot's distinction between a workshop and salerooms is paralleled in the representations of both kinds of spaces in the plates of the *Encyclopaedie*. This sequence of plates represents collectively a hierarchy of the trades symbolized in part by the difference between workshop or shop space, and by the degree of decoration of the interior. The cork-maker and balance-maker's shops, for example, are both open to the street but incorporate a small amount of decoration in the carved wooden panelling in the interior. The furrier's and milliner's shops are depicted as fashionable shop spaces. The gilder's workshop represents several gilders working at benches with frames hanging on the wall, with no decorative woodwork or shop accessories.

The signifiers therefore seem to have comprised, for the workshop, materials, manual work, sometimes conducted in a space open to the street, and for the shop a glazed shop-front, a sales counter, display cabinets and shelving, decorative carving (usually *boiseries* and mirrors), seating, sometimes a stove and some degree of fashionable dress and gesture on the part of the proprietor. For example, in the case of the plate of the goldsmith's shop, the space is divided by a line along the floor which symbolized the difference between the workshop on the left, with goldsmiths working alongside the window and a furnace in the background, and the saleroom on the right, with sales counter, *boiseries*, glazed display cabinets, door and shopfront.

81. *Le tapissier*.
Diderot *L'Encyclopaedie*, vol. IX, 1771, plate 1.
Victoria and Albert Museum, London.

The interior of this *boutique* combines the display of finished goods with some 'clean' work – the women at *l* to the left are stitching tapestries for hangings or curtains. Mattresses are being carried out for delivery at *i* and other finished goods are displayed at *d* (mirrors) and *e* (veneered furniture). Chair frames hang on the wall at *f*. The *tapissier*, rather than working on a piece of furniture or tapestry, is depicted at *m* inspecting the workmanship on an upholstered chair.

The stair to the upper floors (described in the text as *magasins*) is indicated at *g*. In the mercers' inventories, the *magasins* were on the upper floors and were used for the display and storage of finished goods, whilst the smaller *boutique* and sometimes *arrière boutique* were on the ground floor.

82. *Boutique de Mlle S^t^. Quentin, rue Saint-Honoré, Au Magnifique*, French, 1777, Gabriel de St Auban.
Watercolour, signed at lower left *G. de S^t^* Aubin f. 15 janvier 1777.
Dacier 1929–31, vol. II cat. no. 458, plate XVI (Victoria and Albert Museum, London).
Ex Destailleur collection Paris, 26–7 May 1893, sheet 28 in lot 111, *Livre de St. Aubin*, and collection of the Comtesse de Behague, 19–23 May 1896, lot 846.

Mademoiselle de St. Quentin was famous for her fashion dolls, *les poupées de la rue St. Honoré*. The interior of her shop shows the use of large-scale statuary in the form of the statue of Minerva, goddess of stitchery, and also depicts the activities associated with such shops, of the finishing of gowns and fashionable accessories, and of flirtation and seduction. At the left, behind the counter, several women are trimming hats with flowers, and at the rear of the shop a male client appears to be pursuing another of the female shopworkers. Two other male clients are examining a purse towards the front of the shop at the right. The statue of Minerva was the subject of another drawing by Gabriel de St. Aubin (*La Minerve de Saint-Quentin, marchande de modes*, Dacier 1929–31, cat. no. 459).

83. *Marchande lingère dans sa boutique*, French 1688.
Bibliothèque Nationale de France, Paris, cabinet des Estampes, Est Oa 77 (70).

The theme of seduction is also evident in this print. The sexuality of female shopkeepers and workers and the exchange of fashionable wares for sexual favours was frequently the subject of comment. For example, Diderot said ironically of the proprietor of the Traits Galants in the rue St-Honoré, Madame Pagelle (who became a mistress of Louis XV) *si vous n'entendez que les étoffes et l'ajustement, faites vous fille de boutique aux Traits Galants* (cited in Henard 1908–9, 430).

BIBLIOGRAPHY

Where printed material is rare, the library or archive reference to the example consulted is also given. Appendix 2 lists the printed papers recording inter-corporate disputes, and these are not reproduced in this bibliography. Manuscript sources are listed, with full archival references, after the printed sources.

PRINTED SOURCES

A. Adburgham *Shops and Shopping, 1800–1914; where, and in what manner the well-dressed Englishwoman bought her clothes* London 1964.

H. Adhemar 'L'Enseigne de Gersaint par Antoine Watteau, aperçus nouveaux' *Bulletin du Laboratoire du Louvre* (1964) 6–17.

D. Alcouffe (ed.) *Le Mobilier du Musée du Louvre* 2 vols., Paris 1993.

D. Alcouffe *Les Artisans décorateurs du bois au Faubourg St. Antoine sous Louis XIV* (thesis) Ecole de Chartes 1962.

P. Alfassa *L'Enseigne de Gersaint* Paris 1910.

H.R. d'Allemagne *Musée Le Secq de Tournelles à Rouen: Férronerie Ancienne* 2 vols., Paris 1924.

Almanac Dauphin ou Tablettes Royales du vrai mérite des artistes célebres du royaume etc Paris n.d. [published between 1772–1791] (BN V25839).

Almanac général des Marchands, Negotians Armateurs et Fabricans de la France et de l'Europe, et autres parties du Monde Paris 1770 (BN V21444).

Almanac Parisian, en faveur des étrangers et des personnes curieuses Paris 1762 (BM 59975[1]).

S. Arasaratnam *Merchants, Companies and Commerce on the Coromandel Coast 1650–1740* Delhi and Oxford 1986.

Archives Historiques et Litteraires du Nord de la France et du Midi de la Belgique 3rd series, vol. 3, Valenciennes 1852.

Arrest du Conseil Privé du Roy 5 October 1691 (AN AD XI/22).

Arrest de la Cour de Parlement qui omologue une Deliberation de la Communauté des Maîtres et Marchands Tapissiers, 31 August 1723 (AD XI, 27).

Arrest de la Cour de Parlement 7 December 1761 (BN 4° Z Le Senne 992).

Arrest de la Cour rendu en faveur des Marchands Merciers, Grossiers, Jouailliers a Paris . . . 31 mars 1699 (AN AD XI/22).

Arrêt du Conseil d'état du Roi, concernant la nomination d'un Député pour le Commerce, réprésentant les Six Corps de marchands de la Ville de Paris 27 April 1785.

Arts Council of Great Britain *French Eighteenth-Century Furniture Designs. Drawings from the Musée des Arts Décoratifs Paris* London 1960.

J-D. Augarde '1749 Joseph Baumhauer, ébéniste privilgié du roi' *L'Estampille* 20 (4 June 1987) 15–44.

L'Avant Coureur: December 1767, Jan 1768, Jan 1770, April 1770, May 1770, Dec 1770, April 1771, Sept 1771, Oct 1771, July 1772, Nov 1772.

J. Ayers, O. Impey and J. V. G. Mallet *Porcelain for Palaces; the Fashion for Japan in Europe 1650–1750* London 1990.

A. Babeau 'Le Faubourg St. Honoré sous Louis XV' *Bulletin de la Société Historique du 8ème arrondissement de Paris* Paris 1904–1907 (BN 4°2 le Senne 2733 [2]).

M. Baker 'Roubiliac's Argyll Monument and the interpretation of eighteenth-century sculptors' designs' *Burlington Magazine* 134 (December 1992) 785–97.

C.B. Bailey 'Lebrun et le commerce d'art pendant le blocus continental' *Revue de l'Art* 63 (1984) 35–46.

G. Baldwin *Looking at Photographs: a guide to technical terms*, Malibu, California, 1991.

N. Ballu 'Influence de l'Extrême Orient sur le style de Chantilly au XVIII siècle' *Cahiers de la Céramique et des Arts de Feu* 2 (1958) 100–112.

M. Baulant, A.J. Schuurman, P. Servais (eds.) *Inventaires après décès et ventes de meubles: Apports à une histoire de la vie économique et quotidienne (XIVe–XIXe siècle)* Louvain-la-Neuve 1988.

C. Baulez 'Pierre Gouthière' in H. Ottomeyer and P. Proschel *Vergoldeten Bronzen: Die Bronzearbeiten des Spatbarock und Klassizimus* Munich 1986.

C. Baulez 'Toute l'Europe tire ses bronzes de Paris' in Ulrich Leben (ed.) *Bernard Molitor 1755–1833: Ebéniste parisien d'origine luxembourgeoise* (exhibition catalogue) Luxembourg 1995, 77–101.

G. Beard 'Decorators and Furniture Makers at Croome Court' *Furniture History* 29 (1993) 88–110.

W. Beawes *Lex Mercatora Rediviva: or, the Merchant's Directory* 6th edition Dublin 1773.

R. Behamou 'Public and private art education in France 1648–1793' *Studies on Voltaire and the eighteenth century* 308 (1993).

H. Belevitch-Stankevitch *Le Goût chinois en France au temps de Louis XIV* reprinted Geneva 1970.

J.F. Belhoste 'Les entrepeneurs du Dijonval' *La Manufacture de Dijonval et la Draperie Sedanaise 1650–1850: Cahiers de l'Inventaire* 2 (November 1984) 77–97.

G. de Bellaigue *The James A de Rothschild collection at Waddesdon Manor; Furniture, Clocks and Gilt Bronzes* 2 vols., Fribourg 1974.

G. de Bellaigue 1968 'Martin-Eloy Lignereux and England' *Gazette des Beaux-Arts*, 6e période LXXI (May–June 1968) 283–94.

G. de Bellaigue 'George IV and French Furniture' *Connoisseur* 195 (June 1977) 116–25.

G. de Bellaigue 'Daguerre and England' in U. Leben (ed.) *Bernard Molitor 1755–1833: Ebéniste parisien d'origine luxembourgeoise* (exhibition catalogue) Luxembourg 1995, 157–179.

L. Bergeron *Banquiers, Négotiants et Manufacturiers Parisiens du Directoire à l'Empire* Paris 1978.

Berliner Festspiele *Japan und Europa 1543–1929* Berlin 1993.

M. Beurdeley *Porcelaine de la Compagnie des Indes* Fribourg 1962.

Bibliothèque Historique de la Ville de Paris, *Images de Confréries Parisiennes* (exhibition catalogue) Paris 1991–2.

Bibliothèque Nationale, Paris *Trafic d'influences, meubles de lacque et goût extreme-oriental aux XVIIe et XVIIIe* (exhibition catalogue) Paris 1989.

J. Black *Natural and Necessary Enemies: Anglo-French Relations in the Eighteenth Century* London 1986.

N. Blomac *La Gloire et le Jeu: des harmes et des chevaux, 1766–1866* Paris 1991.

A. Blunt *Art and Architecture in France 1500–1700* London 1977.

Boileau 1268: R. Lespinasse and F. Bonnardot (eds.) *Les Métiers et communautés de la Ville de Paris: Le Livre des Métiers d'Etienne Boileau* Paris 1897.

E. Bonnaffé *Le Commerce de la Curiosité* Paris 1895.

C. Boltz 'Hoym, Lemaire und Meissen, ein Betraq zur Geschichte der Dresdener Porzellansammlung' Keramos (April 1980) 3–101.

G. Bossenga 'Protecting merchants: Guilds and Commercial Capitalism in Eighteenth Century France' *French Historical Studies* XV, 4 (Fall 1988) 693–703.

F. Boucher 'Les Sources de l'Inspiration de l'Enseigne de Gersaint' *Bulletin de la Société de l'Histoire de l'Art Français* (1957) 123–129.

F. Braudel *The Wheels of Commerce, Civilisation and Capitalism 15th–18th Century* 2 vols., London 1982.

C. Bremer-David (ed.) *Decorative Arts: an illustrated summary catalogue of the J. Paul Getty Museum* Malibu 1993.

J. Brewer and R. Porter *Consumption and the World of Goods* London and New York 1993.

F. Buckland 'The Marchands Merciers in the eighteenth century' *Partridge: International Year Book* 1988.

H. Burstin *Le faubourg Saint-Marcel à l'époque révolutionnaire: structure économique et composition sociale* (thesis) Université de Paris I, 1977.

S. Bury *Jewellery Gallery: Summary Catalogue, Victoria and Albert Museum*, London 1982.

C. Campbell 'Understanding traditional and modern patterns of consumption in eighteenth century England; a character-action approach' in J. Brewer and R. Porter *Consumption and the world of goods* London and New York 1993.

C. Campbell *The Romantic Ethic and the Spirit of Modern Consumerism* Oxford 1987.

P. Casselle 'Pierre François Basan, marchand d'estampes' *Paris et l'Ile de France, mémoires* XXXIII (1982) 99–185.

Catalogue des Marbres, Bronzes, Agates, Porcelaines composant le Magasin de Julliot, Marchand rue S. Honore, attenant celle du Four Paris 1777.

Chardon *Recueil d'Ordonnances, statuts et reglemens concernant le corps de la mercerie*, Paris 1752 (BN 21036).

R.J. Charleston *The James A. de Rothschild Collection at Waddesdon Manor Meissen and other Porcelain* Fribourg 1971.

S.D. Chassagne *Oberkampf* London 1980.

S.D. Chassagne and S. Chapman *European Textile Printers of the Eighteenth Century: a study of Peel and Oberkampf* London 1981.

J. Chatelus *Peinture et groupes sociaux: les goûts artistique des marchands parisiens 1729–1959* (thesis) Université de Paris X, 1973.

J. Choux 'Notice sur une boîte de Colporteur' *Gazette des Beaux-Arts* XCVI (December 1980) 209–212.

J. Cleret *La Corporation des marchands merciers de leurs origines jusq'au XVIe siècle* (thesis) Ecole de Chartes 1941.

C. Clunas (ed.) *Chinese Export Art and Design* London 1987.

A. Cobban *A History of Modern France* London 1957.

C.W. Cole *Colbert and a century of French Mercantilism,* New York 1939.

W. Cole *A Journal of my Journey to Paris in the year 1765* reprinted London 1931.

Collection des maisons de commerce et des intérieures les mieux décorés Paris 1806.

E. Coornaert *Les corporations en France avant 1789* Paris 1941.

E. Coornaert *Les Compagnonnages en France du Moyen age à nos jours* Paris 1966.

L. Courajod *Livre Journal de Lazare Duvaux, marchand-bijoutier ordinaire du Roi 1748–1758* Paris 1874.

J. Coural and C. Gastinel-Coural 'La Fabrique lyonnaise au XVIIIe siècle: La commande royale de 1730' *Revue de l'Art* 62 (1983) 49–63.

Les Curiositez de Paris et des Environs 3 vols., Paris 1733.

A. Czarnocka 'Vernis Martin: the lacquerwork of the Martin Family in Eighteenth-Century France' *Studies in the Decorative Arts* 1 (1994) 56–74.

E. Dacier *L'Oeuvre Gravé de Gabriel de Saint-Aubin: notice historique et cataloue raisonné* Paris 1914.

E. Dacier *Gabriel de St Aubin, peintre, dessinateur et graveur (1724–1780)* 2 vols., Paris 1921–31.

C.C. Dauterman and J. Parker 'The Kress Galleries of French Decorative Arts' *Metropolitan Museum of Art Bulletin* 18 (May 1960).

C.C. Dauterman, J. Parker and E. Standen *Decorative Art from the Samuel H. Kress Collection at the Metropolitan Museum of Art* London 1964.

D. Davis *A History of Shopping* London 1966.

A. Dawson 'The Eden Service: another Diplomatic Gift' *Apollo* (April 1980) 288–297.

A. Dawson 'Wedgwood and the revolution' *Country Life* (December 21 1989) 64–66.

D. Defoe *The Complete English Tradesman* reprinted New York 1970.

Délégation à l'Action Artistique de la Ville de Paris.

L. Dermigny *La Chine et l'Occident: le Commerce à Canton au XVIIIe siècle, 1719–1833* 3 vols., Paris 1964.

P. Deyon and P. Guignet 'The Royal Manufacturies and Economic and Technological Progress in France before the Industrial Revolution' *Journal of Economic History* 9 (1980) 611–632.

Dictionnaire du citoyen ou abregé historique, théorique et pratique du commerce 2 vols., Amsterdam 1762.

Dictionnaire Portatif du Commerce, Paris, 1777 (8° Z Le Senne 4221).

D. Diderot and J. d'Alembert *L'Encyclopédie, ou dictionnaire raisonné des sciences, des arts et des métiers* 17 vols., Paris 1750–65.

P.J. Donelly *Blanc de Chine, the Porcelain of Dehua in Fukien province* London 1969.

W. Doyle 'The Price of Offices in Pre-Revolutionary France' *The Historical Journal* 27, 4 (1984) 831–860.

Dumont or Butel-Dumont (attributed to), *Théorie du luxe; ou traité dans lequel on entreprend d'établir que le luxe est un ressort non seulement utile mais même indispensable nécessaire à la prosperité des Etats*, Paris 1771? (London, 1775).

N. Elias *The Court Society* reprinted in translation Oxford 1983.

S. Eriksen 'Marigny and 'le goût grec' *The Burlington Magazine* 708, CIV (March 1962) 96–101.

S. Eriksen 'Some letters from the Marquis de Marigny to his cabinet-maker Pierre Garnier' *Furniture History* 8 (1972) 78–85.

S. Eriksen *Early Neoclassicism in France* London 1974.

S. Eriksen *Louis Delanois Menuisier en Sièges* Paris 1968.

Etat des marchands, négocians, armateurs et fabricans de la France et de l'Europe, et autres parties du Monde Paris 1778 (BN).

C. Fairchilds 'The production and marketing of populuxe goods in eighteeenth-century Paris' in J. Brewer and R. Porter *Consumption and the world of goods* London and New York 1993, 228–248.

Felibien *Histoire de la Ville de Paris* 5 vols. 1725.

L. Fontaine *Histoire du Colportage en Europe XVe–XIXe siècle* Paris 1993.

R. Fox and A. Turner (eds.) *Luxury Trades and Consumerism in Ancien Régime Paris, Studies in the Skilled Workforce* forthcoming Oxford 1996.

A. Franklin *La Vie d'Autrefois: Arts et Métiers, Modes, Moeurs, Usages des Parisiens au XVIIe au XVIIIe d'après des documents originaux* Paris 1889.

A. Franklin *Dictionnaire Historique des Arts, Métiers et Professions exercés dans Paris depuis le 13e siècle* (Paris 1908) reprinted New York 1968.

R. Freyburger 'Eighteenth century French furniture from Hamilton Palace' *Apollo* 113, no. 238 (December 1981) 401–409.

P. Fuhring (1986 [1]) 'The Print Privilege in eighteenth-century France I' *Print Quarterly* II (1986), 174–93.

P. Fuhring (1986 [2]) 'The Print Privilege in eighteenth-century France II' *Print Quarterly* 3 (1986), 19–33.

P. Fuhring *Design into Art*, drawings for architecture and ornament: the Lodewijk Houthakker Collection, London 1989.

F. Furet 'Structures sociales parisiennes au XVIIIe siècle' *Annales ESC* 16 (1961) 939–958.

M. Gaffiot 'La théorie du luxe dans l'oeuvre de Voltaire' *Revue d'histoire économique et sociale* 14 (1926) 320–343.

R. Galliani *Rousseau, le luxe et l'idéologie nobiliare, étude socio-historique* Oxford 1989.

M. Garland 'Rose Bertin: Minister of Fashion' *Apollo* 87 (January 1968) 40–45.

D. Garrioch *Neighbourhood and Community in Paris, 1740–1790* Cambridge and New York 1986.

Gaston *Les Images des Confréries Parisiennes* Paris 1910.

C. Gilbert and T. Murdoch *John Channon and brass-inlaid furniture* (exhibition catalogue) New Haven and London 1993.

A. Gobart 'Les merciers de jadis' *Chambre de Commerce de Paris* (July–August 1949) 75–79.

A. Gonzalez-Palacios *Mosaici e Pietre Dure* Milan 1982.

A. Gonzalez-Palacios 'Capricci Gusto: Vecchio Barocco e Nuovo Classicismo' *Casa Vogue Antiques* 13 (May 1991).

A. Gordon and M. Déchery 'The Marquis de Marigny's purchases of English furniture and objects' *Furniture History* 25 (1980) 86–108.

Gournay *Tableau Général du Commerce, des marchands, négocians, armateurs de la France, de l'Europe & des autres Parties du Monde* Paris 1789 & 1790.

J. Grand-Carteret *Les Almanachs Français* 2 vols., Paris 1896.

S. Grandjean *Les Tabatières du Musée du Louvre: catalogue des tabatières, boîtes et étuis des XVIIIe et XIXe siècles du Musée du Louvre* Paris 1981.

S. Grandjean 'Napoleonic Tables from Sèvres' *Connoissseur*, CLXIII, 577 (April 1959) 147–153.

Grangé, Roi, Le Vent *Almanach général des Marchands, Negotians Armateurs et Fabricans de la France de l'Europe et d'autres parties du Monde* Paris 1778 (BN 8° Z Le Senne 4178).

J. Grieder *Anglomania in France 1740–1789: fact, fiction and political discourse* Geneva 1985.

M. Grivel *Le Commerce de l'Estampe à Paris au XVIIe siècle* Geneva 1986.

L. Gueneau 'Paris, les Industries et el commerce de la soie et des soieries à la fin de l'ancien régime' *Revue d'Histoire Moderne* vol. I, no. 4 (1926).

Guide des Corps des Marchands Paris 1766.

E. Harris 'Robert Adam and the Gobelins' *Apollo* 76 (April 1962) 100–116.

J.R. Harris 'Michael Alcock and the Transfer of Birmingham Technology to France before the Revolution' *Journal of European Economic History* 15 (1986) 7–57.

M.G. Hartmann 'Les Anciens Merciers et les Magasins de Nouveautés' *Le Vieux Paris* 17 (1909) 185–196.

H. Havard *Dictionnaire de l'Ameublement et de la Décoration*, 4 vols., Paris n.d. (2nd edition 1894).

E.F. Heckscher *Mercantilism,* London and New York 1955.

R. Henard *La Rue Saint Honoré* 2 vols., Paris 1908–9.

J. de l'Hiberderie *Le Dessinateur pour les fabriques d'étoffes d'or, d'argent et de soie* Paris 1765.

J. Hillairet *Dictionnaire Historique des Rues de Paris* 2 vols., Paris 1963.

C. Hind (ed.), *The Rococo in England* London 1986.

I. Hont 'Free trade and the economic limits to national politics: neo-Machiavellian political economy reconsidered' in J. Dunn (ed.) *The Economic Limits of Modern Politics* Cambridge 1990, 41–120.

D. Howard and J. Ayers *China for the West* 2 vols., London and New York 1978.

H. Huth *Lacquer of the West 1550–1950* London 1971.

O. Impey *Chinoiserie: the impact of oriental styles on Western art and decoration* London 1977.

O. Impey 'Japanese Export Lacquer of the seventeenth century' *Laquerwork in Asia and Beyond: Colloquies on Art and Archeology in Asia* 11 (1981) 124–159.

O. Impey 'Japan: trade and collecting in seventeenth-century Europe' in O. Impey and A. McGregor (eds.) *The Origin of Museums; the Cabinet of Curiosities in sixteenth and seventeenth century Europe* Oxford 1985, 267–273.

O. Impey & Whitehead 'From Japanese box to French royal furniture' *Apollo* 132 (September 1990) 159–165.

O. Impey 'European Additions to Japanese Lacquer on French Furniture' Furniture History Society *European Lacquer* (symposium) Victoria and Albert Museum London, 16 February 1995.

G. Jackson-Stops *Treasure Houses of Great Britain* New Haven and London 1985.

A. Jacquemart 'Une manufacture de lacque a Paris en 1767' *Gazette des Beaux Arts* 6th series 9 (1861) 311–313.

E.L. Jones 'The Fashion Manipulators: Consumer Tastes and British Industries, 1660–1800' L. P. Cain and P. J. Uselding (eds.) *Business Enterprise and Economic Change* Ohio 1973.

E. John *The China here is lovely: the acquisition of French luxury goods by the British in the eighteenth century* (MA thesis) V&A/RCA London 1995.

C.F. Joullain *Réflexions sur la Peinture et la gravure: le Commerce de la Curiosité* Paris 1786.

W. von Kalnein *Architecture in France in the Eighteenth Century* New Haven and London 1995.

S.L. Kaplan 'Les Corporations, les 'faux-ouvriers et le faubourg Saint-Antoine au XVIIIe siècle' *Annales* E.S.C. 43, (1988) 453–78.

S.L. Kaplan 'The luxury guilds in Paris in the eighteenth century' *Francia* 9 (1981) 273–295.

S.L. Kaplan 'Social Classification and Representation in the Corporate World of Eighteenth Century France: Turgot's "Carnival" in S. Kaplan and C. Koepp (eds) *Work in France: Representations, Meaning Organisation and Practice* New York 1986, 176–228.

S. Kaplan and C. Koepp (eds.) *Work in France: Representations, Meaning Organisation and Practice* New York 1986.

D. Kisluk-Grosheide 'A Japanned Secretaire in the Linsky Collection with Decorations after Boucher and Pillement' *Metropolitan Museum Journal* 21 (1986) 139–147.

P. Kjellberg *Le Mobilier Français du XVIIIe siècle: dictionnaire des ébénistes et des menuisiers* Paris 1989.

K. Klappenbach 'La Collection de lustres français en cristal de roche de Fréderic II de Prusse. Les formes du lustre du XVIIIe siècle' *ICOM Newsletter Vienna 1994: Reports of Sessions* March 1995.

M.R. de Labriolle-Rutherford 'L'évolution de la notion du luxe depuis Mandeville jusqu'à la Révolution' *Studies on Voltaire* 26 (1963) 1025–1036.

F. Lacombe *Tableau de Londres et ses Environs* London 1784.

E. Langlade *La Marchande de Modes de Marie-Antoinette: Rose Bertin* Paris 1911.

A. Laurel *L'Enseigne de Gersaint* Paris 1913.

G-C Lavergne *Archives des corporations des arts et métiers* Paris 1879.

U. Leben *Molitor, ébéniste from the Ancien Régime to the Bourbon Restoration: with a catalogue of the furniture* London 1992.

U. Leben 'New Light on the Ecole Royale Gratuite de Dessin: the years 1766–1815' *Studies in the Decorative Arts* vol. 1, no. 1 (Fall 1993) 99–118.

U. Leben (1995 [1]) 'D'Acier: l'art du mobilier et des objets en fer et acier polis' *Connoisseur* 520 (September 1995) 108–120.

U. Leben ed. (1995 [2]) 'La Fondation de l'Ecole royale gratuite de dessin de Paris (1767–1815)' *Francia* 20 (1995) 217–40.

U. Leben *Bernard Molitor 1755–1833: Ebéniste Parisien d'Origine Luxembourgeoise* (exhibition catalogue) Luxembourg 1995.

G. Le Duc 'The porcelain of Chantilly: the collections of the Duke and Duchess of Bourbon Condé and the inventory of the factory in the middle of the factory' *The International Ceramics Fair and Seminar* London (11–14 June 1993) 8–18.

Le Monde Illustré 28 March 1914.

Les Noms des Curieux de Paris reprinted Paris 1866.

Lemattre *Le Musée de Dunkerque* Dunkirk 1913.

Lemattre *Le 'Petit Dunkerque'* Dunkirk 1898.

B. Lemire *Fashion's Favourite: the cotton trade and the consumer in Britain 1660–1800* Oxford 1991.

P. Lemonnier 'Les commodes de Martin Carlin' *L'Estampille* 171–2 (July–August 1984, 6–19.

P. Lemonnier 'Les Julliot: dynastie des marchands merciers' *L'Estampille* 229 (October 1989) 38–48.

P. Lemonnier *Weisweiler* Paris 1983.

P. Leon *Lyon et le Grand Commerce au XVIIIe siècle: Papiers d'Industriels et de Commerçants Lyonnais* (thesis) Université de Lyon II 1976.

Leroudier *Les Dessinateurs de la Fabrique Lyonnaise au XVIIIe siècle* Lyon 1908.

R. Lespinasse *Les Métiers et Corporations de la Ville de Paris*, XIVe–XVIII 3 vols. Paris 1886–94.

Lettres patentes Paris, 1413.

Lettres patentes du roy, par lesquelles il est permis aux Gardes de la Mercerie d'emprunter 340,000 livres 26 February 1762 (BN F23627 [18]).

Lettres patentes du roy portant confirmation des marchands artisans priviligiés suivant la cour sous la charge du prevost de l'hotel 29 October 1725 (AVP V3 192 fo 87).

J.A. Levenson *Circa 1492: Art in the Age of Exploration*, London, New York, Washington, 1991.

Le Vent *Etat des marchands, négocians, armateurs et fabricans de la France et de l'Europe, et autres parties du Monde* Paris 1785, (BN 8o V58825).

L. Maillard *Les menus et programmes illustrés: invitations, billets de faire part, cartes adresses, petites estampes du XVIIe siècle jusqu'à nos jours* Paris 1898.

Mairie de Paris *Paris et ses Rois* (exhibition catalogue) Paris 1988.

J.V.G. Mallet 'European Ceramics and the Influence of Japan' in J. Ayers, O. Impey and J.V.G. Mallet *Porcelain for Palaces; the Fashion for Japan in Europe 1650–1750*, London 1990, 36–55.

L. Manoeuvre *Joseph Vernet 1714–1789: les ports de France* Arcueil 1994.

M. Marion *Dictionnaire des institutions de la France au XVIIe et XVIIIe siècle*, Paris 1923.

J. McCusker *Money and exchange in Europe and America 1600–1775: a handbook* Williamsburg 1978.

N. McKendrick, J. Brewer and J.H. Plumb *The Birth of a Consumer Society: the Commercialisation of Eighteenth Century England* London 1982.

S. Medlam 'A Sèvres misfit' The *Burlington Magazine* 1071 (June 1992) 378–380.

S. Melchior-Bonnet '"Se Mirer aux Glaces" La Vogue du Miroir à partir du règne de Louis XIV' *Annals généologique et Heraldique* (July–August 1995) 5–33.

Memoire à consulter at consultation pour les Srs Tonnelier, Danet, Lorphevre, Vve Gallot & autres mds de la Ville & fauxbourgs de Paris au sujet de l'Ordonnance du 25 mai 1761, portant réformation des Enseignes Paris 1761 (BN 4° Z Le Senne 992).

L.-S. Mercier *Tableau de Paris* 12 vols., Amsterdam 1787.

Mercure de France, December 1723, April 1775, September 1774, January 1776, July 1776, January 1777.

Metropolitan Museum of Art *Notable Acquisitions 1979–1980*, New York 1980.

L.E. Miller *Designers in the Lyonnais Silk Industry 1812–1787* (Phd thesis) Brighton Polytechnic 1988.

L.E. Miller (1995 [1]) 'Dressing down in eighteenth-century Lyon: the wardrobes of twenty-seven silk designers from their *inventaires après décès*' *Costume* (1995) 25–39.

L.E. Miller 'Paris–Lyon–Paris: Dialogue in the Design and Distribution of Patterned Silks in the Eighteenth Century' in R. Fox and A. Turner (eds.) *Luxury Trades and Consumerism in Ancien Régime Paris, Studies in the Skilled Workforce* forthcoming, Oxford 1996.

L.E. Miller (1995 [2]) 'Jean Revel: Silk Designer, Fine Artist, or Entrepreneur?' *Journal of Design History Society* vol. 8, no. 2 1995.

L.E. Miller and C. Sargentson 'Paris–Lyon: modes of distribution of luxury silks in the mid-eighteenth century' (conference) The Achievement Project *The Skilled Trades of Paris in the Seventeenth and Eighteenth Centuries*' Maison Française, Oxford, November 1993.

L.E. Miller and C. Sargentson 'Paris–Lyon – the relationship of the *marchands merciers* and *marchand fabricants* in the design of brocaded silks in the mid 18th century' (conference) l'Institut d'Histoire Moderne et Contemporaine, Paris and the Université de Rouen *Echanges et cultures textiles* May 1993.

M. Miller *The Bon Marché: Bourgeois Culture and the Department Store, 1869–1920* London 1981.

R. Monnier *Le Faubourg Saint-Antoine (1789–1815)* Paris 1981.

B. de Montgolfier 'Charles Lebrun et les Confréries parisiennes: le tableau des *Merciers* de Saint-Sépulchre' *Gazette des Beaux Arts* 6e période, LVI, (July–August 1960), 195–206.

J.M. Montias 'Cost and Value in Seventeenth-Century Dutch Art' *Art History* 10 (December 1987) 455–465.

M. Morgan-Grasselli and P. Rosenberg *Watteau 1684–1721* (exhibition catalogue) Washington D.C. 1984.

B.A. Morisette 'Mlle Desjardins and the Apologie du luxe' *Modern Languages Notes* 56 (1941) 209–11.

H. and L. Mui *Shops and Shopkeeping in Eighteenth Century England* London 1987.

J. Munger 'French Upholstery Practice of the Eighteenth Century' in E.S. Cooke Jr (ed.) *Upholstery in America and Europe from the Seventeenth Century to World War I* New York and London 1987, 121–130.

Musée des Arts et Traditions Populaires *Paris, Boutiques d'Hier* Paris 1977.

Musée Carnavalet *Collection Henriette Bouvier* Paris 1968.

Musée Historique des Tissus *Soieries de Lyon: Commandes Royales au XVIIIe siècle (1730–1800): Dossiers du Musée des Tissus* (exhibition catalogue) Lyon 1989.

Musée du Louvre *Nouvelles Acquisitions du département des Objets d'Art 1990–1994* Paris 1995.

Musée Missim de Camondo, Paris *The Nissim de Camondo Museum*, Paris 1991.

M. Myers *French architectural and ornement drawings of the eighteenth century* New York 1991.

R. Neuman 'Watteau's l'enseigne de Gersaint and Baroque emblematic tradition' *Gazette des Beaux Arts* VIe période 104 (October 1984) 153–164.

H. Nocq *Le Poinçon de Paris* Paris 1926–31.

H.L. Oberkirch *Memoires de la Baronne d'Oberkirch sur la cour de Louis XVI et la société française* reprinted Paris 1970.

L'Objet d'Art *La Folie D'Artois à Bagatelle* Paris 1988.

L'Office de Saint Louis, Roy de France et Confesseur A l'Usage de Messieurs les Marchands Merciers, Grossiers et Jouailliers de la Ville de Paris, Paris 1749 (V&A 111.RC.K.36 and another copy BHVP 90.2.805).

F. Olivier-Martin 'Le déclin et la suppression des corps en France au XVIIIe siècle' *L'Organisation corporative du Moyen Age à la fin de l'Ancien Régime* Louvain 1937.

Ordonnance de Police, concernant les Enseignes et Etalages des Marchands et Artisans, et autres particuliers de la Ville et Fauxbourgs de Paris 17 Dec 1761 (BN 4° Z Le Senne 992).

Ordonnance du bureau des finances de la generalite de Paris, concernant les Enseignes dans toutes l'etendue de la ville et faubourgs de Paris 25 Mai 1761 (BN 4° Z Le Senne 992).

Ordonnance du bureau des finances de la generalite de Paris, concernant les Enseignes dans toutes l'etendue de la ville et faubourgs de Paris 17 December 1761 (BN 4° Z Le Senne 992).

H. Ottomeyer and P. Pröschel *Vergoldete Bronzen: Die Bronzearbeiten des Spatbarock und Klassizimus* Munich 1986.

Palais Galliera *La Mode et des Métiers du XVIIIe siècle à nos jours*, (exhibition catalogue) Paris 1981.

Palais Galliera *La Mode et ses métiers du XVIIIe siècle à nos jours* (exhibition catalogue) Paris 1981.

Palais Galliera *L'Imprimé dans la mode du XVIIIe siècle à nos jours* (exhibition catalogue) Paris 1984.

U-C Pallach *Materielle Kultur und Mentalitaten im 18 Jahrhundert* Munich 1987.

B. Pallot *L'Art du Siège* Courbevoie 1987.

A. Pardailhé-Galabrun *La Naissance de l'Intime* Paris 1988.

H.T. Parker *The Bureau of Commerce in 1781 and its policies with respect to French Industry* Durham, N. Carolina 1979.

J.C. Perrot 'Les Dictionnaires de Commerce au XVIIIe siècle' *Revue d'histoire moderne et contemporaine* 28 (1981) 36–67.

J. Peyrot 'Les Techniques de la Soierie au XVIIIe siècle à travers les documents commerciaux et comptables des fabricants de soieries' *Bulletin du Centre d'Histoire et Société de la Région Lyon* 1 (1973) 29–48.

R. Picard, J.-P. Kerneis and Y. Bruneau *Les Compagnies des Indes: routes de la porcelaine* Paris 1966.

R. De Plinval de Guillebon *Catalogue des Porcelaines Francaises, I: Chantilly, Mennecy, Saint-Cloud, Boissette, Bordeaux, Limoges, Niderviller, Paris, Valenciennes* Musée du Louvre, Paris 1992.

K. Pomian *Collectionneurs, amateurs et curieux Paris, Venise: XVIe–XVIIIe siècle* Paris 1987.

B. Pons *De Paris à Versailles 1699–1736: les sculpteurs ornemanistes parisiens et l'art décoratif des Bâtimens du Roi* Strasbourg 1986.

D. Posner *Antoine Watteau* London 1984.

A. du Pradel *Livre Commode des Adresses* Paris 1692.

A. Pradère 'Boulle du Louis XIV sous Louis XVI' *L'Objet d'Art* 4 (1987) 28–42.

A. Pradère *French Furniture Makers: the Art of the Ebéniste from Louis XIV to the Revolution* London 1991.

A. Pradère 'Les Bonnes Adresses à Paris autour de 1770' *Antologia di Belle Arti* IV (1993) 88–105.

Précis servant de réponse à précis pour le corps des Marchands Drapiers–Merciers . . . contre la Communauté des Maîtres Tabletiers–Luthiers–Evantaillistres . . . en présence du sieur Bierne, Marchand mercier à Paris, aussi appellant et demandeur 1781 (BHVP 132256).

C. Pris *Une Grande Entreprise Française sous l'Ancien Régime; la manufacture royale des glaces de Saint-Aubin 1665–1830* New York 1981.

W. Reddy *The Rise of Market Culture: the Textile Trade and French Society 1750–1900* Cambridge 1984.

Réflexions des six corps des marchands concernant les Enseignes de la Ville de Paris 1761 (BN 4° Z Le Senne 992).

Reiset, Comte de *Le Livre Journal de Madame Eloffe marchande de modes au Temps de Marie Antoinette* 2 vols., Paris 1885.

G. Reitlinger *The Economics of Taste: 1760–1950* London 1961–3. N. de Reyniès *Le Mobilier Domestique*, Paris 1987 *La Rue et Faubourg St. Honoré* Paris 1994.

N. de Reyniès *Le Mobilier Domestique*, Paris 1987 *La Rue et Faubourg St Honoré* Paris 1994.

M. Rimbaud *Documents du Minutier Central concernant l'Histoire de l'Art (1700–1750)* 2 vols., Paris 1964–1971.

Rivière du Frény *Amusemens sérieux et comiques des boutiques de la rue des Bourdonnais* Paris 1731.

H. Roberts 'Gilles Joubert, sub-contractor, some recent discoveries' *Furniture History* 8 (1972) 32–35.

E. Robinson 'Eighteenth-century commerce and fashion: Matthew Boulton's Marketing Techniques' *Economic History Review* 16 (1963–4) 39–60.

E. Robinson 'Matthew Boulton and Josiah Wedgwood, Apostles of Fashion' *Business History* 28 (1986) 98–114.

D. Roche *La Culture des Apparences* Paris 1989.

D. Roche *Le Peuple de Paris* Paris 1981.

N. Rothstein *The Silk Industry in London, 1702–1766* (thesis) University of London 1961.

N. Rothstein 'The Introduction of the Jacquard Loom to Great Britain' in V. Gervers (ed.) *Studies in Textile History in Memory of Harold B. Burnham* Canada 1977.

N. Rothstein 'The Purchase of the Warner Collection by the Victoria and Albert Museum' .

N. Rothstein *L'organisation du commerce des soireries en France et en Angleterre au XVIIIe d'après un livre de commissions lyonnais conservé au Victoria and Albert Museum* Paris.

N. Rothstein *Silk Designs of the Eighteenth Century* London 1990.

E. Ross *The luxury debate in eighteenth century France: a study in the resistance to change* (Phd thesis) Princeton 1975.

J.A. Roubo *L'Art du Menuisier en Meubles* Paris 1772.

Roze de Chantoiseau *[Essai sur] l'almanac général d'indication d'adresse personelle & domicile fixe, des six corps, Arts et métiers* 1769 (BN V25838).

C. Sabel and J. Zeitlin 'Historical Alternatives to Mass Production: Politics, Markets and Technology in Nineteenth-Century Industrialisation' *Past and Present,* 1985.

D.-G. Saint-Joanny *Régistre des déliberations et ordonnances des marchands merciers de Paris, 1596–1696* Paris (BHVP 935270).

E.M. Saint-Léon *Histoire des corps de métiers depuis leurs origines jusqu'à leur suppression en 1791*, Paris 1941.

R.G. Saisselin *The enlightenment against the Baroque: Economics and aesthetics in the eighteenth century*, Berkeley and Oxford 1992.

R.G. Saisselin 'Neoclassicism: Images of Public Virtue and realities of Private Luxury' *Art History* vol. 4 no. 1 (March 1981) 14–36.

J.P. Samoyault *André-Charles Boulle et sa famille: nouvelles recherches, nouveaux documents* Geneva 1979.

F. de Salverte, Comte *Les Ebénistes su XVIIIe siècle, leurs oeuvres et leur marques* Paris and Brussels 1923.

C. Sargentson 'The Continental Context: France' in C. Gilbert and T. Murdoch *John Channon and brass-inlaid furniture* (exhibition catalogue) New Haven and London 1993, 37–45.

C. Sargentson *The marchands merciers: merchants and luxury markets in eighteenth-century Paris* (Phd thesis), University of Glasgow 1996.

C. Sargentson 'Markets for Boulle furniture in early eighteenth-century Paris' *The Burlington Magazine* 1071, CXXXIV (June 1992) 363–7.

C. Sargentson 'The role of the *marchands merciers* in the seventeenth and eighteenth-century Parisian *commerce de luxe*' in R. Fox and A. Turner (eds.) *Luxury Trades and Consumerism in Ancien Régime Paris, Studies in the Skilled Workforce* forthcoming, Oxford 1996.

C. Sargentson 'Second-hand and recycled goods in the luxury economy of 18th-century Paris' V&A/RCA Seminar, Victoria and Albert Museum, November 1994.

A. Sassoon *Vincennes and Sèvres Porcelain: Catalogue of the Collections, The J. Paul Getty Museum* Malibu 1991.

H. Sauval *Histoire et recherches des antiquités de la ville de Paris* 3 vols., Paris 1724.

J. Savary *Le Parfait Negotiant* Paris 1675.

J. Savary des Bruslons *Dictionnaire Universel de Commerce*, Paris 1723.

R. Savill *The Wallace Collection: Catalogue of the Sèvres Porcelain* 3 vols., London 1988.

W. Schaeper *The French Council of Commerce, 1700–1715: A study of mercantilism after Colbert* Columbus, Ohio, 1983.

D.F.L. Scheurleer *Chinese Export Porcelain* London 1974.

M. Schoeser-Boyce 'The Barbier Manuscripts' *Textile History* 12 (1981) 37–58.

M. Schoeser-Boyce *Letters to M. Barbier, Parisian Silk Merchant 1755–97* (MA thesis) Courtauld Institute of Art 1979.

K. Scott *The Rococo Interior: Decorative and Social Spaces in early eighteenth-century Paris* New Haven and London 1995.

K. Scott 'Hierarchy, Liberty and Order: languages of Art and Institutional Conflict in Paris (1766–1776)' *Oxford Art Journal* 12 no. 2 (1989) 59–70.

W.C. Scoville *Capitalism and French Glass Making 1640–1789* California 1950.

De Segur *Le Royaume de la rue Saint Honoré* Paris 1897.

J. Sekora *Luxury: The concept in Western thought, Eden to Smollett* Baltimore and London 1977.

A. Setterwall 'Some Louis XVI Furniture decorated with pietre dure reliefs' *The Burlington Magazine* 681, CI (December 1959) 425–435.

W.H. Sewell *Work and Revolution in France – the language of labour from the Old Régime to 1848* Cambridge 1981.

W.H. Sewell 'Visions of Labor: Illustrations of the Mechanical Arts before, in and after, Diderot's Encyclopaedie' in S. Kaplan and C. Koepp (eds.) *Work in France: Representations, Meaning Organisation and Practice* New York 1986, 258–86.

J. Sgard 'L'Echelle des Revenus' *Dix-Huitième Siècle* 14 (1982) 425–433.

M.D. Sibalis 'Corporatism after the Corporations: the Debate on Restoring the Guilds under Napoleon I and the Restoration' *French Historical Studies* vol. XV, no. 4 (Fall 1988) 718–730.

Snodin & Cornforth 'French style, English mood' *Country Life* (1 October 1992) xx–xx.

A.K. Snowman *Eighteenth Century Gold Boxes of Europe* Woodbridge 1990.

W. Sombart *Luxury and Capitalism* reprinted in translation Michegan 1967.

M. Sonenscher 'The Empire of Taste: Trade, Enterprise and the Trades of Eighteenth Century Paris' *Les métiers d'Art à Paris 1500–1800* (symposium) Bibliothèque Nationale, Paris 2–3 April 1993, a version of which to be published in R. Fox and A. Turner (eds.) *Luxury Trades and Consumerism in Ancien Régime Paris, Studies in the Skilled Workforce* forthcoming Oxford 1996.

M. Sonenscher 'Work and Wages in Eighteenth-Century Paris' in M. Berg, P. Hudson and M. Sonenscher (eds.) *Manufacture in Town and Country before the Factory* Cambridge 1983.

M. Sonenscher 'Journeymen's Migrations and Workshop Organisatin in Eighteenth-Century France' in S. Kaplan and C. Koepp (eds.) *Work in France: Representations, Meaning Organisation and Practice* New York 1986.

M. Sonenscher (1987 [2]) *The Hatters of Eighteenth-Century France* Berkeley California 1987.

M. Sonenscher 91987 [1]) 'Journeymen, the Courts and the French Trades 1781–1791' *Past and Present* 114 (February 1987) 77–109.

M. Sonenscher *Work and Wages; Natural Law, Politics and the Eighteenth Century French Trades* Cambridge 1989.

M. Sonenscher and D. Garrioch 'Compagnonnages, Confraternities and Associations of Journeymen in Eighteenth Century Paris' *European History Quarterly* 16 (1986), 25–45.

H. Sorenson 'Des Ebénistes, Sèvres et les marchands–merciers' *Connaissance des Arts* 322 (December 1978) 85–91.

Statuts, ordonnances et reglemens du corps des marchands merciers, grossiers, joalliers de la ville de Paris Paris 1727 (AN ADXI/22).

M. Sturmer 'An Economy of Delight: Court Artisans of the Eighteenth Century' *Business History Review*, vol. 53, no. 4 (Winter 1979) 496–528.

M. Sturmer '"Bois des Indes" and the economics of Luxury Furniture in the Time of David Roentgen' *The Burlington Magazine* 909, CXX (December 1978) 799–805.

J. Styles 'Design for large-scale production in Eighteenth-Century Britain' *Oxford Art Journal* 11 (1988) 10–16.

J. Styles 'Manufacturing, consumption and design in eighteenth century England' in Brewer and Porter *Consumption and the world of goods*, London and New York 1993.

J. Styles 'Product innovation in early-modern London' forthcoming 1996.

Tablettes Royales de Renommée, ou de correspondance et d'indication générale des principes fabriques, manufactures, et maisons de commerce de draperie, soireries, toileries et lainages de Paris et aures villes de la Royaume & des Pays Etrangers, Paris 1788 (BN Z Lesenne 8418 [1]).

S. Taubert *Bibliopola; Bilder und Texte aus der Welt des Buchhandels*, 2 vols., Hamburg 1966.

The London Goldsmith 1200–1800, 1935.

M. Thomas *Almanac des marchands, négocians et commerçans de la France et du Reste de l'Europe* Paris 1770 (BN Z Le Senne 3995).

P.K. Thornton *Authentic Decor*, London 1984.

P.K. Thornton *Baroque and Rococo Silks* London 1965.

P.K. Thornton 'Jean Revel and the Grand Fabrique' *Gazette des Beaux-Arts* 6th series 56 (July 1960) 71–86.

P.K. Thornton *Seventeenth Century Interior Decoration in England, France and Holland*, New Haven and London 1978.

C. Todd 'French advertising in the eighteenth century' *Studies in Voltaire and the eighteenth century* 268, 1989, 515–548.

Tournier 'La porcelaine des Indes d'après les archives de la Compagnie des Indes' *Bulletin et Mémoire de la Société Archéologique du Département d'Ille et Vilaine* LXX (1953) 17–65.

Ier Trimestre des tablettes royales de renommée, d'adresse perpetuelle et d'indication des négocians, artistes célebres et fabriquans des six corps, arts et métiers de la ville & faubourgs de Paris & autres villes de la Royaume, Paris 1775 (BN Z Lesenne 11630).

A. Turner 'Berthoud in England, Harrison in France: the transmission of horological knowledge in 18th-century Europe *Antiquarian Horology* 3, vol. 20 (Autumn 1993) 219–39.

L. Vardi 'The Abolition of the Guilds during the French Revolution' *French Historical Studies* vol. XV, no. 4, Fall 1988, 404–717.

T. Veblen *The Theory of the Leisure Class* New York 1912.

P. Verlet *Le Mobilier Royal Français* 4 vols., Paris 1990–1994.

P. Verlet 'Le Commerce des objets d'art et les marchands merciers à Paris au 18e siècle' *Annales* E,S.C. 1958, 10–29.

P. Verlet *Les Bronzes Dorés Français du XVIIIe siècle*, Paris 1987.

Victoria & Albert Museum *Catalogue of the Jones collection: Part II – Ceramics, Ormulu, Goldsmith's Work, Enamels, Sculpture, Tapestry, Books and Prints* London 1924.

M. Vidal *Watteau's Painted Conversations: Art, Literature and Talk in seventeenth and eighteenth century France*, New Haven and London 1992.

P. Vidal and L. Duru *Histoire de la Corporation des marchands merciers–joailliers*, Paris 1911.

T. Volvesperges, *Les manufactures de Tole Vernie vers 1765–1775*, Furniture History Society *European Lacquer* (symposium) Victoria and Albert Museum London, 16 February 1995.

C. Wainwright *The Romantic Interior: the British collector at home, 1750–1880* New Haven and London 1989.

W. Walton '"To Triumph before Feminine Taste": Bourgeois Women's Consumption and hand Methods of Production in Mid-Nineteenth-Century Paris' *Business History Review*, vol. 60, no. 4 Winter 1986, 541–563.

W. Walton 'Political Economists and Specialised Industrialisation during the French Second Republic, 1848–1852. *French History*, vol. 3, no. 3, September 1989, 293–311.

O. Walcha, *Meissen Porcelain*, English Edition, Dresden, 1981.

C. Walsh 'Shop Design and the Display of Goods in Eighteenth Century London *Design History Journal* vol. 8, no. 3 (1995) 157–175.

M. Ward *The Dubarry Inheritance* London 1967.

F.J.B. Watson (196] [25) 'The Paris marchands–merciers and French eighteenth-century taste' *Antiques* (September 1965) 347–51.

F.J.B. Watson (1967 [2]) 'Les Marchands merciers et le goût français au XVIIIe siècle' *L'Oeil* 151–3 (September 1967) 12–21.

F.J.B. Watson 'A possible source for the practice of mounting French furniture with Sèvres porcelain' in Nationalmuseum, Stockholm *Opuscula in honorem C. Hernmarck Skriftsein* 15 (1966) 245–254.

F.J.B. Watson (1967 [1]) 'Holland and Daguerre: French undercurrents in English Neo-Classical Furniture Design, *Burlington Magazine* (September 1967) 282–287.

F.J.B. Watson (1965 [1]) 'French Furniture at Woburn 18th and early 19th centuries' *Apollo* 46, LXXXII (December 1965), 472–483.

F. Watson 'Beckford, Mme de Pompadour, the Duc de Bouillon and the taste for Japanese lacquer in eighteenth-century France' *Gazette des Beaux-Arts* 6th series, LX, 1963, 101–127.

F.J.B. Watson *Mounted Oriental Porcelain*, Washington D.C. 1986.

F.J.B. Watson *Catalogue of the Charles B. Wrightsman Collection* 3 vols., New York 1966–70.

F.J.B. Watson 'Chinese Porcelains in European Mounts' *Orientations* 12 (September 1981).

F.J.B. Watson (1967 [3]) 'Walpole and the taste for French porcelain in eighteenth-century England' W.H. Smith (ed.) *Horace Walpole – writer, politician and connoisssseur* 1967.

F.J.B. Watson, G. Wilson & A. Derham *Mounted Oriental Porcelain in the J. Paul Getty Museum* Malibu, California 1982.

F.J.B. Watson and J. Whitehead 'A inventory dated 1689 of the Chinese porcelain in the collection of the Grand Dauphin, son of Louis XIV, at Versailles' *Journal of the History of Collections*, vol. 3 no. 1 1991, 13–52.

J. Whitehead (1993 [1]) *The Eighteenth-Century French Interior*, London 1992.

J. Whitehead 'The marchands merciers and Sèvres' *The International Ceramics Fair and Seminar* London 11–14 June 1993, 36–43.

J. Whitehead (1993 [2]) 'George IV: furnishing in the French taste (the place of Dominique Daguerre in the Royal Collection) *Apollo* 138 (September 1993) 153–9.

J. Whitehead and O. Impey 'Les Lacques du Japon' *Connaissance des Arts* 432 (February 1988) 86–97.

G. Wildenstein, 'Le Goût pour la peinture dans le cercle de la bourgeoisie parisienne autour de 1700' *Gazette des Beaux-Arts*, 6th series, 118 (September 1956) 113–20.

G. Wildenstein 'Simon-Philippe Poirier, fournisseur de Madame du Barry' *Gazette des Beaux-Arts*, 6th series, 110 (1962) 365–377.

R. Williams *Dream Worlds: Mass Consumption in late nineteenth century France* California 1982.

G. Wilson 'Boulle' *Furniture History* 8 1972, 47–69.

G. Wilson *The J. Paul Getty Museum Journal*, 'Acquisitions' 1981.

G. Wilson 'Acquisitions', *The J. Paul Getty Museum Journal*, 1980.

G. Wilson, A. Sassoon and C. Bremer-David 'Selected Acquisitions Made by the Department of Decorative Arts in 1984' *The J. Paul Getty Museum Journal* vol. 13, 1985, 67–88.

P. Word *Paris Shopkeepers and the Politics of Resentment* Princeton 1986.

A. Young *Travels in France* London 1989.

R.E. Zupko *French Weights and Measures before the Revolution* Bloomington and London 1978.

MANUSCRIPT SOURCES

ADR Série B, Commerçants.

ADR Série B, Formations de Societes.

ADR Série B, Fonds de Vitry et Gayet, *liasse* 1.

ADR 3E3866 Dalier (lyon): 11.10.1753 *Société* Pernon, Pernon, Aubert.

ADR, Série B, Fonds Carret, *liasse* 1.

ADR, Série B, Fonds Fayet, *liasse* 1, 17 January 1749 letter Rohault-Fayet.

AML HH139 *Memoire pour les sieurs Ribier et Bertrand contre les sieurs Assada et Reynard c.* 1740, f.2v.

AML CC178 *Rolle de capitation* (grand Fabrique), 1758–9.

AML HH139 Saint-Michel, Dany et Compagnie contre Thevillon et Vingtain, 5 documents 1761–2.

AN F12 54, (Conseil de Commerce) 31 August 1708, *Projet d'Arret . . .*

AN F^{12} 70, fo 195, (Conseil de Commerce) 19 November 1722, *Projet d'Arret . . .*

AN F^{12} 95, fo 35, (Conseil de Commerce) 17 January 1748.

AN F^{12} 54, (Conseil de Commerce) 31 August 1709, *Placet du Dr Braulard . . .*

AN MC XLII, 362, 29 Avril 1732, Baillet.

AN MC LXXV, 672, 26–28 February 1762, Barbier.

AN Y13579, 22 November 1787, Barbier.

AN MC VII, 483, 23 November 1787, Barbier.

AN MC VII, 414, 13 November 1774, Barbier-Tetard.

AN MC VII, 486, 12 June 1788, Bardin.

AN MC VII, 447, 16 August 1780. Bardin-Barbier.

AN MC LXXXIII, 363, 29 September 1738 Bauvin-Aubertin.

AN MC CXV, 711, 7 December 1757 Bazin.

AN MC CXV, 698, 12 October 1756 Bazin-Lair.

AN MC XCIII, 187, 13 August 1790, Beaulard.

AN CXVIII,454, 18 dec 1748, Bentabole-Rohault-Rohault.

AN MC XXII, 60, 21 September 1789, Berrieux.

AN MC LXXVIII, 786, 24 November 1773, Blakey and-Bournisian.

AN MC LXXVIII, 817, 29 December 1776, Blakey-Jousset de Lizy

AN MC LXXXIII, 363, 4 August 1738, Boscheron-Bauvin.

AN MC, CXV, 447, 6 June 1726, Bosseux.

AN MC XXXIV, 758, 14 July 1788, Bourjot.

AN MC XXIV, 980, 14 October 1790, Bourjot.

AN MC XXXIV, 758, 29 April 1788, Bourjot-Pierre Sorte.

AN MC LII, 361, 23 June 1759 Briant.

AN MC LIII, 488, 30 August 1772, Buffault-Lenormand

AN MC LII, 492, 24 October 1772 Buffault-Fayan.

AN MC CXVII, 802, 27 October 1755, Buffault-Peeters.

AN MC VI, 892, 22 brumaire an III, Cavillier.

AN MC XCII, 504, 17 February 1740, Chantilly.

AN MC XXIV, 5 Avril 1741, Cholet.

AN MC XC11, 469, 29 February 1732, Prince de Conty.

AN MC XXXXVI, 633, 15 Frimaire an 5, Daguerre.

AN MC XXXVI, 633, 29 frimaire an 5, Daguerre.

AN MC XXXVI, 633, 21 pluvioise an 5, Daguerre.

AN MC LXXXVIII, 630, 8 October 1753, Darnault-Darnault.

AN MC XXXIX, 217, 26 September 1713 Daustel.

AN MC xxx, xxx, 11 June 1759, David-Eve.
AN MC LXXXIX, 36, 23 May 1742, Davollé.
AN MC CXVII, 800, 23 May 1755, Davollé.
AN MC CXVI, 439, 23 December 1768 Delahoguette.
AN XLII, 543, 26 June 1775, Delaplanche.
AN MC XXIX, 472 14 March 1746 Delaporte.
AN MC LIII, 226, 22 May 1724, Desgodets.
AN MC LXI, 590 10 December 1765. Disnematin.
AN MC LIII, 492, 22 December 1772, Dumont.
AN MC, XCIV, 290, 29 November 1758, Duvaux.
AN MC XXXIII, 641, 1768–1778 Ecole de Dessein.
AN MC CXVIII, 801, 1 September 1755, Fayan-Buffault.
MC AN XXXIX, 353 7 December 1736, Fevrier.
AN MCXXIX, 355, 14 November 1720, de la Fond.
AN MC XXXVIII, 609, Gaillard.
AN MC XCVIII, 517, 8 January 1752, Gaucherel.
AN MC XCVIII, 517, 8 Jan 1752, Gaucherel-Corvoisier-Richer.
AN MC XXVIII, 4111, 7 October 1768 Garnier.
AN MC XXIV, 704, 9 Avril 1746 Gillot.
AN MC 1X, 814, 22 October 1787, Granchez.
AN MC IX, 817, 17 September, Granchez.
AN MC IX, 817, 2 October 1787, Granchez.
AN MC 1X, 816, 28 March 1788 Granchez-Granchez.
AN MC CXVII, 930, 17 Feb 1737, Guerin-Omont.
AN MC XXXVIII, 130, 19 July 1714, Guignard.
AN MC LIII, 502, 15 Jan 1774, Hebert.
AN MC XLII, 521, 24 October 1770, Hennebert.
AN MC XCII, 510, 28 June 1741, Princesse de Hesse Reinfels.
AN MC X, 652, 6 February 1776. 1773, Honnez.
AN MC II, 425, 1 August 1726, Hugot.
AN MC XXVII, 499, 30 Avril 1790, Jacques.
AN MC X, 540, 20 Mar 1760, Julliot.
AN MC LX, 481, 17 January 1759, Lair.
AN MC XXIX, 368, 14 January 1723 Lambert.
AN MC XXIII, 654, 26 Aug 1763, Legras.
AN MC IX, 795, 4 October 1784 Levesque.
AN MC VII, 486, 5 July 1788, Lorieux.
AN MC X, 788, 22 October 1790 Malencourt.
AN MC IX, 666, 5 November 1777 Martin.
AN MC LIV, 927 14 March 1768, Merre.
AN MC LIII, 243, 31 October 1727, Noblin.
AN MC LIII, 535, 30 November 1777, Peeters.
AN MC VII, 462, 29 January 1784, Pingot.

AN MC CXVIII, 627, 9 September 1785 Poirier.

AN MC CXVIII, 857, 15 April 1772, Poirier-Hecquerre.

AN MC III, 928, Potor-Julliot.

AN MC CXVII, 800, 25 May 1755 Pucelle.

AN MC XC, 476, 20 Jan 1778, Richard.

AN MC XCIV, 429 Rozelet-Desmaret-Durand.

AN MC LIII, 286, 24 January 1738, Sailly.

AN MC LIII, 394, 7 January 1765, Thibert.

AN MC CIX,537 5 July 1742, Tremblin.

AN MC, LII, 249, 20 November 1731 Ziegler.

AN 0^{1}3641, 1er semestre 1787.

AN *Placard de décès* 364.

AN *Placard après décès* 2.417, Bourjot.

AN *Placard de décès* 366.

AN S1302 *Terrier de l'Archevêché de Paris*.

AN T1051 Tremouille papers.

AN T186 Fitzjames papers.

AN V3 192 fo 191 r°.

AN Y9331, 9 April 1767.

AN Y11990, 22 August 1775.

AN YII314, 24 December 1751.

AN Y11314, 4 December 1756, de Lerpine-Desmoulins.

AN Y11370, 12 July 1768, Maillard.

AN Y11930, 2 April 1749, Daniel.

AN Y11940 23 December 1757 Riolle-Souris.

AN Y12644, 10 Sept 1789, Laflaîche.

AN Y13702 *Régistre de factures de marchandise tirees de'Angleterre commence le 27 mai 1766*, Blakey.

AN Y13702 *Régistre de factures de marchandise tirees de'Angleterre commence le 27 mai 1766*, Blakey.

AN Y13980 28 April 1788, Bourjot.

AN Y15000, 5 November 1779, Languigneux.

AVP DC^{6} 282, 12 February 1788, Barbier.

AVP 6AZ 1521 12 July 1788, Barbier-Tetard.

AVP $D^{4}B^{6}$ *carton* 14, *dossier* 654, 19 November 1754, Baillet.

AVP $D^{4}B^{6}$ *carton* 44 *dossier* 2490 Blakey.

AVP $D^{4}B^{6}$ *carton* 40, *dossier* 2224, Delahaye.

AVP $D^{4}B^{6}$ *carton* 14 *dossier* 677, 2 April 1755, Delahoguette.

AVP $D^{4}B^{6}$ *carton* 39 *dossier* 2158, 30 October 1770 Dubuisson.

AVP $D^{4}B^{6}$ *carton* 91, *dossier* 6280, 15 September 1787, Granchez.

AVP $D^{4}B^{6}$ *carton* 109 *dossier* 1772, Julien.

AVP $D^{4}B^{6}$ *carton* 12 *dossier* 560, 1753–1768, Porlier.

AVP $D^{5}B^{6}$ *régistre* 1772–1776 Baudouin.

AVP $D^{5}B^{6}$ *régistre* 2813 Blakey.

AVP $D^{5}B^{6}$ *régistre* Claude Carelu.

AVP D^5B^6 *régistre* 690, 1 October 1768–7 September 1770, Dubuisson.

AVP D^5B^6 *régistre* 1967, Dubuisson.

AVP D^5B^6 *régistre* 2464, 5 November 1766–10 November 1767 Dubuisson/Carelu.

AVP D^5B^6 *régistre* 2524 5 Nov 1766–10 Nov 1767, Dubuisson.

AVP D^5B^6 *régistre* 3499, 1 May 1764–1 July 1766 Dubuisson.

AVP D^5B^6 *régistre* 326, 29 April–Oct 1754 Herbert.

AVP D^5B^6 *régistre* 5491 Migeon.

AVP DC6 29 fos 89vo and 176vo Granchez.

BF Moccassi *Exposizione delle Manuffatture di Francia, Inghilterra ed Olanda*. (FN 677.064).

BML 354461 *Memoire sur l'envoi d'echantillons de la fabrique de Lyon*, 1760.

BML Imprimes 113949, *Arret*, 14 July 1787.

BML Fonds Coste ms 1005, f.2v.

BML Imprimés 113923 & 113925 *Arret*.

BML Imprimés 113925 *Arret*.

BN Est. *Echantillons Richelieu* 7 vols., Lh45–45f.

BN F23627 (47).

Livre Journal de Pierre Migeon, 1730–1736 BN Nouv, acq. fr. 4765.

Manson, Lefevre, mds merciers, étalans dans les rues, places et marchés, intervenans dans la cause d'entre M. le procureur général et le Sr Bruer Paris 1780 (BN MSS Mss Joly de Fleury 515, fo 262–274).

Mémoire (BN Mss Joly de Fleury 2018, fo 245).

Mémoire pour les Srs Marchand, Fouquet, Derault, Moulins, Lefevre, Degamaches, Tiphaine, Lizeret, Onfroy, Villegoulet, Cheron, Lemoine, Brousse, Dilieu, Dubois, Magu, Baron, Roussel, Quignon, Boucherelle, Legay, Boucheri, Isselot.

Mémoire générale sur la manufacture des étoffes de soye or et argent qui se fabriquent dans la ville de Lyon, 1731 (BN Mss fr. 11855).

MNS *Régistre de vente*, 54 AQ 5.

MNS *Régistre de vente*, 54 AQ 10.

Valeur, qualite et quantite des marchandises saisies et inventoriees dans une salle des Grands Augustins, et au bureau des Epiciers, notorial act, 22 January 1721 (BN Factums FM 8259).

INDEX

* Note: Plate references appear in bold.